Frontiers
in Econometrics

ECONOMIC THEORY AND MATHEMATICAL ECONOMICS

Consulting Editor: Karl Shell

UNIVERSITY OF PENNSYLVANIA
PHILADELPHIA, PENNSYLVANIA

Franklin M. Fisher and Karl Shell. **The Economic Theory of Price Indices:** *Two Essays on the Effects of Taste, Quality, and Technological Change.*

Luis Eugenio Di Marco (Ed.). **International Economics and Development:** *Essays in Honor of Raúl Presbisch.*

Erwin Klein. **Mathematical Methods in Theoretical Economics:** *Topological and Vector Space Foundations of Equilibrium Analysis.*

Paul Zarembka (Ed.). **Frontiers in Econometrics.**

George Horwich and Paul A. Samuelson (Eds.). **Trade, Stability, and Macro-**economics: *Essays in Honor of Lloyd A. Metzler.*

Frontiers
in Econometrics

Edited by $PAUL\ ZAREMBKA$

STATE UNIVERSITY OF NEW YORK
BUFFALO, NEW YORK

ACADEMIC PRESS   New York and London   1974

A Subsidiary of Harcourt Brace Jovanovich, Publishers

COPYRIGHT © 1974, BY ACADEMIC PRESS, INC.
ALL RIGHTS RESERVED.
NO PART OF THIS PUBLICATION MAY BE REPRODUCED OR
TRANSMITTED IN ANY FORM OR BY ANY MEANS, ELECTRONIC
OR MECHANICAL, INCLUDING PHOTOCOPY, RECORDING, OR ANY
INFORMATION STORAGE AND RETRIEVAL SYSTEM, WITHOUT
PERMISSION IN WRITING FROM THE PUBLISHER.

ACADEMIC PRESS, INC.
111 Fifth Avenue, New York, New York 10003

United Kingdom Edition published by
ACADEMIC PRESS, INC. (LONDON) LTD.
24/28 Oval Road, London NW1

Library of Congress Cataloging in Publication Data

Zarembka, Paul.
    Frontiers in econometrics.

    (Economic theory and mathematical economics)
    Includes bibliographies.
    1.   Econometrics–Addresses, essays, lectures.
I.   Title.
HB141.Z47   330   73-2063
ISBN 0–12–776150–0

PRINTED IN THE UNITED STATES OF AMERICA

Contents

Part I   MODEL SELECTION

Chapter One

Classical Model Selection through Specification Error Tests   **13**

JAMES B. RAMSEY

Chapter Two

Discriminating among Alternative Models: Bayesian and Non-Bayesian Methods   **49**

KENNETH M. GAVER AND MARTIN S. GEISEL

Part II   LINEAR MODELS

Part III MULTIPLE-EQUATION MODELS

List of Contributors

Numbers in parentheses indicate the pages on which the authors' contributions begin.

JAMES M. BRUNDY (215), Federal Reserve Bank of San Francisco, San Francisco, California

KENNETH M. GAVER (49), Department of Economics, University of Rochester, Rochester, New York

MARTIN S. GEISEL (49), Graduate School of Industrial Administration, Carnegie-Mellon University, Pittsburgh, Pennsylvania

ARTHUR S. GOLDBERGER (193), Department of Economics, University of Wisconsin, Madison, Wisconsin

DALE W. JORGENSON (215), Department of Economics, Harvard University, Cambridge, Massachusetts

DANIEL McFADDEN (105), Department of Economics, University of California, Berkeley, California

JAMES B. RAMSEY (13), Department of Economics, Michigan State University, East Lansing, Michigan

P. A. V. B. SWAMY (143), Department of Economics, Ohio State University, Columbus, Ohio

LESTER D. TAYLOR (169), Department of Economics, University of Michigan, Ann Arbor, Michigan

PAUL ZAREMBKA (81), Department of Economics, State University of New York, Buffalo, New York

Introduction

PAUL ZAREMBKA[1]

STATE UNIVERSITY OF NEW YORK AT BUFFALO
BUFFALO, NEW YORK

In the post World War II period, economists have felt sufficiently confident of their theoretical structure to extensively utilize a separate branch of the discipline econometrics to relate economic theory directly to observations. The results of applied econometric research have not been particularly impressive, however. In his 1970 Presidential address to the American Economic Association, Leontief (1971, p. 3) argued that "in no other field of empirical inquiry has so massive and sophisticated a statistical machinery been used with such indifferent results." Large-scale macroeconometric models provide a striking example. Cooper (1972) has compared seven models of the U.S. economy with an autoregressive scheme. An important conclusion is that, for one-quarter predictions, "the econometric models are not, in general, superior to purely mechanical methods of forecasting" and "are, in general, structurally unstable" (p. 920). Nelson (1972) has found that the FRB-MIT-PENN model (considered to be the most neoclassical of the macromodels) does not outperform and, in fact, is worse than an integrated

[1] Comments on drafts of this introduction by M. Brown, A. S. Goldberger, M. S. Geisel, M. Harwitz, P. A. V. B. Swamy, and A. Zellner were most helpful and are gratefully acknowledged.

1

autoregressive moving average process for purposes of one-quarter post-sample prediction.

A major difficulty with assessing applied econometric research is that obtaining empirical results is a complicated interaction of bringing economic theory to data; thus, indifferent performance may result from any one or more of several problems (in descending order of fundamental impact on the economics profession):

1. The neoclassical paradigm of economic theory;
2. Inadequate development of neoclassical theory;
3. Composite commodity problems;
4. Inadequate development of econometric theory;
5. Aggregation problems;
6. Substantial errors in data.

This book is devoted to the development of econometric theory; yet some remarks on economic theory in its relation to empirical work may help to emphasize its importance in the formulation of maintained hypotheses.

The neoclassical paradigm begins with the basic static concept of the isoquant—an abstraction of reality expressing trade-offs between goods while holding all other variables in a posited relationship fixed. Common isoquants are the production isoquant, which expresses trade-offs between chosen factor inputs while holding outputs and other factor inputs fixed, and the consumer indifference curve, which expresses trade-offs between chosen consumed goods while holding consumer satisfaction and other consumed commodities fixed. From this construct it is natural to base choice on a maximization problem of equating marginal trade-off with relative cost. Elements of the system can then be interrelated by the concept of a "market" to yield allocations of factor resources and consumed commodities. Conceptually, this same paradigm can be used for allocations over time to achieve a dynamic theory, but often special simplifying assumptions are introduced for changes in knowledge and in preferences (e.g., no such changes) and for uncertainty (e.g., perfect foresight).

A rising number, but still a proportionately small group, of academic economists reject this paradigm; the group is best represented in the United States by the Union for Radical Political Economics and its *Review*, in Western Europe by the Cambridge critique of neoclassical capital theory, and in many other countries by an acceptance of Marxian economics. One aspect of the radical criticism particularly deserves more attention prior to applied econometric research using the neoclassical paradigm: the extent to which neoclassical marginalism is "marginal." That is, it may be that nonoptimal utilization of factor inputs or nonoptimal consumption of commodities does not lead to substantial changes in costs so that empirical implications of

TABLE 1

Costs to Maintain Given Utility for Nonoptimal
Commodity Consumption Ratios
(Costs at Optimum: 1.00)[a]

Commodity consumption ratio X_1/X_2	Elasticity of indifferent substitution $\sigma = 1/(1-\rho)$					
	10.00	2.00	1.11	0.77	0.53	0.30
0.22	1.02	1.09	1.19	1.32	1.56	2.12
0.31	1.01	1.06	1.12	1.19	1.32	1.64
0.50	1.00	1.02	1.04	1.07	1.10	1.20
0.73	1.00	1.00	1.01	1.01	1.02	1.04
0.86	1.00	1.00	1.00	1.00	1.00	1.01
1.00	1.00	1.00	1.00	1.00	1.00	1.00
1.16	1.00	1.00	1.00	1.00	1.00	1.01
1.33	1.00	1.00	1.01	1.01	1.02	1.03
2.00	1.01	1.03	1.05	1.07	1.11	1.17
3.00	1.01	1.08	1.14	1.20	1.28	1.42
4.00	1.02	1.12	1.23	1.34	1.48	1.69

[a] Computer calculations of costs to maintain given utility U when the utility function is the CES $U = (\frac{1}{3}X_1^\rho + \frac{2}{3}X_2^\rho)^{1/\rho}$ where X_1 and X_2 are commodities consumed. The relative price of X_1 to X_2 is taken to equal 0.50 so that the optimal X_1/X_2 is 1.00 and the relative commodity share at the optimum is 0.50.

neoclassical theory cannot be expected to be sharply defined. For example, costs to maintain constant utility for an individual consuming two commodities are shown in Table 1 to be only slightly affected by substantial departures from the optimal commodity consumption ratio, particularly for higher values of the elasticity of indifferent substitution. If the neoclassical paradigm, by its abstraction from social, political, and psychological factors, is a weak description of economies, applied econometric research based on the paradigm would also be weak; i.e., the maintained hypothesis would not be stable.

On the other hand, inadequate development of neoclassical theory may be best represented by lack of well-articulated theories for technical and taste changes, for uncertainty, and for information and adjustment costs, and, more fundamentally, by lack of theories for motivations of economic actors. These limitations are well-recognized. What is not so commonly recognized for empirical work is that, since the heterogeneity of economic phenomena is enormous, a procedure for relating theory to observations requires some fundamental simplification of the theoretical system. This simplification has been the concept of a "composite" commodity. In purest form in Leontief (1936) and Hicks (1946, pp. 33–34, 312–313), a composite commodity is a grouping together of physically diverse commodities by their *unchanging* relative prices. In impure form, it is the grouping together of those commodities for which index number theory is believed to be relevant (see the recent treatment of index number theory by Fisher and Shell (1972)).[2] Yet theorists and econometricians have offered little advice on the proper choice for composite commodities.

The limitations of economic theory are important to bear in mind for applied econometric research and may very well explain remarks such as Leontief's. Nevertheless, econometric theory can offer much to the broader field of economics, particularly if its development stays in touch with the needs of changing economic theory. Thus, continued development of econometric theory will be an indispensable aid in verifying, refuting, and refining economic hypotheses as they arise.

The first two chapters of this volume, by J. B. Ramsey, and K. M. Gaver and M. S. Geisel, specifically focus on testing economic models with data. Ramsey is concerned with examining *ex post* of data for the validity of the standard econometric model $y = X\beta + \varepsilon$, where y is a vector of observations on a dependent variable, X is a matrix of observations on independent variables, β is a vector of fixed coefficients, and ε is a stochastic error term with zero mean and variance–covariance matrix Ω, and distributed independently of X (the most common case arising from assuming X nonrandom). Ramsey's concern is to test if evidence from estimated disturbances indicates that the assumptions of the linear model (including $\Omega = \sigma^2 I$) obtain for the particular empirical problem being investigated. The procedure he discusses may thus be quite useful for discriminating among alternative models of economic behavior.

Gaver and Geisel are also discussing procedures for model selection. The first part of their chapter summarizes model selection procedures based upon classical statistical inference, while the latter part discusses Bayesian procedures.[3] Bayesian inference, in fact, seems to find a most interesting application in these problems. To take one example, consider an investment theory

---

[2] An example of choice of composite commodities would be the choice of the measurement of "capital" in production economics: aggregate capital, capital in equipment and capital in structures, or a larger number of groupings of capital items. Incidentally, questions of capital aggregation, as asked, for example, by Fisher (1969 and references therein), do not deal with the problem of composite commodities. Rather they deal with the forming of a "consistent" index of several composite commodities—composite commodities that are decided before the index is attempted and that are needed to form the index.

[3] Until recently, econometrics was based almost solely upon classical statistical inference. But in the past decade, and particularly with the publication of the book by A. Zellner (1971), Bayesian inference in econometrics is becoming better understood and accepted. Nevertheless, Bayesian inference faces two fundamental difficulties before being widely adopted: first is the critical problem of appropriately choosing priors, and second is a demonstration that the computationally more difficult Bayesian techniques (stubborn integrations often require numerical integration procedures) have more to offer the advancement of economic knowledge than classical procedures.

such as D. W. Jorgenson's (best summarized in Jorgenson (1965)). In empirical work on investment, Jorgenson, on the one hand, assumes that the elasticity of factor substitution between capital and labor is unity; Eisner and Nadiri (1968), on the other hand, estimate it and find it much closer to zero. Bayesian econometricians might then interpret the resulting dispute over Jorgenson's assumption to say that Jorgenson has a prior on the substitution elasticity which is strongly peaked at unity (based, presumably, on supplementary evidence (Jorgenson, 1972)), while Eisner and Nadiri have a relatively flat prior on it. In other words, Bayesian analysis offers a relatively compact procedure to indicate the manner in which the prior beliefs of an econometrician enter his empirical work. And Bayesian model discrimination can be used for much more divergent models than our example, as Gaver and Geisel show.

Each of the other contributions in the volume generalizes the standard linear econometric model in a specific way: P. Zarembka, through nonlinear transformations on dependent or independent variables; D. McFadden, for models involving discrete choices; P. A. V. B. Swamy, by studying estimation when the β vector is random; L. D. Taylor, by suggesting estimation by minimizing the sum of absolute errors when the covariance matrix Ω is undefined (infinite); A. S. Goldberger, through analyzing models with unobservable variables; and J. M. Brundy and D. W. Jorgenson, by analyzing instrumental variable estimation of simultaneous equation systems.

Economic theory sometimes suggests a nonlinear functional form for a maintained hypothesis. More often theory has little to suggest by way of functional form, but there is little reason to expect linearity in the observed variables to be the appropriate specification. The principal focus of the Zarembka contribution is the possibility that the standard model may only obtain with nonlinear transformations on either the dependent or the independent variables. In particular, as in the CES production function, transformations of variables may be available that attain linearity of the model (implying "additivity"[4]) so that linear techniques can be applied to the transformed variables. The problem in econometric theory then arises from estimating the transformation under assumptions about the error vector.

D. McFadden also considers specification of variables; his particular concern is for economic models involving discrete decision variables, such as choice of urban transformation mode, college attended, and occupation, or for such household decisions as geographical location, housing, and labor

---

[4] Christensen, Jorgenson, and Lau (1973) have discussed additivity and have proposed a functional form that allows additivity of a functional form to be a tested, rather than a maintained, hypothesis. For more than a few independent variables, that functional form involves a linear model in a large number of regressors ($n(n+3)/2$, where n is the number of independent variables).

force participation. Not only are many of these decisions discrete, rather than continuous, but they are described in models partly by the individual's socio-economic characteristics that are themselves discrete. McFadden suggests an approach to such models by first developing an underlying economic theory in which outcomes of decisions are viewed as a *probability* of a particular individual's choice, then setting up a maximum likelihood procedure for estimation.

If models available from economic theory are attempting to capture the essence of reality, as surely they must, rather than reality itself, then econo-metricians cannot have full faith that the β coefficient vector does not vary across observations or that the observations contained in the **X** matrix directly reflect theoretical constructs. Assumptions that β is a fixed vector or that the **X** matrix is measured without error are made in the belief that, in many circumstances, these assumptions do not significantly distort econometric results. In the next decade, both assumptions will probably undergo increasing scrutiny. Thus, we may find it increasingly implausible that all firms have the same cost conditions and technological blueprints or that all consumers have the same preferences. And econometricians may return to regard errors-in-variables at least almost as important as errors-in-equations.

P. A. V. B. Swamy suggests an approach to variations in decision-making units across observations by regarding β as a random vector, distributed independently of **X**. The mean of β can be viewed as a "representative" coefficient vector (as "$v(s, x)$" is the representative tastes in McFadden's work). Swamy's problem is to develop a procedure to estimate the mean of β and its variance–covariance matrix. By assuming β fixed for an individual over time but varying randomly across individuals, panel data become most useful for estimation.[5]

A further important use of random cofficient models, as suggested by Zellner (1969) and mentioned by Swamy, is to regard the β in *aggregate* economic analysis as a mean of microeconomic coefficients.[6] Zellner showed that the standard least squares estimate of β in such circumstances is unbiased if β is distributed independently of **X**, but that the usually calculated standard errors are biased estimates of the standard deviations of the estimated means for the elements of β. Theil (1971, pp. 570–573) extended this analysis to indicate that if the number of microeconomic units composing the aggregate becomes indefinitely large, then the β vector could be treated as fixed.

---

[5] In a yet unpublished work, Hsiao (1972) extends Swamy's problem to allow for random variations over time for an individual, as well as random variations across individuals.

[6] The importance of aggregation problems is mentioned above, but little empirical work is available on aggregation bias. One recent study is that by Feige and Watts (1972) who find that, for U.S. commercial bank data, "the likelihood of bias when data are aggregated up to state means is so great as to make them almost useless" (p. 356).

Note that Swamy's work, as well as Zellner's and Theil's, is most applicable to consumer theory, where it is more reasonable to assume that such variables as income, prices, socioeconomic characteristics, etc., are outside the consumer's (immediate) control. Use of such a random coefficient framework in production theory requires extension to a simultaneous system in which the firm would be expected to know its own technological coefficients (i.e., β) and thus be influenced in its choice of inputs (i.e., X); in other words, distributional independence of β with X would be lacking (thus, see Kelejian (1973)).

As mentioned above, another econometric problem that is receiving increasing attention is errors-in-variables. Thus, the variables suggested by economic theory are often not accurately reflected even in ideal data. Furthermore, many economists are sufficiently skeptical of data quality to doubt most applied econometric reasearch.[7] A leading example of the problem of errors of measurement is in the estimation of production functions with capital and labor as arguments. Leaving aside whether "capital" ought to be regarded as a composite commodity,[8] there are well-known difficulties in measuring the value of capital stock and then interpreting it as a flow of services of "real" input. Virtually all production function estimates, however, do not explicitly recognize the econometric problems created by poor measurement of capital input, perhaps because the error-in-variables problem has been a particularly difficult nut to crack.

The work of A. S. Goldberger seems to offer a breakthrough. In the production function example, suppose we have observations not only on "real" capital input, albeit measured with considerable error, but also observations on electric energy consumed. Suppose that we are willing to argue that electric energy is another measure of the services of real capital and also that the errors in the two measures of capital are distributed with zero mean and constant variance and independently of each other, of the theoretical but unobserved capital, and of the production function disturbance term. Then, if the labor input is measured without error, the maximum likelihood principle can be applied to estimate consistently the parameters of the model, in which measured capital stock, energy, and output are all treated as "indicators" of true capital.

In Goldberger's work, a difficult problem is solved by changing the approach to the problem; i.e., instead of asking how to handle an errors-in-variables problem with a given set of data, Goldberger is suggesting the introduction of additional data sets as measures of the variables subject to error. Also, note that the suggestion for handling measurement errors in a multiple-indicator model arises not out of economics, but rather from the geneticist S. Wright and from psychometrics (as discussed by Goldberger (1972)). In these

[7] The classic reference on the accuracy of economic observations is Morgenstern (1963).

[8] An interpretation of capital as a composite commodity is developed in Zarembka (1973).

disciplines, researchers are not convinced that their models are directly reflected in data and, accordingly, naturally treat observations as "indicators" of cause and effect hypotheses. Perhaps there is a lesson here: if economic data are used more skeptically, maybe economics as a science will advance more rapidly.[9]

An assumption of the standard linear model that is perhaps least obvious is that the variance–covariance matrix of ε is Ω. A direct implication is that this matrix is defined. Some economists, particularly B. Mandelbrot (1963, 1967), argue that the distribution of some economic stochastic processes has sufficiently large tails (i.e., the probability of "outliers" is sufficiently high) that their distributions are better characterized by a probability distribution which has an undefined (or infinite) variance. The stable distribution with an α parameter less than two is a leading example. The point, of course, is not so much that we really care if the variance of a stochastic economic process is infinite rather than very large, but that its variance may be sufficiently large that estimation procedures derived under the assumption of an infinite variance should be more robust to outlying observations. In particular, L. D. Taylor suggests and discusses estimation by minimizing the sum of *absolute* errors (rather than the usual squared errors, i.e., least squares).

The final contribution, by J. M. Brundy and D. W. Jorgenson, draws its inspiration from the problems of estimating moderate- to large-scale econometric models. Two- and three-stage least squares were developed as computationally simpler alternatives to the maximum likelihood principle to consistently estimate part, or all, of a simultaneous economic model. These methods require a "first-stage" regression of each endogenous variable on the full list of all predetermined variables, and, in moderate- to large-scale models, the number of predetermined variables can easily approach or even exceed the number of observations. Brundy and Jorgenson therefore approach the problem of estimating simultaneous equation systems from the point of view of instrumental variable estimators, derive necessary and sufficient conditions for them to be asymptotically efficient, and suggest an instrumental variable estimator that is consistent and asymptotically efficient even in large-scale econometric models. Note that the illustrative example they provide here (Klein's Model I) can also be estimated consistently and efficiently by two- and three-stage least squares (which can be interpreted as instrumental variable estimators); the T. C. Liu model they consider in Brundy and Jorgenson (1971) could also, in principle, but the number of predetermined variables is 46 (!) while the number of observations is 88.

---

[9] A recent, intriguing paper by Hartley and Revankar (1973) on the topic of unobservable variables develops the estimation of a Pareto distributed variable when the observations on the variable are underreported (as, for example, for income reported on tax returns). Thus, in their work the distribution of measurement errors is onesided.

The contributions in this volume define a number of frontiers in econometric theory. Most of them illustrate with empirical applications. It is often through econometrics that theoretical hypotheses are confronted with data, and it is often through econometrics that economists attempt to use theory for purposes of quantitative policy. While applied research cannot be better than the underlying economic theory and available data, it also cannot be better than statistical procedures utilized.

REFERENCES

Brundy, J. M. and D. W. Jorgenson (1971). "Efficient Estimation of Simultaneous Equations by Instrumental Variables," *Rev. Econ. Stat.* **53**, 207–224.

Christensen, L. R., D. W. Jorgenson, and L. J. Lau (1973). "Transcendental Logarithmic Production Frontiers," *Rev. Econ. Stat.* **55**, 28–45.

Cooper, R. L. (1972). "The Predictive Performance of Quarterly Econometric Models of the United States," in *Econometric Models of Cyclical Behavior* (Conference on Research on Income and Wealth, Vol. 36, B. G. Hickman, ed.), pp. 813–926. National Bureau of Economic Research, New York.

Eisner, R. and M. I. Nadiri (1968). "Investment Behavior and the Neoclassical Theory," *Rev. Econ. Statist.* **50**, 369–382.

Feige, E. L. and H. W. Watts (1972). "An Investigation of the Consequences of Partial Aggregation of Microeconomic Data," *Econometrica*, **40**, 343–360.

Fisher, F. M. (1969). "The Existence of Aggregate Production Functions," *Econometrica* **37**, 553–577.

Fisher, F. M. and K. Shell (1972). *The Economic Theory of Price Indices: Two Essays on the Effects of Taste, Quality, and Technological Change*, Academic Press, New York.

Goldberger, A. S. (1972). "Structural Equation Methods in the Social Sciences," *Econometrica* **40**, 979–1002.

Hartley, M. J. and N. S. Revankar (1973). "On the Estimation of the Pareto Law from Under-Reported Data," *J. Econometrics* (forthcoming).

Hicks, J. R. (1946). *Value and Capital*, 2nd ed., Clarendon Press, Oxford (1st ed., 1939).

Hsiao, C. (1972). "Some Estimation Methods for a Random Coefficients Model," Tech. Rep. 77, Economics Series, Institute for Mathematical Studies in the Social Sciences, Stanford.

Jorgenson, D. W. (1965). "Anticipations and Investment Behavior," in *The Brookings Quarterly Econometric Model of the United States*. Rand McNally, Chicago.

Jorgenson, D. W. (1972). "Investment Behavior and the Production Function," *Bell J. Econ. Management Sci.* **3**, 220–251.

Kelejian, H. H. (1973). "Random Parameters in a Simultaneous Equation Framework: Identification and Estimation," *Econometrica* (forthcoming).

Leontief, W. (1936). "Composite Commodities and the Problem of Index Numbers," *Econometrica* **4**, 39–59.

Leontief, W. (1971). "Theoretical Assumptions and Nonobserved Facts," *Amer. Econ. Rev.* **61**, 1–7.

Mandelbrot, B. (1963). "The Variance of Certain Speculative Prices," *J. Business* **36**, 307–332.

Mandelbrot, B. (1967). "The Variance of Some Other Speculative Prices," *J. Business* **40**, 393–413.

Morgenstern, O. (1963). *On the Accuracy of Economic Observations*, 2nd ed., Princeton University Press, Princeton (1st ed., 1950).

Nelson, C. R. (1972). "The Prediction Performance of the FRB-MIT-PENN Model of the U.S. Economy," *Amer. Econ. Rev.* **62**, 902–917.

Theil, H. (1971), *Principles of Econometrics*, Wiley, New York.

Zarembka, P. (1973). "Capital Heterogeneity, Aggregation, and the Two-Sector Model," *Quart. J. Econ.* (forthcoming).

Zellner, A. (1969). "On the Aggregation Problem: A New Approach to a Troublesome Problem," in *Economic Models, Estimation, and Risk Programming: Essays in Honor of Gerhard Tintner* (K. A. Fox, G. V. L. Narasimham, and J. K. Sengupta, eds.), Springer-Verlag, Berlin, Heidelberg, and New York.

Zellner, A. (1971). *An Introduction to Bayesian Inference in Econometrics*, Wiley, New York.

Part I

MODEL SELECTION

Chapter One

Classical model selection through specification error tests

JAMES B. RAMSEY[1]

MICHIGAN STATE UNIVERSITY
EAST LANSING, MICHIGAN

   [1] The author gratefully acknowledges financial support from the National Science Foundation (GS-3291) and from the Social Science Research Council (HR2166/1) in the U.K.

13

To Understand is to Predict; but to Predict is, perhaps, to Err.

Frequently, economists, not noting the difference in objectives between the prediction of economic events and the understanding of the structure of economic systems, confuse the fundamental issues involved in the comparison of economic models. The question is why one should bother with complicated economic models when a simple extrapolation of past trends "does just as well." While it is true that if one merely wishes to predict the value of a variable within a well-specified experimental region, a formal model is not necessary; it is also true that if one wishes to predict outside that region or to modify the system, a formal model is necessary.

The former problem is known as the response surface problem (Box and Hunter, 1962). The idea is that if one has a set of control variables constrained to lie in a well-defined region and if one wishes to predict the values taken by the dependent variables in response to the controls, then any simple function (often a polynomial) that produces a good fit to the data will do. As long as the system and its constraints remain unchanged and one is concerned only with interpolations, accurate predictions will continue to be made. However, efforts to extrapolate results beyond the observed experimental region or to evaluate changes in the constraints and/or the structure of a system require considerable knowledge of that structure; "mathematical French curves" will no longer suffice (Hunter and Reiner, 1965).

Since the use of econometric models invariably involves extrapolation, knowledge of the structure of the system is essential. Yet, unlike in the response surface problem, where high multiple correlation coefficient values usually provide an adequate criterion for choosing between alternative models, a high correlation value in the econometric case is at best an uncertain guide. Indeed, the task is often to choose between models each of which provides "a good fit" to the data; an example is provided by Ramsey and Zarembka (1971), who consider five alternative functional forms for aggregate production functions, all of which had coefficient of determination values of about 0.99. In sum, the econometric problem requires much more sophisticated and sensitive procedures than the relatively simple response surface problem.

This chapter is concerned with the econometric problem. Attention will be given mainly to the single-equation linear regression model, since the complex issues involved in the nonlinear extensions of the theory are best understood in terms of the linear model. It is assumed throughout that the disturbance terms are independent over the sample space. It is also assumed that one has only one nonexperimentally-controlled sample of modest size so that iterative search strategies (Box and Lucas, 1959) and sequential methods (Box and Hill, 1967) are not applicable. The analysis of evaluation criteria for large scale econometric macro models is omitted; the interested reader is referred to Dhrymes *et al* (1972).

I. Some Examples of Specification Errors and Their Effects on Inference

Such concepts as "true model," "specification error," *etc.* will be defined rigorously in the next section. For now, it suffices to rely on the vague idea that there is some model which describes the stochastic behavior of the variables and this is the "true model." Specification errors of various types are committed when one uses some other model to analyze the data.

Errors in the context of the single-equation linear model will be examined first, followed by a general discussion of asymptotic results in the context of single-equation nonlinear models. Then a system of linear equations is considered briefly.

Linear Models

Consider the following model:

$$(1) \qquad\qquad \mathbf{y} = X\boldsymbol{\beta} + \mathbf{u},$$

where $\mathbf{y}$ is an $N \times 1$ regressand vector, X is an $N \times K$ nonstochastic regressor matrix of rank K, $\boldsymbol{\beta}$ is a $K \times 1$ vector of regression coefficients, and $\mathbf{u}$ is an $N \times 1$ vector of independent disturbance terms identically distributed as Normal with mean zero and variance σ^2. Equation (1) specifies the null hypothesis. For each of the specification errors, the alternative hypothesis is defined by specifying that the true model has some other specification. Thus the use of regression Equation (1) to analyze data generated by some other model leads to specification error. The errors considered are: (a) omitted variables, (b) incorrect functional form of the regressors, (c) simultaneous equation problems, (d) heteroskedasticity, (e) nonnormality of the disturbance term, and (f) errors in the variables. Only summary results are given and the reader is referred for further details to Theil (1957), Ramsey (1968a, 1969), Richardson and Wu (1970), and Goldfeld and Quandt (1972). The last reference is particularly recommended for an extensive and detailed discussion of heteroskedasticity.

Under the alternative hypotheses, the specifications of the true models which would give rise to these errors when Equation (1) is used are

$$(2a) \qquad\qquad \mathbf{y} = X\boldsymbol{\beta} + \mathbf{z}\gamma + \mathbf{v},$$

$$(2b) \qquad\qquad \mathbf{y} = Z\gamma + \mathbf{v},$$

$$(2c) \qquad\qquad \mathbf{y} = Z\gamma + W\boldsymbol{\delta} + \mathbf{v},$$

$$(2d) \qquad\qquad \mathbf{y} = X\boldsymbol{\beta} + \mathbf{v}, \quad \mathbf{v} \sim N(\varnothing, \sigma^2\Omega),$$

$$(2e) \qquad\qquad \mathbf{y} = X\boldsymbol{\beta} + \mathbf{v}, \quad v_i \sim \chi_1^2,$$

$$(2f) \qquad\qquad \mathbf{y} = Z\boldsymbol{\beta} + \mathbf{v}.$$

In model (2a), the specification of $\mathbf{y}$, X, and $\boldsymbol{\beta}$ are the same as in Equation (1). $\mathbf{z}$ is an $N \times 1$ nonstochastic regressor vector, γ is the corresponding coefficient, and $\mathbf{v}$ is distributed as $N(\varnothing, \sigma^2 I)$. If one uses Equation (1) to estimate the coefficient vector $\boldsymbol{\beta}$, one has a misspecified model where the misspecification is that of omitting the variable $\mathbf{z}$. In model (2b), where Z is nonstochastic and $\mathbf{v}$ is distributed as $N(\varnothing, \sigma^2 I)$, if one considers a matrix X whose elements are obtained from the elements of the matrix Z by nonstochastic nonlinear transformations and one uses Equation (1) as the regression model instead of (2b), then one would have a misspecified model in which the misspecification is that of incorrect functional form of the regressors. In (2c), let $\mathbf{y}$ be an $N \times 1$ regressand vector, Z an $N \times K_1$ nonstochastic full rank matrix of regressors with γ the corresponding coefficient vector, W an $N \times K_2$ *stochastic* matrix of regressors of rank K_2 in observed samples with $\boldsymbol{\delta}$ the corresponding coefficient vector, and let $\mathbf{v}$ be the $N \times 1$ vector of disturbance terms distributed as $N(\varnothing, \sigma^2 I)$, where the elements of each row of W and the corresponding v_i, $i = 1, 2, \ldots, N$, are statistically *dependent*. Define the $N \times K$ matrix X by $X = (Z : W)$, $K = K_1 + K_2$, and the $K \times 1$ vector $\boldsymbol{\beta}$ by $\boldsymbol{\beta}' = (\gamma', \delta')$. If one were to assume that the model $\mathbf{y} = X\boldsymbol{\beta} + \mathbf{v}$ so defined satisfies the conditions given in Equation (1), one has a misspecified model in which the misspecification is denoted the "simultaneous equation problem." In (2d), all the specifications made for model (1) are correct except that $\sigma^2 \Omega$ is assumed to be diagonal, but with unequal elements on the diagonal. σ^2 is a scaling factor. If one uses a model such as (1), the specification error of heteroskedasticity is said to have been made. In Equation (2e), all the specifications made for model (1) hold except for the normality of the disturbance term's distribution, which in this case is assumed to be distributed as central chi-square with one degree of freedom. The last specification error is illustrated in terms of the simple formulation given in Equations (3) where $K = 2$. In terms of Equation (2f), the specification error lies in the nonzero correlation between the elements of the matrix Z and the vector $\mathbf{v}$.

$$\eta_i = \beta_0 + \beta_1 \xi_i, \qquad E(u_i u_j) = \sigma_u^2, \quad i = j$$
$$= 0, \quad i \neq j$$

(3) $\qquad x_i = \xi_i + u_i, \qquad E(v_i v_j) = \sigma_v^2, \quad i = j$

$$y_i = \eta_i + v_i, \qquad = 0, \quad i \neq j$$

$$E(u_i) = E(v_i) = 0, \qquad E(u_i v_j) = 0 \quad \text{for all} \quad i, j,$$

$$i = 1, 2, \ldots, N,$$

where the variable ξ_i (and hence η_i) is nonstochastic and only x_i, y_i are observed. The potential inferential effects of these errors are best indicated by giving in each case the distributions of $\hat{\boldsymbol{\beta}} = (X'X)^{-1}X'\mathbf{y}$, and of $\hat{\mathbf{u}} = M\mathbf{y}$, $M = [I - X(X'X)^{-1}X']$, where the estimators are obtained from model (1). The mean vectors and covariance matrices of $\hat{\boldsymbol{\beta}}$ and $\hat{\mathbf{u}}$ complete the summary of results which are listed in Table 1. The covariance matrices are the population parameters, not the expected values of the least squares estimates. From the distribution of $\hat{\mathbf{u}}$, one can easily calculate in each case the bias and inconsistency of the estimator $\hat{\mathbf{u}}'\hat{\mathbf{u}}/(N-K)$ for the parameter σ^2.

In models (2a) to (2c) (see Table 1), if $\mathbf{z} \perp X$, $Z \perp X$, and $\boldsymbol{\eta}_{v|x} \perp X$, $\hat{\boldsymbol{\beta}}$ will not be biased, and $\hat{\mathbf{u}}'\hat{\mathbf{u}}/\sigma^2$ will be distributed as central chi-square with $(N-K)$ degrees of freedom. In model (2e) only the constant term is biased, i.e., $E\{\beta_0\} = \beta_0 + 1$. If a constant term is included in regression model (1) for true model (2e), then $M\mathbf{i} = \varnothing$ and $\mathbf{i}'\hat{\mathbf{u}}/2$ is distributed as central chi-square with $(N-K)$ degrees of freedom. The properties of the multivariate distributions $h_a(\cdot)$ and $h_b(\cdot)$ are easily obtained from the corresponding characteristic generating functions since each element of $\hat{\boldsymbol{\beta}}$ and of $\hat{\mathbf{u}}$ are weighted sums of independently and identically distributed chi-square variables.

The distribution of $\hat{\beta}_1$ in model (2f) is $g(\hat{\beta}_1', \beta_1', r, N)$, where $g(\cdot)$ is given explicitly in Richardson and Wu (1970, p. 727). For convenience, the distribution is expressed in terms of standardized parameters; i.e., $\beta_1' = \beta_1 \sigma_u/\sigma_v$ and $\hat{\beta}_1' = \hat{\beta}_1 \sigma_u/\sigma_v$. The term r is given by

$$(4) \qquad\qquad r = \sum_1^N \frac{(\xi_i - \bar{\xi})^2}{2\sigma_u^2}.$$

$E\{\hat{\beta}_1\}$ given in Table 1 can be reexpressed to show the connection with the well-known asymptotic results by considering to terms of $O(n^{-2})$:

$$(5) \qquad\qquad \frac{E(\hat{\beta}_1 - \beta_1)}{\beta_1} \doteq \frac{-1}{1 + 2r/N}\left(1 - \frac{r^2 N/2}{(1 + Nr/2)^2}\right),$$

where the first term in Equation (5) is the well-known asymptotic result. The remaining entries for model (2f) have not been completed since the analysis is extremely complicated.

The results in Table 1 can be summarized by noting that there are three types of error. Group A errors are those which lead to a shift in the central tendency of the estimator; i.e., if the estimator were unbiased, the error leads to bias; or if the estimator were biased, but consistent, the error leads to a different bias and inconsistency. Omitted variables, incorrect functional form, and the simultaneous equations problem (under the appropriate conditions) are examples. Group B errors are those which lead to a change in the covariance matrix of the estimators, an example of which is heteroskedasticity. Group C errors are those in which the distribution of the disturbance terms is not the same as that assumed in the model specification, so that the distribution of the regression coefficient estimators is affected.

TABLE 1

EFFECTS OF SOME EXAMPLES OF SPECIFICATION ERRORS ON OLS ESTIMATORS

Model	Distribution $\hat\beta$	Mean $\hat\beta$	Covariance matrix $\hat\beta$	Distribution $\hat u$	Mean $\hat u$	Covariance matrix $\hat u$
2a	N^a	$\beta + (X'X)^{-1}X'z\gamma$	$\sigma^2(X'X)^{-1}$	N_s^b	$Mz\gamma^a$	$\sigma^2 M$
2b	N	$(X'X)^{-1}X'Z\gamma$	$\sigma^2(X'X)^{-1}$	N_s	$MZ\gamma$	$\sigma^2 M$
2c	N	$(X'X)^{-1}X'\eta_{v|x}{}^c$	$\sigma_{v|x}^2(X'X)^{-1}{}^d$	N_s	$M\eta_{v|x}$	$\sigma_{v|x}^2 M$
2d	N	β	$\sigma^2(X'X)^{-1}(X'\Omega X)(X'X)^{-1}$	N_s	$\varnothing$	$\sigma^2 M\Omega M$
2e	$h_a(\beta)^e$	$\beta + (X'X)^{-1}X'i$	$2(X'X)^{-1}$	$h_b(\hat u)$	Mi	$2M$
2f	$g(\hat\beta_1, \beta_1'; r, N)$	$\beta_1 \dfrac{2r}{N} e^{-r} {}_1F_1\left(\dfrac{N}{2}, \dfrac{N+2}{2}; r\right)^f$	—	—	—	—

[a] N is the normal distribution; $M = I - X(X'X)^{-1}X'$, $i' = (1,1,\ldots,1)$.

[b] N_s is the singular normal distribution; i.e., a multivariate distribution whose covariance matrix is singular.

[c] $\eta_{v|x}$ is the conditional mean of vector v given the regressor matrix $X = (Z:W)$.

[d] $\sigma_{v|x}^2$ is the conditional variance of the disturbance term given the regressor matrix $X = (Z:W)$.

[e] $h_a(\cdot)$, $h_b(\cdot)$, and $g(\cdot)$ are distributions defined in the text.

[f] ${}_1F_1(\cdot)$ is the confluent hypergeometric distribution.

In so far as a specific error is a member of only one of Groups A to C, it is potentially feasible to consider discriminating between the different groups of errors. With the current approach, errors within the same group are observationally unidentifiable.

Asymptotic Results for Nonlinear Models

The conclusions derived in the previous subsection were all exact. In this section some useful asymptotic results will be given only for the case of maximum likelihood estimators that satisfy the usual regularity conditions; see, for example, Kendall and Stuart (1961, Vol. 2, Chapter 18). The analysis presented essentially follows that of Cox (1961).

Let us consider first of all a single parameter parent probability distribution function (p.d.f.) $f(y, \alpha \,|\, x)$, where y is the random dependent variable, x is a non-stochastic variable, and α is the parameter. The alternative model is also assumed to be a single parameter distribution and is denoted by $g(y, \beta \,|\, x)$. It is assumed that $f(y, \alpha \,|\, x)$ designates the true p.d.f. Consider the problem of determining the asymptotic joint distribution of the estimators $\hat{\alpha}$ and $\hat{\beta}$, where $\hat{\alpha}$ is the maximum likelihood estimator of α and $\hat{\beta}$ is defined by the solution to

$$(6) \qquad \frac{\partial Lg(\hat{\beta})}{\partial \hat{\beta}} = 0,$$

where

$$Lg(\hat{\beta}) = \sum_{i=1}^{N} \log g(y_i, \hat{\beta} \,|\, x_i).$$

It will be assumed for the moment that there exists a unique solution to (6) and that $\hat{\beta}$ converges in probability as $N \to \infty$ to a limit β_α. It should be noted that this implies some regularity in the behavior of the sequence $x_1, x_2, \ldots$ and that in general β_α will be a function of the x_i, $i = 1, 2, \ldots$ as well as of α. For example, in the omitted variables case in the linear model, the asymptotic analysis would require a condition of the type

$$(7) \qquad \lim_{N \to \infty} \{N(X'X)^{-1}(1/N) X'\mathbf{z}\gamma\} = \sigma_{xz}\gamma,$$

where σ_{xz} is some finite constant. Expanding Equation (6) around β_α yields

$$(8) \qquad (\hat{\beta} - \beta_\alpha) \doteq \frac{-\partial Lg(\hat{\beta})/\partial \hat{\beta}}{\partial^2 Lg(\beta_\alpha)/\partial^2 \beta},$$

where numerator and denominator are individually sums of N independent terms. Following the usual argument and since $\hat{\beta}$ is consistent for β_α, then the expectation of $\partial \ln g(y, \beta_\alpha \,|\, x)/\partial \beta$ with respect to $f(y, \alpha \,|\, x)$ is zero. Consequently, the statistic $(\hat{\beta} - \beta_\alpha)$ is asymptotically distributed as Normal with mean β_α and variance $\sigma_\alpha^2(\hat{\beta})$ given by

(9)
$$\sigma_\alpha^2(\hat{\beta}) = \frac{E_\alpha\{[\partial Lg(\beta_\alpha)/\partial\beta]^2\}}{[E_\alpha\{\partial^2 Lg(\beta_\alpha)/\partial^2\beta\}]^2},$$

where $E_\alpha\{\cdot\}$ denotes expectation with respect to the distribution $f(\cdot)$ and the partial derivatives are evaluated at $\hat{\beta} = \beta_\alpha$. The covariance between $\hat{\alpha}$ and $\hat{\beta}$ is

(10)
$$\mathrm{Cov}(\hat{\alpha}, \hat{\beta}) = \frac{-d\beta_\alpha/d\alpha}{E_\alpha\{\partial^2 Lf(\alpha)/\partial\alpha^2\}}.$$

Finally, it is clear that $\hat{\alpha}$ and $\hat{\beta}$ are asymptotically bivariate normal with mean vector (α, β_α). In practical cases, one replaces the asymptotic expectations by consistent estimates, i.e., by the mean values of the partial derivatives of the log likelihoods.

Let us now consider the generalization to the situation in which both distributions are defined by a vector of parameters. The true and alternative p.d.f.'s are now $f(y, \alpha | x)$ and $g(y, \beta | z)$, respectively, where x and z are vectors of nonstochastic variables. As before, given $f(\cdot)$ is the true distribution and given appropriate assumptions about the sequences $x_1, x_2, \ldots$ and $z_1, z_2, \ldots$, assume that $\hat{\beta}$ converges in probability to a limit β_α. Let us define

(11)
$$F_i = N^{-1} \sum_{j=1}^N \frac{\partial \log f(y_j, \alpha | x_j)}{\partial\alpha_i}, \qquad i = 1, 2, \ldots, df$$

$$G_i = N^{-1} \sum_{j=1}^N \frac{\partial \log g(y_j, \beta_\alpha | z_j)}{\partial\beta_i}, \qquad i = 1, 2, \ldots, dg$$

$$F_{ij} = \sum_{l=1}^N \frac{\partial^2 \log f(y_l, \alpha | x_l)}{\partial\alpha_i \partial\alpha_j}, \qquad i, j = 1, 2, \ldots, df$$

$$G_{ij} = \sum_{l=1}^N \frac{\partial^2 \log g(y_l, \beta_\alpha | z_l)}{\partial\beta_i \partial\beta_j}, \qquad i, j = 1, 2, \ldots, dg.$$

Let $\mathcal{F} = \{\mathcal{F}^{ij}\}$ be the inverse of the matrix $E_\alpha\{N^{-1}F_{ij}\}$ and $\mathcal{G} = \{\mathcal{G}^{ij}\}$ be the inverse of $E_\alpha\{N^{-1}G_{ij}\}$.

Corresponding to Equation (8), the maximum likelihood normal equations for $\hat{\alpha}$ and $\hat{\beta}$ are

(12)
$$F_i + \sum_j [E_\alpha\{N^{-1}F_{ij}\}](\hat{\alpha}_j - \alpha_j) = 0$$

and

(13)
$$G_i + \sum_j [E_\alpha\{N^{-1}G_{ij}\}](\hat{\beta}_j - \beta_{\alpha j}) = 0$$

or

(14)
$$(\hat{\alpha}_i - \alpha_i) = -\sum_j \mathscr{F}^{ij} F_j$$

and

(15)
$$(\hat{\beta}_i - \beta_{\alpha i}) = -\sum_j \mathscr{G}^{ij} G_j,$$

where F_j; $j = 1, 2, ..., df$ is by assumption the sum of N independently distributed random variables with mean zero. The same is true for G_j, $j = 1, 2, ..., dg$. The multivariate analog to the relationship between the derivative of β_α with respect to α and the partials of the likelihood functions is

(16)
$$\sum_{l=1}^{dg} E_\alpha\{\mathscr{G}_{il}\} \frac{\partial \beta_{\alpha l}}{\partial \alpha_j} + E_\alpha\{G_i F_j\} = 0.$$

Using these relations plus the standard ones involving the expected values of partials of likelihood functions one obtains asymptotically

(17)
$$\text{Cov}(\hat{\alpha}_i - \alpha_i, \hat{\alpha}_j - \alpha_j) = -\frac{1}{N} \mathscr{F}^{ij},$$

(18)
$$\text{Cov}(\hat{\alpha}_i - \alpha_i, \hat{\beta}_j - \beta_{\alpha j}) = -\frac{1}{N}\left(\sum_{l=1}^{dg} \mathscr{F}^{il} \frac{\partial \beta_{\alpha j}}{\partial \alpha_l}\right),$$

(19)
$$\text{Cov}(\hat{\beta}_i - \beta_{\alpha i}, \hat{\beta}_j - \beta_{\alpha j}) = \frac{1}{N} \mathscr{G} E_\alpha\{\mathbf{GG}'\} \mathscr{G},$$

where

$$\mathbf{G}' = (G_1, G_2, ..., G_{dg}).$$

To conclude, the vector $(\hat{\boldsymbol{\alpha}}, \hat{\boldsymbol{\beta}})$ defined by Equations (14) and (15) is asymptotically distributed as multivariate normal with mean vector (α, β_α) and covariance matrix given by Equations (17) to (19).

Another technique which provides some theoretical results needed later in the paper is given by assuming that the true distribution is

(20)
$$y_i = \mathbf{x}_i'\boldsymbol{\beta} + u_i, \qquad i = 1, 2, ..., N$$

where the u_i, $i = 1, 2, ..., N$, are independently and identically distributed as normal with zero mean and variance σ^2. The alternative model is given by

(21)
$$w_i = \ln(y_i) = \mathbf{x}_i'\boldsymbol{\alpha} + v_i.$$

It is assumed that the value of $|\mathbf{x}_i'\boldsymbol{\beta}|$ is sufficiently large relative to the value of σ^2 so that the probability of observing $y_i \leqslant 0$ is negligible. The opposite problem, i.e., where Equation (21) is the true model and Equation (20) is the alternative misspecified model, was analyzed by Theil (1957).

conditioning variables $\mathbf{x}$, and a vector of parameters $\boldsymbol{\theta}$, where $y \in Y$, $\mathbf{x} \in X$, and $\boldsymbol{\theta} \in \Theta$. The specification of $F(\cdot)$ includes specifying the structure of the sets Y, X, and Θ.

This latter point is one frequently overlooked by econometricians. For example, whether $\theta \in [0, 1]$ or $\in (0, 1)$ or $\in \{0, 1\}$ is important for the appropriate choice of estimator and test procedure. The importance for estimation and testing in noting that $Y = \{0, 1\}$, i.e., that y is a binary variable, has received considerable attention only comparatively recently. Finally, careful attention to the structure of the space X may enable one to derive modified procedures which have significant advantages over standard techniques. As an obvious example, there is both a gain in estimating efficiency and a saving in computational effort if the regression matrix in a linear regression is composed of orthogonal vectors.

The function $F(\cdot)$ defined on some subset of the Cartesian product of Y, X, and Θ defines a set, say $\mathscr{F}$, which is known in economics as a model. The class M is the set of all sets isomorphic to the set $\mathscr{F}$. It will be recalled that two sets are said to be isomorphic to each other if they are related by an isomorphism, which is a 1-1 transformation that preserves group compositions; see, for example, Jacobson (1951).

A simple example will clarify this notion. One might specify the model $y = \theta_0 x^{\theta_1} v$, where v is distributed as ln normal. An isomorphism of this model is $\ln y = \ln \theta_0 + \theta_1 \ln x + \ln v$, where $\ln v$ is distributed normally. These two models are equivalent to each other and both are contained in the same equivalence class, M. However, from the point of view of statistical analysis one member of a given class may be preferable to another, as is well illustrated by the cited example.

At this point it is useful to note that models can be defined at various levels of generality. Thus, using the above example, a more general model is defined if v is merely specified to be continuous, and a less general model is specified if $\theta_1 \in [0, 1]$.

With these preliminaries completed, the problem of distinguishing alternative models can be discussed. Basically, there are three cases. If M_1 and M_2 denote two classes of models, then one must consider $M_1 \subset M_2$, $M_1 \cap M_2 \neq \varnothing$, and $M_1 \cap M_2 = \varnothing$. The first situation, i.e., $M_1 \subset M_2$, is the simplest and is the one for which classical procedures are best suited, especially if the distinction between M_1 and M_2 can be expressed in terms of parameters. For example, the class M_1 might be generated by the Cobb–Douglas production function and M_2 by the CES production function. Thus, the choice between M_1 and M_2 can often, but not always, be reduced to a significance test on one or more parameters. The relationship between a specific class of models M_1 and a more general class M_2 is expressed in terms of the above by $M_1 \subset M_2$. The rejection of M_2 implies the rejection of M_1, but not vice versa.

Similarly, the choice involved in the second case, $M_1 \cap M_2 \neq \emptyset$, can sometimes be reduced to a significance test on a parameter or parameters. For example, M_1 might be generated by the CES production function and M_2 by the variable elasticity of substitution (VES) production function; see, for example, Revankar (1966) and Ramsey (1968b) in which the economic implications in distinguishing these two models are discussed. Unlike the previous case, where $M_1 \subset M_2$, there is no simple relationship between the two models in the sense that the rejection of one implies the rejection of the other. Indeed, this situation is the one which provides the most challenging problems in model discrimination. As will be seen below, the successful discrimination between such models demands careful attention to the regressor space X over which the models are to be compared. For it may well be the case that over the subspace of X from which the observations are taken $M_1 = M_2$, but that over the subspace of X over which the model is to be used, $M_1 \cap M_2 = \emptyset$.

The last case is the most interesting and is designated by Cox (1961) and Atkinson (1970) as that of "separate families"; that is, the case where $M_1 \cap M_2 = \emptyset$. Cox (1961; p. 106) defines "separate" hypotheses by saying that an arbitrary model under one simple hypothesis cannot be obtained as a limit of models of simple hypotheses under the alternative hypothesis.

It should also be noted that one can (without further restrictions on the structure of the classes M_i) always find a class M_J such that M_1 and M_2 are both contained in M_J. The simplest example is $M_J = M_1 \cup M_2$. These comments have considerable implications for the problem of statistical discrimination to be discussed in the next section.

Suffice it for now to say that the desired formulation will depend upon which set of alternatives one wishes to consider, the power one wants to achieve against specific alternatives, and the required robustness of the chosen procedures. Loosely speaking, one must usually trade high power against specific alternatives for robustness to unconsidered alternatives. Cox postulated his alternatives in terms of two classes M_f and M_g, $M_f \cap M_g = \emptyset$, in order to achieve high power in testing H_g as an alternative to H_f. There are, of course, quite often advantages in reformulating the choice in terms of more general classes, in particular, when one can express the differences between the models in terms of estimable parameters.

The problem of the analysis of model differences depending on the regressor space X has already been alluded to above. This idea can be formalized in terms of the concepts of "extension" and "restriction" for functions. Suppose M_1 is generated by $F_1(\mathbf{y}, \mathbf{x}, \boldsymbol{\theta})$, $\mathbf{y} \in Y$, $\mathbf{x} \in X_1$, $\boldsymbol{\theta} \in \Theta$, and M_2 is generated by $F_2(\mathbf{y}, \mathbf{x}, \boldsymbol{\gamma})$, $\mathbf{x} \in X_2$, and $\boldsymbol{\gamma} \in \Gamma$. If for $X_1 \subset X_2 \subset X$ there exist subsets $\Theta_0 \subset \Theta$ and $\Gamma_0 \subset \Gamma$ such that

$$F_1(y, x, \theta \in \Theta_0) = F_2(y, x, \gamma \in \Gamma_0)$$

for all $\mathbf{x} \in X_1$ and any $\mathbf{y} \in Y$, then F_1 is said to be the restriction of F_2 to X_1 and F_2 is the extension of F_1 to X_2.

One sees immediately that the above distinctions between the classes M_1 and M_2 cannot in general be made for any spaces X and Θ, but must be made relative to some specified pair of spaces X and Θ. Restricting attention to the set X for the moment, it is clear that whether $M_1 = M_2$, $M_1 \subset M_2$, $M_1 \cap M_2 \neq \varnothing$, or $M_1 \cap M_2 = \varnothing$ will depend upon the set X. Thus, if one wished to choose between two functional forms f_1 and f_2, and f_1 was the restriction of f_2 to the observed sample space as determined by a conditioning variable x, then one would not be able to discriminate between the functions. More important is the idea that an examination of the relationship between, say, M_1 and M_2, over the observed and observable sample spaces, will enable one to evaluate whether one can discriminate between the models using existing data, or whether discrimination would be improved by sampling over a different space. Further, such an examination will determine, for example, whether $M_1 \subset M_2$ or $M_1 \cap M_2 \neq \varnothing$ over an appropriate set X and this information will help in choosing the "optimal" decision rule.

The former point requires amplification, since one of the most serious problems in econometrics is the fact that over the observed regressor space two models may be equivalent, i.e., $M_1 = M_2$, or nearly so; whereas, over the space in which the results are to be used, the models produce substantially different economic conclusions. It is for this reason primarily that so much effort is put into trying to discriminate between models which over the observed space do not differ by very much. Too often the econometrician must rely on highly complicated techniques in an effort to overcome uninformative data.

There is an enormous number of examples of this problem in econometric analysis. To continue a previous example, suppose one wishes to discriminate between a Cobb–Douglas and a CES production function both with constant returns to scale. One's interest centers in the changes in optimal input ratios to changes in relative prices. If, however, one's data are restricted to observations along the expansion path, i.e., X_0 is a restricted subspace of X so that relative to X_0 $M_1 = M_2$, one obviously cannot discriminate between the models on the basis of these data.

A Definition of True Model and Specification Error

Utilizing the above discussion, it is now possible to give fairly rigorous definitions of the concepts "true model," "specification error," *etc.*, which were loosely defined in the first section. The various definitions used earlier in this section hold for the subsequent discussion.

A true model, "m," relative to a given population P is a member of a class of models M such that the distributional characteristics prescribed by M on P are the same as those generated by P. The population P is defined by specifying some subset of the Cartesian product space $Y \otimes X$.

The common statement that there are "many true models" can now be made more precise. First of all, it is recognized that "m" is only a member of an equivalence class of models. Secondly, there is no restriction in the above definition on the "level of generality" of specification of M. Indeed, one can consider a nested set of classes M_i such that $M_1 \subset M_2 \subset M_3 \cdots$ where for each M_i, each member of the ith class is a true model.[3] One may usefully assume that there exists a least element in the sequence $M_1 \subset M_2 \cdots$, in the sense that the members of M_1 are simple, i.e., the p.d.f.'s are fully specified and contain no unknown parameters.

A specification error is said to have been made if one uses a model other than a true model to describe the distributional characteristics of a given population. More precisely, if m_p designates a postulated model and if $m_p \notin M_i$ for any $i \in I$, where I is some index set on the number of classes, m_p is an "incorrect" model and its use in analyzing data generated by P is a specification error.

The analysis of specification error in the previous section proceeded by specifying a true model $m_i \in M_i$ and an alternative model a_i such that m_i and a_i differed in a precise way and $a_i \notin M_i$.

In practice, specification errors can arise in two ways. First and most obviously by specifying a model such as m_p above, i.e., postulating an incorrect model. However, specification error can arise in practical situations in another way. Suppose one wishes to consider a population P and one specifies a correct model $m_i \in M_i$ for some i on the basis of that population. If, however, one draws one's sample not from P, but from say P', then a specification error will have been made since the relevant models are now $m_j' \in M_j'$ for some j relative to the population P'.

A simple, but famous, example will clarify this idea. Suppose one wishes to examine the relationship between permanent consumption and permanent income and one has indeed postulated a "true model" which is, for example, determined according to Friedman's permanent income hypothesis. If, however, one were to sample from the population given by current money income and consumption, then analysis of the true model using data drawn from another population leads to specification error. This is a well-known result. Further illustrative examples of these ideas are contained in Ramsey (1970).

III. Hypothesis Tests and Methods of Model Discrimination

The distinction between hypothesis testing and discrimination is really one of interpretation and strategy, since usually the same statistics are used in both

---

[3] It is convenient at this level of analysis to restrict one's attention to the cases in which there is a countable number of classes.

situations. The differences between these two inference procedures stem from the differences in the amount of presumed information brought to bear on the problem.

In the testing situation, the null hypothesis is the one that is believed to represent the true state of the world and the alternative hypothesis is, as it were, the next most likely alternative. Such a state of belief is presumed to have been acquired through theoretical reasoning and previous empirical research. Under such circumstances, one is willing to reject the null in favor of the alternative *only* if an unlikely event were to occur; otherwise, the test can be said to have provided additional confirmation of the null hypothesis. This is the rationale for the usual choice of low sizes of test. The critical region is chosen in such a way that the null hypothesis will not be confirmed only if an event occurs which under the *null* hypothesis is unlikely. One important aspect to note for this procedure is the essential assymetry in the roles of the null and alternative hypotheses.

The objective of discrimination procedures is different to that of testing. In this situation, one is not committed *a priori* to any of the alternatives. The objective is, in some sense, to choose the most likely alternative, or the most likely subspace of the maintained hypothesis space. When discriminating between alternatives, the specification of null and alternative hypotheses is irrelevant and there is no reason to assign an arbitrarily low probability of incorrect rejection to one of the hypotheses.

The main problem is how to express an order of preference among the alternatives "which may be said to be rationally induced when the observations are known"; see Barnard (1967, p. 27).

One may usefully distinguish three subcases of discrimination. First, from theoretical analysis or prior empirical investigation, one may be confident that one of the alternative models is correct. In this situation the objective is to discover which of the alternatives is the true one. This case might be called "strong relative discrimination."

A potentially useful procedure in this situation is based on the idea of the maximum likelihood ratio. However, as noted by Cox (1961), Barnard (1967), and many others, these procedures are most easily justified and interpreted only in those cases where the numerator is a member of the class defined by the denominator, i.e., in terms of our analysis of models, only when $M_1 \subset M_2$. But, as has been noted, the more interesting and challenging cases of separate models, $M_1 \cap M_2 = \varnothing$, and intersecting models, $M_1 \cap M_2 \neq \varnothing$, are the more common in occurrence. A simple way to overcome this difficulty for separate models is as follows.

Suppose the p.d.f.'s of the K alternative models to be considered are denoted by $f_i(y \mid \theta_i)$, $i = 1, 2, ..., K$. Let Λ be the linear space defined by $0 \leq \lambda_i \leq 1$, $\sum_1^K \lambda_i = 1$, and let $F(y \mid \lambda) = \sum_i \lambda_i f_i(y \mid \theta_i)$ for some $\lambda \in \Lambda$. $F(y \mid \lambda)$ is a density function[4] for each $\lambda \in \Lambda$, so that for all $\lambda \in \Lambda$, $F(y \mid \lambda)$ defines a class of p.d.f.'s of which each of the original p.d.f.'s is a member.

The likelihood function is

$$(27) \qquad L(\lambda, \boldsymbol{\theta}_i, i = 1, 2, ..., K) = \prod_{j=1}^{N} F(y_j \mid \lambda),$$

and let its supremum over $(\lambda, \boldsymbol{\theta}_i, i = 1, 2, ..., K)$ be denoted by L^*. Consider the maximum likelihood ratio statistic 1_i defined by

$$(28) \qquad 1_i = \frac{\sum_{j=1}^{N} f_i(y_j \mid \hat{\boldsymbol{\theta}}_i)}{L^*},$$

where $\hat{\boldsymbol{\theta}}_i$ is the maximum likelihood estimate of $\boldsymbol{\theta}_i$ on the assumption $\lambda_i = 1$. The "most likely" model is chosen quite simply by the condition $\max_i\{1_i\}$, or equivalently $\min_i\{-2 \log(1_i)\}$.

Work is currently under way to obtain the asymptotic joint distribution of the 1_i, $i = 1, 2, ..., K$. The main problem in the derivation is the fact that the parameter space Λ is closed so that the usual arguments in terms of derivatives no longer apply. One could drop the requirement that $0 \leqslant \lambda_i \leqslant 1, i = 1, 2, ..., K$, in which case the asymptotic joint distribution of $\hat{\lambda}_i$, $i = 1, 2, ..., K-1$, since $\hat{\lambda}_K = 1 - \hat{\lambda}_1 - \hat{\lambda}_2 - \cdots - \hat{\lambda}_{K-1}$ by the constraint, is $(K-1)$ variate normal. The distribution of the 1_i, or more easily of $W_i = -2 \log 1_i$, can be obtained by the use of characteristic generating functions from that of the $\hat{\lambda}_i$.

The second situation involves less prior information in the sense that one does not assume that one model is true, but that one wants to infer which model is "most likely" to be true *relative* to the others under consideration. This case might be labeled "weak relative discrimination."

The same basic procedure as that used in the case of strong relative discrimination could be used here, except for the allowance for weaker prior information. In this situation, one would not usually be willing to pick the largest 1_i unless it were in some sense "substantially" larger than $1_j, j \neq i$, since one is not sure to start with that the set of models contains a true model.

A variant of the previous procedure which meets this difficulty is to pick $\max_i(1_i)$ only if $\inf_{j \neq i}(1_i - 1_j) \geqslant a$, for some specified a, $0 < a < 1$. However, such a procedure should not be mechanically applied without examining the observed distribution of the 1_i, $i = 1, 2, ..., K$, since one may have no single 1_i which meets the criterion, but two or more 1_i treated as a group do meet it. In such a case one might prefer to reserve judgement on the distinction between the members of such a group, but to reject the remaining models.

---

[4] Note that if one wished to consider models involving both continuous and discrete variables, no problem arises if one puts the definition of $F(\cdot)$ in terms of cumulative distribution functions instead of density functions. Such "mixed" functions are well defined; see Lukacs (1970).

The third situation involves no assumption that one of the models is true, but does assume that one is willing to set an "absolute" standard of rejection. In the former two situations of relative discrimination one, and only one, model is chosen in each instance. In this situation, in any given trial, any number of models may be "chosen," from none to all of them. This case might be labeled "absolute discrimination."

For example, suppose one applies a given "test" to each of the K models at an assigned α level. More precisely, for each model one calculates a test statistic and compares its observed value with the α level critical value which would obtain if the model were true. Given the observed data, assume K_1 models are "rejected" and $K_2 = (K - K_1)$ models are "not rejected." The interpretation of this procedure is that, given the data, the test statistic at the assigned α level can discriminate between two groups of models, those in the rejected group and those in the nonrejected group. The models in the non-rejected group are "more likely" to contain a true model than the other group. More information is required in order to discriminate between the models in the nonrejected group if the same implied confidence level is to be maintained.

In principle, at least, it is possible to calculate, on the assumption that some model "m" is the correct model, the probabilities of rejection and acceptance for each model; more precisely, one can calculate directly the probabilities associated with the specified critical region and its complement for each model. The model m may, or may not, be included in the original set of models examined. This procedure is nothing more than a simple extension of the idea of calculating power functions. In this situation, however, the power function is not a continuous curve, but a set of discrete points. Using such a set of power points, one can determine the *relative* distance of various models from any given base. A close examination of these relative distances for various models may enable one to get a better understanding of the relationships between the models.

The test statistics originally considered for use in this procedure are the specification error tests to be discussed in the next section. In addition, one could consider using the statistic defined in Equation (28); one specifies a critical region by choosing a value "a" such that for $1_i < a$ the ith model is rejected. However, it should be noted that some generality has been lost and the idea of absolute discrimination weakened by the fact that the test depends crucially on the set of chosen alternatives. In the procedure using specification error tests this is not the case.

IV.   Some Specific Specification Error Tests

Tests in general and specification error tests in particular can be put into two broad categories: general and specific tests; or, to use the related terminology of Goldfeld and Quandt (1972), nonconstructive versus constructive tests. Loosely speaking, general tests are tests against broad diffuse alternatives with modest data requirements. Specific tests are tests against more specific alternatives and usually require much more data than general tests.

An example will clarify this rough distinction. One might compare a general test in the classical linear regression theory against omitted variables versus a specific test on the inclusion in the regression of a variable x_{K+1}. The specific test, for example, a "t" test on the statistical significance of the $(K+1)$th coefficient, is specific in that it tests for the inclusion of a specific variable x_{k+1} using observations on that variable.

The task faced by the general test is considerably more difficult in that one assumes that all information available and relevant has been used and the alternative is that some *unspecified* variable has been omitted. Occasionally, one will need to use a general test, even though a specific omitted variable is being considered, because there are no observations available on the omitted variable.

As a general rule specific tests, in that they usually incorporate more information, both theoretical and empirical, are to be preferred to general tests since the former tests are much more powerful. However, a *caveat* is necessary in that often the price paid for the high power of a specific test is its sensitivity (lack of robustness) to third alternatives.

In the subsequent discussion of specification error tests attention will be paid mainly to general tests, since it will be assumed that the researcher has already included in his analysis all information available to him. For reviews of the literature in this area the reader is referred to Ramsey (1968a) and Goldfeld and Quandt (1972). The latter reference is particularly good for a detailed study of heteroskedasticity.

Some Specification Error Tests for the Classical Linear Model

The specification errors considered in the first part of this subsection are those of omitted variables, incorrect functional form of the regressors, simultaneous equation problems, and heteroskedasticity. The null hypothesis is that specified as the true model in Equation (1) of the first section. The errors listed above were discussed in terms of Equations (2a) to (2d) in Section I.

The distributional properties of OLS residuals are well known and the effects of specification errors were discussed in the first section, so little needs to be added to the discussion. The dissatisfaction with OLS residuals in the classical normal linear regression model is that under the null hypothesis of no specification error, the residual vector has a singular distribution with a nonscalar covariance matrix whose elements are functions of the regressors. These characteristics tend to complicate the distributional analysis of test statistics based on such residuals.

To counter balance these points, the claim has been made that for large N the distribution of the OLS residuals is approximately that of the original disturbances given the consistency of the regression coefficient estimators. However, this asymptotic result is only correct under suitable conditions; the proviso is an important one. Durbin (1970) points out that although statistics based on OLS residuals are (under suitable regularity conditions) asymptotically unbiased and normally distributed, their covariance matrix will in general differ substantially from that of the corresponding statistics using the actual disturbance terms. The error is always towards the underestimation of significance.

A general class of residuals in linear regression models is defined with respect to an orthonormal base, Putter (1967). Recalling the model specified in Equation (1), an orthonormal residual vector is defined by

$$(29) \qquad\qquad \mathbf{v} = A'\mathbf{y} = A'\mathbf{u}$$

for any $(N-K) \times N$ matrix A' satisfying

$$(30) \qquad\qquad A'X = \varnothing, \qquad A'A = I_{N-K}.$$

If the disturbance term vector defined in Equation (1) is distributed as multivariate normal, then the $(N-K)$ dimensional vector $\mathbf{v}$ is also distributed as multivariate normal with null mean vector and scalar covariance matrix. If, however, the disturbance term vector is nonnormal in distribution, then in general the elements of $\mathbf{v}$, though uncorrelated, will not be distributed independently.

Theil's (1965) BLUS residual vector ($\tilde{\mathbf{u}}$) is a special case of orthonormal residuals in that $\tilde{\mathbf{u}}$ is obtained by finding that matrix that subject to the restrictions in Equation (30) is a solution to

$$(31) \qquad \min_{A} E\{\mathbf{u}'(A-J)'\mathbf{u}\} = 2\sigma^2 \min_{A} [N-K-tr(A'J)],$$

where $(A-J)'\mathbf{u}$ denotes the "error in predicting" $\mathbf{u}$, J is an $N \times (N-K)$ matrix which is obtained by deleting K columns from the identity matrix I_N.

The relationship between the Theil and OLS residuals is given by

$$(32) \qquad\qquad \tilde{\mathbf{u}} = HQ\hat{\mathbf{u}},$$

where Q is an orthonormal basis for the eigenvectors of the matrix M and the matrix H extracts the $(N-K)$ rows of Q that correspond to the nonzero eigenvalues of M. Another way of interpreting Theil residuals is that they are the (nonzero) OLS residuals from a regression transformed to an orthonormal basis; see Ramsey (1968a, p. 58).

In Ramsey (1969) it is shown that the distributional properties under the alternative hypotheses of the Theil (BLUS) residuals are similar to those of the

OLS residuals with the $(N-K) \times N$ matrix A' replacing M. This is illustrated in the next few paragraphs.

In Ramsey (1969) it was shown that for the models specified in Equations (2a) to (2c) the use of Equation (1) as the true regression model leads to a BLUS residual vector $\tilde{u}$ distributed as $(N-K)$-variate normal with mean vector given by $A'\xi$, where ξ is a nonstochastic vector, the precise definition of which depends upon the particular misspecification. Furthermore, under quite general conditions, the mean vector of $\tilde{u}$ can be approximated by

$$(33) \qquad A'\xi \doteq \alpha_0 + \alpha_1 \mathbf{q}_1 + \alpha_2 \mathbf{q}_2 + \cdots,$$

where the $(N-K) \times 1$ dimensional vectors $\mathbf{q}_j$, $j = 1, 2, \ldots$, are defined by

$$(34) \qquad \mathbf{q}_j = A'\hat{\mathbf{y}}^{(j+1)}, \qquad j = 1, 2, \ldots$$

where the $1 \times N$ vector $\hat{\mathbf{y}}^{(j+1)'} = (\hat{y}_1^{j+1}, \hat{y}_2^{j+1}, \ldots, \hat{y}_N^{j+1})$; i.e., the vector $\hat{\mathbf{y}}^{(j+1)}$ is the vector obtained by raising each element of the estimated vector of the conditional mean of the regressand to the $j+1$ power.

In the case that model (2d) is the true model, the distribution of $\tilde{u}$ derived from the use of model (1) is $(N-K)$-variate normal with null mean vector and a covariance matrix given by $A'\Omega A$.

For each of the tests considered below, the null hypothesis, say H_0, can be expressed in terms of the BLUS residuals as

$$H_0 : \tilde{u} \sim N(\varnothing, \sigma^2 I_{N-K}).$$

The various alternative hypotheses, H_i, $i = 1, 2$, can also be expressed in terms of the distributional properties of the BLUS residuals as shown below:

$H_1 : \tilde{u} \sim N(A'\xi, \bar{\sigma}^2 I)$, where $\bar{\sigma}^2$ is the variance of $\tilde{u}_i$ and $A'\xi$ is as given above;

$H_2 : \tilde{u} \sim N(\varnothing, \Theta)$, where Θ is a diagonal positive-definite matrix.

Thus, alternative hypothesis H_1 refers to Group A errors and hypothesis H_2 to the Group B errors which were defined in Section I.

From the above, it is clear that the fundamental idea underlying the tests is that the effect of specification error is to alter the distribution of the residuals from that postulated under the null hypothesis. For example, in the omitted variables problem [shown in Equation (2a)], the vector ξ is given by $\gamma \mathbf{z}$. The implication of the assumption made in Equation (33) is that the vector $\mathbf{z}$ can be approximated by a polynomial in the vector $\hat{\mathbf{y}}$. It is at this point that some *caveats* are necessary. First, it may not be possible to express $\mathbf{z}$ in terms of a polynomial in $\hat{\mathbf{y}}$ because the implicit functional relationship between $\mathbf{z}$ and $\hat{\mathbf{y}}$ is not analytic. Secondly, if $\mathbf{z}$ is a linear combination of the included regressors (so that inclusion of $\mathbf{z}$ would yield a multicollinear regression model), then the vector $A'z$ is null. A more detailed discussion of these problems together with a simple example is given in Ramsey (1969, pp. 359–361). With these preliminaries the following three specification error tests are easily summarized.[5]

Regression Specification Error Test (RESET)

Consider the regression equation

(35) $$\mathbf{u} = \alpha_0 + \alpha_1 \mathbf{q}_1 + \alpha_2 \mathbf{q}_2 + \cdots + \alpha_k \mathbf{q}_k + \mathbf{e},$$

where one assumes that $\mathbf{e}$ is a vector of independent disturbance terms distributed as normal with zero mean and constant variance. The test procedure is simply to apply the usual F test for the hypothesis that all the α's are zero. Under the null hypothesis H_0, the F test statistic is distributed as central F with $k+1$ and $(N-K-k-1)$ degrees of freedom. Under the alternative hypothesis H_1 the F test statistic is distributed approximately as noncentral F. RESET is obviously insensitive to the alternative H_2.

Bartlett's M Specification Error Test (BAMSET)

This test is designed specifically to test the null hypothesis against the alternative H_2. If the alternative hypothesis is that the $\tilde{u}_i^2$, $i = 1, 2, ..., N-K$, are distributed as $\sigma_i^2 \chi_1^2$, one can consider as a test of heterogeneity the following modification of Bartlett's M test; see, for example, Kendall and Stuart (1961, Vol. II, pp. 234–236). One defines the maximum likelihood ratio test statistic by

(36) $$l^* = \sum_{i=1}^{k} \frac{(s_i^2)^{v_i/2}}{s^2},$$

where k is the number of subgroups of squared residuals, $s_i^2 = (1/v_i) \sum_{j=1}^{v_i} \tilde{u}_j^2$, each v_i is an integer approximately equal to $(N-K)/k$, $\sum_{i=1}^{k} v_i = v = (N-K)$, and $s^2 = (1/v) \sum_{j=1}^{N-K} \tilde{u}_j^2$. In practice k is usually set equal to three as was recommended in Ramsey (1969). The choice of three subgroups is taken for convenience as a useful compromise between the need for a number of subgroups and the need for a large sample size in each group so that the asymptotic limits will be quickly attained. The actual statistic used is $M = -2\ln l$ which under the null hypothesis is asymptotically distributed as central chi-square with $(k-1)$ degrees of freedom.

A Monte Carlo analysis of the small sample properties, in particular power,

---

[5] The curious titles to these tests are meant to be indicative of the test so named. The ending SET stands for Specification Error Test and was suggested by Arnold Zellner.

of these tests[6] is reported in Ramsey and Gilbert (1972).[7] The basic conclusion is that RESET and BAMSET are reasonably powerful tests against their respective alternatives. In addition, a comparison was made between the performance of the test statistics using OLS and BLUS residuals. For BAMSET, the conclusion is that OLS residuals provide the more powerful test for heteroskedasticity. With respect to RESET the situation is not so clear. Although the ratio of powers of the tests using the two residuals was in favour of the BLUS residuals, it must be noted that the use of OLS residuals lowers the size of the test significantly. Consequently, further research designed to compare the BLUS and OLS based tests at equal test sizes may well show that OLS tests are more powerful.

In terms of the statistical dependence under the null hypothesis of the two test statistics, F and M, the result seems to be that F and M are independent under Theil residuals, but that there is some weak evidence in favor of dependence for OLS residuals.

It should be noted that for each of the two tests some further information is used in the form of assumptions. The basic additional assumption (and therefore assumed added information) in RESET is that the error can be expressed analytically in $\hat{y}$. The added information used in BAMSET is that one can find an indexing $\{i\}$ such that the variances σ_i^2, $i = 1, 2, ..., N - K$, can be usefully grouped into three categories as shown above. These two examples illustrate a general problem in this area which is that usually some type of further information is needed. The trick, of course, is to try to get as much power as possible with the most general assumption. Inevitably, one must consider the trade off between power and generality.

The Shapiro–Wilk Test for Normality (WSET)

The next specification error to be considered is that of nonnormality in the distribution of the disturbance terms. An example of such a situation was given in Equation (2e) in Section I. The currently[8] recommended test is WSET, which is based on the Shapiro–Wilk W test; see Shapiro and Wilk (1965). The

---

[6] The test RASET discussed in Ramsey (1969) is not recommended to be retained in these types of situations since in every model examined in Ramsey and Gilbert (1969, 1972), this test had less power than either RESET or BAMSET and sometimes less than both.

[7] The Monte Carlo run size in Ramsey and Gilbert (1969, 1972) was 1000 so that the various inferences drawn from the experiments should be reasonably accurate. Checks on the accuracy of the Monte Carlo estimates were made wherever exact analytical results could be obtained relatively easily. The results were very encouraging; in many cases the estimates approximated theoretical values within three significant digits.

[8] In Ramsey (1968a) a variant of Kolmogorov's test was used. However, on the basis of considerable efforts in evaluating the power of this test and in conjunction with Durbin's (1961) comments, this test was dropped from further consideration in favor of WSET.

test's small sample powers against a number of alternative tests was examined in Shapiro, Wilk, and Chen (1968).

Let $n = (N - K)$, $\bar{\tilde{u}} = n^{-1} \sum \tilde{u}_i$, and $S^2 = \sum_1^n (\tilde{u}_i - \bar{\tilde{u}})^2$, where $\tilde{u}_i$ is the ith BLUS residual. The W test statistic is defined by

$$(37) \qquad W = \frac{(\sum_1^n a_i y_i)^2}{S^2},$$

where y_i, $i = 1, 2, ..., n$, are the order statistics obtained from $\tilde{u}_i$, $i = 1, 2, ..., n$, and a_i, $i = 1, 2, ..., n$, are coefficients provided by Shapiro–Wilk (1965, pp. 603–604). The authors provide critical bounds for the test statistic for various α levels and $n = 3(1)50$.

The critical region is given by small values of W, $na_1^2/(n-1) \leqslant W \leqslant 1$. The null hypothesis is the same H_0 as given above. The alternative hypothesis, H_3, is that the distribution of $\tilde{u}_i$ is nonnormal in so far as nonnormality will affect the regression of sample order statistics on the mean values of order statistics obtained from an $N(0, 1)$ distribution. The test in this form is known as WSET.

The small sample behavior of the W statistic was examined by Monte Carlo means in the same work in which the previous two tests were initially examined; see Ramsey and Gilbert (1969). Consequently, it was possible to examine the statistical dependence of the W statistic with the other statistics. Under Theil residuals it would appear that W and M are not independently distributed, but do appear to be so under OLS residuals.

As predicted, the W statistic had considerable power against the alternative given in Equation (2e), in which the alternative (true) hypothesis is that the distribution is central chi-square with one degree of freedom. For example, the estimated probabilities of rejection at an α level 0.05 are 0.70, 0.89, and 0.99 for sample sizes 20, 30, and 50, respectively. Interestingly, the power of the test using OLS residuals was even greater. This is especially interesting in the light of the fact that the use of OLS residuals seems to have no observable effect on the distribution of W under the null hypothesis.

The effect of the errors summarized in Equations (2a) to (2d) on the distribution of the W statistic was negligible with the exception of model (2b) in which the estimated probabilities of rejection for small sample sizes were less than the assigned α level.

An interesting result was the application of the W test statistic to the specification error problem defined in Equation (21), i.e., the situation in which $\ln y$ is regressed instead of y, which is itself normally distributed. The analysis in Section I indicates that WSET should have relatively low power except at large sample sizes and that both RESET and BAMSET should reject with high power. The Monte Carlo estimates confirm these conclusions; the estimated probabilities of rejection of the null hypothesis at the 5% level by WSET,

BAMSET, and RESET were 0.10, 0.45, and 0.98, respectively, for sample size 50.

This completes the discussion on the set of tests for which some comparative analysis was made of the small sample behavior, both over tests and with respect to Theil and OLS residuals for a number of interesting specification errors. The above three tests are essentially tests for situations in which $M_1 \not\subset M_2$, and M_2 is a very broad class of alternatives.

Other Tests for Specification Errors

The likelihood test proposed by Cox (1961) and extended by Atkinson (1970) is a test most useful in nonlinear situations and with respect to "separate families." However, the test is a specific, not a general, one.

The statistic used is defined by

$$(38) \qquad T_f = L_{fg} - E_{\hat{\alpha}}(L_{fg}),$$

where one is comparing the distribution $f(y, \alpha)$ with the distribution $g(y, \beta)$, and $E_{\hat{\alpha}}(\cdot)$ indicates taking the expectation with respect to $f(y, \hat{\alpha})$. L_{fg} is given by

$$(39) \qquad L_{fg} = \log\left(\frac{f(y, \hat{\alpha})}{g(y, \hat{\beta})}\right),$$

where $\hat{\alpha}$ and $\hat{\beta}$ are the maximum likelihood estimators of α and β under $f(\cdot)$ and $g(\cdot)$, respectively. The asymptotic distribution theory discussed in Section I is used to evaluate the distribution of the statistic T_f. Note that this test is asymmetric in $f(y, \alpha)$ and $g(y, \beta)$, which is a distinct disadvantage in discrimination procedures. For example, tests based on T_f and T_g, which is defined analogously, may indicate respectively rejection of H_f in favor of H_g and rejection of H_g in favor of H_f, where H_f and H_g are the hypotheses that $f(y, \alpha)$ and $g(y, \beta)$ respectively are the true p.d.f.'s.

A final problem with the test is that in many common situations the joint distribution of $(\hat{\alpha}, \hat{\beta})$ is singular normal so that the apparent variance of T_f is zero; see Cox (1961, p. 120).

De-Min Wu (1971) has developed a useful set of alternative tests for the nonindependence of regressors and disturbance terms with an interesting application to "errors in the variables" models. An example of this type of error is given in Equations (2f) and (3). The general model considered by De-Min Wu is

$$\mathbf{y}_1 = Y_2\boldsymbol{\beta} + Z_1\boldsymbol{\gamma} + \mathbf{u},$$

$$(40) \qquad Y_2 = M + V, \qquad Z = (Z_1, Z_2),$$

$$\Sigma(u_i, v_i) = \begin{pmatrix} \sigma_{11} & \boldsymbol{\delta} \\ \boldsymbol{\delta} & \Sigma_{22} \end{pmatrix}, \qquad i = 1, 2, \ldots, N$$

where the elements $\{u_i, v_{11i}, ..., v_{GGi}\}$, $i = 1, 2, ..., N$, are multivariate normally distributed with null mean vector. $\mathbf{y}_1$ is an $N \times 1$ regressand vector, Y_2 is $N \times G$, $\boldsymbol{\beta}$ is a $G \times 1$ coefficient vector, Z_1 is an $N \times K_1$ matrix of non-stochastic regressors, $\boldsymbol{\gamma}$ is the corresponding coefficient vector, $\mathbf{u}$ is an $N \times 1$ vector of disturbance terms, M is an $N \times G$ matrix of constants, V is an $N \times G$ matrix of random variables, and Z_2 is an $N \times G$ matrix of nonstochastic instrumental variables. Σ is a $(G+1)^2$ dimensional positive-definite matrix. The hypothesis to be tested is that $\delta = \varnothing$ against the alternative $\delta \neq \varnothing$.

Since the alternative tests are all related in quite a simple manner, one need only examine one of them. The test statistic T_2 is defined by

$$T_2 = \frac{Q^*/G}{(Q_4 - Q^*)/(N - K_1 - 2G)},$$

(41) $\quad Q^* = (\hat{\boldsymbol{\beta}}_1 - \hat{\boldsymbol{\beta}}_2)'[(Y_2'A_2 Y_2)^{-1} - (Y_2'A_1 Y_2)^{-1}]^{-1}(\hat{\boldsymbol{\beta}}_1 - \hat{\boldsymbol{\beta}}_2),$

$\qquad A_1 = I - Z_1(Z_1'Z_1)^{-1}Z_1', \qquad A_2 = Z(Z'Z)^{-1}Z' - Z_1'(Z_1'Z_1)^{-1}Z_1',$

$\qquad \hat{\boldsymbol{\beta}}_i = (Y_2'A_i Y_2)^{-1} Y_2'A_i \mathbf{y}_1, \qquad i = 1, 2$

and

$$Q_4 = (\mathbf{y}_1 - Y_2 \hat{\boldsymbol{\beta}}_1)' A_1 (\mathbf{y}_1 - Y_2 \hat{\boldsymbol{\beta}}_1).$$

$\hat{\boldsymbol{\beta}}_1$ is the OLS estimator of $\boldsymbol{\beta}$ and $\hat{\boldsymbol{\beta}}_2$ is the instrumental variables estimator using the instrumental matrix Z. Terms of the form $(Y_2'A_i Y_2)$, $i = 1, 2$, are the matrices of residuals from the regression of Y_2 on Z_1 and Z, respectively. The statistic T_2 is distributed as F with G and $(N - K_1 - 2G)$ degrees of freedom.

The last specification error discussed in Section I was that of incorrect inclusion or omission of variables from a system of simultaneous equations. In this connection, Byron (1972) has applied the methods of Aitchison and Silvey (1958) for tests of restrictions on the parameter space to tests for identifying restrictions.

The Aitchison and Silvey approach is in principle quite simple and follows naturally from the maximum likelihood analysis extensively discussed in previous sections. Suppose the p.d.f. of a random variable y is known and is denoted by $f(y, \boldsymbol{\alpha})$, where $\boldsymbol{\alpha}$ is a K dimensional vector of parameters contained in some space A. The hypothesis to be tested is that the space A is restricted by r, $r < K$, relationships of the form $h_j(\boldsymbol{\alpha}) = 0$, $j = 1, 2, ..., r$. Let $\mathbf{h}$ denote the r dimensional vector function of restrictions. This hypothesis can be tested quite easily by reformulating the likelihood function in terms of a Lagrangian function. Thus, if $L(y, \boldsymbol{\alpha})$ designates the unconstrained likelihood, one considers the constrained likelihood

(42) $$L^*(\mathbf{y}, \boldsymbol{\alpha}, \lambda) = L(\mathbf{y}, \boldsymbol{\alpha}) + \lambda'\mathbf{h},$$

which is to be maximized with respect to α and λ. The null hypothesis is that $\lambda = \varnothing$ and the alternative is that $\lambda \neq \varnothing$. Under the usual regularity conditions the statistic A_s is defined by

$$(43) \quad A_s = -N^{-1}\hat{\lambda}'D^{-1}\hat{\lambda}, \quad D^{-1} = -(RV^{-1}R'), \quad R' = \{r_{ij}\}, \quad r_{ij} = \frac{\partial h_i(\alpha)}{\partial \alpha_j},$$

where V is the information matrix and the unknown parameters are replaced by their restricted maximum likelihood estimates. Asymptotically, the distribution of A_s is chi-square with r degrees of freedom under the null hypothesis.

In Dhrymes *et al.* (1972), this test is compared with the usual F test for linear restrictions in the context of the classical normal linear model. If the scale factor, σ^2, in the disturbance vector's covariance matrix is known, the two tests are mathematically equivalent; whereas if σ^2 is unknown, the two tests are asymptotically equivalent.[9] The advantage of the test statistic A_s is, of course, its use outside the context of the classical normal linear model.

Byron (1972) uses this procedure to test for the presence of overidentifying restrictions, where the maintained hypothesis is that the system is at least identified. The model is formulated in the usual manner, namely,

$$(44) \qquad\qquad YB + ZC = U,$$

where Y is an $N \times M$ matrix of endogenous variables, M_1 equations are stochastic and $M - M_1$ equations are (nonstochastic) identities, Z is an $N \times K$ matrix of exogenous variables, U is the $N \times M$ matrix of disturbance terms with null column vectors corresponding to the identities, and B and C are the corresponding matrices of coefficients. By rearranging the *a priori* unspecified coefficients in B and C in an $[M_1 \times (M + K)]$ dimensional vector, θ, the zero restrictions can be represented by $H\Theta = \varnothing$, where the matrix H has r rows corresponding to r restrictions on the parameters of the M_1 stochastic equations.

Using the estimation method of full information maximum likelihood (FIML), the concentrated log-likelihood function incorporating the restrictions is

$$(45) \qquad L^*(\theta, \lambda) = N \log|B| + \tfrac{1}{2}N \log|V|^{-1} + \lambda'H\theta,$$

where L^* is to be maximized with respect to θ and λ and V is the residual covariance matrix. At the maximum point, the *sample* Lagrange coefficients are the gradients of the log-likelihood function with respect to the constrained parameters. As above, one uses the asymptotic distribution theory to test the hypothesis $\lambda = \varnothing$. For further details, the reader is referred to Byron (1972).

Cox (1962) noted in passing that an alternative to the test using the statistic

---

[9] The usual F test is to be preferred in this special case since it is exact.

T_f is to introduce a general model which includes H_f and H_g as special cases, namely, to consider $\{f(y,\alpha)\}^\lambda \{g(y,\beta)\}^{1-\lambda}$ as being proportional to the generalized p.d.f. Atkinson (1970) examined this suggestion. He defined a generalized p.d.f. $f_\lambda(y)$ relative to a set of separate alternatives $f_i(y,\theta_i)$ by

$$(46) \qquad\qquad f_\lambda(y) = \frac{\prod_{i=1}^{K} \{f_i(y,\theta_i)\}^{\lambda_i}}{\int_u \prod_{i=1}^{K} \{f_i(u,\theta_i)\}^{\lambda_i} \, du},$$

so that $f_\lambda(y)$ is a p.d.f. and $f_i(y,\theta_i)$ is obtained from $f_\lambda(y)$ by setting $\lambda_i = 1$ and $\lambda_j = 0, j \neq i$. The procedure is to estimate $\lambda_i, i = 1, 2, ..., K$ jointly with the $\theta_i, i = 1, 2, ..., K$ and discriminate between hypotheses on the basis of tests of hypotheses about the values of $\lambda_i, i = 1, 2, ..., K$.

V. Use of Specification Error Tests for Model Discrimination

In Section III three types of discrimination were distinguished; weak and strong relative discrimination, and absolute discrimination. The first section here deals with three basic procedures for relative discrimination, which are all generalizations of maximum likelihood ratios. The second section considers the use of specification error tests for absolute discrimination.

Procedures for Relative Discrimination

The generalized (linear) likelihood procedure was discussed in the third section. The main disadvantage to this procedure lies in the potential computational complexities inherent in its use. However, the procedure is intuitively appealing, is easily extended to more than two alternatives, and with it all alternatives are treated equally. This is usually an important consideration in discrimination procedures.[10,11]

Further, with this procedure, one chooses one, and only one, model. Thus, there is no question of trying to modify the existing set of models in light of the results in order to produce a "better" model. This is, of course, a disadvantage when the test is being used in the weak relative case. Further, even if one uses the modification mentioned in footnote 11, the procedure yields no information as to how best to alter the model.

The procedure using Cox's statistic T_f [defined in Equation (38)], can yield three results interpretable as consistency with H_f, evidence of departure

[10]This situation presumes that *a priori* one is indifferent between the models.

[11] One might wish to modify this procedure by specifying a critical minimum value for the likelihood ratio. This modified approach incorporates elements of both relative and absolute discrimination. Logically, however, this makes sense only with weak relative discrimination.

from H_f in favor of H_g, and evidence of departure from H_f away from H_g. If, in addition, one also calculates T_g, the corresponding statistic assuming H_g is the true hypothesis, then there are nine possibilities, one of which is logically inconsistent; see Cox (1962, p. 407).

The further problems with this approach are that the test is asymmetric in the hypotheses, depends crucially on a specific alternative H_g, and may be sensitive to unconsidered third alternatives; that is, by its design it is more useful for strong relative discrimination than for weak. It is not easily extended to multiple comparisons, and, in common with the generalized (linear) likelihood ratio, it is of not much use in helping one to discover the specific aspects of H_f that lead to its rejection.

The third procedure for relative discrimination is the generalized likelihood procedure of Atkinson defined in Equation (46). Despite the analytical convenience due to the exponential combination being additive in the log likelihoods, values of λ_i not equal to zero or unity are not easily interpretable. Further, the analysis in Section II would indicate that the claim that equal values of λ_i, $i = 1, 2, ..., K$, indicate that the models describe the data equally well is unjustified.[12] As the reader will recall, two models can be said to "fit data equally well" if relative to a given conditioning variable space X_0, the two models yield the same probability distributions. More precisely, if relative to X_0, $M_1 = M_2$; that is, if the two models are equivalent in the sense defined in Section II, then they will "fit the data equally well." Atkinson provides no explicit justification for the statement that equal exponents of different p.d.f.'s represent a set of models, each of which fits the data as well as each of the others.

Finally, the main problem with this procedure for discrimination is that the discrimination problem has merely been transformed from a choice between the original models to a choice between the λ_i, $i = 1, 2, ..., K$. If the statistics $\hat{\lambda}_i$, $i = 1, 2, ..., K$, were analytically more convenient than the original models, an improvement would have been made.

Procedures for Absolute Discrimination

Essentially, procedures for absolute discrimination are modifications of specification error tests; or rather, the differences between testing and discrimination occur in the interpretation and use of the test statistics. With respect to each test, the question asked is in a sense whether the model as formulated is "consistent" with the data with respect to certain specified characteristics. Thus, the main feature common to these procedures is that

---

[12] The interested reader is referred to the Discussion following the 1970 paper for further details on this point.

they are all constructed to test for the presence of one or more important characteristics, rather than being, in some sense, summary measures of fit. More precisely, the various specification error tests test for certain specific characteristics such as homoskedasticity, normality, means of estimators independent of the regressor space, and so on.

Although this usually means that a battery of tests must be applied, it does enable one to consider the feasibility of discriminating between models in terms of a number of alternative characteristics. As a consequence, it becomes possible to narrow the range of "unconsidered" alternatives when seeking to modify models and to concentrate on key characteristics in order to make finer selections.

The first problem to be solved in using specification error tests for discrimination is the appropriate choice of critical region, i.e., how much deviation in the observed result from each model is to be regarded as being inconsistent with that model. Given the natural wish to rely on published tables, one will normally choose the critical region to correspond with a conventional α level.

If the value of the observed statistic lies in the critical region one is faced with the disjunction: Either the model, say M_1, is not a true model, or it is a true model with respect to the characteristic being tested, and an event of low probability has occurred. As Barnard (1967) notes, it is our unwillingness to believe in events of low probability that encourages us to "reject" the model in such circumstances. Continuing to use Barnard's language, the α level chosen is a chosen critical bound on the credibility of the "hypothesis" that the model M_1 is a true model. This is in the sense that "as α ranges from 1 down to 0 our disposition to think of some alternative will increase"; see Barnard (1967, p. 28). Thus, one will in general tend to choose low values of α in that one's willingness to reformulate the model is greater the smaller the value of α at which the observed data lie in the critical region.

Having chosen an α level, one calculates the test statistic with respect to each of the models. The possible decisions for only two models are obviously reject either, neither, or both. One should be careful to note that even if one model is not rejected by the given test, another test for some other characteristic of the model may indicate rejection with the same data. This is, of course, a reflection of the fact that all but the simplest of models have a number of characteristics, and a misspecified model may be in agreement with the true model with respect to some of them.

The above procedure can be "evaluated," that is, probabilities can be attached to the various decisions in a manner analogous to the usual hypothesis testing framework. To do this, one must specify a specific model, say M, as the true model and with this information the probability of taking each decision can be calculated. Indeed, it is important to do this in order to ensure one has chosen a "sensible" procedure with respect to the models under consideration.

Ideally, one would like to have a procedure such that for any model M, the probability of rejecting the incorrect models is greater than the chosen α. It is well known in conventional hypothesis testing that some tests are biased. The problem here is the same, but somewhat more complicated.

The application of a set of simultaneous specification error tests is similar to that of a simple test. However, in these circumstances one must be concerned with the appropriate composition of the joint α level. The interested reader is referred to Miller (1966) for an introduction to the problems of simultaneous inference. The appropriate choice of the composition of the joint α level is such a problem.

The application of specification error tests in the classical normal linear single-equation model is quite simple. In nonlinear models, one must in general rely on applying the tests to the asymptotic distributions of the residuals. Given the discussion in Sections I and II, it is clear that once the asymptotic distributions have been obtained, all of the above tests can be applied directly in a manner analogous to the linear case. Further, using the asymptotic theory one can immediately extend the use of these tests to the simultaneous equation framework.[13]

It should be noted that reliance on asymptotic results with modest sample sizes can be most misleading. Currently, work is underway to obtain approximations to the required distributions that are of a higher order of approximation than the normal. Such results at the very least will be useful in evaluating the degree of approximation in using the normal distribution.

One of the main advantages of the use of specification error tests in absolute discrimination is the potential information to be obtained from them for modifying rejected models. As an example, consider the problem of distinguishing between the alternative hypotheses H_1 and H_2 defined in Section IV. The following procedure indicates that the tests RESET and BAMSET can be used to give at least some weak indication of whether H_0 is rejected in favor of H_1 or H_2 when a joint test is made. Apply both RESET and BAMSET. If only RESET indicates rejection at a given α level, one infers that the null hypothesis is rejected in favor of H_1. If, however, BAMSET indicates rejection, but *not RESET*, one infers that the null hypothesis is rejected in favor of H_2. If both tests indicate rejection, one cannot distinguish between H_1 and H_2 nor between H_1 and H_3, where H_3 is the union of H_1 and H_2. Since the distributions of the RESET and BAMSET test statistics under the null hypothesis are apparently independent, the size of the joint test is given by $\alpha_J = 1 - (1-\alpha_R)(1-\alpha_B)$, where α_J is the size of the joint test and α_R, α_B are the

---

[13] A word of warning is needed here. The above results can be relied upon only if care is taken to derive the asymptotic distributions. The reader should note that in many instances the asymptotic distributions may not be normal. What is worse, is that in some cases there will be no limiting distributions.

test sizes for RESET and BAMSET, respectively. Similarly, under the null hypothesis the probabilities of rejecting the null hypothesis in favor of alternative H_1 is $\alpha_R(1-\alpha_B)$, and in favor of alternative H_2 is $\alpha_B(1-\alpha_R)$.

Despite the previous theoretical arguments, the main criterion for the acceptance of any test procedure is its performance in actual situations. Specification error tests have been applied in a variety of circumstances and the number of reported uses will grow as the computer programmes developed at Michigan State become more widely available. Unfortunately, much of the work done to-date is either unfinished or unpublished.

The earliest use of the specification error tests discussed in the first part of Section IV is reported in Ramsey (1968a). The tests were used in an attempt to discriminate between alternative models of the relationship between value added per unit of labor and the wage rate. The results are interesting in that they illustrate the use of the tests in an effort to discover appropriate modifications of the original rejected hypotheses. In all, eight variants of the original model were considered. Despite the low sample sizes involved (all of the data sets had less than 50 observations and most had less than 20), the results indicated that the tests were sensitive to the various alternatives and that the tests enabled one to select one model in preference to the others.

Gilbert (1969) provides an example of the use of the specification error tests in attempting to discriminate between a very large number of alternative formulations of the demand for money. Lee (1972) found the tests successful in discriminating between four alternative production functions using data on manufacturing industries at the three-digit level which were compiled by the U.N.

In Ramsey and Zarembka (1971), the tests were used to discriminate between the Cobb–Douglas, CES, VES, GPF, and a quadratic production function defined on data referring to U.S. manufacturing industries by state in 1957. The interesting point to note with this study is that, even though almost all of the coefficient estimates were statistically significant at the 5% level and that all of the R^2 values were greater than 0.99, the test results enabled the researchers to select the CES form of the production function in preference to the others. It is also interesting to note that the quadratic form had the highest value of R^2 (even after allowing for differences in degrees of freedom) and was the model most strongly rejected by the tests.

An example of the use of the tests as tests of the appropriateness of a model, instead of their use in discrimination, is provided in Ramsey (1971). As described in Ramsey (1972) a very specific model for market demand curves was hypothesized and the "adequacy" of that model was tested in Ramsey (1971) with respect to several sets of data. Note that what was under test was the formulation of the model itself, not hypotheses about the values of the parameters. This work illustrates one of the most important uses of specification error tests, the testing of the adequacy of a model. One must be reasonably sure that the model itself is correctly specified before one can proceed to carry out tests of hypotheses about the values of the parameters. Specification error tests provide the empirical evidence.

VI.   A Suggested Research Strategy and Problems for Future Research

The preceding arguments are best summarized by stating the research strategy implied by the above analysis. It is assumed that the researcher has brought to the problem a set of alternative models suggested by theory and previous research together with all the available data relevant to the problem. The question is now how to proceed in the face of several alternative models purporting to explain the same phenomena.

The first step is a careful evaluation of the relationships between the models on the observed regressor space X_0 and over the space X_1 in which the models are to be used. This analysis will enable the researcher to determine precisely in what ways the models differ, whether data from X_0 will allow inferences to be made over X_1, and the extent to which differences can be expressed in terms of parameters. Attempts to distinguish between certain models may well be dropped at this stage if it is clear that the implicit sample design is inadequate for the purpose. For the same reasons, the researcher may also have to limit the number and variety of points about which inferences are to be made.

The second step is to decide on the appropriate form of discrimination for the purposes in hand. The results of these two steps enable him to determine the appropriate set of discrimination procedures, the specification error tests to be used, and the choice of α levels.

The third step is relatively simple and mechanical. Carry out the procedures and take the appropriate decisions. A fourth step might then be to analyze the results obtained in an effort to further modify the models. The extent to which this can be effective will be determined by the analysis performed in the first step.

Further research in these problems needs to proceed from two different points. The first departure point is in model formulation. The previous discussion should have made it clear that the more specific the models, the easier is the statistical task of choosing between the alternatives. One of the major problems in inference in economics relative to the physical sciences is that in economics the models are incompletely specified by current theory. Consequently, models are often given a specific form without theoretical justification and inferences are made about model parameters when it is not clear that the general model is relevant. An example of an approach that yields a highly specific model is Ramsey (1972) in which limit theorems are used to derive not only the distribution of the disturbance terms, but also (and more importantly) the functional form of the conditional mean.

The second point of departure is to improve the statistical techniques and the underlying methodology. With respect to the former there are five basic needs.

(i) To derive small sample results, especially for nonlinear equations.

(ii) To investigate the joint distributions of various tests.

(iii) To make further power comparisons in order to choose an "optimal" set of procedures.

(iv) To extend the current work to nonrandom samples.

(v) To examine the feasibility of distinguishing various types of specification error.

REFERENCES

Aitchison, J. and S. D. Silvey (1958). "Maximum Likelihood Estimation of Parameters Subject to Restraints," *Ann. Math. Statist.* **29**, 813–828.

Atkinson, A. C. (1970). "A Method of Discriminating between Models (with Discussion)," *J. Roy. Statist. Soc.* **32**, No. 3, 323–353.

Barnard, G. A. (1967). "The Use of the Likelihood Function in Statistical Practice," *Proc. Berkeley Symp. Math. Statist. Probability, 5th*, 27–40.

Box, G. E. P. and H. L. Lucas (1959). "Design of Experiments in Nonlinear Situations," *Biometrika* **46**, 77–90.

Box, G. E. P. and W. G. Hunter (1962). "A Useful Method of Model-Building," *Technometrics* **4**, 301–318.

Box, G. E. P. and W. J. Hill (1967). "Discrimination among Mechanistic Models," *Technometrics* **9**, No. 1, 57–71.

Byron, R. P. (1972). "Testing for Misspecification in Econometric Systems Using Full Information," *Int. Econ. Rev.* (forthcoming).

Cox, D. R. (1961). "Tests of Separate Families of Hypotheses," *Proc. Berkeley Symp., 4th* **1**, 105–123.

Cox, D. R. (1962). "Further Results on Tests of Separate Families of Hypotheses," *J. Roy. Statist. Soc., Ser. B* **24**, 406–424.

Cragg, J. G. (1968). "Some Effects of Incorrect Specification on the Small-Sample Properties of Several Simultaneous Equation Estimators," *Int. Econ. Rev.* **9**, 63–86.

Dhrymes, P. J., E. P. Howrey, S. H. Hymans, J. Kmenta, E. E. Leamer, R. E. Quandt, J. B. Ramsey, H. J. Shapiro and V. Zarnowitz (1972). "Criteria for Evaluation of Econometric Models," *Ann. Econ. Soc. Measurement* **1**, 291–324.

Durbin, J. (1961). "Some Methods of Constructing Exact Tests," *Biometrika* **48**, 41–54.

Durbin, J. (1970). "Testing for Serial Correlation in Least Squares Regression When Some of the Regressors Are Lagged Dependent Variables," *Econometrica* **38**, 410–421.

Fisher, F. M. (1961). "On the Cost of Approximate Specification in Simultaneous Equation Estimation," *Econometrica* **29**, 139–170.

Gilbert R. F. (1969). "The Demand for Money: An Analysis of Specification Error," unpublished Ph.D. Thesis, Michigan State Univ., East Lansing, Michigan.

Goldfeld, S. M. and R. E. Quandt (1972). *Nonlinear Methods in Econometrics*. North-Holland Publ., Amsterdam.

Hunter, W. G. and A. M. Reiner (1965). "Designs for Discriminating between Two Rival Models," *Technometrics* **7**, 307–323.

Jacobson, N. (1951). *Lectures in Abstract Algebra*, Vol. 1. Van Nostrand Reinhold, Princeton, New Jersey.

Kendall, M. G. and A. Stuart (1961). *The Advanced Theory of Statistics*, Vols. 1 and 2. Griffin, London.

Lee, K. W. (1972). "An International Study of Manufacturing Production Functions," unpublished Doctoral Thesis, Michigan State Univ., East Lansing, Michigan.

Lukacs, E. (1970). *Characteristic Functions.* Hafner, New York.

Miller, R. G., Jr. (1966). *Simultaneous Statistical Inference.* McGraw-Hill, New York.

J. Putter (1967). "Orthonormal Bases of Error Spaces and Their Use for Investigating the Normality and Variances of Residuals," *J. Amer. Statist. Ass.* **62**, 1022–1036.

Ramsey, J. B. (1968a). "Tests for Specification Errors in Classical Linear Least Squares Regression Analysis," Ph.D. Thesis, Univ. of Wisconsin, Madison, Wisconsin.

Ramsey, J. B. (1968b). "A Comment on the Marginal Physical Product Curves for the CES and VES Production Functions," *Amer. Econ. Rev.* **58**, 482–485.

Ramsey, J. B. (1969). "Tests for Specification Errors in Classical Linear Least Squares Regression Analysis," *J. Roy. Statist. Soc., Ser. B* Pt. 2, 350–371.

Ramsey, J. B. (1970). "Models, Specification Error, and Inference: A Discussion of Some Problems in Econometric Methodology," *Bull. Oxford Inst. Econ. Statist.* **32**, No. 4, 301–318.

Ramsey, J. B. (1971). "Limiting Forms for Demand Functions: Preliminary Tests of Some Specific Hypotheses," paper presented at the Meeting of the Western Econ. Ass., Vancouver, B.C.

Ramsey, J. B. (1972). "Limiting Functional Forms for Market Demand Curves," *Econometrica* **40**, No. 2, 327–341.

Ramsey, J. B. and R. Gilbert (1969). "A Monte Carlo Study of Some Small Sample Properties of Tests for Specification Error," Econometrics Working Paper, No. 6813, Michigan State Univ., East Lansing, Michigan.

Ramsey, J. B. and P. Zarembka (1971). "Specification Error Tests and Alternative Functional Forms of the Aggregate Production Function," *J. Amer. Statist. Ass.* **66**, 471–477.

Ramsey, J. B. and R. Gilbert (1972). "Some Small Sample Properties of Tests for Specification Error," *J. Amer. Statist. Ass.* **67**, 180–186.

Revankar, N. (1966). "The Constant and Variable Elasticity of Substitution Production Functions. A Comparative Study in U.S. Manufacturing Industries," Paper presented at the annual meeting of the Econometric Soc. in December.

Richardson, D. H. and De-Min Wu (1970). "Alternative Estimators in the Errors in Variables Model," *J. Amer. Statist. Ass.* **65**, 724–748.

Shapiro, S. S. and M. B. Wilk (1965). "An Analysis of Variance Tests for Normality (Complete Samples)," *Biometrika* **LII**, 591–611.

Shapiro, S. S., M. B. Wilk and H. J. Chen (1968). "A Comparative Study of Various Tests for Normality," *J. Amer. Statist. Ass.* **LXIII**, 1343–1373.

Theil, H. (1957). "Specification Errors and the Estimation of Economic Relationships," *Rev. Int. Statist. Inst.* **XXV**, 41–51.

Theil, H. (1965). "The Analysis of Disturbances in Regression Analysis," *J. Amer. Statist. Ass.* **60**, 1067–1079.

Wu, De-Min (1971). "Alternative Tests of Independence between Stochastic Regressors and Disturbances," *Econometrica* (forthcoming).

Chapter Two

Discriminating among alternative models: Bayesian and non-Bayesian methods

KENNETH M. GAVER[1]

UNIVERSITY OF ROCHESTER
ROCHESTER, NEW YORK

MARTIN S. GEISEL[1]

CARNEGIE–MELLON UNIVERSITY
PITTSBURGH, PENNSYLVANIA

[1] We have benefited from the comments of Jay Kadane, Ed Leamer, Tim McGuire, P. A. V. B. Swamy, and Arnold Zellner on a preliminary draft of this paper.

Empirical researchers are often confronted with the problem of making choices among alternative statistical models of the process they are investigating. What variables should be included in a regression equation? Is a log-linear functional form more appropriate than a linear regression? What error structure is appropriate for the model? Some such issues may be mainly ones of statistical "tidiness" within the framework of a fixed substantive model or maintained hypothesis; however, problems of comparing alternative or rival theories also arise. Examples are the comparison of simple Quantity Theory models with simple Keynesian models by Friedman and Meiselman (1963) and the comparison of alternative investment theories by Jorgenson and Siebert (1968).

In many such situations, conventional statistical methods offer little guidance since these procedures assume that the model is given. In cases where the specific alternative models can be nested in a more general model, standard estimation and testing procedures, both Bayesian and non-Bayesian, can fruitfully be employed. Often, however, such general models do not readily present themselves, and other considerations may dictate against their use.

In recent years, considerable progress has been made on the development of statistical procedures for comparing alternative nonnested models. In this paper we provide an exposition of what we see as the major lines of activity, both Bayesian and non-Bayesian, in this area. We give numerous references, but do not attempt an exhaustive literature review. Since much of the Bayesian development is very recent and not yet available in published form elsewhere, we cover it in more detail than we provide for non-Bayesian procedures. Before proceeding to consideration of the various procedures themselves, we provide some additional introductory remarks in the remainder of this section of the paper.

The term "model" is sufficiently familiar to economists to make a formal definition unnecessary; nevertheless, we remind the reader that an econometric or statistical model is fundamentally a characterization (in terms of parameters and exogenonous variables) of the probability distribution of some random variable(s) of interest. In the Bayesian framework, prior information about the parameters of the model, expressed in the form of a prior distribution, is explicitly part of the model. Most non-Bayesian analyses, while making use of such information informally, do not incorporate it into the model in an explicit fashion.

Our analysis deals with the comparison of *econometric* or *statistical* models. It is important, however, to bear in mind the relationships between econometric models and *theoretical* (economic) models. Theoretical models typically involve some degree of abstraction from reality. Econometric or statistical models reflect this abstraction; however, they need not bear a one-to-one correspondence with theoretical models. For example, one theoretical model may be consistent with several different functional forms which constitute different econometric models. The question addressed in model selection is, "Which model among those being considered provides the best characterization in some statistical sense of the process under consideration?" The term "correct model," which appears often in model-selection analyses, thus encompasses both statistical and substantive considerations.

Substantive theory bears on the problem of comparing statistical models in another important way. The development of new theoretical models, perhaps combining or generalizing models that had been viewed as separate ones, may alter the *model space*, the set of statistical models to be compared. Of course, substantive theory may also be a source of prior information about various aspects (e.g., possible parameter values) of the statistical models.

In addition to the impact of substantive theory on the delineation of the elements of the model space, the possibility of a more mechanical combination of separate models should be considered. This, like the development of new theoretical models, may result in elimination of a model-comparison problem. A single, albeit more complicated, model may then be analyzed by conventional statistical methods. Such generalization may also introduce new models that are superior to those originally under consideration. For example, in some cases, such as the choice of functional form in a regression equation, the introduction of one or a small number of new parameters will accomplish such generalization (see, for example, Paul Zarembka's paper in this volume). Also, mechanistic generalizations, such as including all possible explanatory variables in a single regression equation, may be available.

New theoretical models that combine separate rival models are not always attainable. Mechanistic combination may produce generalizations that are not of substantive interest. Also, statistical considerations such as a limited data base or difficulties of analysis and estimation of a complicated model with many parameters may restrict the usefulness of such models. Even when generalizations can be obtained, they may not be unique. In these situations, the analysis and comparison of separate models is dictated. The procedures discussed here provide methods for statistical inference in such situations.

I. Non-Bayesian Methods for Discriminating Among Models

In this section we consider non-Bayesian procedures for discriminating among alternative statistical models. While some of these procedures are applicable to a broader class of problems, we emphasize their application to the problem of choosing among *linear models*.

Roughly speaking, these procedures fall into three categories. The first category consists of those procedures that use informal decision rules for discriminating among linear models. Such rules are characterized as owing their *raison d'etre* primarily to their intuitive appeal or certain other *ad hoc* considerations.

The second category includes those procedures that employ classical hypothesis testing theory to discriminate among models. In reviewing these techniques, we shall place particular emphasis on the recent developments in this area stemming from the theory developed by Cox (1961, 1962) for testing separate families of hypotheses. We shall not consider the use of specification error tests in model selection. On that subject see James Ramsey's chapter in this volume.

Finally, we relegate to the last category those procedures that deal specifically with the special problem of choosing the best subset of a set of possible regressors. Kennedy and Bancroft (1971) have labeled this subject as the *analysis of incompletely specified models.*[2] While there is some overlap between this and the second category, they are sufficiently distinct to warrant separate treatment in our opinion.

Informal Decision Rules

There are several informal decision rules for choosing among alternative linear models. Of these, the rule of maximizing R^2 is the most frequently used.

R^2 (or the coefficient of multiple determination) in a linear model with fixed, nonstochastic explanatory variables is nothing more than a measure describing the proportion of variance in the dependent variable which is "explained" by the linear relationship. Since one can increase R^2 by adding more variables, the "maximize R^2" rule is usually replaced by "maximize $\bar{R}^2$," where $\bar{R}^2 = R^2 - [(k-1)/(T-k)](1-R^2)$, T is the sample size, and k is the number of explanatory variables.[3]

One justification for this procedure is that it minimizes the estimated fraction of variance unexplained. Theil (1957) provides a more formal justification for the $\bar{R}^2$ rule. His argument may be summarized as follows: Suppose we are considering two models of the same process.

$$\text{Model } i: \quad \underset{(T\times 1)}{\mathbf{y}} \ = \ \underset{(T\times k_i)}{X_i} \quad \underset{(k_i\times 1)}{\boldsymbol{\beta}_i} + \underset{(T\times 1)}{\boldsymbol{\varepsilon}_i} \ , \quad i=1,2.$$

The first model is in fact the "correct" one. Assume X_1 and X_2 have full column rank with real nonstochastic elements, $E(\boldsymbol{\varepsilon}_1) = 0$ and $E(\boldsymbol{\varepsilon}_1 \boldsymbol{\varepsilon}_1') = \sigma^2 I$. Let

$$(T-k_i)s_i^2 = \mathbf{y}'[I - X_i X_i' X_i)^{-1} X_i']\mathbf{y}.$$

---

[2] More specifically, we may view this as analysis of a model in which the prior information on the parameters of the model has not been completely specified.

[3] This adjustment approximately corrects for the bias in R^2 as an estimate of the fraction of (population) variance explained; see Barten (1962). Also note that $\bar{R}^2$ is increased by the addition of variables if and only if the F statistic for the hypothesis that their coefficients are all zero is greater than one; see Edwards (1969).

Theil shows that $E(s_2{}^2) \geqslant E(s_1{}^2)$. From this he concludes that choosing the model with the higher $\bar{R}^2$ (i.e., the lower s^2) will lead "on the average" to the correct choice. Kloek (1970) shows that while $\text{plim}_{T\to\infty} s_1{}^2 = \sigma^2$ (under suitable conditions on X_1) $\text{plim}\, s_2{}^2 > \sigma^2$ or that $s_2{}^2$ does not converge at all. Thus, as $T \to \infty$, minimizing s^2 will lead to the correct choice with high probability.

Pesaran (1972) points out, however, that there are many other quadratic forms of the least squares residuals, say $v_i{}^2 = \hat{\varepsilon}_i' W_i \hat{\varepsilon}_i$, that satisfy $E(v_1{}^2) \leqslant E(v_2{}^2)$ if the first model is the correct specification. A sufficient condition for this is that $\text{tr}[(I - X_i(X_i'X_i)^{-1}X_i')W_i] = 1$. Each such $v_1{}^2$ is an unbiased estimator of σ^2 but different W_i's may imply different probabilities of correctly selecting model 1. Also, Koerts and Abrahamse (1969) point out that the distribution of R^2 depends not only on $\boldsymbol{\beta}$ and σ^2 but also on X. In small samples this dependency can have a sizeable influence on the probability of choosing the correct model.

Theil did not make clear the precise meaning of obtaining the correct model "on the average." One way of giving content to that statement is to consider the distribution of $s_2{}^2/s_1{}^2$. The frequency with which the correct model is chosen is the probability that this random variable is greater than one. For the case in which X_2 is included in X_1, this probability is given by a noncentral F distribution. See Schmidt (1973) for further discussion and illustrative calculations.

The maximize $\bar{R}^2$ rule is often applied to choose one from a large set of models. Suppose, for example, that there are 10 possible explanatory variables, that all 1023 possible combinations of them are tried, and the combination with the minimum s^2 is chosen. Under this procedure the probability of selecting the correct model (i.e., the probability that *none* of the 1022 incorrect alternatives has an s^2 smaller than that of the correct model) is very low.[4] Finally, it should be noted that the $\bar{R}^2$ rule includes no consideration of the loss structure associated with choosing incorrect models.

Another informal procedure for model selection which is widely used in psychology is cross-validation. In this procedure the sample is split into two parts, usually of roughly equal size. The first part is used for selecting a model and estimating its parameters. These estimated parameters are then used to predict the dependent variable in the second sample, and a simple correlation between these predictions and the actual values of the dependent variable is computed.[5] This correlation is usually smaller than the R^2 in the first sample.

---

[4] If the comparisons were independent, the probability of selecting the correct model would be $\prod_{i=1}^{1022} p_i$, where p_i is the probability than $s_c{}^2$ (correct) $< s_i{}^2$. They are not independent and this simple formula probably understates the probability of choosing the right model.

[5] In double cross validation, this procedure is repeated interchanging the roles of the two samples.

If there is a large reduction ("shrinkage"), the model is deemed unsatisfactory. For a detailed study of cross-validation, see Herzberg (1969).[6]

The use of the cross-validation procedure implies a loss of efficiency in parameter estimation. This loss may be partially offset by fitting the chosen model with all the data after the predictive tests have been performed. Further, this reduction of efficiency will not be too important in large samples, and if there is substantial uncertainty about the appropriate model it may be worthwhile to give up some precision in parameter estimation in order to gain information about the model.[7] While this splitting-the-sample procedure may be quite useful, it should be noted that in principle it does not make optimal use of the data, since all the data contain information about *both* the model and the parameter values.

Residual analysis and goodness-of-fit tests are another set of informal techniques that are used to examine the adequacy of a (currently entertained) model. The purpose of these tests is to discover if "something is wrong" with the model. The alternative model or hypothesis is not well defined although some of the test statistics employed are designed to detect the presence of specific classes of departures from assumptions. For extensive discussion of these procedures, see Anscombe (1963) and Anscombe and Tukey (1963). For a likelihood-ratio interpretation of goodness-of-fit tests, see DeGroot (1972).

Hypothesis Testing Procedures

There have been several attempts to develop procedures for choosing a model that fit into the classical hypothesis testing framework. One of the earliest of these is a study by Hotelling (1940), which deals with the problem of selecting variables for use in prediction. Healy (1955) and Williams (1959) give additional discussions of the procedure.

Specifically, the Hotelling test is applied to the following problem. Suppose interest centers in predicting y using a linear forecasting equation and that two predictor variables, x_1 and x_2, are available. For reasons of economy, only two models are being considered. These are

$$\text{(model 1)} \quad y = \alpha_1 + \beta_1 x_1 + u_1,$$

$$\text{(model 2)} \quad y = \alpha_2 + \beta_2 x_2 + u_2.$$

---

[6] Economists often employ a test procedure similar to cross validation, namely, Chow's test for equality of coefficients in two separate regressions; see Chow (1960) and Fisher (1970).

[7] Christ (1966, pp. 546–548) offers additional comments on the use of hold out samples for predictive testing. He argues against their use in small samples because he feels they yield nothing not obtainable from examination of the residuals and because the researcher cannot avoid being "familiar" with the hold out sample and taking advantage of this "familiarity" in choosing the model. However, he recommends their use in large cross-sectional samples. Apparently, laziness overcomes dishonesty in large samples.

The problem is to decide which of these two models to use to estimate the forecasting equation.

Hotelling develops a test to indicate the significance of the difference between the R^2's in these two models. This provides a measure to take into account the possibility that by maximizing R^2 a wrong choice has been made because of chance fluctuations in the sample correlation coefficients. If a choice is necessary, however, one would choose the model with the higher R^2, even if it was not significantly greater than the other.

Hotelling's test is based on the statistic

$$t = (r_1 - r_2)\left[\frac{(T-3)(1+r_0)}{2D}\right]^{1/2},$$

where r_1 and r_2 are the sample correlations between y and x_1 and x_2, respectively, r_0 is the sample correlation between x_1 and x_2, T is the sample size, and

$$D = \begin{vmatrix} 1 & r_1 & r_2 \\ r_1 & 1 & r_0 \\ r_2 & r_0 & 1 \end{vmatrix}.$$

This statistic has a student t distribution with $T-3$ degrees of freedom under the hypothesis that both x_1 and x_2 are equally correlated with y.

Hotelling generalizes this result by deriving a similar test that can be applied to the problem of choosing one predictor from among three or more alternatives. However, he is unable to construct a similar test for choosing among alternatives with more than one explanatory variable.

In general, most approaches which use hypothesis testing to discriminate among linear models use the technique of embedding specific alternative models into one general model. This model is confronted with the relevant data, and hypotheses concerning specific values of the model's parameters are tested to decide which of the models to accept.[8]

The following illustration of this procedure can be found in Malinvaud (1970) and Goldberger (1968). Suppose one is contemplating two theories of the consumption function,

$$\text{model 1:} \quad C_t = \beta_0 + \beta_1 Y_t + \beta_2 Y_{t-1} + \varepsilon_t,$$

$$\text{model 2:} \quad C_t = \beta_0{}^* + \beta_1{}^* Y_t + \beta_2{}^* C_{t-1} + \varepsilon_t{}^*,$$

---

[8] There are large literatures on two related problems in which nesting of alternatives in a larger model appears to be a "natural" mode of analysis. These are the choice of the degree of polynomial in polynomial regression [see, e.g., Anderson (1962) and Graybill (1961)] and the determination of the maximum lag in an autoregressive equation [see, e.g., Anderson (1963) and Box and Jenkins (1970)]. While we shall not discuss these problems, we note that they illustrate well the difficulties with nesting, which we point out below. These problems are also related to the problem of choosing a best subset of regressors, which we consider below.

where C_t and Y_t are the levels of consumption and income respectively at time t. One can form the following general model of the consumption function that embodies both of these specific models as special cases:

$$C_t = \beta_0^{**} + \beta_1^{**}Y_t + \beta_2^{**}Y_{t-1} + \beta_3^{**}C_{t-1} + e_t^{**}.$$

This model specializes to model 1 when $\beta_3^{**} = 0$; similarly, for $\beta_2^{**} = 0$, model 2 is obtained. One can test which of the two alternatives is correct by testing (separately) the hypotheses that $\beta_2^{**} = 0$ and $\beta_3^{**} = 0$.

This procedure does not always yield a clear-cut decision. As shown in Table 1, there are four possible outcomes for the above tests.

TABLE 1

POSSIBLE TEST OUTCOMES

Outcome	H: $\beta_2^{**} = 0$	H: $\beta_3^{**} = 0$
1	Reject	Accept
2	Accept	Reject
3	Reject	Reject
4	Accept	Accept

If one of the first two outcomes occurs, either model 1 or model 2 is selected. If either of the last two outcomes occurs, an unambiguous decision is not obtained. One is inclined to interpret these outcomes as evidence in favor of or against the general model. However, a joint test of the hypothesis that $\beta_2^{**} = \beta_3^{**} = 0$ may lead to conclusions contrary to those suggested by the outcomes of the separate tests for $\beta_2^{**} = 0$ and $\beta_3^{**} = 0$.[9]

Furthermore, the occurrence of the fourth outcome above may be due largely to the way the general model has been specified. If, for example, the explanatory variables C_{t-1} and Y_{t-1} in the general model are highly colinear, then precise estimation of β_2^{**} and β_3^{**} will be hampered. In addition, if either of the two simple alternatives is the "correct" specification, then the general model will contain an irrelevant variable. This misspecification also reduces the precision of the parameter estimates. [See, e.g., Rao (1972).] These potential difficulties become more prominent as the number of alternative models being considered increases. Thus, while offering an intuitively appealing approach for choosing among models, these mechanical nesting procedures do involve statistical problems that reduce their discriminatory power.

[9] Computing the probability of a correct decision is rather complicated. It depends on the explanatory variables as well as the probabilities of error in the individual tests. On a related subject, see Graybill (1961, pp. 127–128).

We now turn to the consideration of procedures for testing separate families of hypotheses. Suppose two hypotheses about the probability density function of a random variable, y, are being entertained. Under the first hypothesis, H_1, y is assumed to have a p.d.f. $f_1(y; \theta_1)$, where $\theta_1 \in \Omega_1$. Under the second hypothesis, H_2, y has a p.d.f. $f_2(y; \theta_2)$, where $\theta_2 \in \Omega_2$. In addition, assume that $\Omega_1 \cap \Omega_2$ is not equal to either Ω_1 or Ω_2. Under these circumstances we say that H_1 and H_2 are nonnested or separate hypotheses. Note that, unlike the case of nested hypotheses, it may not be possible to obtain an arbitrarily close approximation to $f_1(y; \theta_1)$ by $f_2(y; \theta_2)$ for any $\theta_2 \in \Omega_2$.

The seminal work on this subject is that of Cox (1961, 1962). Before discussing the major aspect of his work, we consider two recent applications motivated by his suggestions for embedding separate hypotheses into a single model. One of these suggestions was to form a p.d.f. for the general model as

$$f(y; \theta_1, \theta_2, \lambda) \propto \{f_1(y; \theta_1)\}^\lambda \{f_2(y; \theta_2)\}^{1-\lambda}.$$

Inferences about the two specific models are made through the new parameter λ.

Atkinson (1970) applies this procedure to the problem of comparing two alternative one-variable models. Suppose these models are

$$(\text{model } i) \qquad y_t = b_i x_{it} + u_{it}, \qquad i = 1, 2.$$

Under the first hypothesis, y_t is distributed normally with mean $b_1 x_{1t}$ and variance σ^2. Under the second hypothesis, y_t is distributed normally with mean $b_2 x_{2t}$ and variance σ^2.[10]

Atkinson writes the combined p.d.f. of y as

$$f_\lambda(\mathbf{y}; \boldsymbol{\theta}) = k^T \prod_{t=1}^{T} \{f_1(y_t; b_1 x_{1t})\}^{\lambda_1} \{f_2(y_t; b_2 x_{2t})\}^{\lambda_2},$$

where k^T is a normalizing constant defined by[11]

$$k = \frac{1}{\int_{-\infty}^{\infty} \{f_1(y_t; b_1 x_{1t})\}^{\lambda_1} \{f_2(y_t; b_2 x_{2t})\}^{\lambda_2} \, dy_t}.$$

For the models above, the p.d.f. is

$$f_\lambda(\mathbf{y}; \theta) = k' \exp\left(\frac{-\sum_{t=1}^{T} (y_t - c_1 x_{1t} - c_2 x_{2t})^2}{2\tau^2} \right),$$

where

$$c_1 = \frac{b_1 \lambda_1}{\lambda_1 + \lambda_2}, \qquad c_2 = \frac{b_2 \lambda_2}{\lambda_1 + \lambda_2}, \qquad \tau^2 = \frac{\sigma^2}{\lambda_1 + \lambda_2}, \qquad \text{and} \quad k' = \left(\frac{\lambda_1 + \lambda_2}{2\pi\sigma^2} \right)^{T/2}.$$

[10] The procedure may be generalized without great difficulty to handle models with more explanatory variables. Also, $\text{var}(y_t)$ need not be the same for both models.

[11] In general, k may be difficult to compute for nonnormal data densities.

It is not possible to estimate the λ_i's, b_i's, or σ since these parameters are not identified in the combined model.[12] However, inferences about the component models can be made via tests on the estimable functions, c_1 and c_2, of the original parameters. For example, testing $c_1 = 0$ is equivalent to testing the adequacy of model 2. We observe that this procedure leads to the same results as the informal embedding procedure discussed above. Exactly the same tests are used; it is also subject to the same limitations.[13]

As an alternative to Atkinson's procedure, Quandt (1972) suggests that a linear combination of the separate p.d.f.'s for a single observation, y_t,

$$f(y_t; \theta_1, \theta_2, \lambda) = \lambda f_1(y_t; \theta_1) + (1 - \lambda) f_2(y_t; \theta_2),$$

be used as the p.d.f. for the general model. He notes the following advantages that this formulation offers: (1) It is capable of intuitively easier interpretation; (2) it is formally identical to the p.d.f. of a random variable that is produced by a mixture of two distributions, λ being the probability that nature has chosen the p.d.f. f_1 for generating a value of y; (3) there is no computational problem in obtaining the normalizing constant as there is in Atkinson's formulation.

Quandt's likelihood function, based on a sample of T-independent observations, is the product of the linear combinations above. A conceptually important aspect of Quandt's formulation is that it implies that we may view the "correct" model as changing from observation to observation [see the display above and statement (2) below it]. Most other formulations that involve combining p.d.f.'s assume a stable "correct" model.

In this model it is possible to construct examples in which λ is not identified and in which maximum likelihood estimators do not exist [see Kiefer and Wolfowitz (1956, p. 905)]. Also, the estimation procedure entails a high dimensional nonlinear optimization problem. For example, if θ_1 and θ_2 each contain four parameters, the combined model contains nine parameters. Furthermore, the restriction $0 \leqslant \lambda \leqslant 1$ must be imposed, since it is possible for the combined "p.d.f." to take on negative values if it is not.

Quandt performs some sampling experiments using two linear models with different explanatory variables to examine the distributions of the maximum likelihood estimator of λ and the likelihood ratio statistic. Interpretation of his results is hampered by the frequent occurrence of computational problems and a small number of replications. Considerable further work is required to obtain an accurate evaluation of Quandt's procedure.

We now consider the main aspect of Cox's analysis, namely, the study of the

<hr>

[12] Atkinson does not require that $\lambda_1 + \lambda_2 = 1$. However, even if this restriction were imposed, the parameters would still be unidentified.

[13] However, for problems other than those in which linear models are compared, Atkinson's procedure may yield useful results. See his paper for several other applications.

asymptotic distribution of a function of the generalized log-likelihood ratio in the case of nonnested hypotheses.[14] He shows that this statistic is asymptotically normal, computes the mean and variance of the asymptotic distribution, and indicates how it may be used to test for departures from H_1 in the direction of H_2. He also works out the form of the statistic in some specific problems.

Cox's test may indicate one of three outcomes: (1) consistency with H_1, (2) departure from H_1 in the direction of H_2, or (3) departure away from H_2. Moreover, the test is not symmetric in the hypotheses. When H_2 instead of H_1 is made the reference hypothesis, different conclusions may result. Thus, great care must be exercised in interpreting the results of the test. Finally, the test does not readily generalize to cases involving more than two alternatives.

Dhrymes *et al.* (1972) outline the computation of Cox's statistic for the case of two linear models with different explanatory variables. Pesaran (1972) performs a similar computation and also considers the case in which the linear models have serially correlated errors. He also employs the procedure to compare models of U.S. demand for imports.

The procedures of Atkinson, Cox, and Quandt offer potentially useful alternatives to *ad hoc* selection rules and mechanical embedding procedures. Further investigation of their properties and interrelationships is necessary in order to permit their routine use.

The Best Subset Problem

There are numerous methods, mostly non-Bayesian, for dealing with the problem of selecting a best subset of regressors from some larger set. It is perhaps preferable to view these procedures as dealing more with *model simplification* rather than model selection because many of them assume (at least implicitly) that the "correct" model is the one containing all the regressors under consideration. The objective is to simplify by deletion of variables while still retaining a model which is "good" in some sense not always specified.

Many of these simplification procedures involve sequential testing of hypotheses. Among these are the forward selection, backward elimination, forward and backward ranking, and stepwise and stagewise regression procedures. In these procedures the next step of the process (adding and/or deleting a variable or variables) is based on the outcome of some (preliminary) test of significance. The procedures terminate when the test suggests no further changes are desirable. Often different procedures will lead to different final results. See, for example, Draper and Smith (1966) and the references therein.

---

[14] The function considered is the generalized log-likelihood ratio itself minus the expected value (under the first hypothesis H_1) of the difference between the sample log-likelihood given H_1 and the sample log-likelihood given H_2, the likelihoods and the expectation being evaluated at the maximum likelihood estimates, $\hat{\theta}_1$ and $\hat{\theta}_2$.

Also, see Kennedy and Bancroft (1971) and the references therein for a discussion of the consequences for estimation and prediction, in terms of bias and mean squared error, of using sequential procedures such as these.[15]

The efficiency of preliminary testing procedures has also been examined by comparison of the risk function of preliminary test estimators with that of various Stein-like estimators. In particular, Sclove et al. (1972) show that a modified Stein–James positive part estimator has everywhere lower risk than the preliminary test estimator.[16]

These criticisms of ad hoc sequential searches do not imply that model simplification is necessarily undesirable. What is needed, however, is a well-specified, understandable criterion for simplification and avoidance of situations in which error rates of individual tests or comparisons compound so as to make a "good" end result unlikely.

There are several model simplification procedures that include a formal criterion as a basis for selection. These recognize, in one form or another, the bias-variance tradeoff inherent in the simplification process. The first of these is the C_p statistic developed by C. Mallows in unpublished work and popularized by Gorman and Toman (1966). The C_p statistic is an estimate of the expected scaled (by $1/\sigma^2$) sum of squared errors associated with using a particular estimator as an estimator of the conditional expectation $(X\beta)$ of $\mathbf{y}$. In particular,

$$C_p = \frac{RSS_p}{\hat{\sigma}^2} - T + 2p,$$

where p is the number of explanatory variables included, RSS_p is the error sum of squares for a particular p variable regression, and $\hat{\sigma}^2$ is the estimate of the disturbance variance obtained when all variables are included. When the bias associated with a particular subset regression is small $C_p \doteq p$.[17]

---

[15] A clear exposition for the case of two explanatory variables is given in Wallace and Ashar (1972).

[16] It should be noted, however, that preliminary test estimators do dominate ordinary least squares estimators over certain regions of the parameter space. For more on Stein estimators and risk comparisons, see Judge et al. (1972) and references therein.

[17] Let $\hat{\beta}_i$ be the least squares estimator obtained when certain columns of X (dimension $T \times k$) are deleted and let X_i (dimension $T \times k_i$) be the matrix of included variables. Further, let $\gamma_i(k \times 1)$ have as jth entry the corresponding element of β if the column of X is deleted and 0 if included. Then

$$E[(\hat{\beta}_i - \beta)'X'X(\hat{\beta}_i - \beta)] = k_i\sigma^2 + B_i,$$

with $B_i = \gamma_i'X'[I - X_i(X_i'X_i)^{-1}X_i']X\gamma_i$. If no variables are excluded B_i (the bias) is zero. Now, letting $RSS_i = (y - X_i\hat{\beta}_i)'(y - X_i\hat{\beta}_i)$, we see that

$$E(RSS_i) = (T - k_i)\sigma^2 + B_i.$$

When for a particular regression with p explanatory variables B is small, RSS is a nearly unbiased estimator of $(T-p)\sigma^2$ and $RSS_p/(T-p) = \hat{\sigma}_p^2 \doteq \hat{\sigma}^2$. Thus, $C_p \doteq p$. Use of $\hat{\sigma}^2$ from the complete equation presumes that none of the variables is irrelevant.

In practice, C_p is computed for all possible subsets and one of the equations with $C_p \doteq p$ or less is chosen.[18] No fixed rules such as "minimize C_p" is advocated by these authors. In fact, Mallows (1972) shows that with orthogonal regressors and large T the "minimize C_p" rule (which is equivalent to discarding variables with t-statistics $< \sqrt{2}$ in absolute value) yields an expected scaled sum of squares 1.65 times that obtained when the full equation is always used. While the orthogonal case may be more unfavorable to the "minimize C_p" rule than the case $X'X \neq I$, this result supports our criticism above of choosing the minimum s^2 from all subsets.

Allen (1971) considers the problem of choosing the best subset when the criterion is minimum mean squared error of prediction. He obtains an expression for the mean square prediction error (MSE) (for given values of the explanatory variables) when various variables are deleted. It differs from the MSE for predicting with all explanatory variables by the addition of two terms, one positive and one negative. It is thus possible that dropping variables leads to smaller mean squared prediction error. This expression involves, in addition to the values of the predictor variables, the unknown parameters β and σ^2. Allen suggests estimating the MSE by plugging in the full least squares estimates of the parameters. He then compares the MSE estimates for various subsets and chooses the subset with the smallest estimated MSE.

Allen's procedure is subject to the difficulties mentioned above since the minimum of a set of estimates need not correspond to the minimum of the true values. In addition, since the MSE expressions involve a specific future $\mathbf{x}$ value, the "optimal" subset need not be the same for different future values of the regressors. In one sense this may be regarded as an advantage since, in contrast to the previous procedures, the purpose for which the model is to be used is explicitly incorporated.

Before proceeding to Bayesian model selection procedures, we give a brief discussion of a Bayesian analysis of the choice of a best subset problem. Lindley (1968) considers both the problem of selecting predictors for a future value of y and the problem of selecting variables for controlling y at a specified value. The analyses and results in the two cases are different; we discuss only the prediction problem. In Lindley's analysis the x's are stochastic, distributed independently of β (σ^2 is assumed known). There are two important differences between this and the apparently similar studies above. First, a cost of observing variables in the future is included. Secondly, the criterion is minimization of expected (with respect to the distribution of β) mean square error of prediction (plus observation cost). For a given set of (values of the) included variables,

---

[18] When the total number of explanatory variables is large, this computation is burdensome. LaMotte and Hocking (1970) devise an algorithm for finding models with good C_p statistics without doing all possible regressions. Also, Schatzoff *et al.* (1968) provide an efficient algorithm for running all possible subsets.

say $\mathbf{x}_I$, the optimal predictor is the mean of the predictive density of y. This is given by $E(y \mid \mathbf{x}_I) = E(\boldsymbol{\beta})' E(\mathbf{x} \mid \mathbf{x}_I)$, where $\mathbf{x}$ is an observation on all regressors. Then $E[\{y - E(y \mid \mathbf{x}_I)\} \mid \mathbf{x}_I]$ is averaged over $\mathbf{x}_I$ and a general expression to be minimized by numerical evaluation over possible subsets is obtained.

Lindley specializes to the case in which the x's have a multivariate normal distribution and where prior information on all the parameters of the model is diffuse. In this case the subset is chosen for which the sum of the observation cost and the excess of the residual sum of squares fitting the subset over the residual sum of squares from fitting with all the x's is minimum. Lindley's procedure in this case thus employs the same quantity as the conventional test statistic for significance of additional variables except that it is compared with observation cost rather than some fractile of a chi-square distribution. He also notes that if the observation costs for all variables are equal to $2\sigma^2/T$, his procedure chooses the same subset as the "minimize C_p" rule. On the other hand, if costs of obtaining observations are negligible, Lindley's procedure suggests inclusion of all variables under the conditions stated above.

In summary, we see that the problem of model simplification has received much attention. This study has resulted in both a better understanding of the problem and in the development of new methods for dealing with it. Informal sequential tests have been studied extensively and new methods which include an explicit criterion to govern the simplification process have been introduced. Lindley's treatment of the problem especially serves to point out the importance of formal consideration of the purposes for which the model will be used.

II. Bayesian Procedures for Comparing and Choosing among Alternative Models

The fundamental feature of Bayesian statistics, as is now well known, is the use of probability to measure uncertainty even in situations in which the usual repetitive element is absent. In the Bayesian framework, it is natural to consider in a nontrivial way the concept of the probability of a model. Bayesian approaches to "hypothesis testing" problems have been developed by Jeffreys (1961), Edwards et al. (1963), Cornfield (1966), and Dickey (1971a, b), among others. These studies consider mainly alternative hypotheses that are nested in a general model. Bayesian model-selection procedures largely constitute the application of the same concepts and methods to situations in which the alternatives are nonnested.

This part of the paper is divided into three parts. First, we present a general outline of the probability and decision calculus for Bayesian model-selection procedures. Secondly, we apply this to the problem of comparing single-equation linear models with alternative sets of explanatory variables. Finally, we discuss extensions to other common econometric problems such as distributed lags and serial correlation.

Probability Calculus for Model Comparisons

In this section we discuss two somewhat different approaches to model selection. The first is a purely inferential one that focuses on the predictive performance of the competing models. The second sets up a decision framework for selecting the "best" model. Throughout the discussion we presume that the model space is given, and for convenience of exposition we deal with the case where it consists of two models, denoted M_1 and M_2. We denote the random variable of interest by Y, and a particular observation on it by y. The parameters of M_i are denoted by θ_i and the parameter space is taken to be finite dimensional. We deal with the case in which all distributions of Y and θ_i have densities, also for expositional convenience. Densities of observations will be indicated by p, densities of parameters by π, and the mass function of the models by P. Conditioning "events," whether parameters, observations, or models, appear to the right of a vertical mark in the list of arguments for a density or mass function.

In this discussion we do not consider the details of the statistical analysis of a given model. Such analysis is, of course, a component of the procedure. Conventional procedures for examining the appropriateness of the assumed data and prior densities may be used as part of model comparison procedures. We also point out again that enumeration of the elements of the model space is important in the sense that the results of the comparisons depend on it. These *caveats* apply equally to non-Bayesian procedures as well.

A central quantity in the discussion is the *marginal density of the observations* or *predictive p.d.f.*, which is denoted $p(y \mid M_i)$ and is given by

$$(1) \qquad p(y \mid M_i) = \int p(y \mid \theta_i, M_i) \, \pi(\theta_i \mid M_i) \, d\theta_i,$$

where $p(y \mid \theta_i, M_i)$ is the usual sampling density that is conditional on the model and the values of its parameters and $\pi(\theta_i \mid M_i)$ is a (prior) density for the parameters of M_i. $p(y \mid M_i)$ depends on the model, but is marginal of its parameters since the conditional sampling densities have been averaged with respect to the prior π. When y is fixed and θ_i variable, $p(y \mid \theta_i, M_i)$ is called the likelihood function of the parameters (given the model). Similarly, for given y, $p(y \mid M_i)$ is often called the *marginal likelihood* or weighted likelihood of the model.

We now presume that the prior mass function of the models (and density functions for the parameters of the models) have been assessed [with $P(M_2) = 1 - P(M_1)$ and both $P(M_1)$ and $P(M_2)$ positive] and consider how sample evidence causes our opinions about the models to be revised. The discussion follows Roberts (1965), who deals with a problem of comparing forecasters, and (more directly) Geisel (1970).

Given the form of the conditional sampling densities, $p(y \mid \theta_i, M_i)$, we may compute $p(y \mid M_i)$ via Equation (1) in advance of obtaining the observations. This density expresses our opinions, conditional on M_i, regarding the as-yet-to-be-observed data. Unconditional of the models, our opinion is expressed by

$$(2) \qquad p(y) = P(M_1)p(y \mid M_1) + P(M_2)p(y \mid M_2),$$

a weighted average of the densities that depend on the models.

Suppose now we observe a particular (set of) value(s) of the random variable Y, say y. Then Bayes' Rule is used to revise the prior probabilities of the models. That is,

$$(3) \qquad P(M_i \mid y) = \frac{P(M_i)p(y \mid M_i)}{p(y)}.$$

Thus, by Equations (2) and (3), the revision of the probabilities of the models is governed by the relative weighted likelihoods of the models given the observed data.[19]

Suppose we contemplate future sample evidence, Y_F. Our opinions about it are expressed by a predictive density entirely analogous to Equation (2), namely,

$$(4) \qquad p(y_F \mid y) = P(M_1 \mid y)p(y_F \mid M_1, y) + P(M_2 \mid y)p(y_F \mid M_2, y),$$

where $p(y_F \mid M_i, y)$ [as in Equation (1)] is given by

$$p(y_F \mid M_i, y) = \int p(y_F \mid \theta_i, M_i)\pi(\theta_i \mid M_i, y)\,d\theta_i.$$

When we observe $Y_F = y_F$ we may again revise the probabilistic weights for the models in accord with Equation (3) and compute a new predictive p.d.f. via Equation (4). Once again, the models' probabilities are revised according to the weighted likelihood (or predictive density) of the models given the observed data.

The computations involved in this procedure are in principle straightforward if each model implies a proper density for y or y_F. In general, however, $p(y)$ will have to be obtained by adding its components, $p(M_i)p(y \mid M_i)$, numerically, because the conditional (on the model) densities usually will not

---

[19] Of course, the densities $\pi(\theta_i \mid M_i)$ may be updated in the usual manner via Bayes' rule, i.e.,

$$\pi(\theta_i \mid y, M_i) = \frac{p(y \mid \theta_i, M_i)\pi(\theta_i \mid M_i)}{p(y)}.$$

add to a tractable expression. The moments of $p(y)$ or $p(y_F \mid y)$ in terms of the moments of the conditional densities are readily obtainable, however.

We now see the central role of prediction in Bayesian procedures for comparing models. The procedure outlined above also provides a framework for viewing procedures, Bayesian or otherwise, that select one model as "true" or "best." If a model has positive probability, it contributes to our knowledge of future observations and there is no reason to neglect this contribution. Procedures that select one model are thus seen as approximations undertaken for simplicity of view or ease of computation. The sensitivity of prediction to the choice of model is also made clear by this procedure.

We now turn to discussion of a decision-theoretic procedure for choosing one model from a set of models. The exposition follows those of Thornber (1966) and Geisel (1970). The decision criterion adopted is minimization of posterior expected loss (MEL). This criterion is equivalent to the minimization of expected risk (a Bayes' decision rule) if expected risk is finite.[20]

We employ the following simple loss structure for the model-selection problem:

		accept	
		M_1	M_2
	M_1	0	L_{12}
"correct"			
	M_2	L_{21}	0

where L_{12} and L_{21} are positive numbers. This loss structure is of the type used in the decision-theoretic analysis of simple dichotomy problems. It is a simple loss function in that it involves neither estimation nor prediction errors of the models. Clearly, it is not the only possible appropriate loss structure for discriminating among alternative models.

Now, the posterior expected loss of choosing M_1 is

$$EL(M_1) = 0 \cdot P(M_1 \mid y) + L_{21} \cdot P(M_2 \mid y),$$

with a corresponding expression for $EL(M_2)$. To minimize posterior expected loss we choose M_1 if

$$L_{21} P(M_2 \mid y) < L_{12} P(M_1 \mid y)$$

and M_2 otherwise. An equivalent way of expressing this condition is by choosing M_1 if

(5)
$$\frac{P(M_1 \mid y)}{P(M_2 \mid y)} > \frac{L_{21}}{L_{12}}$$

[20] See, for example, Ferguson (1967) or Raiffa and Schlaifer (1961) for detailed expositions of statistical decision theory.

and M_2 otherwise. Thus, if $L_{21} = L_{12}$ we simply choose the model with the larger posterior probability. Making use of Equation (3) we see that M_1 is chosen if

$$(6) \qquad \frac{p(y \mid M_1)}{p(y \mid M_2)} > \frac{P(M_2) L_{21}}{P(M_1) L_{12}}.$$

That is, we choose M_1 if the weighted likelihood ratio of M_1 relative to M_2 is greater than the ratio of the *prior* expected loss of choosing M_1 to that of choosing M_2. Expressions (5) and (6) are "Bayesianized" versions of Jeffreys' testing procedures; see Jeffreys (1961, esp. Chap. V) and, for example, Roberts (1964, Chap. 11) and Zellner (1971, Chap. 10).[21]

It is frequently convenient to employ the concept of odds ratios in discussion of Bayesian model comparisons. By Equation (3), the posterior odds for M_1 are given by

$$(7) \qquad \frac{P(M_1 \mid y)}{P(M_2 \mid y)} = \frac{P(M_1)}{P(M_2)} \frac{P(y \mid M_1)}{P(y \mid M_2)}$$

and are thus the product of the prior odds ratio and the weighted likelihood ratio. Note that this ratio is the same even if there are more than two models under consideration.

The behavior of the posterior odds as the sample size changes is thus governed by the behavior of the likelihood ratio. The study of the large sample behavior of the weighted likelihood ratio has largely been confined to the case in which the alternative models are single-equation linear models. In that case, if M_1 is the true model, $\text{plim}_{n \to \infty} P(M_1 \mid y) = 1$ under rather mild conditions on the matrices of explanatory variables; see Lempers (1971, pp. 37–41). It seems reasonable to anticipate that similar results may be obtained for other classes of models, but a general result is perhaps precluded because we have imposed no conditions on the nature of the alternative models.[22]

Comparison of Single-Equation Linear Models with Alternative Sets of Explanatory Variables

In this section, we focus on the calculation of $p(y \mid M_i)$ for single-equation linear models under various assumptions about the prior p.d.f.'s of the

---

[21] It may be noted that the entire development of this section can be applied if M_1 and M_2 are submodels nested within a general model.

[22] This statement may be too pessimistic. Lindley (1965) and Zellner (1971, pp. 31–33), among others, have examined the large sample behavior of posterior distributions of parameters. If the model is correct, then under certain regularity conditions (similar to those employed in establishing consistency of maximum likelihood estimators) the limiting posterior distribution is concentrated on a point. Berk (1966) shows that this is not the case if the model is incorrect. It may be possible to obtain similar general results for $p(y \mid M_i)$.

parameters of the models. We call $p(y \mid M_1)/p(y \mid M_2)$ the posterior odds ratio, thus assuming that $P(M_1)/P(M_2)$ is one [see Equation (7)]. Further, in discussion of rules for choosing one of the models, we assume $L_{12} = L_{21}$ so that the MEL decision is to select the model with the higher posterior probability.

We use the notation

$$M_i: \quad \mathbf{y} = X_i \boldsymbol{\beta}_i + \mathbf{u}_i, \qquad i = 1, 2,$$

where $\mathbf{y}$ is a $T \times 1$ vector of observations on a random variable, X_i is a $T \times k_i$ matrix of explanatory variables for M_i assumed to be nonstochastic or, if stochastic, distributed independently of $\mathbf{u}_i$ with a distribution not involving $\boldsymbol{\beta}_i$ or σ_i (see below), $\boldsymbol{\beta}_i$ is a $k_i \times 1$ vector of unknown parameters of M_i, and $\mathbf{u}_i$ is a $T \times 1$ vector of unobservable disturbances for M_i. The elements of u_i (given M_i) are assumed to be independently and normally distributed, each with mean zero and variance σ_i^2, which is unknown.

First, we compute the posterior odds ratio on the assumption that the prior density of $\boldsymbol{\beta}_i$ and σ_i (given M_i) is of natural conjugate form. Then we consider the case in which the prior information on the parameters is "diffuse" or vague.

In the natural conjugate case[23] we break up the prior p.d.f. of $\boldsymbol{\beta}_i$ and σ_i as

$$\pi(\boldsymbol{\beta}_i, \sigma_i \mid M_i) = \pi_1(\boldsymbol{\beta}_i \mid \sigma_i, M_i) \pi_2(\sigma_i \mid M_i)$$

with π_1 a multivariate normal p.d.f. with mean vector $\mathbf{b}_i$ (arbitrary) and covariance matrix $\sigma_i^2 h C_i^{-1}$, where C_i is an arbitrary $k_i \times k_i$ positive-definite symmetric matrix and h is a scale parameter [to be discussed below, but may be ignored for now (set equal to unity)] independent of the models. π_2 is an inverted gamma-2 p.d.f. with parameters η_i and v_i.[24]

To compute $p(\mathbf{y} \mid M_i)$ we simply combine $p(\mathbf{y} \mid \boldsymbol{\beta}_i, \sigma_i, M_i)$ with $\pi(\boldsymbol{\beta}_i, \sigma_i \mid M_i)$ and integrate out $\boldsymbol{\beta}_i$ and σ_i. Define

$$A_i = \frac{1}{h} C_i + X_i' X_i,$$

$$\hat{\hat{\boldsymbol{\beta}}}_i = A_i^{-1} \left(\frac{1}{h} C_i \mathbf{b}_i + X_i' X_i \hat{\boldsymbol{\beta}}_i \right),$$

[23] This exposition follows most closely that of Geisel (1970) but roughly parallels that of Leamer (1970, 1972), Lempers (1971, Chap. 3), and Zellner (1971, Chap. 10).

[24] For properties of this p.d.f. see Raiffa and Schlaifer (1961, Chap. 7). η_i is a prior "degrees of freedom" parameter and v_i a location parameter. For natural conjugate analysis of the normal linear model, see Chap. 11 of that book.

with $\hat{\boldsymbol{\beta}}_i = (X_i'X_i)^{-1}X_i'\mathbf{y}$ being the usual least squares estimator of $\boldsymbol{\beta}_i$ and

$$v_i''s_i''^2 = \eta_i v_i^2 + \frac{1}{h}\mathbf{b}_i'C_i\mathbf{b}_i + \mathbf{y}'\mathbf{y} - \hat{\hat{\boldsymbol{\beta}}}_i'A_i\hat{\hat{\boldsymbol{\beta}}}_i,$$

with $v_i'' = T + \eta_i$.

On combining the prior and the likelihood, noting that

$$(\mathbf{y} - X_i\boldsymbol{\beta}_i)'(\mathbf{y} - X_i\boldsymbol{\beta}_i) + (\boldsymbol{\beta}_i - \mathbf{b}_i)'C_i(\boldsymbol{\beta}_i - \mathbf{b}_i)\frac{1}{h}$$

$$= (\boldsymbol{\beta}_i - \hat{\hat{\boldsymbol{\beta}}}_i)'A_i(\boldsymbol{\beta}_i - \hat{\hat{\boldsymbol{\beta}}}_i) + \frac{1}{h}\mathbf{b}_i'C_i\mathbf{b}_i + \mathbf{y}'\mathbf{y} - \hat{\hat{\boldsymbol{\beta}}}_i'A_i\hat{\hat{\boldsymbol{\beta}}}_i$$

and performing the required integrations, we have

$$(8)\quad p(y\,|\,M_i) = \pi^{-T/2}\frac{(\eta_i v_i^2)^{\eta_i/2}}{\Gamma(\eta_i/2)}\Gamma\left(\frac{T+\eta_i}{2}\right)\left(\frac{1}{h}\right)^{k_i/2}\frac{|C_i|^{1/2}}{|A_i|^{1/2}}(v_i''s_i''^2)^{-(T+\eta_i)/2}.$$

It may be noted that $p(\mathbf{y}\,|\,M_i)$ is a multivariate-Student p.d.f. (see Raiffa and Schlaifer again), although our notation is somewhat different from that normally employed.[25] It is a proper sampling density if $\eta_i > 0$, the number of finite moments depending on the value of η_i.

Examination of Equation (8) indicates that the posterior odds ratio depends on η_i, v_i, C_i, A_i, and $v_i''s_i''^2$. Substantial simplification obtains if we take the priors on σ_1 and σ_2 to be the same. Then the posterior odds ratio depends solely on the ratio of "posterior error sums of squares" and on the determinantal ratios, $|C_i|/|A_i|$. These latter ratios may be interpreted as the ratio of the prior generalized variance of $\boldsymbol{\beta}_i$ to the posterior generalized variance.

Zellner (1971, pp. 309–311) and Leamer (1970, 1972) provide some further interpretations of $p(y\,|\,M_i)$. Zellner shows that the $v_i''s_i''^2$ term reflects what the sample information has to say about goodness of fit of the models (via the sample error sum of squares), as well as the discrepancies $[p(y\,|\,M_i)$ decreases as the discrepancies increase] between the prior mean $\mathbf{b}_i$ and the posterior mean $\hat{\hat{\boldsymbol{\beta}}}_i$ and between the sample mean $\hat{\boldsymbol{\beta}}_i$ and the posterior mean. A final component of the $v_i''s_i''^2$ term relates to the discrepancy between v_i^2 and s_i^2, the sample estimate of σ_i^2. Leamer shows that the penalties for discrepancies between $\mathbf{b}_i$, $\hat{\hat{\boldsymbol{\beta}}}_i$, and $\hat{\boldsymbol{\beta}}$ can be viewed as a single penalty for a discrepancy between the prior and sample means.

We note that the above procedure may be applied without modification in the case in which one of the X_i matrices is a subset of the other, although in

---

[25] The required integrations may be performed in any of several ways, perhaps the easiest of which is to first recognize that the part of the integral depending on $\boldsymbol{\beta}_i$ is a constant times a multivariate normal p.d.f. and then use a change of variable $u = v_i''s_i''^2/2\sigma_i^2$ and the definition of the gamma function to do the σ_i integral.

this case particular attention must be given to the consistent assessment of the prior on the common elements of $\boldsymbol{\beta}$.

Dickey (1971a, b) and Leamer (1970, 1972) have questioned the appropriateness of assuming *a priori* dependence of $\boldsymbol{\beta}_i$ on σ_i, which is incorporated in the natural conjugate approach above. Leamer employs a normal prior for $\boldsymbol{\beta}_i$ which is independent of σ_i. The computation of $p(y \mid M_i)$ now requires numerical integration or approximation of the integrand by a function that can be integrated analytically [see Zellner (1971, Chap. 4 Appendix 2)]. Leamer gives a limiting approximation to $p(y \mid M_i)$ that is valid when information about σ_i is nearly perfect, and compares it with a corresponding approximation for the natural conjugate case. The two expressions are the same except for the obvious changes due to the different prior covariance structure of $\boldsymbol{\beta}_i$. Dickey uses similar priors for which the computation of $p(y \mid M_i)$ also requires numerical evaluation of a one-dimensional integral.

We now examine the posterior odds ratio in the case where the prior information about $\boldsymbol{\beta}_i$ and σ_i is "diffuse." We first consider a "limiting natural conjugate" approach of Geisel (1970) and then review alternative approaches by several other authors.

Our starting point is Equation (8). Let us simplify matters by taking $\eta_i = \eta$ and $v_i = v$ for both models. The former restriction is crucial; the latter is unimportant but simplifies the algebra. A weakening of prior information corresponds to letting h become large and η small.[26] As $h \to \infty$,

$$(a) \qquad \frac{1}{h} \mathbf{b}_i' C_i \mathbf{b}_i \to 0,$$

$$(b) \qquad A_i \to X_i' X_i,$$

and

$$(c) \qquad \hat{\hat{\boldsymbol{\beta}}}_i \to \hat{\boldsymbol{\beta}}_i.$$

As $\eta \to 0$, $\eta v^2 \to 0$ and $v_i'' \to T$. Thus, $v_i'' s_i''^2 \to (y - X\hat{\boldsymbol{\beta}})'(y - X\hat{\boldsymbol{\beta}})$ and

$$(9) \qquad p(\mathbf{y} \mid M_i) \doteq c \left(\frac{1}{h}\right)^{k_i/2} \left(\frac{|C_i|}{|X_i' X_i|}\right)^{1/2} [(y - X\hat{\boldsymbol{\beta}})'(y - X\hat{\boldsymbol{\beta}})]^{-T/2},$$

where c is a constant that does not depend on the model. Since $h \to \infty$, $p(\mathbf{y} \mid M_i) \to 0$ everywhere. Furthermore, if $k_1 \neq k_2$, it approaches zero much faster for the larger model. This problem has frequently been recognized before in Bayesian approaches to comparing a sharp hypothesis with a vague alternative; see, e.g., Cornfield (1966). If $k_1 = k_2$, the situation is not so bad since the "flattening out" occurs at the same rate for the two models. Also, if

---

[26] A widely dispersed normal distribution is quite different from a uniform distribution since it possesses a monotone likelihood ratio. That is, illustrating with a univariate $\mathbf{x} \sim N(\mu, \sigma)$, $f(\mathbf{x} = \mu + k\sigma)/f[x = \mu + (k+\delta)\sigma]$ is an increasing function of $|k|$ for any $\delta > 0$.

$|C_i|/|X_i'X_i|$ is the same[27] for both models, the approximate posterior odds ratio depends only on the ratio of the error sums of squares for the two models. The model with the higher posterior probability is the model with the larger coefficient of determination. Kadane, in work in progress, has pointed out that this result holds (given all the other assumptions) for any prior on σ_i as long as it is the same for both models.

This coincidence of the Bayesian result with classical practice (maximizing R^2) clearly occurs only with specific, perhaps unreasonable, assumptions about the prior distribution of parameters.[28] In particular, this approach does not yield an "adjusted" R^2 rule when $k_1 \neq k_2$. Although this lack of correspondence between conventional practice and Bayesian theory may be displeasing to some, more disturbing is the failure of this limiting natural conjugate to produce sensible results at all when $k_1 \neq k_2$. We shall now review other attempts to deal with this problem.

Thornber (1966) uses the prior suggested by Jeffrey's invariance theory.[29] That is,

$$(10) \qquad \pi_T(\boldsymbol{\beta}_i, \sigma_i \,|\, M_i) \propto \frac{|X_i'X_i|^{1/2}}{\sigma_i^{k_i+1}} .$$

This prior is not integrable. Thus, neither is $p(\mathbf{y} \,|\, M_i)$. While this may not totally damn the approach since we are interested in the $\mathbf{y}$ actually observed rather than any possible values, we should note that one is in principle free to replace Equation (10) by an arbitrary positive constant multiple of it with different constants for different models. Doing this, we can get any results we wish.[30] Thornber takes both constants to be the same and proceeds. For the case $k_1 = k_2$, his procedure chooses the model with the smaller error sum of squares. When $k_1 \neq k_2$, the sum-of-squares rule is altered so as to favor the model with more parameters (by an increasing amount as the difference between k_1 and k_2 increases).[31]

---

[27] A way in which this will occur is to let $C_i = X_i'X_i$. It is hard to argue why sample quantities should appear in one's prior. For further details on this condition, see Zellner (1971, p. 311).

[28] We do not claim that there exist no other priors that yield this result. However, within the natural conjugate class the conditions above are necessary.

[29] See Jeffreys (1961, esp. pp. 117–122 and pp. 179–192) and Zellner (1971, pp. 41–53).

[30] Lempers (1971, Chaps. 3 and 5) comments extensively on this problem.

[31] This result does not appear in Thornber (1966). In fact, his results show a correction to the sum-of-squares rule that favors the model with fewer parameters, though not by an amount equal to the conventional degrees of freedom correction. However, he made an error in computing $p(y \,|\, M_i)$ that accounts for the difference between our statement of his results and his own. Dagenais (1972a) employs a prior similar to Thornber's, though based on other considerations, and obtains results similar to his. Dagenais (1972b) employs somewhat different prior considerations and obtains an error sum-of-squares rule (for $k_1 = k_2$).

Lempers (1971, Chaps 3.5 and 5.3) starts with a uniform prior over a finite interval on $\boldsymbol{\beta}_i$ and $\log \sigma_i$, which he then "spreads out."[32] For $k_1 = k_2$ his limiting result differs from the error sum-of-squares rule only in that the posterior odds ratio contains $(|X_2'X_2|/|X_1'X_1|)^{1/2}$, since the inverse of that factor is not in the priors as it was in Thornber's case.

When $k_1 \neq k_2$, Lempers' limiting result is

$$\frac{p(\mathbf{y}\,|\,M_1)}{p(\mathbf{y}\,|\,M_2)} \propto \frac{|X_2'X_2|^{1/2}}{|X_1'X_1|^{1/2}} \cdot \frac{\Gamma(v_1/2)}{\Gamma(v_2/2)} \frac{(\tfrac{1}{2}v_2\, s_2{}^2)^{v_2/2}}{(\tfrac{1}{2}v_1\, s_1{}^2)^{v_1/2}} \frac{(2\pi)^{k_1/2}}{(2\pi)^{k_2/2}}.$$

This expression involves some seemingly arbitrary constants that affect the likelihood ratio. Considering first the term involving $v_i s_i{}^2$, we see that the exponents are such that the model with more parameters is favored. The other terms can reinforce or negate this effect depending on v_1 and v_2.

Lempers recognizes the inherent arbitrariness of improper priors, but his suggestions for dealing with it [(i) ignore it, (ii) use part of the sample to get a proper prior, and (iii) go back to natural conjugate priors] do not seem helpful. Lempers also points out that Thornber's procedure does not yield the same result if the sample is analyzed in two parts sequentially as it does when analyzed all at once.

Leamer (1970, 1972) also examines the weak prior information case extensively. He obtains results similar to those above when using a limiting proper prior approach. While recognizing the arbitrariness inherent in the problem, he feels it worthwhile to search for some solution that might be appealing and generally acceptable. He examines the behavior of $p(y\,|\,M_i)$ when the sample information vastly dominates the prior information. For a natural conjugate prior, an expression similar to Equation (9) results, while for the independent normal prior a considerably different expression, which builds in a preference for larger models, is obtained. Leamer regards neither result as satisfactory.

Leamer continues his search for reasonable weak priors by studying the case in which both models have the same known variance. He suggests that the prior should be such that $p(y\,|\,M_i)$ is invariant to location and scale changes and that the prior expected posterior probability of both models is the same.[33] He assumes the prior of β_i is normal with mean zero and determines the covariance matrix to satisfy the preposterior indifference criterion. One such matrix is $c_i X_i'X_i$, where c_i depends on k_i. The model with the highest posterior probability is that for which a weighted average of the error sum of squares and the total sum of squares, $\mathbf{y}'\mathbf{y}$, is minimum. Several other ways of attaining preposterior indifference are examined. They involve allocating high prior

---

[32] Box and Hill (1967) employ improper uniform priors in their analysis of a problem in which the next period's explanatory variable is picked so as to maximize a measure of discrimination between alternative functional forms.

[33] A similar notion is employed in Box and Hensen (1969).

probability to the larger model and assuming that the prior covariance matrix depends on the sample size. Leamer concludes that there does not seem to be any unambiguous criterion for choice among models with vague prior information on the parameters.

In summary, we feel, as does Leamer, that none of these procedures for model selection with vague prior information is generally satisfactory. The minimum error sum-of-squares rule probably represents a useful approximation for the $k_1 = k_2$ case when prior information on the parameters is relatively vague, but its users should regard it as such. Resolution of the problem that develops when $k_1 \neq k_2$ may be possible, but it certainly has defied substantial efforts in that direction to date. However, the Bayesian approach does provide a useful method for comparing models when nondiffuse prior information on the parameters is included.

Extensions to Other Econometric Problems

Several other model-selection problems may be analyzed using the methods of the previous subsection. First, suppose that the models have different but functionally related dependent variables (with the other assumptions unaltered). Let $z_t = f(y_t)$, $t = 1, ..., T$, be the dependent variable for M_2 with $f(\cdot)$ a one-to-one function. Then $p(y \mid M_2)$ may be obtained by transforming $p(z \mid M_2)$ into a density in y. That is,

$$p(y \mid M_2) = p(z \mid M_2) \prod_{t=1}^{T} |f'(y_t)|,$$

where f' is the first derivative of f. Secondly, suppose that $E\mathbf{u}_i \mathbf{u}_i' = \sigma_i^2 \Omega_i$, where Ω_i is a known matrix. Such comparisons may be handled by a trivial extension of the above methods inserting Ω_i^{-1} where appropriate in the sampling densities, or by a simple extension of the change-of-variable method above. Also, we note that the problem of comparing alternative finite lag distributions (as in the polynomial distributed lag model) is a problem of choosing among alternative X matrices.

Gaver and Geisel (1972) consider comparisons of alternative single-equation linear models that have unknown covariance matrices. In particular, they concentrate on the case in which the disturbances follow a first order autoregressive scheme. That is, using the notation of the previous subsection,

$$u_{it} = \rho_i u_{it-1} + \varepsilon_{it}, \quad i = 1, 2,$$

where u_{it} is the disturbance of model i for observation t and the ε_{it} are independently and normally distributed, each with mean zero and variance σ_i^2.

The following prior densities for the parameters are used:

$$\pi(\boldsymbol{\beta}_i, \sigma_i, \rho_i \mid M_i) = \pi_1(\boldsymbol{\beta}_i \mid \sigma_i, \rho_i, M_i) \pi_2(\sigma_i \mid M_i) \pi_3(\rho_i \mid M_i),$$

where π_i is a multivariate normal p.d.f. with mean vector $\mathbf{b}_i$ and covariance $h\sigma_i^2 (X_i'\Sigma_i^{-1}X_i)^{-1}$. Here,

$$\Sigma_i = \frac{1}{1-\rho_i^2} \begin{bmatrix} 1 & \rho_i & \cdots & \rho_i^{T-1} \\ \rho_i & 1 & \cdots & \rho_i^{T-2} \\ \vdots & \vdots & \vdots & \vdots \\ \rho_i^{T-1} & & \cdots & 1 \end{bmatrix}$$

π_2 is an inverted gamma-2 p.d.f. with parameters η and v. π_3 is a uniform p.d.f. over the interval $(-1, 1)$. It is assumed that $k_1 = k_2$.

In obtaining $p(y\,|\,M_i)$, the $\boldsymbol{\beta}_i$ and σ_i integrals are done as in the preceding section. The integral over ρ_i is done numerically. When h is large and η small,

$$(11) \qquad p(\mathbf{y}\,|\,M_i) \doteq c \int [SSE(\rho_i)]^{-T/2}\,d\rho_i,$$

where

$$SSE(\rho_i) = (\mathbf{y} - X_i\hat{\boldsymbol{\beta}}_i)'\Sigma_i^{-1}(\mathbf{y} - X_i\hat{\boldsymbol{\beta}}_i),$$

with

$$\hat{\boldsymbol{\beta}}_i = (X_i'\Sigma_i^{-1}X_i)^{-1}X_i'\Sigma_i^{-1}\mathbf{y}.$$

Gaver and Geisel then compare the posterior probabilities of the models obtained in this fashion with those obtained under the assumption that $\rho_i = 0$, $i = 1, 2$. That is, they examine the error involved in ignoring the serial correlation. Let $P(M_1\,|\,\mathbf{y})$ be the posterior probability of M_1 computed on the basis of Equation (11), $P_0(M_1\,|\,\mathbf{y})$ the probability computed assuming $\rho_i = 0$ ($i = 1, 2$), and $\hat{\rho}_i$ the mode of the posterior density of ρ_i. Then, via sampling experiments and a Taylor series approximation to Equation (11), they find that

$$P_0(M_1\,|\,\mathbf{y}) \lesseqqgtr P(M_1\,|\,\mathbf{y}) \qquad \text{according as} \quad \hat{\rho}_1^2 \lesseqqgtr \hat{\rho}_2^2.$$

Further, for a fixed difference between $\hat{\rho}_1^2$ and $\hat{\rho}_2^2$, the difference between $P_0(M_1\,|\,\mathbf{y})$ and $P(M_1\,|\,\mathbf{y})$ increases as $\hat{\rho}_1^2$ increases.

Zellner and Geisel (1970) apply Bayesian model comparison methods to the problem of discriminating among alternative error structures in a distributed lag consumption function model. In their analysis, the regression coefficients are constrained *a priori* to a finite interval; thus, additional numerical integrations are required. Their results show very sharp discrimination between the assumption of independent errors and first order autoregressive errors and moderate discrimination between two second order autoregressive processes. They also examine the sensitivity of the posterior odds to different prior p.d.f.'s on the regression parameters. Courville and Geisel (1971) extend this analysis to consider alternative rational lag distributions as well as alternative error structures.

Finally, Gaver (1972) studies the comparison of multivariate regression models. When the two models have the same number of parameters and the prior p.d.f.'s are widely dispersed natural conjugate densities,

$$p(Y \mid M_i) \doteq c \mid S_i \mid^{-T/2}, \qquad i = 1, 2,$$

where

$$S_i = (Y - X_i \hat{\beta}_i)'(Y - X_i \hat{\beta}_i)$$

with

$$\hat{\beta}_i = (X_i' X_i)^{-1} X_i' Y.$$

Thus, [for $P(M_1) = P(M_2)$] the model with the higher posterior probability is the model with the smaller coefficient of vector alienation [see Dhrymes (1970, pp. 246–252) for discussion of the vector alienation measure].

In summary, the examples of this subsection indicate that it is feasible to use Bayesian model-comparison techniques for single-equation models in the presence of complicating factors such as serial correlation. The development of procedures for comparing multiple-equation models is just beginning.

III.   Concluding Remarks

The problem of choosing an appropriate model has long faced applied researchers. Historically, the selection process has been governed by informal procedures whose main virtue was intuitive appeal. Apart from certain restricted problems where conventional hypothesis testing procedures could be employed, the model-selection problem was regarded as being outside the domain of the methods of mathematical statistics.

This state of affairs has been substantially altered in the past decade. The properties of popular informal procedures have been systematically examined. These examinations, in addition to yielding information about the informal procedures, have suggested new comparison procedures. A method for comparing nonnested hypotheses has been developed and applied to a range of specific classes of models. Use of subjectivist Bayesian methodology has led to the development of alternative model-selection procedures that are also readily applicable to a considerable variety of problems.

Much remains to be done, however. The problem of comparing alternative multiple-equation models has barely been considered. The sensitivity of the procedures to various kinds of specification errors has been examined only in special cases. The finite-sample behavior of both the Bayesian and non-Bayesian procedures requires study. The mechanics of handling vague prior information in the Bayesian schemes need to be resolved.

The progress to date, though, warrants an optimistic forecast that the development and extension of useful model-selection methods will continue.

REFERENCES

Allen, D. M. (1971). "Mean Square Error of Prediction as a Criterion for Selecting Variables," *Technometrics* **13**, 469–475.

Anderson, T. W. (1962). "The Choice of the Degree of a Polynomial Regression as a Multiple Decision Problem," *Ann. Math. Statist.* **22**, 255–266.

Anderson, T. W. (1963). "Determination of the Order of Dependence in Normally Distributed Times Series," *Symp. Time Ser. Anal.* (M. Rosenblatt, ed.). Wiley, New York.

Anscombe, F. J. (1963). "Tests of Goodness of Fit," *J. Roy. Statist. Soc. Ser. B* **25**, 81–94.

Anscombe, F. J. and J. W. Tukey (1963). "The Examination and Analysis of Residuals," *Technometrics* **5**, 141–160.

Atkinson, A. C. (1970). "A Method for Discriminating between Models," *J. Roy. Statist. Soc. Ser. B* **32**, 323–353.

Barten, A. P. (1962). "Note on Unbiased Estimation of the Squared Multiple Correlation Coefficient," *Statist. Neerland.* **16**, 151–163.

Berk, R. H. (1966). "Limiting Behavior of Posterior Distributions When the Model is Incorrect," *Ann. Math. Statist.* **37**, 51–58.

Box, G. E. P. and W. J. Henson (1969). "Model Fitting and Discrimination," Tech. Rep., 211, Dept. of Statist., Univ. of Wisconsin, Madison, Wisconsin.

Box, G. E. P. and W. J. Hill (1967). "Discriminating among Mechanistic Models," *Technometrics* **9**, 57–71.

Box, G. E. P. and G. M. Jenkins (1970). *Time Series Analysis: Forecasting and Control.* Holden-Day, San Francisco, California.

Chow, G. C. (1960). "Tests of Equality between Subsets of Coefficients in Two Linear Regressions," *Econometrica* **28**, 591–605.

Christ, C. F. (1966). *Econometric Models and Methods.* Wiley, New York.

Cornfield, J. (1966). "A Bayesian Test of Some Classical Hypotheses—With Applications to Sequential Clinical Trials," *J. Amer. Statist. Ass.* **61**, 577–594.

Courville, L. and M. S. Geisel (1971). "Comparison of Alternative Lag Distribution and Error Structures," unpublished manuscript. Graduate School of Ind. Administration, Carnegie-Mellon Univ., Pittsburgh, Pennsylvania.

Cox, D. R. (1961). "Tests of Separate Families of Hypotheses," *Proc. Berkeley Symp. Math. Statist. Probability*, *4th* **1**, 105–123. Univ. of California Press, Berkeley, California.

Cox, D. R. (1962). "Further Results on Tests of Separate Hypotheses," *J. Roy. Statist. Soc. Ser. B* **24**, 406–424.

Dagenais, M. G. (1972a). "Choosing among Alternative Linear Regression Models: A General Bayesian Solution With Non-Informative Priors," unpublished manuscript. Ecole des Hautes Etudes Commerciales, Univ. de Montreal., Montreal, Quebec.

Dagenais, M. G. (1972b). "Comparing Linear Regression Models with Diffuse Prior Information," unpublished manuscript. Ecole des Hautes Etudes Commerciales, Univ. de Montreal, Montreal, Quebec.

De Groot, M. H. (1972). "Doing What Comes Naturally: Interpreting a Tail Area as a Posterior Probability or as a Likelihood Ratio," Tech. Rep. No. 64, Dept. of Statist., Carnegie-Mellon Univ., Pittsburgh, Pennsylvania.

Dhrymes, P. J. (1970). *Econometrics: Statistical Foundations and Applications.* Harper, New York.

Dhrymes, P. J., E. P. Howrey, S. H. Hymans, J. Kmenta, E. E. Leamer, R. E. Quandt, J. B. Ramsey, H. T. Shapiro and V. Zarnowitz (1972). "Criteria for Evaluation of Econometric Models," *Ann. Econ. Soc. Measurement* **1**, 291–324.

Dickey, J. M. (1971a). "The Weighted Likelihood Ratio, Linear Hypotheses on Normal Location Parameters," *Ann. Math. Statist.* **42**, 204–223.

Dickey, J. M. (1971b). "The Bayesian Alternatives to the F Test," Res. Rep. 50, Statistics Department, State Univ. of New York at Buffalo, Amherst, New York.

Draper, N. R. and H. Smith (1966). *Applied Regression Analysis.* Wiley, New York.

Edwards, J. B. (1969). "The Relationship between the F-Test and $\bar{R}^2$," *Amer. Statistician* **23**, No. 5, 28.

Edwards, W., H. Lindman and L. J. Savage (1963). "Bayesian Statistical Inference for Psychological Research," *Psycholog. Rev.* **70**, 193–242.

Ferguson, T. (1967). *Mathematical Statistics: A Decision Theoretic Approach.* Academic Press, New York.

Fisher, F. M. (1970). "Tests of Equality between Sets of Coefficients in Two Linear Regressions: An Expository Note," *Econometrica* **38**, 361–366.

Friedman, M. and D. Meiselman (1963). "The Relative Stability of Monetary Velocity and the Investment Multiplier in the United States 1897–1958," in the Commission on Money and Credit Research Study, *Stabilization Policies.* Prentice-Hall, Englewood Cliffs, New Jersey.

Gaver, K. M. (1972). "Choosing Among Alternative Multivariate Regression Models," unpublished manuscript, Univ. of Rochester (in progress), Rochester, New York.

Gaver, K. M. and M. S. Geisel (1971). "Comparing Linear Regression Models with Serially Correlated Errors," unpublished manuscript. Graduate School of Ind. Administration, Carnegie-Mellon Univ., Pittsburgh, Pennsylvania.

Geisel, M. S. (1970). "Comparing and Choosing among Parametric Statistical Models: A Bayesian Analysis with Macroeconomic Applications," unpublished doctoral dissertation, Univ. of Chicago, Chicago, Illinois.

Goldberger, A. S. (1968). *Topics in Regression Analysis.* Macmillan, New York.

Gorman, J. W. and R. J. Toman (1966). "Selection of Variables for Fitting Equations to Data," *Technometrics* **8**, 27–51.

Graybill, F. A. (1961). *An Introduction to Linear Statistical Models*, Vol. 1. McGraw-Hill, New York.

Healy, M. J. R. (1955). "A Significance Test for the Difference in Efficiency between Two Predictors," *J. Roy. Statist. Soc. Ser. B* **17**, 266–268.

Herzberg, P. A. (1969). "The Parameters of Cross Validation," *Psychometrika* **34**, No. 2, part 2.

Hotelling, H. (1940). "The Selection of Variates for Use in Prediction with Some Comments on the Problem of Nuisance Parameters," *Ann. Math. Statist.* **11**, 271–283.

Jeffreys, H. (1966). *Theory of Probability*, 3rd ed. Oxford Univ. Press (Clarendon), London and New York.

Jorgenson, D. W. and C. D. Siebert (1968). "A Comparison of Alternative Theories of Corporate Investment Behavior," *Amer. Econ. Rev.* **58**, 681–712.

Judge, G. G., M. E. Bock and T. A. Yancey (1972). "On Post Data Model Evaluation," unpublished manuscript, Univ. of Illinois, Urbana, Illinois.

Kennedy, W. J. and T. A. Bancroft (1971). "Model Building for Prediction in Regression Based upon Repeated Significance Tests," *Ann. Math. Statist.* **42**, 1273–1284.

Kiefer, J. and J. Wolfowitz (1956). "Consistency of the Maximum Likelihood Estimator in the Presence of Infinitely Many Incidental Parameters," *Ann. Math. Statist.* **27**, 887–906.

Kloek, T. (1970). "Note on Consistent Estimation of the Variance of the Disturbances in the Linear Model," Rep. 7003, Netherlands School of Econ., Econometrics Inst., Rotterdam.

Koerts, J. and A. P. J. Abrahamse (1969). *On the Theory and Application of the General Linear Model.* Rotterdam Univ. Press, Rotterdam.

LaMotte, L. R. and R. R. Hocking (1970). "Computational Efficiency in the Selection of Regression Variables," *Technometrics* **12**, 83–93.

Leamer, E. E. (1970). "Bayesian Model Selection with Applications," unpublished manuscript, Harvard Univ., Cambridge, Massachusetts.

Leamer, E. E. (1972). "Probabilities of Linear Hypotheses," unpublished manuscript, Harvard Univ., Cambridge, Massachusetts.

Lempers, F. B. (1971). *Posterior Probabilities of Alternative Linear Models.* Rotterdam Univ. Press, Rotterdam.

Lindley, D. V. (1965), *Introduction to Probability and Statistics from a Bayesian Viewpoint, Part 2, Inference.* Cambridge Univ. Press, London and New York.

Lindley, D. V. (1968). "The Choice of Variables in Multiple Regression," *J. Roy. Statist. Soc. Ser. B* **30**, 31–66.

Malinvaud, E. (1970). *Statistical Methods of Econometrics,* 2nd ed. North-Holland Publ., Amsterdam.

Mallows, C. (1972). "Some Comments on Cp," Bell Lab. manuscript, Murray Hill, New Jersey.

Pesaran, M. H. (1972). "On the General Problem of Model Selection," unpublished manuscript, Trinity College, Cambridge.

Quandt, R. E. (1972). "Testing Nonnested Hypotheses," Econometric Res. Program, Memorandum No. 140, Princeton Univ., Princeton, New Jersey.

Raiffa, H. and R. Schlaifer (1961). *Applied Statistical Decision Theory,* Div. of Res. Graduate School of Business Administration, Harvard Univ., Boston, Massachusetts.

Rao, P. (1971). "Some Notes on Misspecification in Multiple Regression," *Amer. Statistician* **25**, No. 5, 37–39.

Roberts, H. V. (1964). *Statistical Inference and Decision.* Univ. of Chicago manuscript, Chicago, Illinois.

Roberts, H. V. (1965). "Probabilistic Prediction," *J. Amer. Statist. Ass.* **60**, 50–62.

Schatzoff, M., R. Tsao and S. Fienberg (1968). "Efficient Calculation of All Possible Regressions," *Technometrics* **10**, 769–779.

Schmidt, P. (1973). "Calculating the Power of the Minimum Standard Error Choice Criterion," *Inter. Econ. Rev.* **14**, 253–255.

Sclove, S. L., C. Morris and R. Radhakrishnan (1972). "Non Optimality of Preliminary Test Estimators," *Ann. Math. Statist.* (to appear).

Theil, H. (1957). "Specification Errors and the Estimation of Economic Relationships," *Rev. Int. Statist. Inst.* **25**, 41–51.

Thornber, E. H. (1966). Applications of Decision Theory to Econometrics, unpublished doctoral dissertation, Univ. of Chicago, Chicago, Illinois.

Wallace, T. D. and V. G. Ashar (1972). "Sequential Methods in Model Construction," *Rev. Econ. Statist.* **LIV**, 172–179.

Williams, E. J. (1959). *Regression Analysis.* Wiley, New York.

Zellner, A. (1971). *An Introduction to Bayesian Inference in Econometrics.* Wiley, New York.

Zellner, A. and M. S. Geisel (1970). "Analysis of Distributed Lag Models with Applications to Consumption Function Estimation," *Econometrica* **38**, 865–888.

Part II

LINEAR MODELS

Chapter Three

Transformation of
variables in econometrics

PAUL ZAREMBKA[1]

STATE UNIVERSITY OF NEW YORK AT BUFFALO
BUFFALO, NEW YORK

Although natural considerations of convenience or technique may dictate that the observations be made on a variable y, it still has to be decided which function of y is to be used for the purpose of the analysis. There is no reason why the quantity measured, rather than some function of it, should be best suited to the assumptions of the model (Kendall and Stuart, 1968, p. 85).

[1] A first draft of this paper was completed while the author was on sabbatical leave from the University of California, Berkeley, Spring 1972, at the Ibero–American Institute, Göttingen University. Research support from the National Science Foundation (GS-2822) is gratefully acknowledged.

Part of the beauty of the Arrow *et al.* (1961) and Brown and de Cani (1963) CES production function is that the functional form for the production function is generalized with a parameter (ρ) directly related to the elasticity of factor substitution. Furthermore, the authors argue that the generalizing parameter should be estimated and not assumed (e.g., as in the Cobb–Douglas assumption of an elasticity of substitution equal to unity).

For statisticians, the CES production function is simply a problem in transformation of variables in which the same transformation is applied to all variables. Thus, suppose that the CES production function is first written

$$Y = (a_1 K^\rho + a_2 L^\rho)^{1/\rho}, \qquad \rho < 1$$

where Y is output, K is capital, and L is labor, and where a_1, a_2, and ρ are parameters in which the elasticity of substitution is given by $1/(1-\rho)$, $\rho < 1$. Then the function may be rewritten

$$(1) \qquad\qquad Y^\rho = a_1 K^\rho + a_2 L^\rho.$$

Thus, each variable is transformed by the power ρ. [For the nonconstant returns-to-scale case with v the returns-to-scale parameter,

$$Y = (a_1 K^\rho + a_2 L^\rho)^{v/\rho},$$

we have

$$(2) \qquad\qquad Y^{\rho/v} = a_1 K^\rho + a_2 L^\rho.$$

Equation (2) merely applies a different transformation to the dependent variable than to the independent variables.]

In other areas of economic research we are less fortunate than to have a direct link between economic theory and choice of functional form, yet we may have some beliefs about the functional relationship. For example, utility theory is insufficiently developed to provide a functional form for estimating the food consumption function, but we do have the belief, based on previous empirical work, that the income elasticity for food does not rise as income rises. Since the linear form exhibits a rising elasticity when the elasticity is below one, three common forms for estimating the food consumption function are the logarithmic

$$\ln c = a_0 + a_1 \ln y,$$

the semi-log

$$c = a_0 + a_1 \ln y,$$

and the log-inverse

$$\ln c = a_0 - a_1/y,$$

where c is food consumption, y is income, and a_0 and a_1 are parameters. The income elasticity in the logarithmic case is a_1; in the semi-log case, a_1/c; and in the log-inverse case, a_1/y. In any case, these three functional forms are actually special cases of the general transformation-of-variables form in which

$$(3) \qquad c^{\lambda_0} = a_0 + a_1 y^{\lambda_1},$$

with x^λ at $\lambda = 0$ defined as the logarithm of a variable x $[\lim_{\lambda \to 0}(x^\lambda - 1)/\lambda = \ln x$, using L'Hospital's rule]. For the logarithmic case, $\lambda_0 = \lambda_1 = 0$; for the semi-log case, $\lambda_0 = 1$ and $\lambda_1 = 0$; and for the log-inverse case, $\lambda_0 = 0$ and $\lambda_1 = -1.$[2]

Finally, economic theory often fails almost completely to suggest a functional form. As Dhrymes *et al.* (1972, p. 294) assert, "Economic theory gives preciously few clues as to the functional forms appropriate to the specification of economic relationships, and the presence of random error terms in stochastically specified equations adds an additional element of functional ambiguity." A common practice in econometrics then is to choose between a linear functional form

$$y = a_0 + a_1 x_1 + \cdots + a_K x_K$$

and linear-in-logarithms functional form

$$\ln y = a_0 + a_1 \ln x_1 + \cdots + a_K \ln x_K.$$

Again, however, both are special cases of the general transformation-of-variables problem

$$(4) \qquad y^{\lambda_0} = a_0 + a_1 x_1^{\lambda_1} + \cdots + a_K x_K^{\lambda_K}$$

in which $\lambda_0 = \lambda_1 = \cdots = \lambda_K = 1$ in the linear case and $\lambda_0 = \lambda_1 = \cdots = \lambda_K = 0$ in the logarithmic case.

In this paper it is suggested that transformation of variables is a powerful procedure in econometrics to handle the general problem of choice of functional form, particularly when functional form is not suggested by theory. The first section discusses the relevant statistical literature concerning transformation of variables. In particular, it is shown that transformations can be estimated simply with least squares regression programs. Section II extends the statistical theory of the analysis of transformations to include heteroskedasticity of the error term. Two subsequent sections discuss previous econometric

---

[2] Even the log-log-inverse functional form for food consumption

$$\ln c = a_0 - \frac{a_1}{y} - a_2 \ln y$$

is a special case of transformation of variables in which $\lambda_0 = \lambda_2 = 0$ and $\lambda_1 = -1$ in

$$c^{\lambda_0} = a_0 - a_1 y^{\lambda_1} - a_2 y^{\lambda_2}.$$

applications of transformation of variables, while the last section suggests extensions and new directions in the use of transformation of variables in econometrics.

I. Transformation of Variables in Statistics

Tukey (1957) is perhaps the first to undertake a general analysis of transformations of variables. He argues that the purpose of a transformation is to increase the degree of approximation to which three desirable properties for statistical analysis hold. These properties are that (p. 609)

(1) effects are additive;
(2) the error variability is constant;
(3) the error distribution is symmetrical and possibly nearly normal.

In other words, he argues that transformation of variables may lead to a more nearly linear model, may stabilize the error variance, and/or may lead to a model for which a symmetrically, perhaps normally, distributed error term is acceptable. Of course, a transformation may increase the degree of approximation to two or three of these properties simultaneously.

Tukey then considers the rather wide family of transformations $(x+d)^\lambda$. For $\lambda = 0$, this transformation is defined as $\ln(x+d)$. For $d = 0$, we have the simple power transformation x^λ, defined as $\ln x$ when $\lambda = 0$. Also, Tukey shows (pp. 622–623) that if $\lambda = md$ ($m < 0$), then the transformation approaches e^{my} as $d \to \infty$.

While the Tukey article does discuss the properties of the transformation, the transforming parameter is assumed to be known or else subject to relatively easy choice. Thus, it need not be estimated. In econometrics, we often act as if this were the case by assuming $\lambda = 1$ (the linear case) or $\lambda = 0$ (the logarithmic case). Turner *et al.* (1961) and Box and Tidwell (1962, particularly pp. 535–536), however, do discuss estimation, but on *independent* variables only. Thus, they suggest an iterative least squares procedure for estimation of the $(x_i+d_i)^{\lambda_i}$ transformations, based on a Taylor series. For the $d_i = 0$ ($i = 1, ..., K$) case, this procedure can be interpreted as follows: After choosing initial guesses λ_i^0 ($i = 1, ..., K$), regress the dependent variable on the initial guesses for each of the $x_i^{\lambda_i^0}$ and $x_i^{\lambda_i^0} \ln x_i$ ($i = 1, ..., K$). If a_i^1 is the regression coefficient for $x_i^{\lambda_i^0}$ and b_i^1 is that for $x_i^{\lambda_i^0} \ln x$, then the new estimate of each λ_i is $\lambda_i^1 = \lambda_i^0 + b_i^1/a_i^1$. The process is then repeated with the new estimates of λ_i; Box and Tidwell (1962, pp. 536 ff.) provide some examples indicating that convergence is rapid.

Confidence intervals for the λ's can also be obtained. Consider the single independent variable case discussed extensively by Turner *et al.* (1961)

$$(5) \qquad y = a_0 + a_1(x+d)^\lambda + \varepsilon, \qquad x + d > 0$$

where ε is normally and independently distributed with zero mean and variance σ^2. Then, asymptotic confidence limits for the parameters can be based directly upon the likelihood approach [see Turner *et al.* (1961, pp. 132–133)]. For example, if d is taken as zero, the asymptotic standard errors of the $\hat{a}_0$ and $\hat{a}_1$ are the same as reported in the final iteration

$$(6) \qquad \hat{y} = \hat{a}_0 + \hat{a}_1 x^{\lambda} + \hat{b}_1 x^{\lambda} \ln x,$$

while the asymptotic standard error for $\hat{\lambda}$ is $\hat{a}_1$ divided into the standard error for $\hat{b}_1$. (Note that $\hat{b}_1$ itself is very close to zero in the final iteration; see the previous paragraph.) For small samples, Box and Tidwell (1962, pp. 547–548) discuss an improved procedure based upon a theorem of Fieller.

Box and Cox (1964) apparently are the first to systematically consider transformation of the dependent variable in the context of the power family. While they consider transformations of the form y^{λ} as well as $(y+d)^{\lambda}$, we focus attention on the former. The latter can be handled similarly to the discussion here. First, Box and Cox define their transformation as

$$(7) \qquad y^{(\lambda)} = \begin{cases} (y^{\lambda}-1)/\lambda, & \lambda \neq 0 \\ \ln y, & \lambda = 0. \end{cases}$$

The virtue of this definition is that the limit for the $\lambda \neq 0$ case as $\lambda \to 0$ is $\ln y$ so that the transformation is continuous around $\lambda = 0$. (Also, the division by λ implies a somewhat simpler Jacobian in the likelihood transformation discussed below.) Unfortunately, however, Schlesselman (1971) has pointed out that the estimation of this transformation is not invariant to units for measuring y *unless* a constant term is included in the regression model.[3] Thus, the CES production function given by Equation (1) or Equation (2) must utilize either the transformation y^{λ} or y^{λ}/λ, not $(y^{\lambda}-1)/\lambda$; similarly, for capital and labor. Nevertheless, when a constant term is included, continuity is probably a worthwhile property so that the $y^{(\lambda)}$ definition is discussed below.

Box and Cox then consider the model

$$(8) \qquad \mathbf{y}^{(\lambda)} = \mathbf{X}\boldsymbol{\beta} + \boldsymbol{\varepsilon},$$

where $\mathbf{y}^{(\lambda)}$ is the vector of dependent variables transformed according to Equation (7), $\mathbf{X}$ is the matrix of untransformed independent variables including a constant term, $\boldsymbol{\beta}$ is a coefficient vector, and $\boldsymbol{\varepsilon}$ is a vector of normally and independently distributed random variables, each with zero mean and variance σ^2. They then formulate the likelihood for the original observations $\mathbf{y}$:

$$(9) \qquad (2\pi\sigma^2)^{-N/2} \exp\left(-\frac{(\mathbf{y}^{(\lambda)}-\mathbf{X}\boldsymbol{\beta})'(\mathbf{y}^{(\lambda)}-\mathbf{X}\boldsymbol{\beta})}{2\sigma^2}\right) J,$$

---

[3] Incidentally, it can be shown that the Schlesselman result also obtains in the more general case in which the covariance matrix for ε in Equation (8) is $\sigma^2\boldsymbol{\Omega}$, not merely $\sigma^2\mathbf{I}$.

where N is the number of observations and J is the Jacobian of the inverse transformation from the dependent variable $y_i^{(\lambda)}$ to the actually observed y_i,

$$(10) \qquad J = \prod_{i=1}^{N} \left| \frac{dy_i^{(\lambda)}}{dy_i} \right| = \prod_{i=1}^{N} y_i^{\lambda-1}.$$

Estimates of λ, $\boldsymbol{\beta}$, and σ^2 can be obtained by maximizing the likelihood (9). This is most easily done by noting that for a given λ (9) is the standard least squares problem of regressing $\mathbf{y}^{(\lambda)}$ on $\mathbf{X}$. The maximized log-likelihood, for fixed λ, is then, except for a constant,

$$(11) \qquad L_{\max}(\lambda) = -\tfrac{1}{2}N \ln \hat{\sigma}^2(\lambda) + (\lambda-1) \sum_{i=1}^{N} \ln y_i,$$

where the second term is obtained from the Jacobian. Zarembka (1968, p. 505, fn. 8) notes that by appropriate units of measurement for y, $\sum \ln y_i$ is zero and the maximized log-likelihood, for fixed λ, is therefore

$$(12) \qquad L_{\max}(\lambda) = -\tfrac{1}{2}N \ln \hat{\sigma}^2(\lambda).$$

To maximize over the entire parameter space, we only need to choose alternative values of λ over a reasonable range and regress $\mathbf{y}^{(\lambda)}$ on $\mathbf{X}$, then find that transformation which maximizes Equation (11) or, in the case of Equation (12), minimizes the calculated error variance after obtaining appropriate units of measurement for y. The estimates of $\boldsymbol{\beta}$ and σ^2 can be obtained from the regression results at $\hat{\lambda}$. Conditional upon $\lambda = \hat{\lambda}$, the estimate of $\boldsymbol{\beta}$ is unbiased and standard errors for each β_i can be obtained from the output of the regression program.

Box and Cox (1964, p. 216) indicate that an approximate $100(1-\alpha)\%$ confidence region for λ can be obtained from

$$(13)' \qquad L_{\max}(\hat{\lambda}) - L_{\max}(\lambda) < \tfrac{1}{2}\chi_1^2(\alpha).$$

This result can be explained as follows: A null hypothesis on λ (i.e., $H_0: \lambda = \lambda_0$) can be tested by forming the logarithm of the ratio of the likelihood valuated at the maximum likelihood estimate of $\boldsymbol{\beta}$ and σ^2, conditional upon $\lambda = \lambda_0$, to the likelihood valuated at $\hat{\boldsymbol{\beta}}$, $\hat{\sigma}^2$, $\hat{\lambda}$. On the null hypothesis, this logarithm is asymptotically distributed as $\tfrac{1}{2}\chi^2$ with one degree of freedom (for λ). Thus, the $100(1-\alpha)\%$ confidence region for λ is obtained by finding that value of λ on either side of $\hat{\lambda}$ such that (13) is an equality for the given confidence level α. For $\alpha = 0.05$, $\tfrac{1}{2}\chi_1^2(0.05) = 1.92$.[4]

----

[4] For a general discussion of likelihood ratio tests, the reader can consult Kendall and Stuart (1967, Chap. 24). Incidentally, this author tried to obtain the information matrix for the Box and Cox model as an alternative procedure to obtaining an asymptotic confidence interval for λ. However, it was found to be too complicated to be interesting (expectations of nonlinear functions are required).

Box and Cox were thus able to provide a procedure for estimating a transformation of the dependent variable. Their procedure is particularly convenient because it requires a search over alternative λ's—a procedure which is applicable to any computer regression package. However, three difficulties remained. First, as pointed out by J. B. Ramsey, the error term ε cannot be strictly normal since a power transformation does not in general permit negative real values. In other words, large negative real values for the error term are prohibited. However, if the probability of such large negative values is quite low, the error term may still be approximately normal; and Draper and Cox (1969) show that the above method of estimating the power transformation can be quite useful, even when normality does not obtain precisely. (Further discussion of the Draper–Cox paper appears in Section II.)

Second, the Box and Cox procedure is only applied to the dependent variable. Of course, if there are only one, or perhaps two, transforming parameters for the independent variables, then a grid of transforming parameters can be searched to maximize the log-likelihood. Thus, Zarembka (1968) applies the same λ transformation to the dependent variable and each of the independent variables; special cases are therefore the standard linear and linear-in-logarithms models. The maximum likelihood technique can then be used in an identical way to the Box and Cox transformation on the dependent variable only. The CES production function falls into this category. If nonconstant returns to scale are permitted, a different transformation is applied to the dependent as to the two independent variables [see Equation (2)] and a grid is searched (see Section IV).

For more complicated problems, Box and Cox (p. 242) suggest that their procedure be extended by searching for the transformation on the dependent variable while applying for each choice of λ the Turner *et al.* and Box and Tidwell technique on the transformations on the independent variables. This extension, of course, can involve rather large amounts of computational time.

A third difficulty with the Box and Cox formulation is that the error term is assumed to have constant variance σ^2 across observations; but the transformation on the dependent variable may not lead simultaneously both to additivity of effect and to homoskedasticity. This important issue is discussed in the next section.

II. Estimation of λ under Heteroskedasticity in ε

In the statistical literature transformations of variables are considered useful so that effects are additive, so that error variability is constant, and/or so that the error distribution is approximately normal. On the one hand, transformations of *independent* variables are only focusing on additivity of effect since these variables are conditioning the value of the dependent variable.

On the other hand, the dependent variable is random and assumptions on the error term focus on this variable.

In econometrics, the transforming parameter or parameters are often of inherent interest (as in the CES production function), and thus the inclusion of transformations focuses only on additivity of effect. In this case, we do not wish estimation of transforming parameters to integrate the search for additivity of effect with the search for transformations that lead to a more closely normal error term or to a constant error variance. In other words, if Equation (8) is the correct model (ignoring, for the time being, transformations on the independent variables since we shall see that they do not affect our results), to what extent is the estimate of the transformation of dependent variable influenced by nonnormality or heteroskedasticity of the error term ε? If it should turn out that estimates of λ are robust to nonnormality and heteroskedasticity, then the Box and Cox procedure is fundamentally focusing on additivity of effect (i.e., nonlinearities).

In this section it is shown that the Box and Cox procedure is robust to nonnormality as long as the error term is reasonably symmetric [a result first obtained by Draper and Cox (1969)], but it does not seem to be robust to heteroskedasticity in the error term. In the latter case, it is shown that there is a bias in estimating λ toward that transformation of the dependent variable which leads a more nearly homoskedasticity error variance for ε. A procedure is then discussed to obtain consistent estimates of λ under assumptions with respect to the level of heteroskedasticity. (Thus, information on the magnitude of the bias is available.)

The model, as postulated by Box and Cox, assumes that for some λ

$$(14) \qquad\qquad y_i^{(\lambda)} = \mathbf{X}_i \boldsymbol{\beta} + \varepsilon_i,$$

where $y_i^{(\lambda)}$ is the transformed dependent variable defined by Equation (7) for the ith observation, $\mathbf{X}_i$ is a vector of independent nonrandom variables for the ith observation, $\boldsymbol{\beta}$ is a vector of unknown coefficients, and the error term ε_i is assumed independently and similarly distributed as normal with zero mean and variance σ^2 constant across observations. In the following it is convenient to write $y_i^{(\lambda)}$ as z_i and $\mathbf{X}_i \boldsymbol{\beta}$ as μ_i so that

$$(15) \qquad\qquad z_i = \mu_i + \varepsilon_i.$$

It is also convenient to assume $\lambda \neq 0$.

Under this model the log-likelihood L for N observations is, except for a constant,

$$(16) \qquad L = -\tfrac{1}{2}N \ln \sigma^2 - \frac{1}{2\sigma^2} \sum_i (z_i - \mu_i)^2 + (\lambda - 1) \sum_i \ln y_i.$$

The condition for consistent estimation of λ by the maximum likelihood method when ε_i in Equation (15) follows some other law than the assumed normality with constant variance is that, at least asymptotically,

$$(17) \qquad E\left(\frac{\partial L}{\partial \lambda_0}\right)_{\lambda_0 = \lambda} = 0,$$

where λ_0 refers to some arbitrary choice of the transforming parameter. To examine whether λ, and thus other parameters, is consistently estimated when ε_i obeys some other law than normality with constant variance, we need to ascertain the conditions under which Equation (17) is or is not equal to zero. If the equation still approximately obtains, then the model assuming normality and constant variance would lead to approximately consistent (even if not asymptotically efficient) estimates of λ and thus $\boldsymbol{\beta}$.

First,

$$\frac{\partial L}{\partial \lambda_0} = -\frac{1}{\sigma^2} \sum_{i=1}^{N} (z_i - \mu_i)\frac{\partial z_i}{\partial \lambda_0} + \sum_{i=1}^{N} \ln y_i,$$

where

$$\frac{\partial z_i}{\partial \lambda_0} = \frac{1}{\lambda_0^{\,2}}[(1 + \lambda_0 z_i)\ln(1 + \lambda_0 z_i) - \lambda_0 z_i].$$

Therefore, Equation (17) becomes

$$(18) \quad E\left(\frac{\partial L}{\partial \lambda_0}\right)_{\lambda_0 = \lambda} = E\left(-\frac{1}{\lambda^2 \sigma^2}\sum_i (z_i - \mu_i)[(1 + \lambda z_i)\ln(1 + \lambda z_i) - \lambda z_i]\right.$$
$$\left. + \frac{1}{\lambda}\sum_i \ln(1 + \lambda z_i)\right).$$

Without loss of generality, the units of measurement for y_i can be supposed to be such that $E \sum_i \ln(1 + \lambda z_i) = 0$. Letting $Z_i = \lambda \varepsilon_i$, we have, therefore,

$$E\left(\frac{\partial L}{\partial \lambda_0}\right)_{\lambda_0 = \lambda} = -\frac{1}{\lambda^3 \sigma^2}E\left(\sum_i Z_i[(1 + \lambda \mu_i + Z_i)\ln(1 + \lambda \mu_i + Z_i) - \lambda \mu_i - Z_i]\right).$$

Note that $E(Z_i) = 0$, $\operatorname{var}(Z_i) = \lambda^2 \sigma^2 = \lambda^2 m_i^{(2)}$, and $E(Z_i^r) = \lambda^r m_i^{(r)}$, where $m_i^{(r)}$ is the rth moment of ε_i and may vary across observations.

Letting $v_i = Z_i/(1 + \lambda \mu_i)$, we can now write

$$E\left(\frac{\partial L}{\partial \lambda_0}\right)_{\lambda_0 = \lambda} = -\frac{1}{\lambda^3 \sigma^2}E\left(\sum_i Z_i(1 + v_i)\frac{Z_i}{v_i}[\ln(1 + v_i) + \ln(1 + \lambda \mu_i)]\right)$$
$$+ \frac{\lambda^2}{\lambda^3 \sigma^2}\sum_i \sigma_i^{\,2}.$$

Furthermore, v_i can be treated as small since, for $y_i > 0$ (as required if y_i is to be subjected to a power transformation), $z_i + 1/\lambda > 0$ or $(\mu_i + 1/\lambda)/\sigma_i =$

$(1+\lambda\mu_i)/(\lambda\sigma_i) \gg 1$. Therefore, we can expand $\ln(1+v_i)$ as a power series to obtain

$$E\left(\frac{\partial L}{\partial \lambda_0}\right)_{\lambda_0 = \lambda} = -\frac{1}{\lambda^3\sigma^2} E\left[\sum_i Z_i^2\left(1+\frac{1}{v_i}\right)\left(\sum_{r=1}^{\infty}(-1)^{r+1}\frac{v_i^r}{r} + \ln(1+\lambda\mu_i)\right)\right]$$

$$+ \frac{\lambda^2}{\lambda^3\sigma^2}\sum_i \sigma_i^2$$

$$= -\frac{1}{\lambda^3\sigma^2} E\left\{\sum_i Z_i^2\left[1 + \sum_{r=3}^{\infty}(-1)^{r+1}\frac{v_i^{r-2}}{(r-1)(r-2)}\right.\right.$$

$$\left.\left. + \left(1+\frac{1}{v_i}\right)\ln(1+\lambda\mu_i)\right]\right\} + \frac{\lambda^2}{\lambda^3\sigma^2}\sum_i \sigma_i^2$$

$$= -\frac{1}{\lambda^3\sigma^2}\sum_i\left(\sum_{r=3}^{\infty}(-1)^{r+1}\frac{\lambda^r m_i^{(r)}}{(r-1)(r-2)(1+\lambda\mu_i)^{r-2}}\right.$$

$$\left. + \lambda^2\sigma_i^2\ln(1+\lambda\mu_i)\right)$$

after substituting for v_i and then taking expectations.

Now let $\alpha_i \equiv 1+\lambda\mu_i$, $\theta_i \equiv \lambda\sigma_i/\alpha_i$, $\gamma_i \equiv m_i^{(3)}/\sigma_i^3$, and $\kappa_i \equiv m_i^{(4)}/\sigma_i^4 - 3$. Thus α_i is the mean of y_i^{λ}, θ_i is the coefficient of variation[5] of y_i^{λ}, γ_i is the skewness of z_i, and κ_i is the kurtosis of z_i. Then, taking the first two terms of the power series, we have

$$E\left(\frac{\partial L}{\partial \lambda_0}\right)_{\lambda_0 = \lambda} = -\frac{1}{\lambda^3\sigma^2}\sum_i\left(\frac{\lambda^3 m_i^{(3)}}{2\alpha_i} - \frac{\lambda^4 m_i^{(4)}}{6\alpha_i^2} + \lambda^2\sigma_i^2\ln(1+\lambda\mu_i)\right)$$

$$= -\frac{1}{\lambda\sigma^2}\sum_i \sigma_i^2\left[\tfrac{1}{2}\theta_i\gamma_i - \tfrac{1}{6}\theta_i^2\kappa_i - \tfrac{1}{2}\theta_i^2 + \ln(1+\lambda\mu_i)\right].$$

Finally, note that

$$\lambda E(\ln y_i) = E[\ln(1+\lambda z_i)]$$

$$= E\left[\ln\left(1 + \frac{Z_i}{1+\lambda\mu_i}\right)\right] + \ln(1+\lambda\mu_i)$$

$$\approx E\left(\frac{Z_i}{1+\lambda\mu_i} - \frac{Z_i^2}{2(1+\lambda\mu_i)^2}\right) + \ln(1+\lambda\mu_i)$$

$$= -\frac{\theta_i^2}{2} + \ln(1+\lambda\mu_i).$$

[5] Draper and Cox (1969, p. 473) incorrectly label θ_i as the coefficient of variation of z_i.

Thus, we have

(19) $$E\left(\frac{\partial L}{\partial \lambda_0}\right)_{\lambda_0 = \lambda} = -\frac{1}{\lambda \sigma^2} \sum_i \sigma_i^2 [\theta_i(\tfrac{1}{2}\gamma_i - \tfrac{1}{6}\theta_i \kappa_i) + \lambda E(\ln y_i)].$$

Equation (19) is the basic equation to be used to address the question of the consistency of estimates of λ under nonnormality or heteroskedasticity of the error term ε_i.

In the first case, suppose that the error terms are nonnormal but identically distributed with constant variance (the question asked by Draper and Cox). Then, $\sigma_i = \sigma^2$, $\gamma_i = \gamma$, and $\kappa_i = \kappa$ for all i and, since units of measurement have been chosen so that $E\sum_i \ln(1 + \lambda z_i) = 0$, we have

(20) $$E\left(\frac{\partial L}{\partial \lambda_0}\right)_{\lambda_0 = \lambda} = -\frac{1}{\lambda} \sum_i \theta_i(\tfrac{1}{2}\gamma - \tfrac{1}{6}\theta_i \kappa).$$

To the first order in θ_i, this equation is zero when $\gamma = 0$, i.e., to the first order in the coefficient of variation in y_i^λ, θ_i, the transforming parameter λ is consistently estimated as long as the distribution of the error term is symmetric. To the second order in θ_i, the condition is $3\gamma \sum_i \theta_i = \kappa \sum_i \theta_i^2$. However, if the θ_i's are reasonably stable across observations, say, due to only moderate variation in $E(y_i^\lambda) = 1 + \lambda \mu_i$, then the second-order condition is approximately $\gamma = \tfrac{1}{3}\kappa\theta$. Thus, since $(\lambda \mu_i + 1)/(\lambda \sigma) = 1/\theta_i \gg 1$ (see p. 90) so that θ_i is small, the second-order expansion also corresponds to a low level of skewness (presuming that the kurtosis coefficient κ is not large). In sum, as long as the distribution of ε_i is reasonably symmetric, the Box–Cox procedure leads to approximately consistent estimates of λ. This result, combined with a study of the precision of estimating λ (which indicates that additivity and constancy of variance contribute to estimating λ), leads Draper and Cox (1969, p. 475) to conclude that "the effect of distributional form is likely to be secondary when complex models are fitted."

Second, suppose that normality does obtain but that the error variance is not constant across observations. Then, γ_i and κ_i are both equal to zero and Equation (19) reduces to

(21) $$E\left(\frac{\partial L}{\partial \lambda_0}\right)_{\lambda_0 = \lambda} = -\frac{1}{\sigma^2} \sum_i \sigma_i^2 E(\ln y_i).$$

Since σ_i^2 refers to the variance of the transformed y_i, it should help to relate σ_i^2 to the variance of the observed variable y_i. Thus, recall that for a function $g(y_i)$,

$$\text{var}[g(y_i)] \approx \left(\frac{\partial g(y_i)}{\partial y_i}\right)^2_{y_i = Ey_i} \text{var}(y_i)$$

so that

$$\sigma_i^2 = \text{var}[y_i^{(\lambda)}] \approx [E(y_i)]^{2\lambda - 2} \text{var}(y_i).$$

Therefore, Equation (21) becomes

$$(22) \qquad E\left(\frac{\partial L}{\partial \lambda_0}\right)_{\lambda_0 = \lambda} = -\frac{1}{\sigma^2} \sum_i \frac{\text{var}(y_i)}{[E(y_i)]^{2(1-\lambda)}} E(\ln y_i).$$

The condition for consistency of estimating λ is, therefore, that $\text{var}(y_i)/[E(y_i)]^{2(1-\lambda)}$, or $[\text{var}(y_i)]^{1/2}/[E(y_i)]^{1-\lambda}$, is constant across observations, remembering that $\sum_i E(\ln y_i) = 0$ by our units of measurement for y_i. For example, if the true model is linear so that $\lambda = 1$, then the variance of y_i must be constant. If the true model is approximately logarithmic in y_i so that $\lambda \approx 0$ (we have, in fact, excluded the $\lambda = 0$ case for convenience), then the variance of y_i must grow with y_i^2—i.e., the coefficient of variation of y_i must be constant. And so on. Thus, if the same transformation that leads to $Ey_i^{(\lambda)} = \mathbf{X}_i\boldsymbol{\beta}$ also leads to homoskedasticity of the error ε_i, then λ and other parameters are consistently estimated.

However, suppose that the transformation which leads to $Ey_i^{(\lambda)} = \mathbf{X}_i\boldsymbol{\beta}$ does not lead to a homoskedastic error variance. Then λ, and other parameters, are not consistently estimated. In particular, if $\text{var}(y_i)/[E(y_i)]^{2(1-\lambda)}$ rises with y_i [for example, if $\lambda = 1$ and $\text{var}(y_i)$ rises with $E(y_i)$], then $\hat{\lambda}$ is asymptotically negatively biased since Equation (22) is negative [and positively biased if $\text{var}(y_i)/[E(y_i)]^{2(1-\lambda)}$ falls with $E(y_i)$]. In other words, $\hat{\lambda}$ is biased in the the direction toward stabilizing the error variance. One particularly interesting example is the case in which the variance of y_i is constant. Then, Equation (22) is proportional to $-\sum_i [E(y_i)]^{2(\lambda - 1)} E(\ln y_i)$ and, in general, the bias is toward $\lambda = 1$. Another interesting example is the case in which the coefficient of variation of y_i is constant. Then the bias is toward $\lambda = 0$.

A couple of extensions of this analysis might be noted before turning to the question of consistent estimation under heteroskedasticity in ε. First, we have already noted in Section I that estimates of λ in the transformation $(y^\lambda - 1)/\lambda$ are not invariant to units for measuring y if a constant term is not included in the model. When a constant term is not included, estimation of the transformation y^λ or y^λ/λ is nevertheless invariant to units, with the latter having the same Jacobian of transformation as the Box and Cox transformation. Then, although it is unnecessary to formally derive the results here, the analysis for nonnormality and heteroskedasticity obtains exactly as derived in this section.

Second, suppose that transformations on independent variables are included. If the relevant transforming parameters are different from that for the dependent variable, then Equation (18) and the subsequent analysis still obtain, as long as a consistent estimating procedure is used to estimate μ_i conditional on $\lambda_0 = \lambda$. (Of course, if under heteroskedasticity λ is not consistently estimated, then neither are the other parameters.) If the same transforming parameter is used on independent variables as for the dependent variable, then $\partial L/\partial \lambda_0$, leading to Equation (18), requires a term in $\partial \mu_i/\partial \lambda_0$ along with $\partial z_i/\partial \lambda_0$: $\partial z_i/\partial \lambda_0 - \partial \mu_i/\partial \lambda_0$. However, again results are unaffected since in $\partial L/\partial \lambda_0$ the nonrandom term $\partial \mu_i/\partial \lambda_0$ is multiplied by $\varepsilon_i = z_i - \mu_i$, which upon taking expectations is zero.

We have shown, above, that estimation of transformation of variables by maximum likelihood methods are robust to nonnormality, but not heteroskedasticity, of the error term ε. In the latter case, the estimate of a λ transformation on the dependent variable is biased in the direction of stabilizing the error variation. This potential bias would be particularly troublesome if its magnitude were unknown. Equation (22), however, provides enough information to assess the magnitude of the bias for any given empirical problem; in particular, given an assumption (or alternative assumptions) concerning the relationship of the variance of y_i (the observed variable) to its expectation, Equation (22) can be valuated with respect to alternative λ's. Thus, Equation (22) provides an implicit equation with which an approximately consistent estimate of λ can be obtained, given an assumption concerning the heteroskedasticity in y_i.

First, let h represent a parameter for the relationship of the square root of the variance of y_i to its expectation: $[\text{var}(y_i)]^{1/2} = \sqrt{c}[E(y_i)]^h$, where c is some constant. Then, Equation (22) becomes

$$E\left(\frac{\partial L}{\partial \lambda_0}\right)_{\lambda_0 = \lambda} = -\frac{c}{\sigma^2}\sum_i [E(y_i)]^{2(h+\lambda-1)}E(\ln y_i).$$

(As discussed above, this equation is zero only when $h = 1 - \lambda$.) Now, σ^2 can be interpreted as the average value of the variance of σ_i^2 [see, e.g., Goldberger (1964, p. 235)], or

$$\sigma^2 = \frac{1}{N}\sum_i \sigma_i^2 = \frac{c}{N}\sum_i [E(y_i)]^{2(h+\lambda-1)}.$$

Therefore, we can now write

$$E\left(\frac{\partial L}{\partial \lambda_0}\right)_{\lambda_0 = \lambda} = -\frac{N\sum_i [E(y_i)]^{2(h+\lambda-1)}E(\ln y_i)}{\sum_i [E(y_i)]^{2(h+\lambda-1)}}.$$

By a series expansion on $[E(y_i)]^{2(h+\lambda-1)}$, we have

$$E\left(\frac{\partial L}{\partial \lambda_0}\right)_{\lambda_0 = \lambda}$$
$$= -\frac{N\sum_i \{1 + 2(h+\lambda-1)[\ln E(y_i)] + 2(h+\lambda-1)^2 [\ln E(y_i)]^2\} E(\ln y_i)}{\sum_i \{1 + 2(h+\lambda-1)[\ln E(y_i)] + 2(h+\lambda-1)^2 [\ln E(y_i)^2]\}}$$
$$= -\frac{N\sum_i \{2(h+\lambda-1)[E(\ln y_i)]^2 + 2(h+\lambda-1)^2 [E(\ln y_i)]^3\}}{\sum_i \{1 + 2(h+\lambda-1)^2 [E(\ln y_i)]^2\}}$$

after taking $\ln E(y_i) = E(\ln y_i)$ as an approximation and remembering that $\sum_i E(\ln y_i) = 0$, by our units for measuring y_i. Now $\sum_i [E(\ln y_i)]^2/N$ is the sample variance of $E(\ln y)$ and $\sum_i [E(\ln y_i)]^3/N$ is the third moment. If $E(\ln y)$ is reasonably symmetric, the third moment is close to zero, and we have

$$E\left(\frac{\partial L}{\partial \lambda_0}\right)_{\lambda_0 = \lambda} = -(h+\lambda-1)\,N\frac{\text{var}[E(\ln y)]}{\tfrac{1}{2} + (h+\lambda-1)^2\,\text{var}[E(\ln y)]}.$$

Finally, to relate this result to the sample, first, note that

$$\text{plim}\left(\frac{\partial L}{\partial \lambda_0}\right)_{\lambda_0 = \lambda} = \text{plim}\left(\frac{dL_{\max}(\lambda_0)}{d\lambda_0}\right)_{\lambda_0 = \lambda}.$$

(See Equations (18) above and (24) below and note that $\text{plim}\,\hat{\sigma}^2 = \sigma^2$; Goldberger [1964, p. 239, Equation (4.52) as sample size grows].) The equality also obtains when an independent variable is transformed by the same λ as the dependent variable, but the computation is more tedious. (The equation also, of course, obtains when a different transformation on an independent variable is used.) Second, note that the $\text{var}[E(\ln y)]$ can be approximated by the $\text{var}(\ln y)$ if the variance of the deterministic portion of y is much larger than the error variance (in practice, the approximation is good if R^2 is high). To the extent that the approximation is in error, the bias due to heteroskedasticity is somewhat overestimated since $\text{var}[E(\ln y)] < \text{var}(\ln y)$. A consistent estimate of λ under heteroskedasticity in ε can now be obtained by finding that λ such that

$$(23) \qquad \frac{dL_{\max}(\lambda)}{d\lambda} = (1-\lambda-h)\,N\frac{\text{var}(\ln y)}{\tfrac{1}{2} + (1-\lambda-h)^2\,\text{var}(\ln y)}.$$

This equation is independent of units of measurement for y since $\text{var}(\ln ky) = \text{var}(\ln y)$ for constant $k > 0$.

In the usual maximum likelihood problem we seek solutions of the partial derivatives of the likelihood function (with respect to each parameter) set equal to zero. In this problem, when we believe that heteroskedasticity of ε may lead to inconsistent estimates of λ and thus of other parameters, we seek that value of λ which yields a value of the derivative of the likelihood function (with respect to λ) given by Equation (23). Then λ, $\boldsymbol{\beta}$, and σ^2 are consistently estimated. [Of course, consistent estimates for the standard errors of $\boldsymbol{\beta}$ cannot be obtained from $\hat{\sigma}^2(\mathbf{X}'\mathbf{X})^{-1}$ as long as ε is heteroskedastic.]

In sum, two procedures for consistently estimating λ under heteroskedasticity of ε are available. First, given the plot of the maximized log-likelihood function provided by Equation (11) or Equation (12), a consistent estimate of λ is given by that value of the transformation, conditional upon a belief about the degree of heteroskedasticity in y_i, such that the slope of the likelihood function at, say, $\hat{\lambda}(h)$, is given by Equation (23). This is thus basically a graphical procedure. Second, the derivative of the likelihood function (11) is

$$(24) \qquad \frac{dL_{\max}(\lambda)}{d\lambda} = -\frac{N}{\lambda} \frac{\mathbf{y}^{(\lambda)'}\mathbf{Mw}^{(\lambda)}}{\mathbf{y}^{(\lambda)'}\mathbf{My}^{(\lambda)}} + \frac{N}{\lambda} + \sum_i \ln y_i,$$

where $\mathbf{M} = \mathbf{I} - \mathbf{X}(\mathbf{X'X})^{-1}\mathbf{X'}$ and $\mathbf{w}^{(\lambda)}$ is the vector of components $\{y_i^\lambda \ln y_i\}$. The numerator of the first term is the residual sum of products in the analysis of covariance of $\mathbf{y}^{(\lambda)}$ and $\mathbf{w}^{(\lambda)}$, while the denominator is $N\hat{\sigma}^2$. [With appropriate units for y_i the last term of Equation (24) drops out.] Thus, we can, on a computer, find that value of λ such that Equation (24) equals Equation (23), for a given value for h.

In two empirical problems reported upon in the next section, a consistent estimate of λ is obtained when $h = 1$ [the standard deviation of y_i rising with $E(y_i)$] using the first approach. We find that in fact the departure of $\hat{\lambda}(h = 1)$ from $\hat{\lambda}(h = \lambda - 1)$, the homoskedastic case in ε, depends upon the problem; in one case (for money demand) the departure is important, in the other case (for food consumption) it is unimportant. The result seems to imply that non-linearities are estimated if they are important; if not, the estimate of λ also reflects estimating heteroskedasticity. Thus, for any particular problem, it is important to ascertain the robustness of estimates of λ to heteroskedasticity in ε.

III. Applications in Econometrics: Demand Studies

The study of the demand for money is an area of econometric research where the central problem has often been the appropriate determinants of that demand, rather than upon its functional relationship (an exception would be estimation of the liquidity trap; see below). Thus, either the linear or linear-in-logarithms functional form has been the usual functional relationship on grounds of simplicity [Eisner (1963), Chow (1966), and Chetty (1969) use both]. Zarembka (1968), however, considers the appropriate functional form as a transformation-of-variables problem in which money demand M_t^D raised to the power λ is a linear function of current income Y_t and current interest rate r_t, both also raised to a power λ:

$$(25) \qquad M_t^{D\lambda} = a_0 + a_1 Y_t^\lambda + a_2 r_t^\lambda,$$

where a_0, a_1, and a_2 are parameters. Thus, the linear and linear-in-logarithms functional forms are special cases (when $\lambda = 1$ and $\lambda \to 0$, respectively).

Equation (25) is first estimated using the Box and Cox transformation on both the dependent and independent variables, as in Equation (7). The maximum likelihood estimate and 95% confidence interval for λ are -0.08 ± 0.31

for 1915–1963 data when money is defined as currency plus demand deposits; -0.42 ± 0.32 for 1915–1963 data when money also includes time deposits; and 0.19 ± 0.10 for 1869–1963 data again when money also includes time deposits. However, the Durbin–Watson statistics calculated at the points of maximum likelihood are all below 0.5, suggesting some misspecification of the model.

Before turning to alternative specifications of the model, let us examine the robustness of the estimates of λ to heteroskedasticity. In particular, since the reported estimates are close to $\lambda = 0$ and since Section II indicates that the estimates are biased toward $\lambda = 0$ when the standard deviation of money demand rises with the level of money demand (i.e., $h = 1$ in Section II), suppose we assume that $h = 1$. For the 1915–1963 data on currency plus demand deposits a consistent estimate of λ using Equation (23) is then -0.3, for the 1915–1963 data on currency plus demand deposits plus time deposits it is 1.2, and for the 1869–1963 data it is 0.45. Thus, the original estimates do *not* appear to be robust to heteroskedasticity (the bias being greater the farther h is from $h = 1 - \hat{\lambda}$). Apparently the data do not indicate important nonlinearities so that estimating heteroskedasticity is at least equally as important.

Given the Durbin–Watson statistics in the original estimates, Zarembka (1968) considers three alternative specifications of the money demand model: (i) The error term is in fact generated by an autoregressive process; (ii) current income is replaced by a measure of expected income or permanent income; or (iii) money stock does not adjust immediately to money demand. The first implies that lagged money, lagged income, and lagged interest rate should all be included as additional regressors, although only one additional parameter is introduced; the second implies that only lagged money and lagged interest rate are additional regressors, again with only one additional parameter; and the third implies that only lagged money need be included with one additional parameter. Thus, the first two models are overidentified; the third is just identified. With the same transformation applied to all variables, the maximum likelihood estimates for λ under the different definitions of money and length of time series are very close to the respective estimates for the initial simple model, and in each case the stock adjustment model is indicated to be the most appropriate.

The most interesting result, however, is reproduced here as Table 1, which provides the signs and t-ratios for the coefficient of each variable *conditional* upon choice of functional form (conditional upon λ). The maximum likelihood estimate for the 1870–1963 data with money defined as currency plus demand deposits plus time deposits gives $\hat{\lambda} = 0.13$, and thus the coefficients of both lagged income and lagged interest rate being statistically insignificant at the 5% level—leading to acceptance of the stock adjustment model. However, an *a priori* choice of the logarithmic form ($\lambda = 0$) would have led to acceptance of the expected income model (the coefficient of lagged interest rate is statistically

TABLE 1

Signs, t-Ratios, and R^2 for Given Values of λ, $C + D + T$, 1870–1963[a]

λ	Signs and t-ratios for the coefficient of					R^2
	$M_{t-1}^{(\lambda)}$	$Y_t^{(\lambda)}$	$r_t^{(\lambda)}$	$Y_{t-1}^{(\lambda)}$	$r_{t-1}^{(\lambda)}$	
1.10	20.46	2.15	−2.80	1.24	−0.10	0.9965
0.95	20.50	2.45	−3.18	1.21	−0.04	0.9971
0.80	20.46	2.79	−3.61	1.22	0.06	0.9977
0.65	20.37	3.20	−4.07	1.25	0.21	0.9982
0.50	20.37	3.70	−4.48	1.20	0.50	0.9985
0.35	20.77	4.25	−4.66	0.85	1.00	0.9988
0.20	22.03	4.74	−4.44	0.01	1.64	0.9989
0.05	24.36	5.05	−3.90	−1.09	2.11	0.9989
−0.10	27.17	5.17	−3.25	−2.08	2.23	0.9989
−0.25	29.34	5.19	−2.61	−2.75	2.06	0.9988

[a] From Zarembka (1968, p. 509).

significant and has the correct positive sign), while an *a priori* choice of $\lambda = -0.25$ would have led to acceptable of the autoregressive model. Thus, choice of functional form appears to be crucial in discriminating among alternative models; yet, for this problem, heteroskedasticity appears to be an important influence in estimating λ.

White (1972) has generalized Equation (25) by allowing for the possibility of a liquidity trap in the demand function for money; that is, he considers the more general transformation on the interest rate variable $(r - d)^\lambda$, where d is the asymptotic liquidity trap rate. His maximum likelihood estimate for λ, using 1900–1958 data on currency plus demand deposits while his Y_t in Equation (25) here refers to total assets or wealth, is -0.32 and for d is 1.5%. The joint 95% confidence region for λ and d excludes $\lambda = 0$ but includes $d = 0$. Particularly interesting is White's figure (reproduced here as Figure 1), which portrays estimates of the liquidity trap rate d conditional on λ (as well as estimates of λ conditional on d). The figure highlights the importance of functional form, particularly in estimating the liquidity trap d.

Choice of functional form has been a particularly important problem in studies of the demand function for food. Basically the issue is that empirical evidence strongly suggests the income elasticity of food demand to be below unity and falling as income level rises. However, since previously used functional forms have some deficiencies [see Zarembka (1972, pp. 207–208)], Zarembka (1972, p. 208) has suggested the form

$$(26) \qquad c^\lambda = a_0 + a_1 y^\lambda,$$

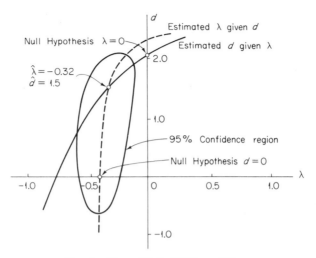

FIG. 1.   From White (1972, p. 196).

where c is food consumption and y is income. Thus, an additional parameter λ is introduced to describe the behavior of the income elasticity as income level changes; the income elasticity is $a_1 (y/c)^\lambda$ so that, if $\lambda < 0$ and the elasticity is less than unity, the elasticity falls as income rises according to the value of λ.

Using the particular transformation suggested by Box and Cox, Zarembka estimates Equation (26) with Philippine household survey data for 1961 and 1965. Consumption and income are divided by average household size, while household size, transformed by the same λ, is also included as a separate regressor since there has been prior evidence that larger families are able to economize somewhat in purchasing, storing, and preparing food. Also, since the data are "grouped," each observation (after any transformations) is weighted by multiplying by the square root of the number of individuals in the grouped observation to allow for heteroskedasticity of the error term due to the grouping. The estimates and 95% confidence intervals for λ, with 72 observations, are -0.53 ± 0.14 for food defined as total food expenditures and -0.46 ± 0.22 for food defined as cereals only. For the range of the Philippine data the resultant income elasticity varies from a high of 0.88 for low income levels to 0.59 for high income levels (and 0.58 to 0.25 for cereals only).

As a check for robustness to heteroskedasticity, a consistent estimate of λ using Equation (23) can be calculated under the assumption that the standard deviation of food consumption per capita rises with the level of food consumption [$h = 1$ in Equation (23)]. The estimate of λ for total food is then -0.60 and for cereals is -0.52. Thus, unlike the money demand example reported above, the estimates of λ appear to be robust to heteroskedasticity so that the estimates of λ are primarily reflecting the nonlinearities of the structure.

IV. Applications in Econometrics: Production Studies

The CES production function is the clearest example of transformation of variables in economics in which the transforming parameter is of inherent interest; it is the parameter for the elasticity of substitution. In the introduction the equation for the CES function is written

$$(27) \qquad Y = (a_1 K^\rho + a_2 L^\rho)^{1/\rho}, \qquad \rho < 1$$

where the elasticity of substitution is $1/(1 - \rho)$. This function can of course be transformed as in Equation (1), an additive error term u appended, which is assumed normally and independently distributed with zero mean and constant variance,

$$(28) \qquad Y^\rho = a_1 K^\rho + a_2 L^\rho + u, \qquad u \sim NID(0, \sigma^2)$$

and then estimated by the maximum likelihood method. While there is no constant term so that the Box and Cox transformation cannot be applied, the transformation can be written Y^ρ/ρ and still lead to the same maximized log-likelihood function, Equation (11) or Equation (12).

As developed in Section II above, a conceptual problem is whether a homo-skedastic error in Equation (28) is a reasonable specification. For example, a lognormally distributed error term in Equation (27) might be thought appropriate so that the error variability around the conditional value of output grows linearly with output; i.e., the error term expresses the percentage departure of output in a sample drawing from its deterministic value. For firm observations, this says that large firms have proportionately larger stochastic errors than small firms (although, indeed, this can be questioned—larger firms may have greater flexibility to adjust to exogenous disturbances). In this case, we have

$$Y = (a_1 K^\rho + a_2 L^\rho)^{1/\rho} e^{u/\rho}, \qquad u \sim NID(0, \sigma^2)$$

or, after transformation,

$$Y^\rho = (a_1 K^\rho + a_2 L^\rho) e^u.$$

For small u, we therefore have

$$(29) \qquad Y^\rho = a_1 K^\rho + a_2 L^\rho + E(y^\rho) u,$$

since $e^u \approx 1 + u$. Thus, the error term in Equation (28) is not in general homo-skedastic; it is only homoskedastic when $\rho = 0$, the Cobb–Douglas case.

In Section II we saw that the estimate of ρ in an equation such as (29) is biased toward $\rho = 0$ when the estimating procedures of Section I are used. For this problem, we could then use the estimating procedure suggested at the end of Section II with $h = 1$.

Aggregate observations may lead to a different formulation. On the one hand, if all firms are the same size with the same variance of the (independent) error term, then the variance of the error term in an aggregate observation grows with the number of firms in the aggregate (not the square of the number of firms). Since the firms are the same size, this suggests that the variance grows with the expected value of output so that $h = \frac{1}{2}$ in Section II. On the other hand, if each observation has the same number of firms but at different output levels, then the variance of the aggregate output observation grows with the sum of the squares of the expected firm output levels (less than the square of the aggregate output observation). In general, aggregate observations depend upon both factors, and so the expected degree of heteroskedasticity in output y_i is rather hard to valuate. However, it is probably reasonable to suppose that the h of Section II lies between one-half and unity.

In any case, Ramsey and Zarembka (1971) have estimated the nonconstant returns-to-scale CES production function as a transformation-of-variables problem; i.e., they estimate[6]

$$(30) \qquad \frac{Y^{\rho/\nu}}{\rho/\nu} = a_1 \frac{K^\rho}{\rho/\nu} + a_2 \frac{L^\rho}{\rho/\nu} + u, \qquad u \sim NID(0, \sigma^2).$$

The data are aggregate observations on United States manufacturing across states for 1957. The maximum likelihood estimate of ρ is 0.38, implying an estimate of the elasticity of substitution of 1.61, and of ν is 1.04. Both the Cobb–Douglas case of $\rho = 0$ and the constant returns-to-scale case of $\nu = 1$ are outside the 1% confidence region. Furthermore, their tests on the error term lead to acceptance of the maintained hypothesis on the included variables, the functional form, and the homoskedasticity and normality of the error term. (However, see footnote 10 below, which suggests that the estimate of ρ, and thus σ, probably reflects stabilizing the error variance.)

Mukerji (1963) and Dhrymes and Kurz (1964, pp. 289–292) have proposed a generalized production function that, in fact, is precisely a general transformation-of-variables problem. Thus, they propose the production function

$$(31) \qquad Y = \left(\sum_{i=1}^{K} a_i X_i^{\lambda_i} \right)^{1/\lambda_0},$$

where Y is output, the X_i's are K factor inputs, λ_0 and λ_i's are transforming parameters, and a_i's are parameters. If $\lambda_i = \lambda$ $(i = 1, ..., K)$, then Equation (31) is a general CES production function with returns-to-scale λ/λ_0. In general the

---

[6] When writing Zarembka (1970), this author attempted to estimate the CES production function using the Box and Cox transformation. Nonsensical results were obtained. The Schlesselman (1971) contribution now makes the reason clear: As already noted, the Box and Cox transformation cannot be used when a constant term is not included in the equation.

elasticities of substitution between inputs are not constant but rather stand in fixed proportion to each other. However, the function is not homogeneous of any degree.[7] In any case, Equation (31) can be written into the general transformation-of-variables problem

$$(32) \qquad Y^{\lambda_0} = \sum_{i=1}^{K} a_i X_i^{\lambda_i}.$$

It can then be estimated by the technique suggested at the end of Section I (remembering not to apply the specific transformation suggested by Box and Cox since there is no constant term in the formulation).

Finally, we should note one other application of transformation of variables in production theory. When Arrow *et al.* (1961) developed the CES production function, they considered (p. 228) two functional forms for the relationship between value added per worker V/L and the wage rate w—the linear form and the logarithmic form. With "the logarithmic form being somewhat better," they generated a new class of production functions based upon it, which has the property that the elasticity of substitution between capital (as a second factor input) and labor is a constant. If, however, the functional form between value added per unit of labor and the wage rate is opened up to specific consideration, then the possibility of a variable elasticity of substitution is introduced. In particular, if the functional form is written

$$(33) \qquad \left(\frac{V}{L}\right)^{\lambda} = a_0 + a_1 w^{\lambda},$$

the elasticity of substitution is given by $a_1 (V/L/w)^{\lambda}$. (This elasticity is always greater than or less than unity.) A test for a constant elasticity of substitution is then a test for $\lambda = 0$.

Lovell (1973) has taken this approach with respect to the K/L to w/r relationship, where r is the cost of capital (measured by the value of output less labor costs per net book value of capital). Using two-digit U.S. manufacturing data for 1958, the 95% confidence region for λ excludes the logarithmic $\lambda = 0$ assumption of Arrow *et al.* for three out of ten industries with data between 17 and 40 observations only (p. 718).

V. New Directions

All of the applications of transformation of variables that have been considered here refer to the single-equation context, not to a simultaneous equation system. If different λ transformations are permitted within such a system, the

---

[7] The limitation of nonhomogeneity of this production function has been removed in an article by Hanoch (1971), at the cost of having only an implicit, not explicit, production function.

identification problem within the nonlinear system is quite serious. Some progress on the simultaneous system, however, has been made by Tintner and Kadekodi (1971). They consider the case in which all variables in the system are transformed by the same λ transformation so that the linear and linear-in-logarithms forms of the whole system are special cases. In other words, if "(λ)" expresses the transformation given by Equation (7), then they consider the simultaneous system

$$(34) \qquad\qquad \mathbf{B}\mathbf{y}_i^{(\lambda)} + \mathbf{C}\mathbf{X}_i^{(\lambda)} = \mathbf{u}_i,$$

where $\mathbf{y}_i^{(\lambda)}$ is the vector of transformed endogenous variables for the ith observation, $\mathbf{X}_i^{(\lambda)}$ is the vector of transformed predetermined variables, $\mathbf{B}$ and $\mathbf{C}$ are fixed matrices in which $\mathbf{B}$ is square and has an inverse $\mathbf{B}^{-1}$, and $\mathbf{u}_i$ is a vector of random variables.

Tintner and Kadekodi obtain the reduced form of the system

$$(35) \qquad\qquad \mathbf{y}_i^{(\lambda)} = \mathbf{G}\mathbf{X}_i^{(\lambda)} + \mathbf{v}_i,$$

where $\mathbf{G} = -\mathbf{B}^{-1}\mathbf{C}$, $\mathbf{v}_i = \mathbf{B}^{-1}\mathbf{u}_i$, and $\mathbf{v}_i$ is assumed to be multivariate normal with mean zero and a covariance matrix Σ invariant over observations and with all other covariances zero. The maximized log-likelihood function, conditional on λ, analogous to Section I above, is thus

$$(36) \qquad L_{\max}(\lambda) = -\tfrac{1}{2}N \ln |\Sigma| + (\lambda-1) \sum_{j=1}^{M} \sum_{i=1}^{N} \ln y_{ji},$$

where N is the number of observation sets, M is the number of endogenous variables, and y_{ji} is the ith observation on the jth endogenous variable.[8] An approximate confidence interval can again be obtained using (13). Using the estimate of λ Tintner and Kadekodi then suggest estimating the system (34) by indirect least squares, limited information maximum likelihood, or two-stage least squares.

Tintner and Kadekodi illustrate their suggestion using Tintner's (1952, pp. 168–172, 176–178) American meat market model with data for 19 years, 1949–1967. Unfortunately, the 95% confidence interval for λ is very large; for the just-identified meat market model, it is -1.7 and 2.5 with a maximum likelihood at $\hat{\lambda} = 0.5$. The cause is probably the limited number of observations.

While further work on estimating a simultaneous system of transformed variables would be useful, the problem of heteroskedasticity of ε_i as discussed in Section II commands more attention. First, of course, an asymptotically *efficient* procedure for estimating λ and $\boldsymbol{\beta}$ under heteroskedasticity needs to be developed; Section II only developed a *consistent* procedure. The problem is

---

[8] Tintner and Kadekodi actually have another term in their maximized log-likelihood function since they consider the transformation $y^{(\lambda)} = y^\lambda$, not y^λ/λ or $(y^\lambda - 1)/\lambda$.

complicated by the fact that the heteroskedasticity in ε_i depends upon the heteroskedasticity in y_i as well as upon the unknown parameter λ. Thus, an equation to be estimated cannot simply be transformed to homoskedasticity in ε_i, even if we know the heteroskedasticity in y_i.

A more important problem may be to develop a tool to separate out the influence of additivity in contributing to estimating transformations of the dependent variable from the influence of stabilizing the error variance [in this connection, see Box and Cox (1964, pp. 226 ff.)].[9] Unlike the hunches of some statisticians [e.g., Tukey in his discussion (p. 247) of the Box and Cox paper, and Kendall and Stuart (1968, p. 88)], we have found that a transformation to additivity may not also stabilize the error variance. My sense, from checking for robustness to heteroskedasticity of the estimates reported in Section III, is that the influence of additivity dominates over stabilizing the error variance in estimating a transformation on a dependent variable whenever underlying nonlinearities are important. But the notion of dominance needs to be formalized.

In any case, an estimate and a confidence region for a transformation on a dependent variable cannot be viewed as derived only from additivity of effect, but also includes, to a greater or lesser extent, stabilizing the error variance. For example, if a CES production function is estimated without enough variability in the capital/labor ratio, then the elasticity of substitution cannot be accurately estimated (although returns-to-scale can be) and the estimate of ρ may mainly reflect stabilizing the error variance.[10] Thus, if the researcher has an inherent interest in a transformation on a dependent variable, he needs to examine the results with regard to the analysis discussed in Section II here. Nevertheless, even if nonlinearities are unimportant, transformations can still be useful for estimating β. For then we can have a more nearly stable error variance and thus more reliable hypothesis tests on parameters in β.

REFERENCES

Arrow, K. J., H. B. Chenery, B. S. Minhas and R. M. Solow (1961). "Capital-Labor Substitution and Economic Efficiency," *Rev. Econ. Statist.* **43**, 225–250.

Box, G. E. P. and D. R. Cox (1964). "An Analysis of Transformations," *J. Roy. Statist. Soc. Ser. B* **26**, 211–243.

Box, G. E. P. and P. W. Tidwell (1962). "Transformation of the Independent Variables," *Technometrics* **4**, 531–550.

[9] This problem does not seem to be particularly connected with sample size since both Equation (23) and Equation (24) rise linearly with N.

[10] This observation probably explains the high estimate of the elasticity of substitution reported in Section IV. In connection with the variability in the capital/labor ratio required to estimate the CES production function, see Griliches and Ringstad (1971, pp. 77–81).

Brown, M. and J. S. de Cani (1963). "Technological Change and the Distribution of Income," *Int. Econ. Rev.* **4**, 289–309.

Chetty, V. K. (1969). "On the Long-Run and Short-Run Demand for Money: Some Further Evidence," *J. Political Econ.* **77**, 921–931.

Chow, G. C. (1966). "On the Long-Run and Short-Run Demand for Money," *J. Political Econ.* **74**, 111–131.

Dhrymes, P. J. and M. Kurz (1964). "Technology and Scale in Electricity Generation," *Econometrica* **32**, 287–315.

Dhrymes, P. J., E. P. Howrey, S. H. Hymans, J. Kmenta, E. E. Leamer, R. E. Quandt, J. B. Ramsey, H. T. Shapiro, and V. Zarnowitz (1972). "Criteria for Evaluation of Econometric Models," *Ann. Econ. Soc. Measurement* **1**, 291–324.

Draper, N. R. and D. R. Cox (1969). "On Distributions and Their Transformation to Normality," *J. Roy. Statist. Soc. Ser. B* **31**, 472–476.

Eisner, R. (1963). "Another Look at Liquidity Preference," *Econometrica* **31**, 531–538.

Goldberger, A. S. (1964). *Econometric Theory.* Wiley, New York.

Griliches, Z. and V. Ringstad (1971). *Economies of Scale and the Form of the Production Function: An Econometric Study of Norwegian Manufacturing Establishment Data.* North-Holland Publ., Amsterdam.

Hanoch, G. (1971). "CRESH Production Functions," *Econometrica* **39**, 695–712.

Kendall, M. G. and A. Stuart (1967). *The Advanced Theory of Statistics, Vol. 2, Inference and Relationship*, 2nd ed., Griffin, London.

Kendall, M. G. and A. Stuart (1968). *The Advanced Theory of Statistics, Vol. 3, Design and Analysis, and Time-Series*, 2nd ed., Griffin, London.

Lovell, C. A. K. (1973). "CES and VES Production Functions in a Cross-Section Context," *J. Political Econ.* **81**, 705–720.

Mukerji, V. (1963). "A Generalized SMAC Function with Constant Ratios of Elasticities of Substitution," *Rev. Econ. Stud.* **30**, 233–236.

Ramsey, J. B. and P. Zarembka (1971). "Specification Error Tests and Alternative Functional Forms of the Aggregate Production Function," *J. Amer. Statist. Ass.* **66**, 471–477.

Schlesselman, J. (1971). "Power Families: A Note on the Box and Cox Transformation," *J. Roy. Statist. Soc. Ser. B* **33**, 307–311.

Tintner, G. (1952). *Econometrics.* Wiley, New York.

Tintner, G. and G. Kadekodi (1971). "Note on the Transformation of Variables in Simultaneous Equations Systems," *J. Indian Soc. Agr. Statist.* **23**, 163–173.

Tukey, J. W. (1957). "On the Comparative Anatomy of Transformations," *Ann. Math. Statist.* **28**, 602–632.

Turner, M. E., R. J. Monroe and H. L. Lucas (1961). "Generalized Asymptotic Regression and Non-Linear Path Analysis," *Biometrics* **17**, 120–143.

White, K. J. (1972). "Estimation of the Liquidity Trap with a Generalized Functional Form," *Econometrica* **40**, 193–199.

Zarembka, P. (1968). "Functional Form in the Demand for Money," *J. Amer. Statist. Ass.* **63**, 502–511.

Zarembka, P. (1970). "On the Empirical Relevance of the CES Production Function," *Rev. Econ. Statist.* **52**, 47–53.

Zarembka, P. (1972). *Toward a Theory of Economic Development.* Holden-Day, San Francisco, California.

Chapter Four

Conditional logit analysis
of qualitative choice behavior

DANIEL McFADDEN[1]

UNIVERSITY OF CALIFORNIA AT BERKELEY
BERKELEY, CALIFORNIA

A fundamental concern of economics is understanding human choice behavior. Models or hypotheses are formed on the nature of decision processes, and are evaluated in the light of observed behavior. This task is complicated

[1] The research for this paper was done with the support of National Science Foundation Grant GS-27226, the Ford Foundation, the University of Chicago, and the U.S. Department of Transportation. I am indebted to P. Cottingham, J. Craig, G. Debreu, T. Domencich, R. Hall, M. Richter, and B. Saffran for useful comments at various stages of this research, but retain sole responsibility for errors.

105

because the econometrician cannot observe or control all the factors influencing behavior, and because the process of observation itself influences acts of the decision-maker through the vehicle of experience. It becomes necessary to make statistical inferences on a model of *individual* choice behavior from data obtained by sampling from a *population* of individuals (or sampling from a population of "experience levels" for a single individual). When the model of choice behavior under examination depends on unobserved characteristics in the population, the testable implications of the individual choice model are obscured. However, it is possible to deduce from the individual choice model properties of population choice behavior which can be subjected to empirical test.

The link between models of individual behavior and data on population choices is most critical when the decision-maker's alternatives are qualitative, or "lumpy." In conventional consumer analysis with a continuum of alternatives, one can often plausibly assume that all individuals in a population have a *common* behavior rule, except for purely random "optimization" errors, and that systematic variations in aggregate choice reflect common variations in individual choice at the *intensive* margin. By contrast, systematic variations in aggregate choice among lumpy alternatives must reflect shifts in individual choice at the *extensive* margin, resulting from a *distribution* of decision rules in the population.

This paper outlines a general procedure for formulating econometric models of population choice behavior from distributions of individual decision rules. A concrete case with useful empirical properties, conditional logit analysis, is developed in detail. The relevance of these methods to economic analysis can be indicated by a list of the consumer choice problems to which conditional logit analysis has been applied: choice of college attended, choice of occupation, labor force participation, choice of geographical location and migration, choice of number of children, housing choice, choice of number and brand of automobiles owned, choice of shopping travel mode and destination.

Section I of this paper derives the relation between individual behavioral models and the distribution of population choices, and discusses the behavioral axiom which leads to the conditional logit model. Section II discusses estimation of the conditional logit model, and Section III discusses its statistical properties. Section IV summarizes an application of the method to the problem of shopping travel mode and destination choice.

I. Preferences and Selection Probabilities

A study of choice behavior is described by (1) the objects of choice and sets of alternatives available to decision-makers, (2) the observed attributes of decision-makers, and (3) the model of individual choice and behavior and distribution of behavior patterns in the population. Observed data are assumed to be generated by the *trial* of drawing an individual randomly from the population and recording his attributes, the set of alternatives available to him, and his actual choice. A sample is obtained by a sequence of independent trials, with or without *replications* in which a sequence of choices are observed for individuals with the same measured attributes and alternative sets.

We let X denote the universe of objects of choice, S the universe of vectors of measured attributes of decision-makers. An individual drawn at random from the population will have some attribute vector $s \in S$ and will face some set of available alternatives, which we now assume to be finite and denote by $B \subseteq X$. Let $P(x \mid s, B)$ denote the conditional probability that an individual drawn at random from the population will choose alternative x, given that he has measured attributes s and faces the alternative set B. The observed choice in a trial with attributes s and alternatives B can then be viewed as a drawing from a multinomial distribution with selection probabilities $P(x \mid s, B)$ for $x \in B$.

An individual behavior rule is a function h which maps each vector of measured attributes s and possible alternative set B into a chosen member of B. A *model* of individual behavior is a set of behavior rules H. For example, h may be a demand function resulting from maximization of a specific utility function, and H may be the set of demand functions which result from maximization of *some* utility function. With unmeasured attributes varying across the population, a model H can contain many behavior rules.

If a model H truly describes a population, then there exists a probability π defined on the (measurable) subsets of H specifying the distribution of behavior rules in the population.[2] The selection probability that an individual drawn at random from the population will choose x, given measured attributes s and alternative set B, equals the probability of occurrence of a decision rule yielding this choice, or

(1) $$P(x \mid s, B) = \pi[\{h \in H \mid h(s, B) = x\}].$$

An econometric model of qualitative choice behavior can be constructed for a specified model of individual behavior by assuming π to be a member of a

---

[2] To be precise, each trial represents a drawing of a triple (s, B, ω) from an underlying universe, where s is a vector of measured attributes, B is an alternative set, and ω determines a unique decision rule h_ω, with $h_\omega(s', B') \in B'$ for all possible arguments (s', B'). A probability defined on the underlying universe induces a probability π on the set of h_ω, conditioned on values of (s, B). When the pair (s, B) and ω are statistically independent [e.g., the underlying probability is a product of a probability defined on the universe of (s, B) and a probability defined on the universe of ω], the probability π is independent of the conditioning values (s, B). We confine our attention to this case, noting that satisfaction of this condition is one of the criteria for a carefully designed laboratory experiment or sample survey.

parametric family of probability distributions and using the fact that the observed choices are multinomially distributed with the probabilities (1) to obtain estimators of the underlying parameters. The following paragraphs carry through this program for the classical model of the utility-maximizing economic consumer.

Suppose an individual in the population has a vector of measured attributes s, and faces J alternatives, indexed $j = 1, ..., J$ and described by vectors of attributes x_j. The individual has a utility function that can be written in the form

$$U = V(s, x) + \varepsilon(s, x),$$

where V is nonstochastic and reflects the "representative" tastes of the population, and ε is stochastic and reflects the idiosyncracies of this individual in tastes for the alternative with attributes x. The individual chooses the alternative which maximizes utility; let h_ε denote his behavior rule, and $B = \{x_1, ..., x_J\}$. The probability that an individual drawn randomly from the population, with attributes s and alternative set B, will choose x_i equals

$$P_i \equiv P(x_i \,|\, s, B) = \pi[\{h_\varepsilon \in H \,|\, h_\varepsilon(s, B) = x_i\}]$$

(2)
$$= P[\varepsilon(s, x_j) - \varepsilon(s, x_i) < V(s, x_i) - V(s, x_j) \quad \text{for all} \quad j \neq i].$$

The probability π induces a joint cumulative distribution function $F(\varepsilon_1, ..., \varepsilon_J)$ over the values $\varepsilon_j = \varepsilon(s, x_j)$ for $j = 1, ..., J$; i.e.,

$$F(\varepsilon_1, ..., \varepsilon_J) = \pi[\{h_\varepsilon \in H \,|\, \varepsilon(s, x_j) \leqslant \varepsilon_j \quad \text{for} \quad j = 1, ..., J\}].$$

Let F_i denote the partial derivative of F with respect to its ith argument, and let $V_i = V(s, x_i)$. Then Equation (2) can be written

(3)
$$P_i = \int_{\varepsilon = -\infty}^{+\infty} F_i(\varepsilon + V_i - V_1, ..., \varepsilon + V_i - V_J) \, d\varepsilon.$$

We may proceed by specifying a joint distribution, such as joint normal, which will yield a family of probabilities depending on the unknown parameters of the distribution. It will generally be necessary to impose rather stringent maintained hypotheses on the unknown parameters to make them identifiable in a choice experiment, particularly in the absence of repetitions.

In practice, it is difficult to define joint distributions F which allow the computation of econometrically useful formulas for the P_i in Equation (3). An alternative approach is to specify formulas for the selection probabilities and then examine the question of whether these formulas could be obtained via Equation (3) from *some* distribution of utility-maximizing consumers. This problem is the population analog of the conventional theory of revealed preference for individual consumers. The author and Professor Marcel K.

Richter have elsewhere (1971) characterized the necessary and sufficient condition on selection probabilities for satisfaction of Equation (3). We shall follow this method, using a particular specification of the selection probabilities that allows direct verification of condition (3).

We consider a powerful axiom on selection probabilities introduced by Luce (1959) which states that the relative odds of one alternative being chosen over a second should be independent of the presence or absence of unchosen third alternatives. Formally, we make the following assumption.

AXIOM 1. (Independence of Irrelevant Alternatives). For all possible alternative sets B, measured attributes s, and members x and y of B,

$$(4) \qquad P(x \mid s, \{x, y\}) \, P(y \mid s, B) = P(y \mid s, \{x, y\}) \, P(x \mid s, B).$$

We show below that this axiom is consistent with condition (3) and leads to a simple econometric specification of the selection probabilities. Luce has presented evidence that the axiom is consistent with behavior in some choice experiments; we shall point out later some of its limitations.

When $P(x \mid s, B)$ is positive, Equation (4) implies $P(x \mid s, \{x, y\})$ positive, and

$$(5) \qquad \frac{P(y \mid s, \{x, y\})}{P(x \mid s, \{x, y\})} = \frac{P(y \mid s, B)}{P(x \mid s, B)}.$$

This condition states that the odds of y being chosen over x in a multiple choice situation B, where both are available, equals the odds of a binary choice of y over x.

Since empirically a zero probability is indistinguishable from one that is extremely small, there is little loss of generality in assuming that the selection probabilities are all positive for the possible alternative sets in an experiment.

AXIOM 2 (Positivity). $P(x \mid s, B) > 0$ for all possible alternative sets B, vectors of measured attributes s, and $x \in B$.

Consider a choice set B containing alternatives x, y, z, and let $p_{xy} = P(x \mid s, \{x, y\})$. Define $p_{xx} = \frac{1}{2}$. From Equation (4),

$$(6) \qquad P(y \mid s, B) = \frac{p_{yx}}{p_{xy}} P(x \mid s, B)$$

and

$$(7) \qquad 1 = \sum_{y \in B} P(y \mid s, B) = \left(\sum_{y \in B} \frac{p_{yx}}{p_{xy}} \right) P(x \mid s, B).$$

Hence, the multiple choice selection probabilities can be written in terms of binary odds,

$$(8) \qquad P(x\,|\,s,\,B) = \frac{1}{\sum_{y \in B}(p_{yx}/p_{xy})}.$$

Permuting the indices x, y, z in Equation (6) and multiplying yields the condition

$$(9) \qquad \frac{p_{yx}}{p_{xy}} = \frac{p_{yz}/p_{zy}}{p_{xz}/p_{zx}}.$$

Taking z to be a "benchmark" member of the alternative set B and defining $V(s, x, z) = \log(p_{xz}/p_{zx})$, Equation (8) can be written

$$(10) \qquad P(x\,|\,s,\,B) = \frac{e^{V(s,x,z)}}{\sum_{y \in B} e^{V(s,y,z)}}.$$

In the function $V(s, x, z)$, one may think of the argument s as giving a "measured taste effect," the argument x as giving a "choice alternative effect," and the argument z as giving an "alternative set effect." In an experiment with sufficient variation in measured attributes s and the alternative set B, and replications for each (s, B) pair, one can normally identify each of these effects. In the absence of replications, it is impossible to identify the "alternative set effect," and an identifying restriction is necessary to isolate the "choice alternative effect"; we shall assume the following.[3]

AXIOM 3   (Irrelevance of Alternative Set Effect).   The function $V(s, x, z)$ determining the selection probabilities in Equation (10) has the additively separable form

$$(11) \qquad V(s, x, z) = v(s, x) - v(s, z).$$

Then, Equation (10) becomes

$$(12) \qquad P(x\,|\,s,\,B) = e^{v(s,x)} \Big/ \sum_{y \in B} e^{v(s,y)},$$

and the function v can be interpreted as a "utility indicator" of "representative" tastes. The following result justifies this terminology in terms of the behavior of a population of consumers.

---

[3] Axiom 3 follows from Axioms 1 and 2 if there exists some "universal benchmark" alternative z such that if B is a possible alternative set, then $B \cup \{z\}$ is also. This follows by noting that Equation (9) holds for $z \notin B$, provided Axioms 1 and 2 holds for $B \cup \{z\}$. Then, taking z to be the universal benchmark in Equation (10) and defining $v(s, x) = V(s, x, z)$ for all alternative sets yields the result.

LEMMA 1.   Suppose each member of a population of utility-maximizing consumers has a utility function $U(s, x) = v(s, x) + \varepsilon(s, x)$, where v is a non-stochastic function reflecting "representative" tastes and $\varepsilon(s, x)$ is a function that varies randomly in the population with the property that in each possible alternative set $B = \{x_1, \ldots, x_J\}$, the values $\varepsilon(s, x_j)$ are independently identically distributed with the Weibull (Gnedenko, extreme value) distribution[4]

$$P\big(\varepsilon(s, x_j) \leqslant \varepsilon\big) = e^{-e^{-\varepsilon}}. \tag{13}$$

Then the selection probabilities given by Equation (3) satisfy Equation (12).

Proof: From Equation (13), letting $V_i = v(s, x_i)$,

$$F_i(\varepsilon + V_i - V_1, \ldots, \varepsilon + V_i - V_J)$$

$$= \exp(-\varepsilon) \prod_{j=1}^{J} \exp\big(-\exp(-\varepsilon - V_i + V_j)\big)$$

$$= \exp(-\varepsilon) \exp\left\langle -[\exp(-\varepsilon)]\left[\sum_{j=1}^{J} \exp(V_j - V_i)\right]\right\rangle.$$

Substituting this expression in Equation (3) yields the result.

A nonconstructive proof of this result was first given by Marschak (1959); the argument above appears in Luce and Suppes (1965), and is attributed to E. Holman and A. Marley. The next lemma establishes that under mild conditions the distribution (13) characterizes the population choice models whose selection probabilities satisfy Equation (12). A random variable ε is said to be *translation complete* if for a function h of bounded absolute variation with $h(\pm\infty) = 0$, the condition $Eh(\varepsilon + a) = 0$ for all real a implies $h \equiv 0$ (except possibly on a set of measure zero). Most common distributions have this property; in particular, the Weibull distribution above is translation complete.[5]

---

[4] Monotone increasing transformations of the utility function $U(s, x)$ do not affect utility maximization or the selection probabilities, but transform the distribution of the random component. In particular, $e^{U(s, x)} = e^{V(s, x)}\eta(s, x)$ has η distributed with the reciprocal exponential distribution $P(\eta \leqslant y) = e^{-1/y}$ $(y \geqslant 0)$; $-e^{-U(s, x)} = e^{-V(s, x)}\eta(s, x)$ has η distributed with the negative exponential distribution $P(\eta \leqslant y) = e^{y}$ $(y \leqslant 0)$; and $e^{-\beta \exp[-U(s, x)]} = \eta(s, x)^{\exp[-V(s, x)]}$ has η distributed with the power distribution $P(\eta \leqslant y) = y^{1/\beta} (0 \leqslant y \leqslant 1)$. These examples demonstrate that the moments of the distribution of utility in the population (or their existence) do not provide a useful guide to the degree of dispersion of tastes. We note for later reference that the Weibull distribution (13) has the characteristic function $\Gamma(1 + it)$, which is nonzero for real t, and has all positive moments finite.

[5] A distribution whose characteristic function is nonzero for real arguments is translation complete [apply Feller (1966), p. 479]; the Weibull distribution satisfies this condition.

LEMMA 2. Suppose selection probabilities are given by Equation (12) for all finite alternative sets B in a universe X, and suppose that for each vector of measured attributes s, the values of $v(s, x)$ range over the real line; i.e., $v(s, X) = (-\infty, +\infty)$. Suppose the selection probabilities satisfy Equation (3) with independently identically distributed $\varepsilon(s, x_i)$ having a translation complete cumulative distribution function G. Then, $G(\varepsilon) = e^{-\alpha \exp(-\varepsilon)}$, where α is an arbitrary positive parameter. Fixing the parameter α by specifying $G(0) = e^{-1}$ yields the distribution (13).

Proof: Consider the choice between an alternative yielding "utility" $v_x = v(s, x)$ and K alternatives, each yielding v_y. Equations (3) and (12) imply that the probability P_x of choosing x is

$$(14) \qquad P_x = \frac{e^{v_x}}{e^{v_x} + K e^{v_y}} = \int_{\varepsilon = -\infty}^{+\infty} G(\varepsilon + v_x - v_y)^K \, dG(\varepsilon).$$

On the other hand, consider a binary choice between x and an alternative z yielding $v_z = v(s, z) = v_y + \log K$, implying

$$(15) \qquad P_{xz} = \frac{e^{v_x}}{e^{v_x} + e^{v_z}} = \int_{\varepsilon = -\infty}^{+\infty} G(\varepsilon + v_x - v_z) \, dG(\varepsilon).$$

The construction of v_z makes Equations (14) and (15) equal, implying

$$\int_{\varepsilon = -\infty}^{+\infty} [G(\varepsilon + v_x - v_y - \log K) - G(\varepsilon + v_x - v_y)^K] \, dG(\varepsilon) = 0.$$

But this can be true for all values of $v_x \in (-\infty, +\infty)$ only if the term in brackets is zero, since G is translation complete, implying

$$G(v_x - \log K) = G(v_x)^K.$$

Taking $v_x = 0$ implies $G(-\log K) = e^{-\alpha K}$, where $\alpha = -\log G(0) > 0$, and taking $v_x = \log K - \log L$ implies $G(-\log L) = G(\log K/L)^K$. Hence, $G(\log K/L) = e^{-\alpha L/K}$ for all positive integers K, L. Since G is monotone, it follows in the limit that $G(\log k) = e^{-\alpha/k}$ for all positive real k. Then $G(\varepsilon) = e^{-\alpha \exp(-\varepsilon)}$.

We summarize the advantages, and then the limitations, of the axioms leading to the formula (12) for the selection probabilities. First, this formula allows a ready interpretation of the selection probabilities in terms of the relative representative utilities of alternatives, and is relatively amenable to computation. Second, the formula makes it simple to ascertain the effect of introducing a new alternative to an alternative set; the proportional decrease in the selection probability of each old alternative equals the selection probability of the new alternative. This also points out a weakness of the model in that one cannot postulate a pattern of differential substitutability and complementarity between alternatives. Third, the axioms provide the identifying restrictions necessary to estimate choice alternative effects without replications, and to predict choice behavior resulting from extrapolation of observed alternative sets. Any set of identifying restrictions meeting these conditions will require powerful axioms on behavior, and care must be exercised in avoiding application of these models in situations where the axioms are implausible. The model above is subject to this general caveat.

The primary limitation of the model is that the independence of irrelevant alternatives axiom is implausible for alternative sets containing choices that are close substitutes. An example illustrates this point. Suppose a population faces the alternatives of travel by auto and by bus, and two-thirds choose to use auto. Suppose now a second "brand" of bus travel is introduced that is in all essential respects the same as the first. Intuitively, two-thirds of the population will still choose auto, and the remainder will split between the bus alternatives. However, if the selection probabilities satisfy Axiom 1, only half the population will use auto when the second bus is introduced. The reason this is counter-intuitive is that we expect individuals to lump the two bus alternatives together in making the auto-bus choice. This example suggests that application of the model should be limited to situations where the alternatives can plausibly be assumed to be distinct and weighed independently in the eyes of each decision-maker.

II. Conditional Logit Estimation

Formula (12) for the selection probabilities, obtained from Axioms 1–3, can be adapted for empirical analysis by specifying the functional form of "representative" utility $v(s, x)$. A particularly convenient assumption is that v is linear in unknown parameters.

AXIOM 4.   The function $v(s, x)$ has the form

$$v(s, x) = \theta_1 v^1(s, x) + \cdots + \theta_K v^K(s, x),$$

where the $v^k(s, x)$ are specified numerical functions and the θ_k are unknown parameters.

A choice experiment yields observations on N distinct trials (s_n, B_n), where s_n is a vector of measured attributes of an individual and B_n is an alternative set. Let B_n contain J_n alternatives, indexed $j = 1, ..., J_n$, with vectors of attributes x_{jn}. Define $z_{jn}^k = v^k(s_n, x_{jn})$ and $z_{jn} = (z_{jn}^1, ..., z_{jn}^K)$. From Equation (12), the selection probabilities then satisfy

(16)
$$P_{in} = P(x_{in} \mid s_n, B_n) = \frac{e^{z_{in}\theta}}{\sum_{j=1}^{J_n} e^{z_{jn}\theta}},$$

where $\theta' = (\theta_1, ..., \theta_K)$.[6] The experiment provides R_n repetitions of trial n, and the ith alternative is observed to be chosen S_{in} times. Of particular interest is the case without repetition,

$$R_n = \sum_{j=1}^{J_n} S_{jn} = 1.$$

We term this the *conditional logit model*. Note that it is an immediate generalization to the case of unequal, possibly unranked, alternatives of the multinomial logit model appearing in the literature.[7] The derivation of this model from a theory of population choice behavior appears to be new.

---

[6] The generality and limits of this form deserve emphasis. A variable $z^k = v^k(s, x)$ may be a component of x, a function specifying a nonlinear transformation or interaction between components of x, or a function specifying an interaction between x and s variables. It cannot be a component of s (or x) that is invariant over each alternative set, as this shifts the origin of the "representative" utility function leaving all the selection probabilities unchanged, and the associated θ_k is nonidentified. In general, the alternatives x_j have no natural ranking, and the indexing j is arbitrary. We would then say the attributes of the alternatives are generic, or "hedonic." However, in some application the alternatives are ranked, and the rank j is a component of the vector of attributes of alternative x_j summarizing the "unique" characteristics of this position. Then z^k may be a variable such that $z_j^k = 1$ and $z_l^k = 0$ for $l \neq j$, yielding a "specific jth alternative" effect θ_k. Further, the interaction of such a variable with other components of x can give variable alternative-specific interaction effects. An extreme case is that in which the specific alternative effect is the only attribute varying across the alternative set, and all variables are as an example of the form $z_j^j = s^1$ and $z_l^j = 0$ for $l \neq j$, implying $v(s, x_j) = \sum_{j=1}^J s^1 \theta_j$, where only the parameters θ_j vary in j. Since translation of all θ_j leaves the selection probabilities unchanged, identification requires a normalization, say $\theta_1 = 0$.

[7] Binomial logit analysis was popularized by Berkson (1951, 1955) and has been analyzed extensively in the statistical literature: Antle (1970), Cox (1958, 1966, 1970), Gart (1967), Gilbert (1968), Grizzle (1962, 1971), Gupta (1967), Harter and Moore (1967), and Walker and Duncan (1967). Multinomial logit was developed for a special case by Gurland (1960), and more generally by Bloch (1967), Bock (1969), Rassam (1971), McFadden (1968), Stopher (1969), and Theil (1969, 1970). An analogous development has occurred for probit analysis, in which the cumulative normal rather than logistic distribution is used to determine the selection probabilities (Aitchison and Silvey, 1957; Aitchison and Bennett, 1970; Amemiya, 1972).

The notion of a distribution of tastes in a population of consumers as a source of stochastic components of demand has been implicit in much of the literature on consumer demand theory, particularly in random coefficients models of demand. The use of this concept in analyzing qualitative choice has been made explicit in the work of Quandt (1968, 1970; Quandt and Young, 1969; Quandt and Baumol, 1966), where selection probabilities are assumed to result from maximization of a log-linear utility function with random parameters. The relationship of logit models to distributions of utility functions was worked out in the context of models of stochastic choice behavior by Marschak (1960) and Block (1960), and explored further by Luce and Suppes (1965); the econometric implications of this work were apparently first noted by the author (1968). The foundations of the theory of testing hypotheses on individual behavior from population data were developed in a later paper by the author and Richter (1971).

The vector $(S_{1n}, \ldots, S_{J_n n})$ can be viewed as the result of R_n independent drawings from a multinomial distribution with probabilities given by Equation (16) for $i = 1, \ldots, J_n$. Hence, the likelihood of the given sample is a function $L = L(\theta) = L((S_{jn}, z_{jn}); \theta)$ satisfying

$$(17) \qquad e^L = \prod_{n=1}^{N} \frac{R_n!}{S_{1n}! \cdots S_{J_n n}!} \prod_{i=1}^{J_n} P_{in}^{S_{in}}.$$

Substitution of Equation (16) yields the log-likelihood function

$$(18) \qquad L = C - \sum_{n=1}^{N} \sum_{i=1}^{J_n} S_{in} \log \sum_{j=1}^{J_n} e^{(z_{jn} - z_{in})\theta}$$

$$= C + \sum_{n=1}^{N} \left[\left(\sum_{j=1}^{J_n} S_{jn} z_{jn} \right) \theta - R_n \log \sum_{j=1}^{J_n} e^{z_{jn}\theta} \right],$$

where

$$C = \sum_{n=1}^{N} \left[\log R_n! - \sum_{j=1}^{J_n} \log S_{jn}! \right].$$

An estimator for θ with good large sample properties under very general conditions is obtained by a vector $\hat{\theta}$, depending on the observations, which maximizes the likelihood (18) of the given sample. We discuss the computation and statistical properties of the maximum likelihood estimator. Several alternative estimation methods are discussed at the end of this section.

Differentiation of Equation (18) with respect to θ yields the formulas

$$(19) \qquad \frac{\partial L}{\partial \theta} = \sum_{n=1}^{N} \left[\sum_{j=1}^{J_n} (S_{jn} - R_n P_{jn}) z_{jn} \right],$$

$$(20) \qquad \frac{\partial^2 L}{\partial \theta \, \partial \theta'} = - \sum_{n=1}^{N} R_n \sum_{j=1}^{J_n} (z_{jn} - \bar{z}_n)' P_{jn}(z_{jn} - \bar{z}_n),$$

where

$$\bar{z}_n = \sum_{i=1}^{J_n} z_{in} P_{in}.$$

Since Equation (20) is the negative of a weighted moment matrix of the independent variables, it is negative semidefinite and the log-likelihood function is concave in θ. Then L is maximized at any critical point θ where $\partial L / \partial \theta = 0$.

Binomial logit and probit analyses have been used in a number of economic applications: Allouche (1972), Amemiya and Boskin (1972), Fisher (1962), Korbel (1966), Lave (1968), Lee (1963), Lisco (1967), McGillivray (1970), Moses *et al.* (1967), Reichman and Stopher (1971), Stopher (1969), Stopher and Lisco (1970), Talvitie (1972), Thomas and Thompson (1971), Uhler (1968), Walker (1968), Warner (1967), and Zellner and Lee (1965).

If, further, the matrix $\partial^2 L/\partial\theta \, \partial\theta'$ is nonsingular, L has a unique maximum in θ (provided one exists). A necessary and sufficient condition for $\partial^2 L/\partial\theta \, \partial\theta'$ to be negative definite is the following.

AXIOM 5 (Full Rank). The $\sum_{n=1}^{N} J_n \times K$ matrix whose rows are $(z_{in} - \bar{z}_n)$ for $i = 1, \ldots, J_n$ and $n = 1, \ldots, N$ is of rank K.

Since N linear dependency conditions are present in this matrix due to the subtraction of weighted means, a necessary order condition is $\sum_{n=1}^{N} J_n \geqslant K + N$. This will hold in particular if $N \geqslant K$ since $J_n \geqslant 2$, but may also hold for $N < K$ if the J_n are large. Analogously to the hypothesis of full rank in the linear statistical model, we can expect Axiom 5 to hold when the order condition is satisfied provided the data vary across alternative sets and are not collinear.

We next introduce an inequalities condition that guarantees the existence of a vector θ maximizing L.

AXIOM 6. There exists no nonzero K-vector γ satisfying $S_{in}(z_{jn} - z_{in})\gamma \leqslant 0$ for $i, j = 1, \ldots, J_n$ and $n = 1, \ldots, N$.

Note that there is a positive probability that Axiom 6 may fail in a finite sample since the S_{in} are random. We show later that this probability is negligible in samples of reasonable size and approaches zero asymptotically. The following result establishes the existence of a θ maximizing L.

LEMMA 3. Suppose Axioms 1–5 hold. Then Axiom 6 is necessary and sufficient for the existence of a vector θ maximizing L.

Proof: We first show Axiom 6 to be necessary. Suppose L has a maximum at $\hat{\theta}$, but Axiom 6 fails for some $\gamma \neq 0$. Recall that

$$\log P_{in}(\theta) = -\log\left(\sum_{j=1}^{J_n} e^{(z_{jn} - z_{in})\theta}\right).$$

If $S_{in} > 0$, then $(z_{jn} - z_{in})(\hat{\theta} + \gamma) \leqslant (z_{jn} - z_{in})\hat{\theta}$ and $\log P_{in}(\hat{\theta} + \gamma) \geqslant \log P_{in}(\hat{\theta}_n)$. Then $L(\hat{\theta} + \gamma) \geqslant L(\hat{\theta})$. Since L is strictly concave, $L(\hat{\theta} + \gamma/2) > L(\hat{\theta})$, contradicting the definition of $\hat{\theta}$. Hence, Axiom 6 is necessary.

Next suppose that Axiom 6 holds. Define $A = \{\gamma \mid \gamma'\gamma = 1\}$. For each $\gamma \in A$, there exists j, i, n such that $S_{in}(z_{jn} - z_{in})\gamma > 0$. Define

$$(21) \qquad b(\gamma) = \underset{n=1,\ldots,N}{\text{Max}} \ \underset{i,j=1,\ldots,J_n}{\text{Max}} \ S_{in}(z_{jn} - z_{in})\gamma.$$

Then b is a positive continuous function on the compact set A, and has a positive lower bound b^* on this set. Let $|\theta| = (\theta'\theta)^{1/2}$ and define

$$D = \{\theta \mid |\theta| \leqslant [-L(0) + C]/b^*\}.$$

Consider any $\theta \neq 0$, and let $\gamma = \theta/|\theta|$. Then $\gamma \in A$, and there exist indices i, j, n such that $b(\gamma) = S_{in}(z_{jn} - z_{in})\gamma$. From Equation (18),

$$L(\theta) - C \leqslant S_{in} \log P_{in} = -S_{in} \log \sum_{k=1}^{J_n} e^{(z_{kn} - z_{in})\gamma|\theta|}$$

$$\leqslant -S_{in}(z_{jn} - z_{in})\gamma|\theta| = -b(\gamma)|\theta|$$

$$\leqslant -b^*|\theta|.$$

For $\theta \notin D$, $L(\theta) - C \leqslant -b^*|\theta| < L(0) - C$. Hence, L can be maximized on the compact set D, and an optimal θ exists.

The following lemma establishes that Axiom 6 can be tested by solving a quadratic programming problem. This can be done by using a finite computational algorithm such as Lemke's method. In practice it is unnecessary to carry out this computation for sample sizes N exceeding the number of parameters K, as the probability of nonexistence rapidly becomes negligible.

LEMMA 4. Suppose Axioms 1–5 hold. Then Axiom 6 holds if and only if the minimum in the following quadratic programming problem is zero:

$$\operatorname*{Min}_{y,\,\alpha} y'y$$

subject to

(22) $$y' = \sum_{n=1}^{N} \sum_{i,\,j=1}^{J_n} \alpha_{ijn} S_{in}(z_{jn} - z_{in}) \quad \text{and} \quad \alpha_{ijn} \geqslant 1.$$

Proof: Suppose the program has a zero minimum, achieved at some $y' = 0$, but that Axiom 6 fails. Then there exists $\gamma \neq 0$ such that $S_{in}(z_{jn} - z_{in})\gamma \leqslant 0$, with at least one inequality strict by Axiom 5. Then

$$0 = y'\gamma = \sum_{n=1}^{N} \sum_{i,\,j=1}^{J_n} \alpha_{ijn} S_{in}(z_{jn} - z_{in})\gamma < 0,$$

a contradiction. Thus, if the program has a zero minimum, Axiom 6 holds.

Let K denote the convex cone generated by the vectors $S_{in}(z_{jn} - z_{in})$ for $n = 1, \ldots, N$ and $i, j = 1, \ldots, J_n$. If the origin is in the interior of K, then there exist positive scalars α_{ijn} such that $y' = \sum_{n=1}^{N} \alpha_{ijn} S_{in}(z_{jn} - z_{in}) = 0$, and the quadratic program achieves a minimum of zero. If the origin is not in the interior of K, then there exists a separating hyperplane with normal $\gamma \neq 0$ such that $S_{in}(z_{jn} - z_{in})\gamma \leqslant 0$ for all $n = 1, \ldots, N$ and $i, j = 1, \ldots, J_n$. Hence, Axiom 6 fails. This proves the lemma.

Computation of the maximum likelihood estimator can be carried out using a variety of standard programs for unconstrained nonlinear optimization.

Since the likelihood function is strictly concave, any algorithm which converges will attain the maximum. Experience has shown that a standard Newton–Raphson algorithm may converge slowly for this problem; we have found that one efficient procedure is to use Davidon's variable metric method to determine direction of search and a one-dimensional procedure employing a cubic approximation to determine the optimal step size.[8]

The maximum likelihood procedure has proved practical for problems of up to 20 variables and 2000 observations, but is relatively costly for large samples. A quick procedure which can be used for screening models is to make a linear expansion of the gradient of the likelihood function (19) in θ about some initial vector $\bar{\theta}$, and then solve for the value of θ equating this approximate gradient to zero, or

$$
(23) \qquad \tilde{\theta} = \bar{\theta} + \left[\sum_{n=1}^{N} R^n \sum_{j=1}^{J_n} (z_{jn} - \bar{z}_n)' \bar{P}_{jn}(z_{jn} - \bar{z}_n) \right]^{-1}
$$
$$
\times \left[\sum_{n=1}^{N} \sum_{j=1}^{J_n} (z_{jn} - \bar{z}_n)'(S_{jn} - R_n \bar{P}_{jn}) \right],
$$

where $\bar{P}_{jn} = P_{jn}(\bar{\theta})$ and $\bar{z}_n = \sum_{j=1}^{J_n} z_{jn} \bar{P}_{jn}$. Note that $\tilde{\theta}$ is the result of one iteration of a Newton–Raphson procedure for maximizing the likelihood function, and can also be interpreted as the ordinary least squares estimator in the linear model (with R_n observations for each n)

$$
(24) \qquad (\bar{P}_{jn})^{-1/2}[(S_{jn}/R_n) - \bar{P}_{jn}] = (\bar{P}_{jn})^{1/2}(z_{jn} - \bar{z}_n)(\theta - \bar{\theta}) + \varepsilon_{jn}.
$$

Equation (24) is termed the *linear probability model*, and is sometimes taken as a specification of selection probabilities $P_{jn} = E(S_{jn}/R_n)$. The estimator $\tilde{\theta}$ is not a consistent estimate of the true parameter vector θ when the specification of Axioms 1–6 is valid; however, as a practical matter it usually agrees in magnitude and sign with the maximum likelihood estimator provided the terms $|(z_{jn} - \bar{z}_n)(\theta - \bar{\theta})|$ are less than unity. Equation (24) is inappropriate for use in forecasting selection probabilities because the requirement that the forecasts lie in the unit interval is not met.

When the number of repetitions for each trial is large, a method of estimation developed by Berkson (1951) and generalized to the multinomial case by Theil (1969) can be employed. When S_{in}, S_{ln} are large,[9] $\log(S_{in}/S_{ln})$ is a close approximation to the left-hand side of

$$
(25) \qquad \log(P_{in}/P_{ln}) = (z_{in} - z_{ln})\theta,
$$

and an estimate of θ can be obtained by applying ordinary or weighted least

----

[8] The author is indebted to H. Wills and H. Varian for work on the numerical methods and programming of this problem.

[9] A rule-of-thumb is $S_{in} \geqslant 5$.

squares to the model

$$\log(S_{in}/S_{ln}) = (z_{in} - z_{ln})\theta + \varepsilon_{in}, \tag{26}$$

taking into account linear restrictions across equations.[10] This procedure is asymptotically equivalent to maximum likelihood estimation as the S_{in} approach infinity (for appropriate weights in the regression), and is to be preferred to the maximum likelihood procedure on computational grounds. It should be noted, however, that grouping observations that are not exact replications in order to achieve the cell frequencies required for application of the Berkson–Theil method introduces an "errors in variables" component that makes the estimator inconsistent and may make it seriously biased. In such cases the maximum likelihood procedure should be more reliable.

III. Statistical Properties

Maximum likelihood estimation of the conditional logit model can be shown under very general conditions to provide estimators that are asymptotically efficient and normally distributed. Examples suggest that the approximation is reasonably good even in quite small samples. These results can be used to construct approximate large-sample confidence bounds and tests of hypotheses for the parameters.

We have noted that for finite sample sizes, there will be a positive probability that a maximum of the likelihood function cannot be attained. This corresponds to the case where the system of inequalities in Axiom 6 has a nontrivial solution and the sample is "explained" by maximization of this linear combination of the independent variables. We first show that when the sample is in fact generated by probabilities satisfying Axioms 1–5, then the probability that the likelihood function has a maximum approaches one as the sample size increases. We impose the following condition on the data.

AXIOM 7. The numbers of alternatives J_n are uniformly bounded by an integer J_*. The independent variables z_{in} are uniformly bounded by a scalar

---

[10] Some improvement in the statistical properties of the unweighted Berkson–Theil estimator can be obtained by replacing Equation (26) with the regression equation

$$\log\left(\frac{S_{in} + \frac{1}{2}}{S_{ln} + \frac{1}{2}}\right) = (z_{in} - z_{ln})\theta + \varepsilon_{in}. \tag{26a}$$

This modification, suggested by Haldane (1955) for the binomial logit model, makes $E\log[(S_{in} + \frac{1}{2})/(S_{ln} + \frac{1}{2})]$ equal to $\log(P_{in}/P_{ln})$ up to a term of order $1/R_n^2$, rather than of order $1/R_n$, as R_n approaches infinity. This improves the speed of convergence of the estimators to their large-sample values. Minor modifications of the Haldane argument establish its validity in the multinomial case.

M.[11] The limit of the weighted moment matrix, as $\sum_{n=1}^{N} R_n \to +\infty$,

$$(27) \qquad \lim \left(\sum_{n=1}^{N} R_n \right)^{-1} \sum_{n=1}^{N} R_n \sum_{i=1}^{J_n} (z_{in} - \bar{z}_n)' P_{in} (z_{in} - \bar{z}_{in}) = \Omega,$$

exists and is positive-definite.

The last part of this axiom strengthens the full-rank condition assumed earlier, implying that an infinite number of blocks of K trials can be found satisfying Axiom 5.[12] One can expect Axiom 7 to hold provided the data are not multicollinear and do not tend to become explosive or degenerate as the sample size increases. The following results are proved in the Appendix.

LEMMA 5.   Suppose Axioms 1–4 and 7 hold. Then the probability that Axiom 6 holds and the maximum likelihood estimator exists approaches unity as $\sum_{n=1}^{N} R_n$ approaches infinity.

LEMMA 6.   Suppose Axioms 1–4 and 7 hold, θ^0 is the true parameter vector, and $\hat{\theta}^M$ is the maximum likelihood estimator for a sample of size $M = \sum_{n=1}^{N} R_n$. Then $\hat{\theta}^M$ is consistent and asymptotically normal, with

$$(28) \qquad \left(\sum_{n=1}^{N} R_n \right)^{1/2} \Omega^{1/2} (\hat{\theta}^M - \theta^0),$$

tending to a multivariate normal distribution with mean zero and a covariance matrix equal to the identity matrix.

This lemma implies that $\hat{\theta}^M$ tends to be distributed normally with mean θ^0 and covariance matrix $(\sum_{n=1}^{N} R_n)^{-1} \Omega^{-1}$, and that the quadratic form

$$Q(\hat{\theta}^M) \equiv \left(\sum_{n=1}^{N} R_n \right) (\hat{\theta}^M - \theta^0)' \Omega (\hat{\theta}^M - \theta^0)$$

tends to be chi-square distributed with K degrees of freedom. These statistics can be used to carry out large sample tests of hypotheses on θ^0. In particular, diagonal elements of the inverse of the information matrix $(\sum_{n=1}^{N} R_n)^{-1} \Omega^{-1}$ provide estimates of the variances of the estimators.[13] To test a hypothesis

---

[11] I.e., $|z_{in}| \leqslant M$, where the norm $|A|$ of any array A is the sum of the absolute values of its elements.

[12] Otherwise, all but a finite number of vectors $z_{in} - \bar{z}_n$ can be written as linear combinations of less than K linearly independent vectors. Then, Ω must also have this property, contradicting the hypothesis that it is nonsingular.

[13] Some improvement in the speed of convergence can be attained by multiplying these estimates by a correction factor for degrees of freedom,

$$\frac{\sum_{n=1}^{N} R_n (J_n - 1)}{\sum_{n=1}^{N} R_n (J_n - 1) - K}.$$

that the true parameter vector θ^0 lies in a $(K-K_1)$ dimensional manifold, calculate the maximum likelihood estimator $\hat{\theta}^H$ under the null hypothesis and the unconstrained maximum likelihood estimator $\hat{\theta}$. Then the statistic

$$(29) \quad -2[L(\hat{\theta}^H)-L(\hat{\theta})] = (\hat{\theta}^H-\hat{\theta})' \sum_{n=1}^{N} R_n \sum_{i=1}^{J_n} (z_{in}-\bar{z}_n)' P_{in}(z_{in}-\bar{z}_n)(\hat{\theta}^H-\hat{\theta}),$$

with P_{in} evaluated at $\hat{\theta}$, is distributed approximately chi-square with K_1 degrees of freedom. If the null hypothesis is that θ^0 is zero, or that it is zero except for pure alternative effects, then this statistic provides a test of the significance of an estimation equation, indicating respectively the "mean square error" explained or the "variance" explained. Noting that the extreme case is $L(\hat{\theta}) \approx 0$, we can define a coefficient of determination that is analogous to the multiple-correlation coefficient in the linear statistical model,

$$(30) \qquad\qquad\qquad \rho^2 = 1 - \frac{L(\hat{\theta})}{L(\hat{\theta}^H)}.$$

If $\hat{\theta}^H$ is zero, or if $\hat{\theta}^H$ is zero except for pure alternative effects and the model contains such effects, then ρ^2 lies in the unit interval. If, in the latter case, the model has no pure alternative effects, it is possible for ρ^2 to be negative.

A second measure of goodness of fit is based on deviations of observed from fitted relative frequencies. Define the weighted residuals

$$(31) \qquad\qquad\qquad D_{in} = \frac{S_{in} - R_n P_{in}}{(R_n P_{in})^{1/2}},$$

for $i = 1, \ldots, J_n$ and $n = 1, \ldots, N$, where P_{in} is evaluated at the maximum likelihood estimate. These residuals satisfy the first-order conditions for maximization of the likelihood function,

$$(32) \qquad\qquad \sum_{n=1}^{N} (r_n)^{1/2} \sum_{i=1}^{J_n} D_{in}(P_{in})^{1/2}(z_{in}-\bar{z}_n) = 0,$$

where

$$(33) \qquad\qquad\qquad r_n = \frac{R_n}{\sum_{m=1}^{N} R_m},$$

and the conditions

$$(34) \qquad\qquad\qquad \sum_{i=1}^{J_n} (P_{in})^{1/2} D_{in} = 0,$$

for $n = 1, \ldots, N$, a total of $N+K$ restrictions. Now suppose $\sum_{n=1}^{N} R_n$ approaches infinity, with each r_n approaching a limit. We show in the Appendix that the

D_{in} are distributed asymptotically with mean zero and covariances

$$\Lambda_{in,jm} \equiv ED_{in}D_{jm} = \delta_{nm}[\delta_{ij} - (P_{in}^0 P_{jn}^0)^{1/2}]$$

(35)
$$- (r_m r_n P_{in}^0 P_{jm}^0)^{1/2}(z_{in} - \bar{z}_n)\Omega^{-1}(z_{jm} - \bar{z}_m).$$

Consider the case in which N remains finite and the R_n approach infinity. Then Λ is an idempotent matrix of rank $N^* = \sum_{n=1}^{N} J_n - N - K$, and the asymptotic distribution of the D_{in} is multivariate normal. Hence,

(36)
$$G = \sum_{n=1}^{N} \sum_{i=1}^{J_n} D_{in}^2$$

has an asymptotic chi-square distribution with N^* degrees of freedom.[14] The statistics D_{in} and G can be used to carry out large-sample tests of the model specification. For example, regression of the D_{in} on potential independent variables provides evidence on the validity of their exclusion from the model. A test of the significance of G provides evidence on the validity of the logit specification of the selection probabilities and the absence of "alternative set" effects. Further, one can define an analog of the multiple-correlation coefficient,

(37)
$$R^2 = 1 - G/G^H,$$

where G is given by Equation (36) and G^H is given by the same equation when the numerators of the residuals are evaluated under the hypothesis that the parameter vector is zero, or is zero except for pure alternative choice effects.

In evaluating the results of regressions of the D_{in} on potential independent variables, one should adjust for the nonindependence and heteroskedasticity of the D_{in}. This can be achieved in part by using the linearly transformed residuals

(38)
$$Y_{in} = D_{in} - \frac{D_{1n}(P_{in})^{1/2}[1 - (P_{1n})^{1/2}]}{1 - P_{1n}},$$

defined for $i = 2, ..., J_n$ and $n = 1, ..., N$. The Y_{in} are asymptotically multivariate normal with mean zero and covariances

(39)
$$\Gamma_{in,jm} \equiv EY_{in}Y_{jm} = \delta_{nm}\delta_{ij} - q'_{in}q_{jm},$$

[14] Treating G as a function of θ and minimizing it at a value $\tilde{\theta}$ provides a *minimum chi-square* estimator of the parameter vector. The first-order conditions for this minimization coincide with Equation (32) except for a term, reflecting the effect of changing θ on the weights in the denominator of Equation (31), which has probability limit zero when the $R_n \to +\infty$. Thus, the maximum likelihood and minimum chi-square estimators are asymptotically equivalent under these limiting conditions. On the other hand, the minimum chi-square procedure is not consistent under the limiting conditions that $N \to +\infty$ and R_n remain finite.

where

$$(40) \qquad q'_{in} = (r_n P^0_{in})^{1/2} \left((z_{in} - \bar{z}_n) + \frac{P^0_{1n} - (P^0_{1n})^{1/2}}{1 - P^0_{1n}} (z_{1n} - \bar{z}_n) \right) \Omega^{-1/2}.$$

The matrix Γ is idempotent of rank N^*. When the r_n are small, the matrix Γ is nearly diagonal, and the regression of any subset of N^* of the Y_{in} on potential independent variables can, as a good approximation, be treated as independent and homoskedastic with unit variance.

We next consider the case in which N approaches infinity and the limiting values of the r_n are zero. Then, the residuals D_{in} have an asymptotic multinomial distribution with mean zero and covariances given by Equation (35), with the second term in this expression vanishing. The D_{in} and the transformed residuals Y_{in} defined in Equation (38) are independent across n, and the Y_{in} have zero mean, unit variance, and zero covariances. Suppose integers N_m satisfy $\sum_{m=1}^{M} N_m = N$ and $N_m \to +\infty$. Then the statistics

$$(41) \qquad Y^m = \frac{\sum_{n=N_m'+1}^{N_m'+1} \sum_{j=2}^{J_n} Y_{jn}}{\left(\sum_{n=N_m'+1}^{N_m'+1} J_n - N_m \right)^{1/2}},$$

where $N_m' = N_1 + \cdots + N_{m-1}$, are asymptotically independent standard normal, and can be used to test the specification of the absence of alternative set effects. When the R_n remain small, the distributions of the D_{in} and Y_{in} depart substantially from asymptotic normality. The statistics G and R^2 defined in Equations (36) and (37) remain useful summary measures, although the robustness of the asymptotic distributions obtained in the previous case has not been investigated. Since the Y_{in} satisfy the Gauss–Markov assumptions when the model is specified correctly, the usual asymptotic theory for the linear statistical model can be applied to test the validity of excluding potential independent variables.

The small sample properties of the maximum likelihood estimator of the conditional logit model are unknown except for a few special cases. Monte Carlo studies of related models suggest that maximum likelihood, minimum chi-square, and Berkson–Theil estimators are all reasonably well behaved in small samples, even when the number of repetitions is small.[15] We next consider several simple examples in which the maximum likelihood estimator can be calculated analytically. These examples suggest that the maximum likelihood estimator is well behaved in samples of sizes likely to be encountered in applications, 50 and greater, but may be inferior to the linear probability model estimator in very small samples provided the range of the data is not too large.

[15] Berkson (1955), Gart and Zweifel (1967), Gilbert (1968), and Talvitie (1972).

TABLE 1

SAMPLING PROPERTIES OF THE MAXIMUM LIKELIHOOD ESTIMATOR: EXAMPLE 1

Parameter value (θ_1)	Sample size	Probability of existence of maximum likelihood estimator	Conditional expectation of maximum likelihood estimator	Percent bias	Conditional variance of maximum likelihood estimator	Calculated variance of maximum likelihood estimator	Percent bias	Linear probability model estimator	Percent bias
0.01	5	0.93748	0.00828	−17.2	0.75018	1.21529	62.0	0.01000	a
	10	0.99814	0.01103	10.3	0.49988	0.50943	1.9	0.01000	a
	20	1.0	0.01057	5.7	0.22422	0.22314	−0.5	0.01000	a
	30	1.0	0.01036	3.6	0.14334	0.14308	a	0.01000	a
	50	1.0	0.01021	2.1	0.08343	0.08338	a	0.01000	a
	75	1.0	0.01014	1.4	0.05482	0.05481	a	0.01000	a
	100	1.0	0.01010	1.0	0.04083	0.04082	a	0.01000	a
0.1	5	0.93594	0.08272	−17.3	0.74726	1.21643	67.0	0.09992	−0.1
	10	0.99782	0.11023	10.2	0.50044	0.51128	2.2	0.09992	−0.1
	20	1.0	0.10575	5.8	0.22503	0.22387	−0.5	0.09992	−0.1
	30	1.0	0.10364	3.6	0.14379	0.14349	a	0.09992	−0.1
	50	1.0	0.10211	2.1	0.08366	0.08360	a	0.09992	−0.1
	75	1.0	0.10138	1.4	0.05497	0.05497	a	0.09992	−0.1
	100	1.0	0.10103	1.0	0.04093	0.04093	a	0.09992	−0.1
0.5	5	0.89888	0.40054	−20.0	0.68164	1.24250	83.0	0.48984	−2.0
	10	0.99121	0.54433	8.9	0.50916	0.55472	8.9	0.48984	−2.0
	20	0.99992	0.53020	6.0	0.24536	0.24215	−1.3	0.48984	−2.0
	30	1.0	0.51912	3.8	0.15515	0.15391	−0.8	0.48984	−2.0
	50	1.0	0.51101	2.2	0.08955	0.08922	a	0.48984	−2.0
	75	1.0	0.50720	1.4	0.05865	0.05852	a	0.48984	−2.0
	100	1.0	0.50535	1.1	0.04361	0.04354	a	0.48984	−2.0

1.0	5	0.78978	0.73234	−26.8	0.52531	1.30757	148.0	0.92423	−7.6
	10	0.95639	1.04040	4.0	0.49435	0.67376	36.5	0.92423	−7.6
	20	0.99810	1.06643	6.6	0.30950	0.30826	−0.4	0.92423	−7.6
	30	0.99992	1.04437	4.4	0.19662	0.19146	−2.6	0.92423	−7.6
	50	1.0	1.02525	2.5	0.11041	0.10881	−1.5	0.92423	−7.6
	75	1.0	1.01641	1.6	0.07145	0.07083	−0.8	0.92423	−7.6
	100	1.0	1.01216	1.2	0.05285	0.05252	−0.6	0.92423	−7.6
2.0	5	0.46885	1.12824	−44.5	0.23655	1.44030	510.0	1.5232	−23.8
	10	0.71897	1.71841	−14.1	0.30827	0.95333	209.0	1.5232	−23.8
	20	0.92102	2.04023	2.0	0.37726	0.60123	59.4	1.5232	−23.8
	30	0.97780	2.09760	4.9	0.35233	0.41411	17.6	1.5232	−23.8
	50	0.99825	2.08151	4.0	0.23948	0.23167	−3.3	1.5232	−23.8
	75	0.99993	2.05384	2.2	0.15052	0.14352	−4.7	1.5232	−23.8
	100	1.0	2.03925	2.0	0.10754	0.10383	−3.5	1.5232	−23.8
3.0	5	0.21568	1.28953	−57.1	0.09262	1.51321	1655.0	1.8103	−39.7
	10	0.38484	2.01670	−32.8	0.13505	1.11987	830.0	1.8103	−39.7
	20	0.62158	2.59216	−13.6	0.21698	0.88161	307.0	1.8103	−39.7
	30	0.76721	2.84486	−5.2	0.27726	0.74378	162.0	1.8103	−39.7
	50	0.91191	3.04643	1.5	0.33452	0.54907	64.4	1.8103	−39.7
	75	0.97385	3.10492	3.5	0.32443	0.38745	19.4	1.8103	−39.7
	100	0.99224	3.10337	3.4	0.27741	0.28459	2.5	1.8103	−39.7

[a] Negligible.

Example 1. Suppose N observations are taken of a binary choice with a selection probability $P_1 = 1/(1+e^{-\theta_1})$ for the first alternative, and suppose this alternative is chosen S times. The maximum likelihood estimator exists if $0 < S < N$, and equals $\hat{\theta}_1 = \log[S/(N-S)]$. Table 1 gives the actual expectation and variance of $\hat{\theta}_1$, conditioned on existence, and the large sample variance calculated from the information matrix. The last columns give the linear probability model approximation (23) to the logit model from starting value zero. For sample sizes exceeding 20, the maximum likelihood estimator and its calculated variance have expectations that are within 10% of true values except for extreme selection probabilities (e.g., $\theta_1 = 2.0$ yields $P_1 = 0.88$). The linear probability model approximation is quite accurate for small parameter values, even for small sample sizes. The bias is severe however for extreme selection probabilities, and is independent of sample size. The probability of existence of the maximum likelihood estimator rises rapidly with sample size, even for extreme selection probabilities.

Example 2. Suppose $N = 2R$ observations are taken of a binary choice with selection probabilities $P_{1n} = 1/(1+e^{-\theta_1 - \theta_2 x_n})$, where $x_n = 0$ for $n = 1, ..., R$ and $x_n = 1$ for $n = R+1, ..., N$. Suppose the first alternative is chosen S_1 times in the first R observations and S_2 times in the second R observations. The maximum likelihood estimator exists if $0 < S_1 < R$ and $0 < S_2 < R$, and equals $\hat{\theta}_1 = \log[S_1/(R-S_1)]$ and $\hat{\theta}_2 = \log[S_2/(R-S_2)] - \log[S_1/(R-S_1)]$. Table 2 gives the conditional expectations of these estimators and the expectations of the variances calculated from the information matrix for selected parameter values. The pattern of the biases generally conforms to that of the previous example. For a sample size of 10, the estimator and its calculated variance are substantially biased, the former downward and the latter upward. As sample size increases, the bias in the estimator swings positive, but never more than 10% and then approaches zero. The calculated variances show similar behavior with reversed sign, their bias going from positive to negative as sample size increases and then approaching zero. As the parameter values and selection probabilities become more extreme, there is an increase in the sample size at which the maximum positive bias in the estimator occurs. The linear probability model approximation provides an accurate estimator for small sample sizes and parameter values, and indicates correctly signs and orders of magnitude of parameters even for extreme values, but with substantial biases. In samples of size 100 or 200 the biases and probabilities of non-existence of the maximum likelihood estimator are acceptably small even for extreme selection probabilities.

One must be cautious in generalizing too far the conclusions drawn from these examples. In particular, we have not explored the behavior of the estimators in samples in which the observations are generated by mixtures of

TABLE 2

Sampling Properties of the Maximum Likelihood Estimator: Example 2

	Sample size					
	10	20	40	80	140	200
First parameter (all cases)						
True value	0.10000	0.10000	0.10000	0.10000	0.10000	0.10000
Expect. of M.L. estimate	0.08272	0.11023	0.10575	0.10267	0.10148	0.10103
Per cent bias of est.	−17.28364	10.22808	5.74896	2.66732	1.48170	1.02609
True variance of M.L. est.	0.74726	0.50044	0.22503	0.10576	0.05902	0.04094
Calc. variance of M.L. est.	0.80200	0.40100	0.20050	0.10025	0.05729	0.04010
Per cent bias of var. est.	7.32580	−19.87098	−10.90107	−5.21060	−2.93154	−2.04035
Linear prob. model est.	0.09992	0.09992	0.09992	0.09992	0.09992	0.09992
Per cent bias of linear est.	−0.08325	−0.08325	−0.08325	−0.08325	−0.08325	−0.08325
Second parameter						
True value	−0.50000	−0.50000	−0.50000	−0.50000	−0.50000	−0.50000
Expect. of M.L. estimate	−0.40695	−0.54780	−0.52948	−0.51365	−0.50757	−0.50524
Per cent bias of est.	−18.60931	9.56094	5.89654	2.72972	1.51402	1.04790
True variance of M.L. est.	1.45241	1.00740	0.46265	0.21631	0.12049	0.08353
Calc. variance of M.L. ext.	1.63443	0.81722	0.40861	0.20430	0.11675	0.08172
Per cent bias of var. est.	12.53225	−18.87888	−11.68067	−5.54934	−3.11136	−2.16302
Linear prob. model est.	−0.49467	−0.49467	−0.49467	−0.49467	−0.49467	−0.49467
Per cent bias of linear est.	−1.06652	−1.06652	−1.06652	−1.06652	−1.06652	−1.06652
Prob. of existence of M.L. est.	0.85421	0.99181	0.99996	1.00000	1.00000	1.00000
True value	0.10000	0.10000	0.10000	0.10000	0.10000	0.10000
Expect. of M.L. estimate	0.08204	0.10990	0.10582	0.10270	0.10150	0.10104
Per cent bias of est.	−17.96158	9.90456	5.82398	2.69820	1.49773	1.03691
True variance of M.L. est.	1.48579	1.00250	0.45254	0.21246	0.11852	0.08220
Calc. variance of M.L. ext.	1.61003	0.80501	0.40251	0.20125	0.11500	0.08050
Per cent bias of var. est.	8.36201	−19.69933	−11.05610	−5.27618	−2.96650	−2.06423
Linear prob. model est.	0.09942	0.09942	0.09942	0.09942	0.09942	0.09942
Per cent bias of linear est.	−0.58076	−0.58076	−0.58076	−0.58076	−0.58076	−0.58076
Prob. of existence of M.L. est.	0.87160	0.99496	0.99999	1.00000	1.00000	1.00000

TABLE 2—continued

	Sample size					
	10	20	40	80	140	200
True value	1.00000	1.00000	1.00000	1.00000	1.00000	1.00000
Expect. of M.L. estimate	0.70474	1.01873	1.06783	1.03421	1.01864	1.01282
Per cent bias of est.	−29.52618	1.87276	6.78330	3.42109	1.86412	1.28241
True variance of M.L. est.	1.23857	0.98412	0.55049	0.25613	0.14019	0.09663
Calc. variance of M.L. ext.	1.86941	0.93470	0.46735	0.23368	0.13353	0.09347
Per cent bias of var. est.	50.93327	−5.02084	−15.10210	−8.76667	−4.75197	−3.26642
Linear prob. model est.	0.90112	0.90112	0.90112	0.90112	0.90112	0.90112
Per cent bias of linear est.	−9.88763	−9.88763	−9.88763	−9.88763	−9.88763	−9.88763
Prob. of existence of M.L. est.	0.71254	0.94144	0.99680	0.99999	1.00000	1.00000
First parameter (all cases)						
True value	1.00000	1.00000	1.00000	1.00000	1.00000	1.00000
Expect. of M.L. estimate	0.73234	1.04040	1.06643	1.03222	1.01764	1.01216
Per cent bias of est.	−26.76589	4.04022	6.64324	3.22242	1.76425	1.21578
True variance of M.L. est.	0.52531	0.49435	0.30950	0.14142	0.07686	0.05285
Calc. variance of M.L. est.	1.01723	0.50862	0.25431	0.12715	0.07266	0.05086
Per cent bias of var. est.	93.64346	2.88570	−17.83370	−10.08782	−5.46810	−3.76027
Linear prob. model est.	0.92423	0.92423	0.92423	0.92423	0.92423	0.92423
Per cent bias of linear est.	−7.57657	−7.57657	−7.57657	−7.57657	−7.57657	−7.57657
Second parameter						
True value	−0.50000	−0.50000	−0.50000	−0.50000	−0.50000	−0.50000
Expect. of M.L. estimate	−0.33180	−0.49607	−0.53624	−0.51826	−0.50991	−0.50681
Per cent bias of est.	−33.64020	−0.78652	7.24721	3.65173	1.98177	1.36160
True variance of M.L. est.	1.20695	1.00351	0.55487	0.25493	0.13986	0.09646
Calc. variance of M.L. ext.	1.86828	0.93414	0.46707	0.23354	0.13345	0.09341
Per cent bias of var. est.	54.79349	−6.91277	−15.82285	−8.39383	−4.58190	−3.15818
Linear prob. model est.	−0.43440	−0.43440	−0.43440	−0.43440	−0.43440	−0.43440
Per cent bias of linear est.	−13.12060	−13.12060	−13.12060	−13.13060	−13.12060	−13.12060
Prob. of existence of M.L. est.	0.70992	0.94799	0.99802	1.00000	1.00000	1.00000

True value	0.10000	0.10000	0.10000	0.10000	0.10000	0.10000
Expect. of M.L. estimate	0.05511	0.08855	0.10715	0.10465	0.10248	0.10169
Per cent bias of est.	−44.88654	−11.44656	7.14974	4.65396	2.48035	1.69241
True variance of M.L. est.	1.01662	0.97802	0.63496	0.29179	0.15804	0.10854
Calc. variance of M.L. ext.	2.08464	1.04232	0.52116	0.26058	0.14890	0.10423
Per cent. bias of var. est.	105.05601	6.57426	−17.92244	−10.69591	−5.78006	−3.96928
Linear prob. model est.	0.07681	0.07681	0.07681	0.07681	0.07681	0.07681
Per cent bias of linear est.	−23.19389	−23.19389	−23.19389	−23.19389	−23.19389	−23.19389
Prob. of existence of M.L. est.	0.60127	0.90235	0.99491	0.99999	1.00000	1.00000

True value	1.00000	1.00000	1.00000	1.00000	1.00000	1.00000
Expect. of M.L. estimate	0.39590	0.67801	0.97380	1.06299	1.04043	1.02706
Per cent bias of est.	−60.40966	−12.19939	−2.62020	6.29931	4.04250	2.70572
True variance of M.L. est.	0.76186	0.80262	0.68676	0.43638	0.24022	0.16047
Calc. variance of M.L. ext.	2.92211	1.46106	0.73053	0.36526	0.20872	0.14611
Per cent bias of var. est.	283.54796	82.03495	6.37315	−16.29632	−13.11233	−8.94926
Linear prob. model est.	0.59895	0.59895	0.59895	0.59895	0.59895	0.59895
Per cent bias of linear est.	−40.10460	−40.10460	−40.10460	−40.10460	−40.10460	−40.10460
Prob. of existence of M.L. est.	0.37108	0.68762	0.91927	0.99376	0.99986	1.00000

extreme and nonextreme selection probabilities. On the other hand, we anticipate that the qualitative structure of biases will be unchanged by the addition of independent variables or of multiple-choice alternatives, as the estimator is analogous to a linear statistical estimator except for the nonlinear dependence of the selection probabilities on the parameters.

IV. An Empirical Application

The theory of qualitative choice behavior outlined above has been applied to several areas of consumer choice. The author (1968) has investigated the criteria employed by a state highway department in selecting urban freeway routes. The determinants of college choice have been studied by Professor Miller and Professor Radner (1970), and the results have been used to forecast the effects of changing educational policy on college enrollment. Professor Boskin (1972) has applied the model to the problem of occupational choice. Studies in progress are investigating urban trip generation, distribution, and modal choice; labor force participation and job search decisions; housing location and type; recidivism; child-bearing decisions and the implications of population control policy; choice of consumer durables; and rural-urban migration decisions. To illustrate the method, we reproduce here selected results on shopping trip mode and destination decisions obtained in a study of travel demand models by T. Domencich and D. McFadden (1972).[16]

The objective of this study is to develop disaggregated, policy-oriented, behavioral models of urban trip generation, distribution, and mode. The behavioral unit studied is the individual trip-maker, faced with decisions on whether to take a trip, mode, and destination. The empirical analysis is based on a household survey in Pittsburgh conducted by the Southwestern Pennsylvania Regional Planning Commission in 1967, supplemented with time and cost data collected by the study authors. A detailed description of the sample frame and variables collected is given in the study.

The analysis of shopping travel behavior is separated into three decisions: (1) choice of mode for trips actually made at the observed time and to the observed destination; (2) choice of destination for trips made at an observed time by preferred mode; and (3) choice of whether or not to make a trip, given a preferred time, mode, and destination.[17] The results of each analysis are summarized in turn.

---

[16] The results below are reproduced with the permission of Charles River Associates, Inc.

[17] The separation of these decisions is justified in the study by postulating a "tree" utility structure; we shall not repeat the argument here.

Shopping choice of mode

Choice between public transit and auto mode is examined for a sample of 140 individual shopping trips. For each observation, walk access to transit is available. The sample is drawn from a southern suburban corridor of Pittsburgh and a central city corridor running from downtown to the east. A number of alternative models were fitted; those giving the most satisfactory results in terms of fitting the base data are described in Table 3. All coefficients in these models are of the expected sign. The coefficients of transit walk time, auto in-vehicle less transit station-to-station time, and auto operating costs less transit fares imply a value of walk time of $5.46 per hour and a value of in-vehicle time of $0.95 per hour in Model 1. These values are in close accord

TABLE 3

CONDITIONAL LOGIT MODEL OF SHOPPING MODE CHOICE;
DEPENDENT VARIABLE EQUALS THE LOG ODDS OF CHOICE OF AUTO MODE;
BINARY LOGIT MAXIMUM LIKELIHOOD ESTIMATES; STANDARD ERRORS IN PARENTHESES

Independent variable	Model 1	Model 2	Model 3	Model 4
Pure auto mode preference effect (constant)[a]	−6.77 (1.66)	−6.20 (2.10)	−6.65 (1.54)	−6.37 (1.82)
Transit walk time (minutes)	0.374 (0.328)	0.398 (0.410)	0.30 (0.351)	0.274 (0.612)
Transit wait plus transfer time (minutes)	—	—	0.0647 (0.0403)	—
Transit station-to-station time (minutes)	—	—	—	0.0532 (0.0455)
Auto in-vehicle time (minutes)	—	—	—	−0.0486 (0.0956)
Auto in-vehicle time less transit station-to-station time (minutes)	−0.0654 (0.0320)	−0.0636 (0.0398)	—	—
Auto in-vehicle time less transit line-haul time (minutes)	—	—	−0.0287 (0.0715)	—
Auto operating cost less transit fares (dollars)	−4.11 (1.67)	−4.66 (2.06)	−4.10 (2.13)	−4.06 (1.74)
Ratio of number of autos to number of workers in the household	2.24 (1.11)	2.26 (1.14)	2.01 (1.04)	1.89 (0.76)
Race of respondent (0 if white, 1 if non-white)	—	−2.18 (1.26)	—	—
Occupation of head of household (0 if blue-collar, 1 if white collar)	—	−1.53 (1.10)	—	—

[a] Because of the sample selection procedure and the presence of the last three variables giving socioeconomic-auto mode interaction effects, this constant cannot be interpreted as a "transit" bias that would be replicated in a random sample of the population.

with shopping trip value of time studies. Thus, the estimates seem quite stable despite the relatively large standard errors. The models provide excellent fits of the base-line data; in Model 1, the probability of selecting the actual mode is greater than one-half for 133 of the 140 observations, and greater than 0.9 for 116 of the 140 observations.

Shopping choice of destination

The choice of shopping destination is analyzed for 63 auto-mode trips starting from the southern suburban corridor. The possible alternative destinations for each observation are selected by dividing the city into zones and choosing all destination zones to which there is a trip in the sample from the origin zone. The number of alternatives varies from three to five in this sample.

This model is estimated using only three explanatory variables, an inclusive index of the "price" of a trip in terms of time and cost, an index of the "attractiveness" of each shopping destination, and an interaction of the inclusive price index and a socioeconomic variable, the number of preschool children. The inclusive price is defined from the shopping mode choice Model 1 to be

[Inclusive price] = 0.0654[Auto in-vehicle time] + 4.11[Auto operating cost].

The measure of destination attractiveness is taken to be the retail employment in the zone as a percentage of total retail employment in the region. Because the alternative destinations are unranked and vary from one observation to the next, the explanatory variables enter generically. In particular, it is assumed that there are no "specific destination" effects. The results of the estimation are given in Table 4. The two independent variables above are both found to be

TABLE 4

Conditional Logit Model of Shopping Destination Choice;
Dependent Variable Equals the Log Odds That One Destination
Zone is Chosen over a Second;
Multinomial Logit Maximum Likelihood Estimates;
Standard Errors in Parentheses

Independent variable	Model 5	Model 6
Inclusive price of trip (weighted time and cost using Model 1 weights)	−1.06 (0.28)	−0.602 (0.159)
Index of attractiveness of destination	0.844 (0.227)	0.832 (0.224)
Interaction effect equals the inclusive price of trip times the number of preschool children	—	−0.521 (0.343)

highly significant. Model 6 yields calculated selection probabilities which are maximum for the actual destination in 29 cases, as opposed to a match for 16 cases which would be expected by chance.

Shopping trip frequency

The decision of whether to take a shopping trip on a given day is analyzed for a sample of 80 households in the southern suburban corridor, of whom 59 recorded a shopping trip on the survey day. An inclusive price of a trip for nontrip takers is calculated by assuming that the distribution of destination preferences is that determined in Model 6, and that utility has a separable form implying this distribution is independent of the distribution of tastes for taking auto trips. The independent variables in the model are the preference-distribution-weighted inclusive price, the measure of attractiveness of shopping zone used above, similarly weighted, and a household-income shopping trip

TABLE 5

CONDITIONAL LOGIT MODEL OF SHOPPING TRIP FREQUENCY;
DEPENDENT VARIABLE EQUALS THE LOG ODDS OF MAKING A
SHOPPING TRIP ON SAMPLED DAY;
BINOMIAL LOGIT MAXIMUM LIKELIHOOD ESTIMATES;
STANDARD ERRORS IN PARENTHESES

Independent variable	Model 7	Model 8
Inclusive price of trip (weighted time and cost using Model 6 weights)	−1.72 (0.54)	−2.25 (0.68)
Index of attractiveness of destination	3.90 (1.08)	2.85 (1.19)
Family income	—	−0.199 (0.195)

interaction variable. The estimates are given in Table 5. Model 7 predicts the actual decision with probability 0.5 or better for 60 of the 80 observations.

The models above of shopping mode, destination, and frequency decisions can be combined with distributions of the independent variables in an urban area to produce trip generation and distribution tables by mode.[18] These

---

[18] Such tables could also be generated by aggregating over individuals for a random sample of the population, a procedure that requires a smaller sample than that necessary to obtain accurate cell frequencies for a detailed classification of multiple-independent variables. In particular, the sample used to calibrate the models may be utilized to produce trip tables. On the other hand, when samples of sufficient size are available to obtain cell frequencies, it may be possible to calibrate the model using the Berkson–Theil estimation procedure.

tables are functions of policy variables such as transit fares and wait times, and can be recalculated to forecast the effects of policy changes on the transportation system. Because the parameters are estimated from data at the level of the individual decision, they do not suffer from the "fallacy of composition" that could occur in attempting to infer response elasticities from data on behavior of heterogeneous groups. Thus, this modeling approach has the potential of providing accurate forecasts of the response of shopping travel demand to policy variables, in a framework that exploits the common thread of utility maximization and taste distribution in a variety of choice situations.

The empirical study summarized above represents a typical application of the theory of qualitative choice behavior of populations of consumers, with the conditional logit specification of the distribution of tastes. For applications in which the independence of irrelevant alternatives is plausible, this statistical procedure provides an analog for qualitative dependent variables of the conventional linear statistical model.

Appendix: Proofs of Statistical Properties

This section outlines proofs of Lemmas 5 and 6, and the properties of statistics based on weighted residuals.

LEMMA 5. Suppose Axioms 1–4 and 7 hold. Then the probability that the maximum likelihood estimator exists approaches unity as $\sum_{n=1}^{N} R_n$ approaches infinity.

Proof: As noted in the text, Axiom 7 implies that Axiom 5 holds when $\sum_{n=1}^{N} R_n$ is large. We next show that Axiom 7 implies a second linear independence condition. Let m be a serial index of trials and repetition; e.g., m identifies the r_mth repetition of trial n_m. We shall show that there exists an infinite subset M of the indices m, and integers i_m, j_m satisfying $1 \leqslant i_m$, $j_m \leqslant J_{n_m}$ such that each sequence of K successive vectors $z_{i_m n_m} - z_{j_m n_m}$ for $m \in M$ are linearly independent. We proceed by induction. Axiom 7 implies there is some m, i, j such that $z_{i n_m} - z_{j n_m} \neq 0$; set $M_1 = \{m\}$, $i_1 = i$, and $j_1 = j$. Suppose that we have constructed a set M_{l-1} containing $l-1$ indices that satisfy the required property. Suppose there does not exist an index m_l such that $M_l = M_{l-1} \cup \{m_l\}$ has the desired property. Then, for all $m > m_{l-1}$ and $1 \leqslant i, j \leqslant J_{n_m}$, the vector $z_{i n_m} - z_{j n_m}$ can be written as a linear combination of vectors $z_{i_p n_p} - z_{j_p n_p}$ for the last $K-1$ or fewer elements p of M_{l-1}. But then $z_{i n_m} - \bar{z}_{n_m} = \sum_{j=1}^{J_{n_m}} P_{j n_m} (z_{i n_m} - z_{j n_m})$ also has this property, implying that the limiting matrix Ω in Axiom 7 is singular, for a contradiction. Hence, by induction, the set $M = \bigcup_{l=1}^{\infty} M_l$ has the desired property.

Partition the set M into successive subsets $M^1, M^2, \ldots$, each containing K

elements. Let W^q denote the matrix with rows $z_{i_m n_m} - z_{j_m n_m}$ for $m \in M^q$. Then, W^q is nonsingular and the linear transformation $(W^{q-1})(W^q)^{-1}$ is continuous. Hence, for even q one can define a strictly positive vector a^{q-1} and a vector a^q with no zero elements such that $a^q W^q = a^{q-1} W^{q-1}$.

For q even, consider the event in which alternative i_m is chosen for $m \in M^{q-1}$; alternative i_m is chosen for $m \in M^q$ if $a_m{}^q$ is negative; and alternative j_m is chosen for $m \in M^q$ if $a_m{}^q$ is positive. Suppose this event occurs, but Axiom 6 fails, and let $\gamma \neq 0$ be such that $S_{in}(z_{jn} - z_{in}) \gamma \leqslant 0$ for all i, j, n. Then, $W^{q-1}\gamma$ is a nonnegative vector. Since W^{q-1} is nonsingular, it has at least one component positive. Hence, $a^q W^q \gamma = a^{q-1} W^{q-1} \gamma > 0$. But z^q and $W^q \gamma$ have opposite signs in each component, contradicting the last inequality. Therefore, when this event occurs, Axiom 6 holds and the maximum likelihood estimator exists.

The selection probabilities are bounded below by

$$(42) \qquad P_{in} \geqslant 1/J_* e^{2M|\theta|} \equiv P_* > 0,$$

where J_* and M are the bounds given by Axiom 7. Hence, the probability that the event above occurs for an even q is at least P_*^{2K}, and the probability that this event occurs for some even $q \leqslant 2q'$ is at least $1 - (1 - P_*^{2K})^{q'}$. This last probability approaches unity as $q' \to +\infty$, proving the lemma.

LEMMA 6.   Suppose Axioms 1–4 and 7 hold, θ^0 is the true parameter vector and $\hat{\theta}^m$ is the maximum likelihood estimator for a sample of size $m = \sum_{n=1}^{N} R_n$. Then $\hat{\theta}^m$ is consistent and asymptotically normal as $m \to +\infty$, with

$$\sqrt{m}\, \Omega^{1/2} (\hat{\theta}^m - \theta^0),$$

tending to a multivariate normal distribution with mean zero and identity covariance matrix.

Proof: We shall first establish that $\hat{\theta}^m$ is a consistent estimator of θ^0. From Axiom 7, $|z_{in}| \leqslant M$ for a positive scalar M. Differentiation of Equation (16) yields the bounds

$$\left| \frac{\partial \log P_{in}}{\partial \theta} \right| \leqslant 2M,$$

$$(43) \qquad \left| \frac{\partial^2 \log P_{in}}{\partial \theta\, \partial \theta'} \right| \leqslant 4M^2,$$

$$\left| \frac{\partial^3 \log P_{in}}{\partial \theta\, \partial \theta'\, \partial \theta_k} \right| \leqslant 8M^3,$$

uniform in θ.

Let m be a serial index of trials and repetitions, and let S_{im} equal unity if alternative i is chosen at this observation and zero otherwise, for $1 \leqslant i \leqslant J_{n_m}$. Define a sequence of independent random variables

$$(44) \qquad \lambda^m(\theta) = \sum_{i=1}^{J_{n_m}} S_{im} \log P_{in}(\theta).$$

Then

$$(45) \qquad L^q(\theta) = C_q + \sum_{m=1}^{q} \lambda^m(\theta),$$

with C_q a constant independent of θ, is the log likelihood function. From Equation (43), the dérivatives of λ^m, denoted $\partial \lambda^m / \partial \theta = \lambda_\theta{}^m$, etc., satisfy the uniform bounds $|\lambda_\theta{}^m| \leqslant 2M$, $|\lambda_{\theta\theta'}^m| \leqslant 4M^2$, and $|\lambda_{\theta\theta'\theta_k}^m| \leqslant 8M^3$. Further,

$$(46) \qquad E\lambda_\theta{}^m(\theta^0) = \left[\sum_{i=1}^{J_{n_m}} \frac{\partial P_{in_m}}{\partial \theta} \right]_{\theta^0} = 0.$$

Define

$$\Omega_m = -E\lambda_{\theta\theta'}^m(\theta^0)$$

$$(47) \qquad \qquad = \sum_{i=1}^{J_{n_m}} (z_{in_m} - \bar{z}_{n_m})' P_{in_m}(z_{in_m} - \bar{z}_{n_m}).$$

Then by Axiom 7,

$$(48) \qquad \lim_{q \to \infty} \frac{1}{q} \sum_{m=1}^{q} \Omega_m = \Omega.$$

Let β denote the smallest characteristic value of Ω. Then there exists q_0 such that for $q \geqslant q_0$, the smallest characteristic value of $(1/q)\sum_{m=1}^{q}\Omega_m$ is at least $\beta/2$.

Given a small positive scalar ε, choose $\delta = \min\{\varepsilon, \beta/4(1+4KM^3)\}$. The strong law of large numbers (Feller, 1966, Vol. II, p. 233) implies that there exists $q_1 \geqslant q_0$ such that for $q \geqslant q_1$, $L_\theta{}^q(\theta^0) = \sum_{m=1}^{q} \lambda_\theta{}^m(\theta^0)$ satisfies

$$(49) \qquad \left| \frac{1}{q} L_\theta{}^q(\theta^0) \right| < \delta^2,$$

with probability at least $1 - \varepsilon$.

A second-order Taylor's expansion of $L_{\theta_k}^q$ about θ^0 yields

$$(50) \qquad \frac{1}{q} L_{\theta_k}^q(\theta) - \frac{1}{q} L_{\theta_k\theta}^q(\theta^0)(\theta-\theta^0) = \frac{1}{q} L_{\theta_k}^q(\theta^0) + \frac{1}{2}\frac{1}{q}(\theta-\theta^0)' L_{\theta_k\theta\theta'}^q(\tilde{\theta})(\theta-\theta^0),$$

where $\tilde{\theta}$ lies between θ and θ^0. Consider $q \geqslant q_1$ and θ satisfying

$$(\theta - \theta^0)'(\theta - \theta^0) = \delta^2,$$

and suppose Equation (49) holds. Then

$$(51) \qquad \left| \frac{1}{q} L^q_{\theta_k}(\theta) - \frac{1}{q} L^q_{\theta_k \theta}(\theta^0)(\theta - \theta^0) \right| \leqslant \delta^2 (1 + 4K^2 M^3) \leqslant \delta\beta/4.$$

Hence,

$$(52) \qquad \frac{1}{q} |(\theta - \theta^0)' L_\theta{}^q(\theta) - (\theta - \theta^0)' L_{\theta\theta'}(\theta^0)(\theta - \theta^0)| \leqslant \delta^2 \beta/4.$$

But $(1/q)(\theta - \theta^0)' L_{\theta\theta'}(\theta^0)(\theta - \theta^0) \leqslant -\delta^2 \beta/2$, implying

$$(53) \qquad \frac{1}{q}(\theta - \theta^0)' L_\theta{}^q(\theta) \leqslant -\delta^2 \beta/4.$$

Hence, at each point on the sphere $(\theta - \theta^0)'(\theta - \theta^0) = \delta^2$, the gradient $L_\theta{}^q(\theta)$ is directed inward. Since L^q is concave in θ, this implies that a maximum $\hat{\theta}^q$ of L^q is achieved inside this sphere. Since this event occurs with probability at least $1 - \varepsilon$, we have proved the estimator to be consistent.

We next show that $\sqrt{q} \Omega^{1/2}(\hat{\theta}^q - \theta^0)$ is asymptotically standard multivariate normal. Evaluating the Taylor's expansion (50) at the maximum likelihood estimator yields

$$(54) \qquad 0 = \frac{1}{q} L^q_{\theta_k}(\theta^0) + \frac{1}{q} L^q_{\theta_k \theta}(\theta^0)(\theta - \theta^0) + 4M^3 |\hat{\theta}^q - \theta^0| a_k(\theta - \theta^0),$$

where a_k is a $1 \times K$ vector depending on $\hat{\theta}^q$, which satisfies $|a_k| \leqslant 1$. Letting A denote the matrix with rows a_k and defining

$$(55) \qquad D_q = \Omega^{-1/2} \left(\frac{1}{q} \sum_{m=1}^q \Omega_m - 4M^3 |\hat{\theta}^q - \theta^0| A \right) \Omega^{-1/2},$$

Equation (54) can be written

$$(56) \qquad \frac{1}{\sqrt{q}} \Omega^{1/2} D_q [\sqrt{q} \Omega^{1/2}(\hat{\theta}^q - \theta^0)] = \frac{1}{q} L_\theta{}^q(\theta^0).$$

Then,

$$(57) \qquad \operatorname*{plim}_{q \to \infty} D_q = I - 4M^3 \Omega^{-1/2} A \Omega^{-1/2} \operatorname*{plim}_{q \to \infty} |\hat{\theta}^q - \theta^0| = I.$$

Hence, $\sqrt{q} \Omega^{1/2}(\hat{\theta}^q - \theta^0)$ has the same asymptotic distribution as

$$(58) \qquad \frac{1}{q} \Omega^{-1/2} L_\theta{}^q(\theta^0) = \frac{1}{q} \sum_{m=1}^q \Omega^{-1/2} \lambda_\theta{}^m(\theta^0).$$

But the independent random variables $\Omega^{-1/2}\lambda_\theta{}^m(\theta^0)$ satisfy the Lindeberg–Levy theorem (Feller, 1966, Vol. II, pp. 256–258), implying that Equation (58) is asymptotic standard normal. This proves the lemma.

Since $\sqrt{q}\,\Omega^{1/2}(\hat{\theta}^q-\theta^0)$ is asymptotically standard multivariate normal, it follows that $q(\hat{\theta}^q-\theta^0)'\Omega(\hat{\theta}^q-\theta^0)$ is asymptotically chi-square with K degrees of freedom. Further, a second-order Taylor's expansion of the log-likelihood function about $\hat{\theta}^q$ can be used to establish that $q(\hat{\theta}^q-\theta^0)'\Omega(\hat{\theta}^q-\theta^0)$ and $2[L(\theta^0)-L(\hat{\theta})]$ converge in probability, and hence have the same asymptotic distribution. This argument justifies use of the statistic (29). Details of the proof can be found in Theil (1971, p. 396), Rao (1968, pp. 347–351), and Kendall and Stuart (1967, Vol. II, pp. 230–236). Rao gives several asymptotically equivalent forms for the test.

Consider the weighted residuals D_{in} in Equation (31). Define

$$(59) \qquad D_{in}^0 = \frac{S_{in}-R_n P_{in}^0}{(R_n P_{in}^0)^{1/2}},$$

$$(60) \qquad D_{in}^1 = \sum_{m=1}^{N}\sum_{j=1}^{J_m} (r_n r_m P_{in}^0 P_{jm}^0)^{1/2}(z_{in}-\bar{z}_n)\Omega^{-1}(z_{jm}-\bar{z}_m)'D_{jm}^0,$$

where $P_{in}^0 = P_{in}(\theta^0)$. Then D_{in}^0 has a multivariate distribution with $ED_{in}^0 = 0$ and $ED_{in}^0 D_{jm}^0 = \delta_{nm}[\delta_{ij}-(P_{in}^0 P_{jn}^0)^{1/2}]$, implying $ED_{in}^1 = 0$,

$$(61) \qquad ED_{in}^0 D_{jm}^1 = (r_n r_m P_{in}^0 P_{jm}^0)^{1/2}(z_{in}-\bar{z}_n)\Omega^{-1}(z_{jm}-\bar{z}_m),$$

and asymptotically

$$(62) \qquad ED_{in}^1 D_{jm}^1 = (r_n r_m P_{in}^0 P_{jm}^0)^{1/2}(z_{in}-\bar{z}_n)\Omega^{-1}(z_{jm}-\bar{z}_m).$$

Making Taylor's expansions, one can show that the random variables

$$\frac{(R_n)^{1/2}(P_{in}^0-P_{in})}{(P_{in}^0)^{1/2}} \qquad \text{and} \qquad (r_n P_{in}^0)^{1/2}(z_{in}-\bar{z}_n)\left(\sum_{n=1}^{N} R_n\right)^{1/2}(\theta^0-\hat{\theta})$$

differ from $-D_{in}^1$ by terms with probability limits zero. It then follows, since $(\sum_{n=1}^{N} R_n)^{1/2}(\theta^0-\hat{\theta})$ is asymptotic normal with mean zero and covariance matrix Ω, that these three random variables have a common asymptotic normal distribution. Hence, $D_{in}^0 - D_{in}^1$ has an asymptotic distribution with mean zero and covariance

$$(63) \qquad \begin{aligned} \Lambda_{in,jm} &= \delta_{nm}[\delta_{ij}-(P_{in}^0 P_{jm}^0)^{1/2}] \\ &\quad -(r_n r_m P_{in}^0 P_{jm}^0)^{1/2}(z_{in}-\bar{z}_n)\Omega^{-1}(z_{jm}-\bar{z}_m). \end{aligned}$$

Write

$$(64) \qquad D_{in} = \frac{S_{in}-R_n P_{in}^0}{(R_n P_{in})^{1/2}} + \frac{(R_n)^{1/2}(P_{in}^0-P_{in}^0)}{(P_{in})^{1/2}}.$$

The first term differs from D_{in}^0, and the second from $-D_{in}^1$, by factors with probability limits zero. Hence, D_{in} has the same asymptotic distribution as $D_{in}^0 - D_{in}^1$. When the R_n approach infinity, D_{in}^0 is asymptotically normal, implying D_{in} asymptotically normal. The covariance matrix can be written

$$(65) \qquad \Lambda = I - \sum_{m=0}^{N} q_m q_m',$$

where

$$(q_0)_{in} = (r_n P_{in}^0)^{1/2} (z_{in} - \bar{z}_n) \Omega^{-1/2},$$

$$(q_m)_{in} = \delta_{mn} (P_{in}^0)^{1/2}, \qquad m = 1, ..., N.$$

The vectors q_m are orthonormal, implying Λ idempotent of rank $N^* = \sum_{n=1}^{N} J_n - N - K$. Then $G = \sum_{n=1}^{N} \sum_{j=1}^{J_n} D_{in}^2$ has an asymptotic chi-square distribution with N^* degrees of freedom (Rao, 1968, p. 149).

Next consider the linear transformations

$$(66) \qquad Y_{in} = D_{in} - D_{1n} (P_{in})^{1/2} \alpha_n, \qquad i = 2, ..., J_n,$$

where $\alpha_n = [1 - (P_{1n})^{1/2}](1 - P_{1n})$. Then, Y_{in} has the same asymptotic distribution as the random variable Y_{in}^0 formed by replacing P_{in} with P_{in}^0 in Equation (66), and the latter random variable has asymptotic moments $EY_{in}^0 = 0$ and

$$\begin{aligned}
\Gamma_{in,jm} = EY_{in}^0 Y_{jm}^0 &= ED_{in} D_{jm} - (P_{jm}^0)^{1/2} \alpha_m ED_{in} D_{1m} \\
&\quad - (P_{in}^0)^{1/2} \alpha_n ED_{1n} D_{jm} + (P_{in}^0 P_{jm}^0)^{1/2} \alpha_n \alpha_m ED_{1n} D_{1m} \\
&= \delta_{nm} \delta_{ij} - q_{in}' q_{jm},
\end{aligned}$$

with

$$q_{in}' = (r_n P_{in}^0)^{1/2} \left((z_{in} - \bar{z}_n) + \frac{P_{1n}^0 - (P_{1n}^0)^{1/2}}{1 - P_{1n}^0} (z_{1n} - \bar{z}_n) \right) \Omega^{-1/2}.$$

Then, $\sum_{n=1}^{N} \sum_{i=2}^{J_n} q_{in} q_{in}' = I_K$ and Γ is idempotent of rank N^*. Hence,

$$\sum_{n=1}^{N} \sum_{i=2}^{J_n} Y_{in}^2 = \sum_{n=1}^{N} \sum_{i=1}^{J_n} D_{in}^2$$

has an asymptotic chi-square distribution with N^* degrees of freedom.

REFERENCES

Aitchison, J. and J. Bennett (1970). "Polychotomous quantal response by maximum indicant," *Biometrika* **57**, 253–262.

Aitchison, J. and S. Silvey (1957). "The Generalization of Probit Analysis to the Case of Multiple Responses," *Biometrika* **44**, 131–140.

Allouche, J. (1972). "Approach to Probability Distribution of Value of Walking Time and Pedestrian Circulation Models," *Highway Res. Rec.* **392**, 121–133.

Amemiya, T. (1972). "Bivariate Probit Analysis: Minimum Chi-Square Methods," Dept. of Econ., Stanford Univ., Stanford, California, unpublished.

Amemiya, T. and M. Boskin (1972). "Regression Analysis when the Dependent Variable is Truncated Lugnormal, with An Application to the Determinants of the Duration of Welfare Dependency," Inst. for Math. Stud. in the Soc. Sci., Stanford Univ., Stanford, California, Tech. Rep. No. 75.

Antle, C., L. Klimko and W. Harkness (1970). "Confidence intervals for the parameters of the logistic distribution," *Biometrika* **57**, 397–402.

Atkinson, A. (1972). "A Test of the Linear Logistic and Bradley-Terry Models," *Biometrika* **59**, 37–42.

Berkson, J. (1951). "Why I prefer Logits to Probits," *Biometrics* **7**, 327–339.

Berkson, J. (1955). "Maximum Likelihood and Minimum Chi-Square Estimates of the Logistic Function," *J. Amer. Statist. Ass.* **50**, 130–162.

Bloch, D. and G. Watson (1967). "A Bayesian Study of the Multinomial Distribution," *Ann. Math. Statist.* **38**, 1423–1435.

Block, H. and J. Marschak (1960). "Random Orderings and Stochastic Theories of Response," *In Contributions to Probability and Statistics* (I. Olkin, ed.). Stanford Univ. Press, Stanford, California.

Bock, R. (1969). "Estimating Multinomial Response Relations," *In Contributions to Statistics and Probability: Essays in Memory of S. N. Roy* (R. Bose, ed.). Univ. of North Carolina Press.

Boskin, M. (1972). "A Conditional Logit Model of Occupational Choice," Dept. of Econ., Stanford Univ., Stanford, California, unpublished.

Cox, D. (1958). "The Regression Analysis of Binary Sequences," *J. Roy. Statist. Soc. Ser. B*, **20**, 215–242.

Cox, D. (1966). "Some Procedures Connected with the Logistic Qualitative Response Curve," *Research Papers in Statistics* (F. David, ed.), pp. 55–71. Wiley, New York.

Cox, D. (1970). *Analysis of Binary Data*. Methuen, London.

Cox, D. and E. Snell (1968). "A General Definition of Residuals," *J. Roy. Statist. Soc. Ser B* **30**, 248–265.

Cox, D. and E. Snell (1971). "On Test Statistics Calculated from Residuals," *Biometrika* **58**, 589–594.

Domencich, T. and D. McFadden (1972). *A Disaggregated Behavioral Model of Urban Travel Demand*, Report No. CRA-156-2, Charles River Associates, Inc., Cambridge, Massachusetts.

Ergun, G. (1971). "Development of a Downtown Parking Mode," *Highway Res. Rec.* **369**, 118–134.

Feller, W. (1966). *An Introduction to Probability Theory and Its Applications*, Vol. 2, Wiley, New York.

Finney, D. (1952). *Probit Analysis*. Cambridge Univ. Press, London and New York.

Fisher, J. (1962). "An Analysis of Consumer Goods Expenditures in 1957," *Rev. Econ. Statist.* **44**, 64–71.

Gart, J. and J. Zweifel (1967). "On the Bias of Various Estimators of the Logit and its Variance," *Biometrika* **54**, 181–187.

Gilbert, E. (1968). "On Discrimination Using Qualitative Variables," *J. Amer. Statist. Ass.* **63**, 1399–1412.

Goodman, L. (1970). "The Multivariate Analysis of Qualitative Data: Interactions Among Multiple Classifications," *J. Amer. Statist. Ass.* **65**, 226–256.

Goodman, L. (1972). "A Modified Multiple Regression Approach to the Analysis of Dichotomous Variables," *Amer. Sociolog. Rev.* **37**, 28–46.

Grizzle, J. (1962). "Asymptotic Power of Tests of Linear Hypotheses Using the Probit and Logit Transformation," *J. Amer. Statist. Ass.* **57**, 877–894.

Grizzle, J. (1971). "Multivariate Logit Analysis," *Biometrics* **27**, 1057–1062.

Gupta, S., A. Qureishi and B. Shah (1967). "Best Linear Unbiased Estimators of the Parameters of the Logistic Distribution Using Order Statistics," *Technometrics* **9**, 43–56.

Gurland, J., I. Lee and P. Dolan (1960). "Polychotomous quantal response in biological assay," *Biometrics* **16**, 382–398.

Harter, J. and A. Moore (1967). "Maximum likelihood estimation, from censored samples, of the parameters of a logistic distribution," *J. Amer. Statist. Ass.* **62**, 675–683.

Kendall, M. and A. Stuart (1967). *The Advanced Theory of Statistics.* Vol. 2. Hafner, New York.

Korbel, J. (1966). "Labor Force Entry and Attachment of Young People," *J. Amer. Statist. Ass.* **61**, 117–127.

Lave, C. (1968). Modal Choice in Urban Transportation: A Behavioral Approach. Dept. of Econ., Stanford Univ., Stanford, California, Ph.D. dissertation.

Lee, T. (1963). "Demand for Housing: A Cross-Section Analysis," *Rev. Econ. Statist.* **45**, 190–196.

Leonard, T. (1972). "Bayesian Methods for Multinomial Data," *American College Testing Program*, Tech. Bull. No. 4.

Lisco, T. (1967). The Value of Commuters' Travel Time: A Study in Urban Transportation. Dept. of Econ., Univ. of Chicago, Chicago, Illinois, Ph.D. dissertation.

Luce, R. (1959). *Individual Choice Behavior.* Wiley, New York.

Luce, R. and P. Suppes (1965). "Preference, Utility, and Subjective Probability," *In Handbook of Mathematical Psychology* (R. Luce, R. Bush, and E. Galanter, eds.), Vol. 3. Wiley, New York.

Marschak, J. (1960). "Binary Choice Constraints on Random Utility Indicators," *In Stanford Symp. Math. Methods Soc. Sci.* (K. Arrow, ed.). Stanford Univ. Press, Stanford, California.

McFadden, D. (1968). "The Revealed Preferences of a Government Bureaucracy," Dept. of Econ., Univ. of California, Berkeley, California, unpublished.

McFadden, D. and M. Richter (1971). "On the extension of a set function to a probability on the Boolean algebra generated by a family of events, with applications," Working Paper 14, MSSB Workshop on the Theory of Markets under Uncertainty, Dept. of Econ., Univ. of California, Berkeley, California.

McGillivray, R. (1969). Binary Choice of Transport Mode in the San Francisco Bay Area, Dept. of Econ., Univ. of California, Berkeley, California, Ph.D. dissertation.

McGillivray, R. (1970). "Demand and Choice Models of Modal Split," *J. Transport Econ. Policy* **4**, 192–207.

Miller, L. and R. Radner (1970). "Demand and Supply in U.S. Higher Education," *Amer. Econ. Rev. Papers & Proceedings*, **60**, 326–340.

Miller, L. and R. Radner (forthcoming). *Demand and Supply in U.S. Higher Education*, Carnegie Commission on the Future of U.S. Higher Education.

Moses, L., R. Beals and M. Levy (1967). "Rationality and Migration in Ghana," *Rev. Econ. Statist.* **49**, 480–486.

Quandt, R. (1968). "Estimation of Modal Splits," *Transportat. Res.* **2**, 41–50.

Quandt, R. (1970). *The Demand for Travel.* Heath.

Quandt, R. and W. Baumol (1966). "The Demand for Abstract Transport Modes: Theory and Measurement," *J. Regional Sci.* **6**, 13–26.

Quandt, R. and K. Young (1969). "Cross Sectional Travel Demand Models: Estimation and Tests," *J. Regional Sci.* **9**, 201–214.

Quarmby, D. (1967). "Choice of Travel Mode for the Journey to Work: Some Findings," *J. Transport Econ. Policy.*

Rao, C. (1965). *Linear Statistical Inference and its Applications.* Wiley, New York.

Rassam, P., R. Ellis and J. Bennett (1971). "The n-Dimensional Logit Model: Development and Application," *Highway Res. Rec.* **369**, 135–147.

Reichman, S. and P. Stopher (1971). "Disaggregate Stochastic Models of Travel-Mode Choice," *Highway Res. Rec.* **369**, 91–103.

Stopher, P. (1969). "A Multinomial Extension of the Binary Logit Model for Choice of Mode of Travel," Northwestern Univ., unpublished.

Stopher, P. and T. Lisco (1970). "Modelling Travel Demand: A Disaggregate Behavioral Approach—Issues and Applications," *Transportat. Res. Forum Proc.* pp. 195–214.

Stopher, P. (1969). "A Probability Model of Travel Mode Choice for the Work Journey," *Highway Res. Rec.* **283**, 57–65.

Talvitie, A. (1972). "Comparison of Probabilistic Modal-Choice Models: Estimation Methods and System Inputs," *Highway Res. Rec.* **392**, 111–120.

Theil, H. (1969). "A Multinomial Extension of the Linear Logit Model," *Int. Econ. Rev.* **10**, 251–259.

Theil, H. (1970). "On the Estimation of Relationships involving Qualitative Variables," *Amer. J. Sociol.* **76**, 103–154.

Theil, H. (1971). *Principles of Econometrics*, Wiley, New York.

Thomas, T. and G. Thompson (1971). "Value of Time Saved by Trip Purpose," *Highway Res. Rec.* **369**, 104–113.

Thurstone, L. (1927). "A Law of Comparative Judgment," *Psycholog. Rev.* **34**, 273–286.

Tobin, J. (1958). "Estimation of Relationships for Limited Dependent Variables," *Econometrica* **26**.

Tversky, A. and J. Russo (1969). "Substitutability and Similarity in Binary Choice ," *J. Math. Psychol.* **6**, 1–12.

Uhler, R. (1968). "The Demand for Housing: An Inverse Probability Approach," *Rev. Econ. Statist.* 50, 129–134.

Walker, F. (1968). "Determinants of auto scrappage," *Rev. Econ. Statist.* **50**, 503–506.

Walker, S. and D. Duncan (1967). "Estimation of the Probability of an Event as a Function of Several Independent Variables," *Biometrika* **54**, 167–179.

Warner, S. (1962). *Stochastic Choice of Mode in Urban Travel: A Study in Binary Choice.* Northwestern Univ. Press, Evanston, Illinois.

Zellner, A. and T. Lee (1965). "Joint Estimation of Relationships Involving Discrete Random Variables," *Econometrica* **33**, 382–394.

Zinnes, J. (1969). "Scaling," *Ann. Rev. Psychol.* **20**, 447–478.

Chapter Five

Linear models
with random coefficients

P. A. V. B. SWAMY[1]

OHIO STATE UNIVERSITY
COLUMBUS, OHIO

[1] A copy of the manuscript of the present paper was, upon its completion, sent to Professor Arnold Zellner, who took the time and trouble to subject it to long and detailed criticism which is hereby gratefully acknowledged. Professor Paul Zarembka and Professor Richard D. Porter also read the preliminary write-up and offered helpful comments. I appreciate their help and thank them for it.

143

By far the greater part of empirical work in econometrics is based on the assumption that the coefficients in a relation are fixed and identical from one observation to the next. As was brought out clearly by Klein (1953, pp. 211–218), Theil (1957), and Zellner (1962b), the numerical values of parameters in behavioral models represent a complex of individual responses to changes in numerous variables and the familiar assumptions of parameter constancy, or of constancy save for a few shifts introduced by dummy variables, appear as convenient but suboptimal hypotheses. One will not be too far from truth if he says that individuals differ greatly in their behavior, and the diversity of individual decision units implies parameter variation across units. Consequently, the usefulness of a conventional fixed-parameter regression method in a cross section is limited.

Econometricians, in their attempts to relax the fixed coefficient assumptions, have introduced a number of models with random coefficients. References include Hurwicz (1950), Klein (1953, pp. 211–218), Kuh (1959), Rosenberg (1970), Theil and Mennes (1959), Wald (1947), and Zellner (1966). Mundlak (1963) and Kuh (1963) present a good rationalization for random intercept model. Klein (1953) provides a brief, but illuminating, discussion on random coefficient models, showing that the coefficients of a regression model can be treated as random in cross-section analysis to account for spacial or inter-individual heterogeneity; see also Nerlove (1965, Chap. IV). Theil and Mennes (1959), while analyzing aggregate time series data on British import and export prices, found it appropriate to assume that coefficients fluctuate randomly from one observation to the next. In a path-breaking paper presented at a departmental seminar held at the University of Chicago in 1965, Zellner (1966) has shown that in the context of random coefficient regression (RCR) models, under not very strong assumptions, there is no aggregation bias in the sense that the expectation of a macro coefficient estimator is equal to the common mean of the random micro coefficient vectors. In Zellner's study the vector of coefficients varies randomly across units but, once an individual is selected, a drawing on its coefficient vector is kept the same for all the time series observations on that individual. This type of RCR model for aggregation was also used by Theil (1971, pp. 570–573, 580–587) and a convergence approach to the aggregation problem was developed. A slight modification of this approach is given in Swamy (1971, pp. 15–16). The convergence approach leads to conventional fixed coefficient models at the aggregate level.[2] Recently, Rosenberg (1970) has developed an elaborate scheme of parameter dispersion across individuals and parameter variation over time.

[2] Following a different approach, Houthakker (1957) has shown that in the context of production functions, aggregate models with fixed coefficients give satisfactory approximations to reality if the distribution of micro coefficients across units is stable over time.

Thus, the preference for the type of parameter variation seems to vary with the author. Our point of view is that, since the limitations of economic data, particularly their nonexperimental nature, do not permit us to know *a priori* the correct specification of a model, one need not insist on any one formulation to the exclusion of all others. We may adopt a scheme which is more elaborate than that which we finally expect to hold so as to decide at what point simplification is possible. In any case, there are certainly reasonable econometric problems where some or all the elements of a coefficient vector may be looked upon as independently and identically distributed chance variables. Consequently, the problem of analyzing RCR models is econometrically meaningful and interesting. This is the attitude implicit in Zellner (1966).

The purpose of the present paper is to compare different types of RCR specifications and to describe the procedures of estimating the parameters in a general RCR model under different conditions. We shall begin with the case in which all the independent variables in a RCR model are nonstochastic and develop the minimum variance linear unbiased (MVLU) estimators of the means of coefficients. As usual, these estimators depend on nuisance parameters whose values are unknown. To obtain an operational procedure we replace these unknown parameters by sample estimates. However, this procedure provides only approximations to the MVLU estimators. In large samples these sample estimates will be close to the true values of nuisance parameters and thus the use of approximate MVLU estimators is satisfactory. We then go on to consider a RCR model in which lagged values of the dependent variable appear as explanatory variables and develop an instrumental variable approach to obtain consistent and asymptotically efficient estimates of the means of coefficients.

It is worth noting that there is an element of arbitrariness in the criterion of minimum variance unbiased, particularly with regard to unbiasedness. One reason why econometricians ignore minimum mean square error (MMSE) estimators of fixed coefficients is that they involve the unknown coefficients themselves; see Theil (1971, p. 125, Problem 4.3). But by replacing the coefficients by sample estimates in a MMSE formula we may be able to obtain an estimator that has a smaller mean square error than an approximate MVLU estimator in certain small sample situations; see Zellner and Vandaele (1971). Some approximate MMSE estimators suggested in this paper will be useful in exploring this possibility.

A comparison of different schemes of parameter variation is given in Section I. It is followed by Section II in which procedures of estimating the parameters of a general RCR model are discussed. Section III contains a numerical example. Section IV provides possible directions for further research.

I. Different Schemes of Parameter Variation

Given a time series of cross sections and a model to estimate from it, one should specify a particular scheme of parameter variation. Due to nonexperimental nature of economic data exact specification of parameter changes is rarely possible. More often, information concerning parameter variation will derive from rough notions about the processes involved and occasional studies with sufficient detail to allow precise conclusions.

Error Component Models

Nerlove (1965) considers the problem of estimating the following dynamic equation from a time series of cross sections.

$$(1) \quad y_{it} = \beta_0 + \sum_{g=1}^{G} \gamma_g\, y_{it-g} + \sum_{k=1}^{K-1} \alpha_k z_{kit} + u_{it} \quad (i = 1, 2, ..., n; \; t = 1, 2, ..., T).$$

Observations on y's and z's for n individuals taken over T periods of time are available.[3] The individuals here may be firms, consumers, or regions. The subscript i refers to an observation on an individual, while the subscript t refers to an observation for a year.

Following Kuh (1963) we may decompose the disturbance term u_{it} into three parts and write

$$(2) \qquad\qquad\qquad u_{it} = \mu_i + \tau_t + v_{it}.$$

The term μ_i is a constant through time but differs among individuals—it is a time-persistent attribute of the ith individual, the term τ_t is the same for all individuals at a given time but varies through time—it reflects the effects that are specific to the year but common to all individuals, and the term v_{it} is a remainder that differs among individuals both at a point in time and through time. The μ_i and τ_t are not readily attributable to identifiable causal variables.

Nerlove (1965) sets $\tau_t \equiv 0$ and assumes that μ_i and v_{it} are independent random variables. In this case the intercept may be interpreted precisely as a random coefficient; we may consider the quantity $(\beta_0 + \mu_i)$ as a random variable while the slope coefficients are fixed. The v_{it}'s represent the combined effect on y_{it} of the neglected variables. If the random component τ_t is present, then the intercept $\beta_0 + \mu_i + \tau_t$ varies randomly in both the time and cross-section dimensions.[4] In the time series analysis of cross-section data, if the

---

[3] When $z_{kit} \equiv 0$ for every k, the autoregressive process in Equation (1) is stationary if Theil's (1971, p. 412) Assumption 8.2 is satisfied by $\gamma_1, \gamma_2, ..., \gamma_G$ and the process $\{u_{it}\}$ of the errors is stationary. References to the original works in this area are given in Theil (1971).

[4] The μ_i's and τ_t's can also be treated as fixed parameters obeying the restrictions $\sum_{i=1}^{n} \mu_i = 0$ and $\sum_{t=1}^{T} \tau_t = 0$, in which case model (1) ceases to be a random intercept model; see Hoch (1962) and Mundlak (1961) and references therein.

interindividual and intertemporal parameter variation takes the form of mere shifts in the regression intercept, then the specification of an equation with a random intercept and fixed slopes is adequate.

If we arrange the observations on each variable first by individual and then according to period, we may represent Equation (2) by

$$(3) \qquad \mathbf{u} = (\boldsymbol{\mu} \otimes \boldsymbol{\iota}_T) + (\boldsymbol{\iota}_n \otimes \boldsymbol{\tau}) + \mathbf{v},$$

where

$$\mathbf{u} \equiv (\mathbf{u}_1', \mathbf{u}_2', \ldots, \mathbf{u}_n')',$$

$$\mathbf{u}_i \equiv (u_{i1}, u_{i2}, \ldots, u_{iT})' \qquad (i = 1, 2, \ldots, n),$$

$$\boldsymbol{\mu} \equiv (\mu_1, \mu_2, \ldots, \mu_n)',$$

$$\boldsymbol{\tau} \equiv (\tau_1, \tau_2, \ldots, \tau_T)',$$

$$\mathbf{v} \equiv (\mathbf{v}_1', \mathbf{v}_2', \ldots, \mathbf{v}_n')',$$

$$\mathbf{v}_i \equiv (v_{i1}, v_{i2}, \ldots, v_{iT})' \qquad (i = 1, 2, \ldots, n),$$

and where $\otimes$ denotes the Kronecker product, $\boldsymbol{\iota}$ is a vector of unit elements, and the subscript of $\boldsymbol{\iota}$ indicates its order.

As in Wallace and Hussain (1969) we assume

$$(4a) \qquad\qquad E\boldsymbol{\mu} = \mathbf{0} \quad \text{and} \quad E\boldsymbol{\mu}\boldsymbol{\mu}' = \sigma_\mu^2 I_n,$$

$$(4b) \qquad\qquad E\boldsymbol{\tau} = \mathbf{0} \quad \text{and} \quad E\boldsymbol{\tau}\boldsymbol{\tau}' = \sigma_\tau^2 I_T,$$

$$(4c) \qquad\qquad E\mathbf{v} = \mathbf{0} \quad \text{and} \quad E\mathbf{v}\mathbf{v}' = \sigma_v^2 I_{nT},$$

$$(4d) \qquad E\boldsymbol{\mu}\boldsymbol{\tau}' = 0, \quad E\boldsymbol{\tau}\mathbf{v}' = 0, \quad \text{and} \quad E\boldsymbol{\mu}\mathbf{v}' = 0.$$

Under these assumptions the random vector $\mathbf{u}$ is distributed with mean zero and variance-covariance matrix of the form

$$(5) \qquad \Sigma_1 = \sigma_\mu^2 (I_n \otimes \boldsymbol{\iota}_T \boldsymbol{\iota}_T') + \sigma_\tau^2 (\boldsymbol{\iota}_n \boldsymbol{\iota}_n' \otimes I_T) + \sigma_v^2 I_{nT}.$$

Identification in Error Component Models

The assumption of random variation in the intercept term introduces a kind of serial correlation in the disturbances. That this raises problems for the analysis of identification of parameters is evident in a general way from the fact that if current and lagged disturbances are correlated, then so will be current disturbances and lagged endogenous variables in Equation (1) which cannot be taken as predetermined. An example and, indeed, the problem were stated in Nerlove (1965, Chap. VII), who derived a dynamic model of a production decision process by maximizing total discounted profits (net of costs of changing input levels) over a finite horizon, subject to the constraint imposed by a Cobb–Douglas form of production function with two inputs, namely, capital and labor. The linearized version of this model consists of three equations without exogenous variables; see Nerlove (1965, p. 151). It is, however, identifiable if the lagged values of endogenous variables are independent of the disturbances. Nerlove (1965, p. 153) has noted that the assumption of independence between lagged endogenous variables and the current values of disturbances in a relationship describing cross-section data over time is untenable because in any realistic situation each disturbance is composed of three parts as in Equation (2) and the time-invariant individual effects determine the lagged values of endogenous variables to exactly the same extent as they determine the current values. He did not derive the conditions for the identifiability of his model. A simple transformation of variables shows that his model is identifiable.

Swamy (1971, pp. 67–70) has shown that an orthogonal transformation described in Rao (1965a, pp. 216–217) can be written in a compact form using the Kronecker products of orthogonal vectors.[5] Fortunately, this transformation does not depend on unknown parameters. In cases in which the variance-covariance matrix of disturbances is in the form of Equation (5), this transformation when applied to independent and dependent variables in Equation (1), reduces the problem to one of heteroskedasticity. The disturbances of the transformed equation are uncorrelated but have four distinct variances (see Swamy and Mehta, 1971). We can assume that the elements of transformed disturbances are serially independent. Under these conditions the lagged values of transformed endogenous variables are independent of the current and the succeeding values of transformed disturbances; see Theil (1971, p. 409). We can treat the lagged values of transformed endogenous variables as predetermined. Nerlove's model, written in terms of transformed variables, can be straightforwardly shown to be identifiable using the necessary condition for identification, i.e., the number of excluded predetermined variables should at least be equal to the number of included endogenous variables less one.

Estimation of Parameters in Error Component Models

Swamy and Arora (1972) sketch the generalized least squares procedure for estimating the parameters $(\beta_0, \alpha_1, \ldots, \alpha_{K-1})$ in Equation (1), when the lagged values of the dependent variable do not appear as explanatory variables. Then, for the practical situation where the variances are unknown, they develop an operational version of generalized least squares, in which certain variance functions are replaced by sample estimates. They also indicate the conditions under which the estimates obtained by this procedure are more efficient in

---

[5] See also Nerlove (1971).

small samples than other estimates. When the lagged values of the dependent variable appear as explanatory variables, the above operational procedure can be applied to obtain consistent and asymptotically efficient estimates; see Swamy (1971, p. 83) and Amemiya (1971).

Are Assumptions (4a)–(4d) Plausible?

It can be seen from Equation (5) that assumptions (4a)–(4d) imply homoskedasticity of error variances and a very specific form of serial correlation that may not be plausible in many nonexperimental situations. The contemporaneous covariances $Eu_{it} u_{jt}$ for $i \neq j$ are all equal to σ_τ^2, which is strictly positive. The covariance between a pair of observations on every individual, i.e., $Eu_{it} u_{it'} = \sigma_\mu^2$ for $t \neq t'$ and $i = 1, 2, ..., n$, does not die out no matter how far apart in time the observations are. This contrasts sharply with a general set of assumptions adopted by Parks (1967).[6] These assumptions can be utilized in the analysis of RCR models if we follow Zellner's (1966) procedure of specifying RCR models. While Swamy (1971, p. 88) and Swamy and Mehta (1971) have generalized assumptions (4a)–(4c) to allow for pairwise equal correlation between the elements of each vector $\boldsymbol{\mu}$, $\boldsymbol{\tau}$, and $\mathbf{v}$ (under this generalization the off-diagonal elements of $\sum_1$ can be negative if n and T are small), still this form of $\sum_1$ is not quite as general as that implied by Parks' assumptions.

Random Coefficient Regression Models

In his important study of the aggregation problem, Zellner (1966) considers the following RCR model. Let the economic relationship for the ith unit be given by

$$(6) \qquad \mathbf{y}_i = \iota_T \beta_{0i} + Z_i \boldsymbol{\alpha}_i + \mathbf{u}_i = X_i \boldsymbol{\beta}_i + \mathbf{u}_i \qquad (i = 1, 2, ..., n),$$

where $\mathbf{y}_i \equiv (y_{i1}, y_{i2}, ..., y_{iT})'$ is a $T \times 1$ vector of observations on a dependent variable; $X_i \equiv [\iota_T, Z_i]$, Z_i is a $T \times K-1$ matrix of observations on $K-1$ independent variables, z_{kit} $(t = 1, 2, ..., T; k = 1, 2, ..., K-1)$; $\boldsymbol{\beta}_i = (\beta_{0i}, \boldsymbol{\alpha}_i')'$ is a $K \times 1$ vector of coefficients; $\mathbf{u}_i \equiv (u_{i1}, u_{i2}, ..., u_{iT})'$ is a $T \times 1$ vector of disturbances. Swamy (1971) analyzes model (6) under the following set of assumptions.

(7a)   The rank of X_i is K, $n > K$ and $T > K$.

(7b)   For $i, j = 1, 2, ..., n$:

$$E\mathbf{u}_i = \mathbf{0} \qquad \text{and} \qquad E\mathbf{u}_i \mathbf{u}_j' = \sigma_{ij} \Omega_{ij},$$

---

[6] Parks's (1967) approach is an extension of the joint estimation technique developed by Zellner (1962a) for a system of "seemingly unrelated" equations. Here we are viewing this system as a temporal cross-section regression but not as a system of equations.

where

$$\Omega_{ij} = \frac{1}{1-\rho_i\rho_j} \begin{bmatrix} 1 & \rho_i & \rho_i^2 & \cdots & \rho_i^{T-1} \\ \rho_j & 1 & \rho_i & \cdots & \rho_i^{T-2} \\ \vdots & \vdots & \vdots & \cdots & \vdots \\ \rho_j^{T-1} & \rho_j^{T-2} & \rho_j^{T-3} & \cdots & 1 \end{bmatrix}$$

$$|\rho_i| < 1$$

(7c)   For $i, j = 1, 2, \ldots, n$:

$$E\boldsymbol{\beta}_i = \bar{\boldsymbol{\beta}} \quad \text{and} \quad E(\boldsymbol{\beta}_i - \bar{\boldsymbol{\beta}})(\boldsymbol{\beta}_j - \bar{\boldsymbol{\beta}})' = \begin{cases} \Delta & \text{if } i = j \\ 0 & \text{otherwise,} \end{cases}$$

Δ is positive-definite.

(7d) $\boldsymbol{\beta}_i$ is independent of $\mathbf{u}_j$ for every $i, j = 1, 2, \ldots, n$.

(7e)   The z_{kjt} are exogenous variables distributed independently of the $\boldsymbol{\beta}_i$ and $\mathbf{u}_i$.

These assumptions imply that for given X the random vector $\mathbf{y} \equiv (\mathbf{y}_1', \mathbf{y}_2', \ldots, \mathbf{y}_n')'$ is distributed with mean $X\bar{\boldsymbol{\beta}}$ and variance-covariance matrix Σ_2, where $X \equiv [X_1', X_2', \ldots, X_n']'$ and

$$(8) \quad \Sigma_2 = \begin{bmatrix} X_1\Delta X_1' + \sigma_{11}\Omega_{11} & \sigma_{12}\Omega_{12} & \cdots & \sigma_{1n}\Omega_{1n} \\ \sigma_{21}\Omega_{21} & X_2\Delta X_2' + \sigma_{22}\Omega_{22} & \cdots & \sigma_{2n}\Omega_{2n} \\ \vdots & \vdots & \cdots & \vdots \\ \sigma_{n1}\Omega_{n1} & \sigma_{n2}\Omega_{n2} & \cdots & X_n\Delta X_n' + \sigma_{nn}\Omega_{nn} \end{bmatrix}$$

Assumption (7c) implies that the $\boldsymbol{\beta}_i$ are n different drawings from a K-dimensional distribution with mean $\bar{\boldsymbol{\beta}}$ and variance-covariance matrix Δ. The randomness of coefficient vectors $\boldsymbol{\beta}_i$ may be attributed to the random selection of individuals whose behavior is described by Equation (6).[7] The form of the variance-covariance matrix of $\mathbf{u} \equiv (\mathbf{u}_1', \mathbf{u}_2', \ldots, \mathbf{u}_n')'$ in Equation (6) under assumption (7b) is less restrictive than that of the variance-covariance matrix of the term $[(\iota_n \otimes \tau) + \mathbf{v}]$ in Equation (3) under assumptions (4b)–(4d). In Equation (8) the contemporaneous covariances $\sigma_{ij}/(1 - \rho_i\rho_j)$ for $i \neq j$ can take on negative values and can also depend upon the i and j subscripts. The variance of u_{it} is not restricted to be the same as that of u_{jt} when $i \neq j$. The degree of serial correlation between a pair of observations with different t subscripts not only varies with i and j subscripts but also declines geometrically with the time distance involved. The model in Equation (6) permits random

---

[7] Recently, Porter (1972) utilized RCR models to analyze sample survey data.

variation in all the coefficients including the constant term across units, whereas the model in Equation (1) permits a similar variation in the constant β_0 but not in slope coefficients.

To understand fully the nature of assumptions (7b) and (7c) consider the two independent sets of factors that determine the values taken by the dependent variable: those that are introduced explicitly in the equation as explanatory variables and those that are neglected and only represented by a random disturbance. Assumption (7c) implies that the way in which an individual reacts to the first set of factors is unrelated to the way in which another individual reacts to the same set of factors.[8] Given that the individuals react independently to changes in the first set of determining factors, the lack of independence between β_i and β_j for $i \neq j$ is perhaps not so important for observations drawn according to a random sampling scheme in which the individual units chosen are selected in a mutually independent fashion. Assumption (7b) implies that the second set of factors are contemporaneously and serially correlated. The contemporaneous correlation between these variables will be present if the same subset of neglected factors affect the behavior of more than one individual in the sample.

If we change assumption (7c) to

$$(7c') \quad E\beta_i = \bar{\beta}_i \quad \text{and} \quad E(\beta_i - \bar{\beta}_i)(\beta_j - \bar{\beta}_j)' = \begin{cases} \bar{\Delta} & \text{if } i = j \\ 0 & \text{otherwise,} \end{cases}$$

then the model analyzed by Parks (1967) is the same as Equation (6) when $\bar{\Delta} = 0$. Some feasible generalizations of assumption (7c) are discussed in Swamy (1971, pp. 138–155).

Alternative Specifications of RCR Models

Following Klein (1953, pp. 211–218) and Theil and Mennes (1959), we can specify a RCR model of the following type:

$$(9) \quad y_{it} = \sum_{k=1}^{K-1} z_{kit}(\bar{\beta}_k + \xi_{kit}) + (\bar{\beta}_0 + \xi_{0it}) \qquad (i = 1, 2, ..., n; \, t = 1, 2, ..., T),$$

where y_{it} is an observation on a dependent variable, the z_{kit}'s are the observations on $K-1$ nonstochastic independent variables, the $\bar{\beta}_k$'s are the unknown means of coefficients, and the ξ_{kit}'s are the additive random elements in coefficients. The additive disturbance term cannot be distinguished from the randomly varying intercept and so is not written explicitly. It is assumed that

---

[8] If there are valid economic reasons for the reaction coefficients of different individuals to be correlated, we should divide the n observations into $p(<n)$ independent groups of m observations each and apply the procedures which are appropriate to m-dependent random variables.

for $i, j = 1, 2, ..., n$; $t, t' = 1, 2, ..., T$; and $k, k' = 0, 1, ..., K-1$:

$$(10) \quad E\xi_{kit} = 0 \quad \text{and} \quad E\xi_{kit}\xi_{k'jt'} = \begin{cases} \sigma_{kk'} & \text{if} \quad i = j \quad \text{and} \quad t = t' \\ 0 & \text{otherwise.} \end{cases}$$

Let $\Delta = \{\sigma_{kk'}\}$ be positive-definite. Fisk (1967) analyzes the model in Equation (9) under assumption (10) and the condition that $z_{kit} = z_{kt}$ for every $k = 1, 2, ..., K-1$. This condition is rarely satisfied in nonexperimental situations. As explained by Theil (1971, p. 622) the meaning of Equation (9) under assumption (10) is that if an independent variable increases by one unit with all the other independent variables remaining constant, the dependent variable responds with a random change with a finite mean and a positive variance. For all the nT observations together we can write Equation (9) as

$$(11) \qquad\qquad\qquad \mathbf{y} = X\bar{\boldsymbol{\beta}} + D_x \boldsymbol{\xi},$$

where

$$\mathbf{y} \equiv (\mathbf{y}_1', \mathbf{y}_2', ..., \mathbf{y}_n')', \qquad X \equiv [X_1', X_2', ..., X_n']',$$

$$X_i \equiv (\boldsymbol{\iota}_T, \mathbf{z}_{1i}, ..., \mathbf{z}_{K-1,i}), \qquad \mathbf{z}_{ki} \equiv (z_{ki1}, z_{ki2}, ..., z_{kiT})'$$

$$(k = 1, 2, ..., K-1), \qquad \bar{\boldsymbol{\beta}} \equiv (\bar{\beta}_0, \bar{\beta}_1, ..., \bar{\beta}_{K-1})',$$

$$D_x \equiv \text{diag}[\mathbf{x}_{11}', \mathbf{x}_{12}', ..., \mathbf{x}_{1T}', ..., \mathbf{x}_{n1}', \mathbf{x}_{n2}', ..., \mathbf{x}_{nT}'],$$

$$\mathbf{x}_{it}' \equiv (1, z_{1it}, ..., z_{K-1,it}),$$

$$\boldsymbol{\xi} \equiv (\boldsymbol{\xi}_{11}', \boldsymbol{\xi}_{12}', ..., \boldsymbol{\xi}_{1T}', ..., \boldsymbol{\xi}_{n1}', \boldsymbol{\xi}_{n2}', ..., \boldsymbol{\xi}_{nT}')',$$

$$\boldsymbol{\xi}_{it}' \equiv (\xi_{0it}, \xi_{1it}, ..., \xi_{K-1,it}).$$

Now it is instructive to compare specifications (6) and (7), and (9) and (10). The mean of $\mathbf{y}$ in either specifications is the same. When assumption (10) holds, the variance-covariance matrix of $\mathbf{y}$ in Equation (11) is

$$(12) \quad \text{diag}[\mathbf{x}_{11}' \Delta \mathbf{x}_{11}, \mathbf{x}_{12}' \Delta \mathbf{x}_{12}, ..., \mathbf{x}_{1T}' \Delta \mathbf{x}_{1T}, ..., \mathbf{x}_{n1}' \Delta \mathbf{x}_{n1}, \mathbf{x}_{n2}' \Delta \mathbf{x}_{n2},$$

$$..., \mathbf{x}_{nT}' \Delta \mathbf{x}_{nT}].$$

These elements also appear as diagonal elements in Equation (8), which is the variance-covariance matrix of $\mathbf{y}$ in Equation (6) when assumption (7) holds. This clearly shows that the specification in Equations (9) and (10) does not imply a distribution for $\mathbf{y}$ which is more general than that implied by the specification in Equations (6) and (7). The estimation and testing procedures within the framework of the specification in Equations (9) and (10) are very complicated; see Hildreth and Houck (1967). Swamy (1971) has shown that standard multivariate techniques can be utilized to analyze the model in Equation (6) under assumptions (7a)–(7e).

To avoid possible misinterpretation of our statement we must add that the above conclusion regarding the generality of the conditional distribution of y given X, implied by Equations (6) and (7), should not be crudely applied to all situations. When a set of observations is recorded for "different" groups of individuals in "different" years, specification (6) is not appropriate. One might adopt Equation (11) in this case. Even when we obtain temporal cross-section data by assembling cross sections of several years, with the "same" cross-section units appearing in all years as in Equation (6), specification (9) may be appropriate in some cases. For example, the parameters appearing in a production function may be different for different firms and they may also vary from year to year due to frequent technological changes. As usual, each situation has to be analyzed carefully.

Rosenberg (1970) has developed a convergent-parameter structure in which the coefficient vectors β_{it} evolve stochastically over time, exhibiting a tendency to converge toward the population mean vector and undergoing random shifts as well. The population mean vector also evolves stochastically over time in this scheme. We need lots of prior information to estimate a model under this general scheme.

In conclusion, it should be noted that the RCR model developed by Zellner (1966) possesses maximum simplicity and the minimum number of parameters consonant with representational adequacy of nonexperimental situations that are often encountered by economists. The nature of both the cross-section and time series data can be taken into account within the framework of Zellner's specification. The assumption that the coefficients of an individual are fixed over time may not be serious if shorter time spans are considered. It may frequently happen that, because of inertia in reactions to changes in independent variables, individual coefficients do not change over time. Even if this does not happen, trends, additional variables, and parameter shifts may be used in time series analysis to account for temporal heterogeneity. Such a device is not adequate to account for interindividual heterogeneity because various demographic, environmental, and cultural factors that affect economic behavior, vary widely among individuals in the sample, and it is not possible to represent these factors by a few independent variables in the regression. These factors do not change greatly over time for the whole community; hence these variables may be properly neglected in time series analysis. Zellner's assumption that coefficient vectors of different individuals are the independent drawings from the same multivariate distribution stands between the limiting assumptions that coefficient vectors are fixed and the same and that coefficient vectors are fixed and different. Given that micro units are possibly different in their behavior, the former assumption is often found to be restrictive, while the latter assumption involves the use of very many parameters and is thus not always satisfactory in the time series analysis of cross-section data on many individuals.

II. Estimation of Random Coefficient Regression Models When Disturbances Are Contemporaneously and Serially Correlated

Standard Linear Model

In this section we outline a procedure for estimating the parameters in Equation (6) when the assumptions in Equation (7) are satisfied. Details are given in Swamy (1971, Chap. IV). We may rewrite Equation (6) as

(13) $$\mathbf{y} = X\bar{\boldsymbol{\beta}} + D\boldsymbol{\xi} + \mathbf{u}$$

where $\mathbf{y}$, X, and $\bar{\boldsymbol{\beta}}$ are as defined in Equation (11),

$$D \equiv \mathrm{diag}[X_1, X_2, ..., X_n], \qquad \boldsymbol{\xi} \equiv [\boldsymbol{\xi_1}', \boldsymbol{\xi_2}', ..., \boldsymbol{\xi_n}']',$$

$$\boldsymbol{\beta}_i = \bar{\boldsymbol{\beta}} + \boldsymbol{\xi}_i \quad \text{and} \quad \mathbf{u} \equiv (\mathbf{u_1}', \mathbf{u_2}', ..., \mathbf{u_n}')'.$$

The best linear unbiased estimator of $\bar{\boldsymbol{\beta}}$ can be obtained by applying Aitken's generalized least squares to Equation (13):

(14) $$\bar{\mathbf{b}}(\boldsymbol{\theta}) = (X'\Sigma_2^{-1}X)^{-1}X'\Sigma_2^{-1}\mathbf{y},$$

where $\boldsymbol{\theta}$ is a $\frac{1}{2}[K(K+1)+n(n+3)] \times 1$ vector containing all the distinct elements of Δ, $\{\sigma_{ij}\}$, and ρ_i ($i = 1, 2, ..., n$) arranged in an order.

Any other estimator of $\bar{\boldsymbol{\beta}}$ that is also linear in the vector $\mathbf{y}$ and unbiased has a variance-covariance matrix which exceeds that of $\bar{\mathbf{b}}(\boldsymbol{\theta})$ by a positive-semidefinite matrix. The variance-covariance matrix of $\bar{\mathbf{b}}(\boldsymbol{\theta})$ is $(X'\Sigma_2^{-1}X)^{-1}$.

A difficulty in the computation of the estimator $\bar{\mathbf{b}}(\boldsymbol{\theta})$ is that the elements of $\boldsymbol{\theta}$ are normally unknown. An approximate solution to this problem is the following two-step procedure. First, obtain a consistent estimate of $\boldsymbol{\theta}$. Second, substitute this estimate in Equation (14) to obtain an approximate Aitken estimate of $\bar{\boldsymbol{\beta}}$.

A consistent estimate of ρ_i is given by

(15) $$\hat{\rho}_i = \frac{(T-K)\sum_{t=2}^{T}\hat{u}_{it}\hat{u}_{it-1}}{(T-1)\sum_{t=1}^{T}\hat{u}_{it}^2} \qquad (i = 1, 2, ..., n),$$

where $\hat{u}_{it}$ is the tth element of the least squares residual vector $\hat{\mathbf{u}}_i = \mathbf{y}_i - X_i\mathbf{b}_i$ and $\mathbf{b}_i = (X_i'X_i)^{-1}X_i'\mathbf{y}_i$ is the least squares quantity obtained from a least squares fit of $\mathbf{y}_i$ on X_i; see Theil (1971, p. 254). Let $\hat{\boldsymbol{\varepsilon}}_i \equiv (\hat{\varepsilon}_{i1}, \hat{\varepsilon}_{i2}, ..., \hat{\varepsilon}_{iT})'$, $\hat{\varepsilon}_{i1} = (1-\hat{\rho}_i^2)^{1/2}\hat{u}_{i1}$, and $\hat{\varepsilon}_{it} = \hat{u}_{it} - \hat{\rho}_i\hat{u}_{it-1}$ ($t = 2, 3, ..., T$). We can estimate σ_{ij} consistently by

(16) $$\hat{\sigma}_{ij} = \frac{\hat{\boldsymbol{\varepsilon}}_i'\hat{\boldsymbol{\varepsilon}}_j}{T} \qquad (i, j = 1, 2, ..., n).$$

Since the variance-covariance matrix of the error term $X_i\boldsymbol{\xi}_i + \mathbf{u}_i$ in the ith equation is expressible in the form $X_i\Delta X_i' + \sigma_{ii}\Omega_{ii}$, application of Rao's (1967) theorem immediately shows that the estimator $\mathbf{b}_i(\rho_i) = (X_i'\Omega_{ii}^{-1}X_i)^{-1}X_i'\Omega_{ii}^{-1}\mathbf{y}_i$ is best linear unbiased in the sense that any other estimator of $\bar{\boldsymbol{\beta}}$ that is also linear in the vector $\mathbf{y}_i$ and unbiased has a variance-covariance matrix which exceeds that of $\mathbf{b}_i(\rho_i)$ by a positive-semidefinite matrix. The matrix Δ can be estimated by

(17) $\quad \hat{\Delta} = \dfrac{S_2}{n-1} - \dfrac{1}{n} \sum_{i=1}^{n} \hat{\sigma}_{ii}(X_i'\hat{\Omega}_{ii}^{-1}X_i)^{-1}$

$$+ \frac{1}{n(n-1)} \sum_{\substack{i \neq j \\ i=1}}^{n} \hat{\sigma}_{ij}(X_i'\hat{\Omega}_{ii}^{-1}X_i)^{-1}X_i'\hat{\Omega}_{ii}^{-1}\hat{\Omega}_{ij}\hat{\Omega}_{jj}^{-1}X_j(X_j'\hat{\Omega}_{jj}^{-1}X_j)^{-1},$$

where

$$S_2 = \sum_{i=1}^{n} \mathbf{b}_i(\hat{\rho}_i)\,\mathbf{b}_i'(\hat{\rho}_i) - \frac{1}{n}\sum_{i=1}^{n}\mathbf{b}_i(\hat{\rho}_i)\sum_{i=1}^{n}\mathbf{b}_i'(\hat{\rho}_i),$$

$$\mathbf{b}_i(\hat{\rho}_i) = (X_i'\hat{\Omega}_{ii}^{-1}X_i)^{-1}X_i'\hat{\Omega}_{ii}^{-1}\mathbf{y}_i,$$

and $\hat{\Omega}_{ij}$ is obtained from Ω_{ij} by replacing ρ_i by $\hat{\rho}_i$.

When the disturbances $\mathbf{u}_i$ are serially uncorrelated, i.e., $\rho_i = 0 \, (i = 1, 2, ..., n)$, an unbiased estimator of Δ is

(18) $\quad \tilde{\Delta} = \dfrac{S_1}{n-1} - \dfrac{1}{n}\sum_{i=1}^{n}s_{ii}(X_i'X_i)^{-1} + \dfrac{1}{n(n-1)}\sum_{\substack{i \neq j \\ i=1}}^{n}s_{ij}(X_i'X_i)^{-1}X_i'X_j(X_j'X_j)^{-1},$

where

$$S_1 = \sum_{i=1}^{n}\mathbf{b}_i\mathbf{b}_i' - \frac{1}{n}\sum_{i=1}^{n}\mathbf{b}_i\sum_{i=1}^{n}\mathbf{b}_i',$$

$$\mathbf{b}_i = (X_i'X_i)^{-1}X_i'\mathbf{y}_i,$$

$$s_{ij} = \frac{\mathbf{y}_i'M_iM_j\mathbf{y}_j}{\operatorname{tr} M_iM_j},$$

$$M_i = I - X_i(X_i'X_i)^{-1}X_i'.$$

Note that Equation (13) can be written as

$$\mathbf{y} = X\bar{\boldsymbol{\beta}} + D_1\boldsymbol{\xi}_1 + \cdots + D_n\boldsymbol{\xi}_n + J_1\mathbf{u}_1 + \cdots + J_n\mathbf{u}_n,$$

where D_i is a $nT \times K$ matrix, $D \equiv [D_1, D_2, ..., D_n]$; J_i is a $nT \times T$ matrix such that $I \equiv [J_1, J_2, ..., J_n]$ is an identity matrix of order $nT \times nT$; and $\mathbf{y}$, X, $\bar{\boldsymbol{\beta}}$, D, $\boldsymbol{\xi}_1, ..., \boldsymbol{\xi}_n$, $\mathbf{u}_1, ..., \mathbf{u}_n$ are as defined in Equation (13). In cases where it is reasonable to assume that $\sigma_{ij} = 0$ for $i \neq j$, we can utilize the estimating equations developed by Rao (1972) to obtain the minimum norm quadratic unbiased estimates of Δ and σ_{ii} $(i = 1, 2, ..., n)$.

By employing an appropriate estimate of Σ_2, we can obtain an approximate Aitken estimator of $\bar{\boldsymbol{\beta}}$ as

(19) $\qquad\qquad \bar{\mathbf{b}}(\hat{\boldsymbol{\theta}}) = (X'\hat{\Sigma}_2^{-1}X)^{-1}X'\hat{\Sigma}_2^{-1}\mathbf{y}.$

Application of Theil's (1971, p. 399) Theorem 8.4 immediately shows that under certain general conditions[9] $\bar{\mathbf{b}}(\hat{\boldsymbol{\theta}})$ is consistent and has the same limiting distribution as $\bar{\mathbf{b}}(\boldsymbol{\theta})$. It turns out that the asymptotic distribution of $\bar{\mathbf{b}}(\hat{\boldsymbol{\theta}})$ as $n, T \to \infty$ is normal with mean $\bar{\boldsymbol{\beta}}$ and variance-covariance matrix Δ/n. Furthermore,

$$(20) \qquad \underset{T \to \infty}{\text{plim}} \left| \bar{\mathbf{b}}(\hat{\boldsymbol{\theta}}) - \left(\frac{1}{n}\right) \sum_{i=1}^{n} \boldsymbol{\beta}_i \right| = 0.$$

In words, the estimator $\bar{\mathbf{b}}(\hat{\boldsymbol{\theta}})$ is asymptotically equal to the simple arithmetic mean of micro coefficient vectors. As explained by Theil (1971, p. 561), a macro coefficient may be defined as the simple arithmetic mean of the corresponding micro coefficients. Under this definition $\bar{\mathbf{b}}(\hat{\boldsymbol{\theta}})$ is a consistent estimator of the macro coefficient vector $(1/n) \sum_{i=1}^{n} \boldsymbol{\beta}_i$. It should be emphasized that the above procedure leads to consistent estimates of parameters only if the X_i's satisfy assumption (7e) and the conditions stated in footnote 9. Of course, these conditions can be weakened to allow for variables like time trend; see Theil (1971, p. 365, Problems 1.8 and 1.9).

Autoregressive Models

If Z_i contains some current and lagged values of endogenous variables, we can apply an instrumental variable approach to obtain a consistent estimate of $\bar{\boldsymbol{\beta}}$, provided the random coefficients are independent of all the other random quantities in the equation. Suppose that the model to be estimated is

$$(21) \qquad \mathbf{y}_i = \boldsymbol{\iota}_T \beta_{0i} + Y_i \gamma_{Yi} + Z_{Ri} \gamma_i + Z_{Fi} \boldsymbol{\alpha}_i + \mathbf{u}_i \qquad (i = 1, 2, ..., n),$$

where $\mathbf{u}_i = \rho_i \mathbf{u}_{i,-1} + \boldsymbol{\varepsilon}_i, 0 \leqslant |\rho_i| < 1$; $\mathbf{u}_{i,-1}$ denotes the vector of the one period lagged values of the terms of $\mathbf{u}_i$; Y_i is a $T \times K_Y$ matrix of observations on K_Y current endogenous variables; Z_{Ri} is a $T \times K_R$ matrix of observations on K_R lagged endogenous variables; Z_{Fi} is a $T \times K_F$ matrix of observations on K_F exogenous variables.[10] As before i indexes cross-section observations and t indexes time series observations. Let $X_i \equiv [\boldsymbol{\iota}_T, Y_i, Z_{Ri}, Z_{Fi}]$ and $\boldsymbol{\delta}_i \equiv (\beta_{0i}, \gamma_{Yi}', \gamma_i', \boldsymbol{\alpha}_i')'$.

We assume that the rank of X_i is $K = (K_Y + K_R + K_F + 1)$ and that the $\boldsymbol{\delta}_i$ $(i = 1, 2, ..., n)$ are independently and identically distributed with mean $\bar{\boldsymbol{\delta}}$ and variance-covariance matrix Δ, which is positive-definite. Rewrite

---

[9] These conditions are the following: (1) $\text{plim}_{T \to \infty} T^{-1} X_i' \Omega_{ii}^{-1} X_i$ is finite and positive-definite for every i; (2) $\text{plim}_{T \to \infty} T^{-1} X_i' \Omega_{ii}^{-1} \Omega_{ij} \Omega_{jj}^{-1} X_j$ is finite for every $i \neq j$; (3) the $\boldsymbol{\beta}_i$ are independently and identically distributed; (4) for every i the ε_{it}'s in $u_{it} = \rho_i u_{it-1} + \varepsilon_{it}$ $(t = 1, 2, ..., T)$ have a finite moment of the fourth order; and (5) for every i the elements of $P_i \mathbf{u}_i$, where $P_i' P_i = \Omega_{ii}^{-1}$, are independently and identically distributed.

[10] We assume that for each i the lagged endogenous variables and exogenous variables in Equation (21) satisfy Theil's (1971, p. 486) Assumptions 10.4 and 10.5.

Equation (21) as

(22) $\mathbf{y}_i = \mathbf{\iota}_T \beta_{0i} + (EY_i)\gamma_{Yi} + Z_{Ri}\gamma_i + Z_{Fi}\alpha_i + [\mathbf{u}_i + (Y_i - EY_i)\gamma_{Yi}]$

or

$$(\mathbf{y}_i - r_i\mathbf{y}_{i,\,-1}) = \mathbf{\iota}_T(1-r_i)\beta_{0i} + (EY_i - r_i Y_{i,\,-1})\gamma_{Yi} + (Z_{Ri} - r_i Z_{Ri,\,-1})\gamma_i$$
$$+ (Z_{Fi} - r_i Z_{Fi,\,-1})\alpha_i + [(\rho_i - r_i)\mathbf{u}_{i,\,-1} + \varepsilon_i$$
$$+ (Y_i - EY_i)\gamma_{Yi}] \quad (i = 1, 2, ..., n),$$

where the subscript -1 denotes the one period lagged values of a variable.

Since the coefficient vector δ_i is fixed for given i, we can apply Fair's (1970) iterative instrumental variable approach to each equation in (22) separately and obtain n sets of consistent estimates of coefficients. Let $\tilde{\beta}_{0i}, \tilde{\gamma}_{Yi}, \tilde{\gamma}_i, \tilde{\alpha}_i, \tilde{\rho}_i$, and $\tilde{\sigma}_{ii}$ be the estimates of $\beta_{0i}, \gamma_{Yi}, \gamma_i, \alpha_i, \rho_i$, and σ_{ii}, respectively, obtained in this way. Here the subscript i indicates that the estimate is based only on observations on the ith individual. Similarly, we can estimate σ_{ij} consistently by

(23) $\tilde{\sigma}_{ij} = T^{-1}\tilde{\varepsilon}_i'\tilde{\varepsilon}_j,$

where $i \neq j$ and

$$\tilde{\varepsilon}_i = \mathbf{y}_i - \tilde{\rho}_i\mathbf{y}_{i,\,-1} - (Y_i - \tilde{\rho}_i Y_{i,\,-1})\tilde{\gamma}_{Yi}$$
$$- (Z_{Ri} - \tilde{\rho}_i Z_{Ri,\,-1})\tilde{\gamma}_i - (Z_{Fi} - \tilde{\rho}_i Z_{Fi,\,-1})\tilde{\alpha}_i.$$

A consistent estimator of Δ is given by

(24) $\tilde{\Delta}_a = \dfrac{S_3}{n} = \dfrac{1}{n}\left(\displaystyle\sum_{i=1}^{n} \tilde{\mathbf{b}}_i \tilde{\mathbf{b}}_i' - \dfrac{1}{n}\sum_{i=1}^{n} \tilde{\mathbf{b}}_i \sum_{i=1}^{n} \tilde{\mathbf{b}}_i'\right),$

where $\tilde{\mathbf{b}}_i = (\tilde{\beta}_{0i}, \tilde{\gamma}_{Yi}', \tilde{\gamma}_i', \tilde{\alpha}_i')'$.

Since the X_i's contain observations on stochastic regressors that are correlated with the ε_i's, we find, following Fair (1970), a $T \times K$ matrix W_i of observations on some instruments such that for $i = 1, 2, ..., n$,

(25) $\operatorname*{plim}\limits_{T \to \infty} \dfrac{W_i'\varepsilon_i}{T} = 0,$ and $\operatorname*{plim}\limits_{T \to \infty} \dfrac{W_i'X_i}{T} = Q_{ii}$ exists and is nonsingular.

If q ($< K$) regressors are correlated with the ε_i's, then we need only q instrumental variables satisfying the conditions in Equation (25). The $K - q$ predetermined variables that are not correlated with the ε_i's act as instruments for themselves.

On premultiplying both sides of the ith equation in (21) by W_i' we obtain

(26) $W_i'\mathbf{y}_i = W_i'X_i\delta_i + W_i'\mathbf{u}_i$ $(i = 1, 2, ..., n).$

We assume that for every $i, j = 1, 2, ..., n$, δ_i is independent of X_j and $\mathbf{u}_j$, and the variance-covariance matrix of $(\mathbf{y}_1'W_1, \mathbf{y}_2'W_2, ..., \mathbf{y}_n'W_n)'$ is $\Sigma_3 = ET^2\Sigma_4$ where the probability limit of Σ_4 is given by Equation (27), [see p. 158],

(27)

$$\Sigma_4 = \plim_{T \to \infty} \frac{1}{T^2} \begin{bmatrix} (W_1'X_1\Delta X_1'W_1 + \sigma_{11}W_1'\Omega_{11}W_1) & \sigma_{12}W_1'\Omega_{12}W_2 & \cdots & \sigma_{1n}W_1'\Omega_{1n}W_n \\ \sigma_{21}W_2'\Omega_{21}W_1 & (W_2'X_2\Delta X_2'W_2 + \sigma_{22}W_2'\Omega_{22}W_2) & \cdots & \sigma_{2n}W_2'\Omega_{2n}W_n \\ \cdots & \cdots & \cdots & \cdots \\ \sigma_{n1}W_n'\Omega_{n1}W_1 & \sigma_{n2}W_n'\Omega_{n2}W_2 & \cdots & (W_n'X_n\Delta X_n'W_n + \sigma_{nn}W_n'\Omega_{nn}W_n) \end{bmatrix}$$

which is finite and positive-definite in an interval containing the true values of parameters as an interior point.

Application of Aitken's generalized least squares to Equation (26) yields an estimator of $\bar{\delta}$ which is:

$$(28) \qquad \bar{\delta}(\theta) = (X'W\Sigma_3^{-1}W'X)^{-1}X'W\Sigma_3^{-1}W'\mathbf{y},$$

where $W'X \equiv (X_1'W_1, X_2'W_2, \ldots, X_n'W_n)'$.

If Σ_3 is unknown, we can obtain a consistent estimator $\hat{\Sigma}_3$ of Σ_3 by replacing Δ, σ_{ij}, and ρ_i by $\tilde{\Delta}_a$, $\tilde{\sigma}_{ij}$, and $\tilde{\rho}_i$, respectively. The estimator (28) can be approximated by

$$(29) \qquad \bar{\delta}(\hat{\theta}) = (X'W\hat{\Sigma}_3^{-1}W'X)^{-1}X'W\hat{\Sigma}_3^{-1}W'\mathbf{y}.$$

Under the additional assumptions stated in footnotes 9 and 10 $\bar{\delta}(\hat{\theta})$ is consistent and has the same limiting distribution as $\bar{\delta}(\theta)$. Amemiya and Fuller (1967) have shown in the context of a distributed lag model that when some of the explanatory variables in a regression model are lagged values of the dependent variable and the disturbances are autocorrelated, Aitken's generalized least squares estimator of the coefficient vector based on a consistent estimate of the variance-covariance matrix of disturbances is consistent, but its efficiency, even in large samples, may be far lower than that of Aitken's generalized least squares estimator based on the "true" variance-covariance matrix. We have shown in this section that if the coefficients in an equation with random regressors and with serially and contemporaneously correlated disturbances vary randomly across units and are independent of all the other random quantities in the equation, the result of Amemiya and Fuller is no longer true. Application of an instrumental variable approach leads to consistent and asymptotically efficient estimators of the means of coefficients.[11]

Tests of Hypotheses

Testing procedures for $\bar{\beta}$ and Δ have been developed by Swamy (1971). One hypothesis of considerable interest is $\Delta = 0$ because Equation (6) under this hypothesis reduces to a fixed coefficient model. A method for testing the hypothesis $\Delta = 0$ against the alternative hypothesis $\Delta \neq 0$ is the likelihood ratio test which is described in Swamy (1971, pp. 122–124). It can be easily seen

---

[11] The assumption that the conditional distribution of the γ's given the y's on the right-hand side of Equation (21) is independent of these y's is critical for this result. This assumption, which is usually made in all the studies of economic behavior under uncertainty, may not hold in some instances; see Zellner (1966) and Theil (1971, p. 572). We say that an approximate Aitken estimator based on a consistent estimate of the covariance matrix of disturbances is asymptotically efficient if its limiting distribution is the same as that of the corresponding Aitken estimator.

that Equation (6) under assumption (7c′) reduces to another fixed coefficient model when $\bar{\Delta}$ becomes a null matrix. We cannot test the hypothesis $\bar{\Delta} = 0$ unless $\bar{\Delta}$ is estimable. It is a simple matter to show that $\bar{\Delta}$ can be estimated from the data in Equation (6) if the $\bar{\beta}_i$'s are known. However, one never knows the $\bar{\beta}_i$'s and, as a result, it is difficult in practice to compare the non-nested hypotheses that individual coefficient vectors are fixed but different and that the vectors are random drawings from a given distribution. Further work is required to produce good procedures for comparing non-nested models containing differing numbers of parameters.

Forecasting with RCR Models

Swamy (1971, pp. 133–138) derives an optimal forecasting procedure for a RCR model. It turns out that this procedure is the same whether the coefficient vector in a micro relation is random across units with the same mean vector or fixed but different for different individuals.

III.   Illustrative Example

Swamy (1971, Chaps. V and VI) provides two applications of a simplified version of the techniques discussed in Section II. The first application is in the analysis of micro investment data for 11 large U.S. corporations and the second is in the analysis of consumption and income data through time for a sample of 24 countries. In both these applications the use of RCR models led to theoretically plausible results. The random coefficient approach gave results which were more plausible than those given by the fixed coefficient approach. In this section we discuss one more application.

The equation chosen for our study here is the constant elasticity demand function for demand deposits in the U.S.

$$(30) \qquad \ln D_{it} = \beta_{0i} + \alpha_{1i} \ln r_{dit} + \alpha_{2i} \ln r_{tit} + \alpha_{3i} \ln r_{sit} + \alpha_{4i} \ln Y_{it} + u_{it}$$

$$(i = 1, 2, ..., 49; \; t = 1, 2, ..., 17),$$

where D_{it} is the real per capita commercial bank demand deposits held by individuals, partnerships, and corporations; r_{dit} is the ratio of service charges to average demand deposits; r_{tit} is the weighted average of actual interest yields on commercial bank time deposits and mutual savings bank deposits, the weights being the respective deposit balances for states at the beginning of the year; r_{sit} is the actual interest yield on savings and loan association shares; and Y_{it} is the real per capita disposable income.

The source of our data is Feige and Swamy (1972). Our data base consists of annual time series for 48 continental states in the U.S. plus the District of Columbia, covering all of the 17-year period 1949–1965.

Feige (1964) utilizes the same body of data for the period 1949–1959 to estimate the demand functions for liquid assets under the restriction that the slope coefficients are the same for all states. He introduces dummy variables to allow for separate intercepts for some states. Feige's results show, among other things, that demand deposits and savings and loan association shares are not substitutes and that the permanent income elasticity of demand for demand deposits is higher than that for time deposits or savings and loan association shares. These results were criticized by Lee (1966) who assembled both time series and cross-section evidence to show that savings and loan association shares are close substitutes for demand deposits. Lee's results also show that demand for demand deposits is more elastic with respect to changes in interest rates on savings and loan association shares than to changes in interest rates on other assets. Lee further argued that Feige's results are not plausible and they stem from excessive use of dummy variables that are highly correlated with interest rate variables. Lee re-estimated Feige's equations omitting the dummy variables. Results obtained in this way were in fair agreement with Lee's results. But this procedure is defective in the presence of regional heterogeneity of behavior. Feige and Swamy (1972) have shown that the assumption of identical regression coefficient vectors for states introduces a specification error of the type analyzed by Zellner (1962b). Also, problems of aggregation bias are bound to arise at the macro level if one insists on fixed coefficient models at the micro level because the units are seldom homogeneous with regard to the coefficient vector in a relation.

It would be interesting to see whether Lee's conclusions hold if we relax the assumption of identical coefficient vectors for states. Now we estimate Equation (30) under assumptions (7a)–(7e). To simplify our calculations we impose the restriction that for $i, j = 1, 2, ..., 49$: $\sigma_{ij} = 0$ if $i \neq j$ and $\rho_i = 0$. We also abstract from possible "simultaneous equation" complications. Application of the formula in Equation (19) gave the estimates shown in Tables 1 and 2 for the means of coefficients in Equation (30).

TABLE 1

ESTIMATES OF THE MEAN ELASTICITIES OF LOG-LINEAR DEMAND FUNCTION
FOR DEMAND DEPOSITS

Dependent variable	Independent variables				
	Constant	$\ln r_d$	$\ln r_t$	$\ln r_s$	$\ln Y$
$\ln D$	1.7942 (0.2030)	−0.0860 (0.0199)	−0.0175 (0.0091)	−0.2063 (0.0312)	0.6194 (0.0237)

TABLE 2

ESTIMATED VARIANCE-COVARIANCE MATRIX OF β_i: $\hat{\Delta}$

β_{0i}	α_{1i}	α_{2i}	α_{3i}	α_{4i}
1.0851	0.0427	−0.0629	−0.0307	−0.0965
	0.0144	0.0005	−0.0237	−0.0014
		−0.0057	0.0135	0.0073
			0.0177	−0.0023
				0.0090

The values given in Table 2 were obtained by applying formula (18) to our data. First, we note that the estimated variance of the coefficient of $\ln r_t$ is negative. This is because an unbiased estimator of Δ in Equation (18) is in the form of a difference of two matrices and it can be negative definite with positive probability (see Swamy, 1971, pp. 107–110, 147–149). Feige and Swamy (1972) have indicated a possible cause of this negative estimate. Second, in order to provide a descriptive measure of cross-state variability in the coefficients, we calculated for each coefficient the coefficient of variation, defined as the ratio of the estimated standard deviation of an element of β_i to the estimated mean of the same element. These are 0.58, −1.39, ——, −0.64, 0.15 for the constant term and the coefficients of $\ln r_d$, $\ln r_t$, $\ln r_s$, and $\ln Y$, respectively. These measures reveal considerable variability in the coefficients across states. An assumption that the entire coefficient vector β_i is the same for all states is obviously incorrect.

In Table 1 the values given in parentheses are the asymptotic standard errors obtained by taking the square root of the diagonal elements of $(X'\hat{\Sigma}_2^{-1} X)^{-1}$. Details of these calculations and further results are given in Feige and Swamy (1972). The estimates of price elasticities in Table 1 lend support to Lee's conclusions. However, the income elasticity estimate in Table 1 is substantially smaller than that obtained by Lee (1966) for the fixed coefficient model. His estimates of other coefficients also differ from ours in magnitude.

Notice that, in view of the result in Equation (20), the estimates in Table 1 can be taken as the consistent estimates of coefficients in a macro relation obtained by aggregating Equation (30) across states (see also Swamy, 1971, pp. 187–188). Since the coefficients of Equation (30) are different for different states, the income elasticity estimate obtained by Lee (1966) suffers from a specification error of the type indicated by Zellner (1962b). Consequently, our estimates are better than Lee's estimates. The principal conclusion to be drawn in a general way, from what has been said above is that the use of RCR methods can result in more fruitful and meaningful econometric analyses of micro panel data.

IV. Suggestions for Further Research

In the preceding section we have been concerned with the problem of finding close approximations to the MVLU estimators of the means of coefficients. While the essential simplicity of this approach is attractive, the inference provided by it is intellectually less satisfying than that provided by the Bayesian approach. Although there are some apparent similarities between assumptions (7a)–(7e) and the assumptions made in a Bayesian analysis of a standard linear model, the argument leading to the MVLU estimator (14) is defective in its premises, in that the condition of unbiasedness is not, in general, a reasonable requirement to impose. An approach to the analysis of Equation (13) under assumptions (7a)–(7e) without the requirement of unbiasedness is to develop a MMSE estimator along the lines explained by Chipman (1964).

Consider Equation (13), which can be written as

$$(13a) \qquad\qquad \mathbf{y} = D\boldsymbol{\beta} + \mathbf{u},$$

where $\boldsymbol{\beta} = (\iota_n \otimes \bar{\boldsymbol{\beta}}) + \boldsymbol{\xi}$.

Assumptions (7b)–(7e) will be made throughout this section. We replace assumption (7a) by the weaker assumption that the rank of X_i is less than or equal to K, $n > K$ and $T > K$. We treat $\bar{\boldsymbol{\beta}}$ and Δ as the first two moments of the prior distribution of $\boldsymbol{\beta}_i$. Regarding the prior distribution of $(\bar{\boldsymbol{\beta}}, \Delta, \Omega)$, we assume that it is a point distribution with the whole mass of the distribution concentrated in one known point in the parameter space. Clearly, these assumptions are weaker than those adopted in a Bayesian analysis of a standard linear model. As in Section II we here wish to preserve the "distribution-free" formulation of the problem, expressing our results in terms of means and variances or similar quantities.

The linear estimator of $\boldsymbol{\beta}$, which has the smallest mean square error, is

$$(31) \qquad \check{\boldsymbol{\beta}} = (I_n \otimes \Delta) D' \Sigma_2^{-1} \mathbf{y} + [I_{nK} - (I_n \otimes \Delta) D' \Sigma_2^{-1} D] (\iota_n \otimes \bar{\boldsymbol{\beta}}),$$

where $\Sigma_2 = D(I_n \otimes \Delta) D' + \Omega$ and $\Omega = \{\sigma_{ij}\Omega_{ij}\}$ $(i, j = 1, 2, ..., n)$.

Chipman (1964, pp. 1104–1105) and, independently, Rao (1965b, Lemma 1) proved that $\check{\boldsymbol{\beta}}$ is a MMSE linear estimator in the following sense: Any other estimator of $\boldsymbol{\beta}$ that is also linear in the vector $\mathbf{y}$ has a matrix of second-order sampling moments around $\boldsymbol{\beta}$, which exceeds that of $\check{\boldsymbol{\beta}}$ by a positive-semi-definite matrix. Chipman attributes the estimator $\check{\boldsymbol{\beta}}$ to Foster who solves the problem quite generally without assuming that Δ and Ω are nonsingular.

Application of a matrix result in Rao (1965a, p. 29, Problem 2.9) yields

$$(32) \qquad \Sigma_2^{-1} = \Omega^{-1} - \Omega^{-1} D (D'\Omega^{-1}D + I_n \otimes \Delta^{-1})^{-1} D'\Omega^{-1}.$$

If the expression (32) is substituted in Equation (31), the estimator $\check{\boldsymbol{\beta}}$ can be expressed as

(33) $\check{\beta} = [D'\Omega^{-1}D + (I_n \otimes \Delta^{-1})]^{-1}[D'\Omega^{-1}\mathbf{y} + (\iota_n \otimes \Delta^{-1}\bar{\beta})].$

Let us now assume that the rank of each X_i is K. The estimator $\check{\beta}$ becomes a weighted average of the least squares estimator $\hat{\beta} = (D'\Omega^{-1}D)^{-1}D'\Omega^{-1}\mathbf{y}$ and the prior mean $(\iota_n \otimes \bar{\beta})$, with weights inversely proportional to their variance-covariance matrices.

By well-known Bayesian arguments it follows that the conditional posterior distribution of β, given Ω and the data, is centered at $\check{\beta}$ if the prior distribution of β is normal with mean $(\iota_n \otimes \bar{\beta})$ and variance-covariance matrix $(I_n \otimes \Delta)$, and the conditional distribution of $\mathbf{y}$ given D and β, is also normal with known variance-covariance matrix Ω; see Zellner (1971, p. 240). The posterior mean is an admissible estimator, for a quadratic loss function, see Zellner (1971, p. 24). Consequently, as far as the estimator $\check{\beta}$ is concerned, we may delete the constraint "linear" of MMSE linear if the random variation in β and $\mathbf{u}$ is normal.

As pointed out by Chipman (1964, p. 1107), MVLU estimation is the limiting case of MMSE linear estimation when the prior variances of β become infinite because, as we can see from Equation (33), $\check{\beta}$ tends to $\hat{\beta}$ as the elements of Δ tend to infinity.

The matrix of second-order moments of $\check{\beta}$ around β is

(34) $R(\theta) = G(D'\Omega^{-1}D)^{-1}G' + (I_{nK} - G)(I_n \otimes \Delta)(I_{nK} - G)',$

where $G = [D'\Omega^{-1}D + (I_n \otimes \Delta^{-1})]^{-1}D'\Omega^{-1}D$ and $(D'\Omega^{-1}D)^{-1}$ is the variance-covariance matrix of $\hat{\beta}$.

It can be shown that the matrix $(D'\Omega^{-1}D)^{-1} - R(\theta)$ is nonnegative definite regardless of the true values of fixed parameters.

If $\bar{\beta}$ and Δ are exactly known and Ω is unknown, it is impossible to use the estimator (33) in practice. What we propose to do is to employ an estimate of Ω in constructing the MMSE estimator. This estimate is $\hat{\Omega} = \{\hat{\sigma}_{ij}\hat{\Omega}_{ij}\}$ $(i, j = 1, 2, ..., n)$, where $\hat{\Omega}_{ij} = \Omega_{ij}$ when $\rho_i = \hat{\rho}_i$, $\hat{\rho}_i$ and $\hat{\sigma}_{ij}$ are as shown in Equations (15) and (16). This procedure gives an approximate MMSE linear estimator of β, while an approximate MVLU estimator of β is $\mathbf{b} = (D'\hat{\Omega}^{-1}D)^{-1}D'\hat{\Omega}^{-1}\mathbf{y}$. The matrix of second-order moments of the estimator $\mathbf{b}$ around β will exceed that of the approximate MMSE linear estimator by a positive-semidefinite matrix for every admissible value of the fixed parameter vector; see Mehta and Swamy (1972).

In cases where $\bar{\beta}$ and Δ are also unknown, their estimation presents no serious difficulties if past data on $\mathbf{y}$ and D are available. Formulas (19) and (17), when applied to past data, might yield reasonable estimates of $\bar{\beta}$ and Δ. An approximate MMSE linear estimator of β can be obtained by replacing $\bar{\beta}$, Δ, and Ω in Equation (33) by their respective estimates. This procedure is very much in the spirit of empirical Bayes procedure described in Clemmer and Krutchkoff (1968). Each diagonal element of the second-order moment matrix of the approximate MMSE linear estimator around β can be smaller than the corresponding diagonal element of the second-order moment matrix of the estimator **b** around β in some cases.

In reporting the results of the above analysis, it may not be convenient to provide the estimates of all the nK elements of β, especially when n is large. It is also a good practice to describe the main features of the distribution of β. In the first place, we often want to locate the distribution by finding some value of the variable, which may be conceived as a central point of the distribution. Such a value is given by $\bar{\beta}$.

It follows from a result in Theil (1971, p. 125, Problem 4.3) that the MMSE linear estimator $\bar{\beta}$ in Equation (13) is

$$(35) \qquad \hat{\bar{\beta}}_f = \bar{\beta}\bar{\beta}'X'(X\bar{\beta}\bar{\beta}'X'+\Sigma_2)^{-1}\mathbf{y},$$

where X and $\mathbf{y}$ are as shown in Equation (13) and Σ_2 is as shown in Equation (8).

If the rank of each X_i is K, then it is easy to show that [see Rao (1965a, p. 29, Problem 2.9)]

$$(36) \quad (X\bar{\beta}\bar{\beta}'X'+\Sigma_2)^{-1} = \Sigma_2^{-1} - \Sigma_2^{-1}X(X'\Sigma_2^{-1}X)^{-1}X'\Sigma_2^{-1}$$
$$+ \Sigma_2^{-1}X(X'\Sigma_2^{-1}X)^{-1}[\bar{\beta}\bar{\beta}'+(X'\Sigma_2^{-1}X)^{-1}]^{-1}$$
$$\times (X'\Sigma_2^{-1}X)^{-1}X'\Sigma_2^{-1}.$$

Inserting this back into Equation (35) gives

$$(37) \qquad \hat{\bar{\beta}}_f = \bar{\beta}\bar{\beta}'[\bar{\beta}\bar{\beta}'+(X'\Sigma_2^{-1}X)^{-1}]^{-1}\bar{\mathbf{b}}(\theta) = G_1\bar{\mathbf{b}}(\theta),$$

where $\bar{\mathbf{b}}(\theta)$ is as shown in Equation (14) and $G_1 = \bar{\beta}\bar{\beta}'[\bar{\beta}\bar{\beta}'+(X'\Sigma_2^{-1}X)^{-1}]^{-1}$.

The matrix of second-order moments of $\hat{\bar{\beta}}_f$ around $\bar{\beta}$ is

$$(38) \qquad G_1(X'\Sigma_2^{-1}X)^{-1}G_1' + (G_1-I)\bar{\beta}\bar{\beta}'(G_1-I)'.$$

An approximate MMSE estimator of $\bar{\beta}$ is

$$(39) \qquad \hat{\bar{\beta}} = \bar{\mathbf{b}}(\hat{\theta})\bar{\mathbf{b}}'(\hat{\theta})[\bar{\mathbf{b}}(\hat{\theta})\bar{\mathbf{b}}'(\hat{\theta})+(X'\hat{\Sigma}_2^{-1}X)^{-1}]^{-1}\bar{\mathbf{b}}(\hat{\theta}),$$

where $\bar{\mathbf{b}}(\hat{\theta})$ and $\hat{\Sigma}_2$ are as shown in Equation (19).

It is possible that for some values of the parameters the mean square error of an element of $\hat{\bar{\beta}}$ in Equation (39) is smaller than that of the corresponding element of $\bar{\mathbf{b}}(\hat{\theta})$. Further investigation of the sampling properties of these estimators is needed. We can also use a prior estimate of $\bar{\beta}\bar{\beta}'$ in places of the known value used in Equation (35).

In some circumstances we may find it necessary to go further and let the parameters $\bar{\beta}$, Δ, and Ω also have a prior distribution other than a point distribution. Using this prior distribution in conjunction with the likelihood function we can obtain the joint posterior density function of the parameters $\bar{\beta}$ and θ; see Swamy (1971, p. 141). At this point if our interest centers at the mean vector $\bar{\beta}$, we can integrate the joint posterior density with respect to θ over the appropriate range to get the marginal posterior density of $\bar{\beta}$. Unfortunately, any reasonable prior distributions for $\bar{\beta}$, Δ, and Ω lead to integrals that cannot all be expressed in closed form and, as a result, the Bayesian analysis of Equation (13) is technically most complex to execute (see Lindley and Smith, 1972). One can, therefore, consider an approximation to it that is technically much simpler and yet yields the bulk, though not all, of the information for the estimation. This approximation consists in using the modal values of the conditional posterior distribution of $\bar{\beta}$ given $\theta = \hat{\theta}$, where $\hat{\theta}$ is a sample estimate of θ. If the prior distributions of $\bar{\beta}$ and θ are diffuse, then the estimator $\mathbf{b}(\hat{\theta})$ in Equation (19) will be close to the mean of the conditional posterior distribution of $\bar{\beta}$ given $\theta = \hat{\theta}$.

The following analysis is even simpler than the above approximate Bayesian analysis. Knowing only the first two moments of the prior distribution of $\bar{\beta}$, we can follow the method developed by Chipman (1964). Let $\mathbf{r}$ and ψ be the mean and variance–covariance matrix of the prior distribution of $\bar{\beta}$. Let $\bar{\beta}$ be independent of X and $\mathbf{u}$. The prior distribution of θ is again a point distribution with the whole mass of the distribution concentrated in one known point in the parameter space. Following Chipman (1964) and Rao (1965b), we can show the estimator

$$(40) \qquad \breve{\bar{\beta}}(\theta) = (X'\Sigma_2^{-1}X + \psi^{-1})^{-1}(X'\Sigma_2^{-1}\mathbf{y} + \psi^{-1}\mathbf{r})$$

is a MMSE estimator of $\bar{\beta}$ in the sense that any other estimator of $\bar{\beta}$ that is also linear in the vector $\mathbf{y}$ has a matrix of second order moments around $\bar{\beta}$, which exceeds that of $\breve{\bar{\beta}}(\theta)$ by a positive semidefinite matrix. If Σ_2 is unknown, an estimate of Σ_2 can be used in place of the known value used in Equation (40), [see Swamy (1971, p. 199)]. Thus, $\breve{\bar{\beta}}(\theta)$ can be approximated by

$$(41) \qquad \breve{\bar{\beta}}(\hat{\theta}) = (X'\hat{\Sigma}_2^{-1}X + \psi^{-1})^{-1}(X'\hat{\Sigma}_2^{-1}\mathbf{y} + \psi^{-1}\mathbf{r})$$

where $\hat{\Sigma}_2$ is as shown in Equation (19). It is worth noting that the estimator $\breve{\bar{\beta}}(\hat{\theta})$ completely dominates the estimator $\mathbf{b}(\hat{\theta})$ in Equation (19) and the estimator $\breve{\bar{\beta}}$ in Equation (39).

REFERENCES

Amemiya, T. (1971). "The Estimation of the Variances in a Variance-Components Model," *Int. Econ. Rev.* **12**, 1–13.

Amemiya, T. and W. A. Fuller (1967). "A Comparative Study of Alternative Estimators in a Distributed Lag Model," *Econometrica* **35**, 509–529.

Chipman, J. S. (1964). "On Least Squares with Insufficient Observations," *J. Amer. Statist. Ass.* **59**, 1078–1111.

Clemmer, B. A. and R. G. Krutchkoff (1968). "The Use of Empirical Bayes Estimators in a Linear Regression Model," *Biometrika* **55**, 525–534.

Fair, R. C. (1970). "The Estimation of Simultaneous Equation Models with Lagged Endogenous Variables and First Order Serially Correlated Errors," *Econometrica* **38**, 507–516.

Feige, E. L. (1964). *The Demand for Liquid Assets: A Temporal Cross-Section Analysis.* Prentice-Hall, Englewood Cliffs, New Jersey.

Feige, E. L. and P. A. V. B. Swamy (1972). "A Random Coefficient Model of the Demand for Liquid Assets," Workshop Paper # 7211, Social Syst. Res. Inst., Univ. of Wisconsin, Madison, Wisconsin. *J. Money, Credit and Banking* (forthcoming).

Fisk, P. R. (1967). "Models of the Second Kind in Regression Analysis," *J. Roy. Statist. Soc. Ser. B* **28**, 266–281.

Hildreth, C., and J. P. Houck (1968). "Some Estimators for a Linear Model with Random Coefficients," *J. Amer. Statist. Ass.* **63**, 584–595.

Hoch, I. (1962). "Estimation of Production Function Parameters Combining Time Series and Cross-Section Data," *Econometrica* **30**, 34–53.

Houthakker, H. (1955). "The Pareto Distribution and the Cobb-Douglas Production Function in Activity Analysis," *Rev. Econ. Stud.* **23**, 27–31.

Hurwicz, L. (1950). "Systems with Nonadditive Disturbances," In *Statistical Inference in Dynamic Economic Models* (T. C. Koopmans, ed.), Chapter 18. Wiley, New York.

Klein, L. R. (1953). *A Textbook of Econometrics.* Row Peterson, Evanston, Illinois.

Kuh, E. (1959). "The Validity of Cross-Sectionally Estimated Behavior Equations in Time-Series Applications," *Econometrica* **27**, 197–214.

Kuh, E. (1963). *Capital Stock Growth. A Micro-econometric Approach.* North-Holland Publ., Amsterdam.

Lee, T. H. (1966). "Substitutability of Non-Bank Intermediary Liabilities for Money: The Empirical Evidence," *J. Finance* **21**, 441–457.

Lindley, D. V. and A. F. M. Smith (1972). "Bayes Estimators for the Linear Model," *J. Roy. Statist. Soc. Ser. B* **34**, 1–18.

Mehta, J. S. and P. A. V. B. Swamy (1972). "Efficient Method of Estimating the Level of a Stationary First-Order Autoregressive Process," *Communications in Statistics* (forthcoming).

Mundlak, Y. (1961). "Empirical Production Functions Free of Management Bias," *J. Farm Econ.* **43**, 44–56.

Mundlak, Y. (1963). "Estimation of Production and Behavioral Functions from a Combination of Cross-Section and Time Series Data," In *Measurement in Economics* (C. F. Christ, ed.). Stanford Univ. Press, Stanford, California.

Nerlove, M. (1965). *Estimation and Identification of Cobb-Douglas Production Functions.* Rand McNally, Chicago, Illinois.

Nerlove, M. (1971). "A Note on Error Components Models," *Econometrica* **39**, 383–396.

Parks, R. W. (1967). "Efficient Estimation of a System of Regression Equations when Disturbances are Both Serially and Contemporaneously Correlated," *J. Amer. Statist. Ass.* **62**, 500–509.

Porter, R. D. (1972). "On the Use of Sample Survey Weights in the Linear Models," *Ann. Econ. Soc. Measurement* (forthcoming).

Rao, C. R. (1965a). *Linear Statistical Inference and Its Applications.* Wiley, New York.

Rao, C. R. (1965b). "The Theory of Least Squares when the Parameters are Stochastic and its Application to the Analysis of Growth Curves," *Biometrika* **52**, 447–458.

Rao, C. R. (1967). "Least Squares Theory Using an Estimated Dispersion Matrix and its Application to Measurement of Signals," *Proc. Berkeley Symp. Math. Statist. Probability, 5th*, pp. 355–371. Univ. of California Press, Berkeley, California.

Rao, C. R. (1972). "Estimating Variance and Covariance Components in Linear Models," *J. Amer. Statist. Ass.* **67**, 112–115.

Rosenberg, B. (1970). "Varying Parameter Regression in the Analysis of a Cross-Section of Time-Series—I," Mimeo, Univ. of California, Berkeley.

Swamy, P. A. V. B. (1971). *Statistical Inference in Random Coefficient Regression Models.* Springer-Verlag, New York.

Swamy, P. A. V. B. and J. S. Mehta (1971). "Bayesian Analysis of Error Components Regression Models," presented at the Second NBER-NSF Symp. on Bayesian Inference in Econometrics. *J. Amer. Statist. Ass.* (forthcoming).

Swamy, P. A. V. B. and S. S. Arora (1972). "The Exact Finite Sample Properties of the Estimators of Coefficients in the Error Components Regression Models," *Econometrica* **40**, 261–275.

Theil, H. (1957). "Specification Errors and the Estimation of Economic Relationships," *Rev. Int. Statist. Inst.* **25**, 41–51.

Theil, H. (1971). *Principles of Econometrics.* Wiley, New York.

Theil, H. and L. B. M. Mennes (1959). "Conception Stochatique des Coefficients Multiplicateurs dans l'Ajustement Linéaire des Séries Temporelles," *Publ. Inst. Statist. Univ. Paris* **8**, 211–227.

Wald, A. (1947). "A Note on Regression Analysis," *Ann. Math. Statist.* **18**, 586–589.

Wallace, T. D. and A. Hussain (1969): "The Use of Error Components Models in Combining Cross-Sections with Time Series Data," *Econometrica* **37**, 55–72.

Zellner, A. (1962a). "An Efficient Method of Estimating Seemingly Unrelated Regressions and Tests for Aggregation Bias," *J. Amer. Statist. Ass.* **62**, 348–368.

Zellner, A. (1962b). "Estimation of Cross-Section Relations: Analysis of a Common Specification Error," *Metro-economica* **14**, 111–117.

Zellner, A. (1966). "On the Aggregation Problem: A New Approach to a Troublesome Problem," Rep. # 6628, Center for Math. Studies in Business and Econ., Univ. of Chicago. Published In *Economic Models, Estimation and Risk Programming: Essays in Honor of Gerhard Tintner* (K. A. Fox *et al.*, eds.). Springer-Verlag, New York, 1969.

Zellner, A. (1971). *An Introduction to Bayesian Inference in Econometrics.* Wiley, New York.

Zellner, A. and W. Vandaele (1971). "Bayes-Stein Estimators for k-Means, Regression and Simultaneous Equation Models," presented at the Third NBER-NSF Symp. on Bayesian Inference in Econometrics. To be published in *Studies in Bayesian Econometrics and Statistics* (A. Zellner and S. Fienberg, eds.) North-Holland Publ., Amsterdam.

Chapter Six

Estimation by minimizing the sum of absolute errors

LESTER D. TAYLOR[1]

UNIVERSITY OF MICHIGAN
ANN ARBOR, MICHIGAN

Orthodoxy should not put tradition before inspiration (Edgeworth, 1888, p. 191).

[1] This research was supported by the National Science Foundation, by the Institute for Policy Analysis at the University of Toronto, and by the University of Michigan.

Econometricians have always pretty much taken for granted that the error terms implicit in their models are generated by distributions having a finite variance. However, it would appear that this assumption, at least in some contexts, ought to be given some second thought, for there now exists a considerable body of evidence that attests to distributions with infinite variance being a reality in economics.[2] Of course, it has been known since the time of Pareto that the distribution of income has this property, but recent years have seen the behavior of speculative prices and the distribution of firms by size, among other economic phenomena, added to the list.

The implications of an infinite variance for conventional methods of estimation, least squares in particular, are rather grim. In a finite-variance world, we hardly need remind ourselves of the virtues of least squares: It provides the Gauss–Markov estimator and, in addition, the maximum likelihood estimator in the context of normality. Normality also opens the door to the vast apparatus of classical and Bayesian inference. However, in an infinite-variance world, the Gauss–Markov theorem no longer applies, and least squares becomes just another estimator. And a poor one at that. An infinite variance means thick tails, and thick tails mean a lot of outliers. Least squares, as we know, gives outliers a lot of weight, and accordingly becomes extremely sample-dependent. Thus, in this context, an estimator which gives relatively little weight to outliers is clearly to be preferred.

The purpose of this paper is to provide a survey of one estimator that has this property, namely, the estimator obtained by minimizing the sum of absolute errors, hereafter to be referred to as LAE (for least absolute error).[3] As a method of estimation, LAE, in Gauss and LaPlace, has the same illustrious progenitors as least squares, but, excepting the interest shown it by Edgeworth (1887, 1888, 1923), Rhodes (1930), and Singleton (1940), it has historically never attracted much attention. Primarily, this lack of attention has stemmed from a combination of the mathematical difficulty of working with the absolute value function and the overwhelming popularity of least squares, which has created a strong vested interest on the part of econometricians for the latter's continued use. Except for the simple, two-variable

---

[2] For recent discussions of this evidence, see Granger and Orr (1972) and Mandelbrot (1967). Distributions observed in the real world can, of course, never display an infinite variance. However, as a practical matter, the important issue is not that the second moment is actually infinite, but whether, say, the interdecile range in relation to the interquartile range is sufficiently large that one is justified in acting *as though* the variance is infinite. Assuming that the variance is infinite in such situations is actually easier to deal with than assuming it to be large but finite. For a discussion, see Mandelbrot (1963). See also Fama and Roll (1968).

[3] One also finds in the literature this estimator referred to variously as MSAE, LAR (least absolute residual), MAD (minimum absolute deviation), "least lines," and L_1 (for the L_p estimator with $p = 1$).

model, computation of the LAE estimator was cumbersome at best until the paper of Charnes *et al.* (1955), in which it was shown that the LAE estimator can be obtained as the solution to a linear programming problem.

With the Charnes–Cooper–Ferguson paper, LAE acquired a new lease on life, and papers by Karst (1958), Wagner (1959), and Fisher (1961), the last two further drawing the parallel of LAE estimation with linear programming, soon followed.[4] There was also some empirical application by Charnes *et al.* in their original paper, Arrow and Hoffenberg (1959), Meyer and Glauber (1964), Oveson (1968), and most recently by Sharpe (1971).[5] The Meyer–Glauber investment study is of special interest, since this was the first time that LAE and least squares estimation had been directly compared in a context that is of more or less "bread and butter" importance to econometricians. What Meyer and Glauber did was first to estimate their investment models by LAE as well as by least squares and then to test the equations obtained on post-sample data by using them to forecast the 9 (in some cases, 11) observations subsequent to the period of fit. They found that, with very few exceptions, the equations estimated by LAE outperformed the ones estimated by least squares, even on criteria (such as the sum of squared forecast errors) with respect to which least squares is ordinarily thought to be optimal.

The Meyer–Glauber results, together with the mounting evidence that infinite-variance distributions in fact exist in economics, provide strong support for the view that LAE estimation is something to be taken seriously and is worthy of the intensified attention that it has been receiving. With computation no longer an issue, the biggest problem facing the use of LAE is the absence of a sampling theory. The only test currently available for an LAE equation is the pragmatic one of how well the equation forecasts. Most sampling theory, and certainly that for least squares, is based on the normal distribution, but since the major reason for being interested in LAE is to be able to deal with error terms triggered by long-tailed distributions, the sampling theory for LAE must begin along nonnormal lines. But even this is only part of the difficulty. Unlike least squares estimators, which are functions of all of the observations in the sample, LAE estimators depend on only a subset of observations, but a subset that in general varies from one realization of the error term to the next. Among other things, this means that in deriving the distribution of an LAE estimator, it is necessary to "go through" the

---

[4] Karst's paper, however, was essentially a retracing of the solution of Rhodes's (1930) for one independent variable, and, also, was apparently written without knowledge of the paper of Charnes *et al.*

[5] There have also been a number of Monte Carlo studies comparing the sampling properties of LAE with least squares in the presence of errors generated by thick-tailed distributions. These include Oveson (1968), Glahe and Hunt (1970), and Blattberg and Sargent (1971).

distribution of the "solution" subset of observations. A good part of this paper is devoted to this problem.

The format of the paper is as follows: The next section presents the mechanics of computation of the LAE estimator, while Section II discusses and summarizes its known statistical properties. I emphasize the "known" in this context, because there is much about the sampling behavior of the LAE estimator that remains to be discovered. The results reported in this section are based primarily on my own research, that of Gilbert Bassett, a student at the University of Michigan doing his Ph.D. thesis under my direction, and on an as yet unpublished paper of Rosenberg and Carlson (1971). A geometrical interpretation of LAE estimation is presented in Section III, while Section IV is devoted to some final observations.

I.   Mechanics of Least Absolute Error Estimation

Let the model to be estimated be given by

$$(1) \qquad\qquad y = X\beta + u,$$

where y and u are $T \times 1$ vectors, X a $T \times n$ matrix, and β an $n \times 1$ vector of constants. As usual, it is assumed that u is a random variable with mean zero. At this point, we make no assumptions about its variance or the form of its distribution. We wish to estimate β by minimizing the expression

$$(2) \qquad\qquad S = \sum |u_i|$$
$$= \sum_i \left| y_i - \sum_j \beta_j x_{ij} \right|$$

with respect to β. It is evident that because of the absolute value function we cannot proceed with conventional calculus methods as with least squares. This is the reason for transforming the problem to an equivalent linear programming problem.

To motivate this, however, it will be useful to consider the case of a single independent variable and an intercept, viz,

$$(3) \qquad\qquad Y_i = a + bX_i + u_i, \qquad i = 1, T.$$

The task is thus to find $\hat{a}$ and $\hat{b}$ so as to minimize

$$(4) \qquad\qquad S = \sum |Y_i - \hat{Y}_i|,$$

where $\hat{Y}_i = \hat{a} + \hat{b}X_i$. Suppose for the moment that $\hat{a}$ is chosen so as to force the regression line to include the point of means, which is to translate the origin to $(\bar{Y}, \bar{X})$.[6] Then, letting $y_i = Y_i - \bar{Y}$ and $x_i = X_i - \bar{X}$, Equations (3) and (4)

---

[6] The choice of any other point would not change the argument.

become

(5) $$y_i = bx_i + u_i, \qquad i = 1, T$$

(6) $$S = \sum |y_i - \hat{y}_i|$$
$$= \sum |y_i - \hat{b}x_i|.$$

The typical element in S is

(7) $$S_i = |y_i - \hat{b}x_i|,$$

which is a broken line in the (S, b) plane composed of two half-lines, with a minimum (equal to zero) at

(8) $$\hat{b}_i = \frac{y_i}{x_i}.$$

The slope of the half-line to the left of $\hat{b}_i$ is equal to $-|x_i|$, while to the right of b_i it is equal to $|x_i|$. This means that S_i is always convex upward. Consequently, S_i considered in the (S, b) plane, being the sum of connected half-lines, will consist of connected line segments. Its slope at any point b will be the sum of the slopes of the individual S_i at that value of b and, since these change only at the minimum points of the S_i, the slope of S also can change only at these points. Moreover, since each S_i is convex, so also must S.

It is evident from the foregoing that in minimizing S only those points corresponding to the minimum points of the individual S_i need to be considered. These are finite in number, and are, as already noted, equal to y_i/x_i for each observation. Thus, the regression line will go through the point of means and will have for slope the $\hat{b}_i$ that minimizes S. This implies, of course, that the regression line must also pass through the observation corresponding to the minimizing i. The regression line, therefore, is determined by the point of means and the observation associated with the minimizing $\hat{b}_i$.

Consider now the case where the regression line is not forced to go through the point of means. The estimation problems accordingly become to find $\hat{a}$ and $\hat{b}$ such that

(9) $$S = \sum |Y_i - \hat{a} - \hat{b}X_i|$$

is minimized. The typical element of S,

(10) $$S_i = |Y_i - \hat{a} - \hat{b}X_i|,$$

is now composed of two half-planes in (S, a, b) space that intersect in the (a, b) plane. It is evident that S_i is convex upward and also that it reaches a minimum on the line of intersection of the two half-planes in the (a, b) plane. Thus, there is a family of (a, b) corresponding to the minimum of S_i given by the equation

(11) $$Y_i - a - bX_i = 0.$$

Since the surface S is an addition of half-planes, it consists of connected plane segments and, because the S_i are convex, so, too, is S. Consequently, S will have a unique minimum region, which will be a point, a line, or a closed polygon. A point represents a unique solution to the estimation problem, while a line or closed polygon represents multiple solutions. The boundaries of the plane segments that compose S will lie directly above the set of lines,

$$(12) \qquad\qquad Y_i - a - bX_i = 0, \qquad i = 1, T$$

in the (a, b) plane. This is because the direction cosines of the constituent half-planes of the S_i change only at their lines of intersection. Consequently, a unique solution to the estimation problem must lie above one of the points of intersection of the lines in Equation (12). Since each of these lines corresponds to a particular observation, there will be two observations that lie on the regression line. These two observations in fact determine the regression line. A nonunique solution to the estimation problem will correspond to the minimum of S lying above either a line segment or a closed polygon in the (a, b) plane. In the first case, the solutions will lie on a closed interval of a line in Equation (12) formed by the intersections of that line with two others that are parallel, while the solutions in the second case will lie in a closed polygon formed by three or more of the lines.

The extension to n independent variables is straightforward. Each S_i in this case will consist of two n-dimensional half-hyperplanes in $(S, \beta_1, ..., \beta_n)$ space intersecting in the $(\beta_1, ..., \beta_n)$ hyperplane and, as before, is convex upward.[7] S, being the addition of all of these half-hyperplanes, will therefore form a polygonal surface whose edges lie above the $(n-1)$-dimensional hyperplanes generated by the intersections of the constituent half-hyperplanes of S with the $(\beta_1, ..., \beta_n)$ hyperplane. Since the S_i are convex, so, too, is S. The minimum of S_i, if the solution to the estimation problem is unique, will lie above the intersection of n of these $(n-1)$-dimensional hyperplanes.[8] Indeed, these n observations, in fact, determine the regression hyperplane.

Since with n independent variables, it is a subset of n observations (assuming no degeneracy) that determines the regression hyperplane, the estimation problem is thus reduced to a combinatorial one, namely, to find the subset out of the $\binom{T}{n}$ possible subsets of n observations that renders S a minimum. Linear programming provides an efficient way of arriving at this optimal subset.

---

[7] Convex "upward" in this context means convex in the direction of the S axis.

[8] This means, as a consequence, that n observations must lie in the regression hyperplane. If the solution to the estimation problem is not unique, the minimum of S will consist of a closed polygonal segment parallel to the $(\beta_1, ..., \beta_n)$ hyperplane and lying above the closed segment in the latter formed by its intersection with $n+1$ or more of the S_i.

Least Absolute Error as a Linear Programming Problem

In matrix notation, the format of a linear programming problem is to minimize the quantity

$$(13) \qquad\qquad Q = p'\alpha$$

subject to the restrictions

$$(14) \qquad\qquad A\alpha \geqslant b,$$

$$(15) \qquad\qquad \alpha \geqslant 0.$$

Our first task, quite clearly, is to convert the function being minimized in Equation (2) into an equivalent linear form. This is done by writing u_i as the difference between two nonnegative variables[9]:

$$(16) \qquad\qquad u_i = v_i - w_i, \qquad v_i, w_i \geqslant 0,$$

and then minimizing the quantity

$$(17) \qquad\qquad S^* = \sum v_i + \sum w_i,$$

Equation (17) is equivalent to Equation (2) in the sense that, while S and S^* are different functionals, the values of v and w that minimize S^* give the value of u that minimizes S. Moreover, it will be seen in a moment that in the optimal solution S^* and S will actually be equal.

Turning now to the constraints in Equation (14), these are given by the T observations, which it will be useful to rewrite in the form of Equation (18) [see p. 176]. Note that u has been replaced by $v - w$ and also that each independent variable appears twice, once as x and again as $-x$. The coefficients for these n "new" independent variables are $\beta_1^*, \ldots, \beta_n^*$. (The reason for this procedure will become apparent in a moment.) In the present context, x and $-x$ correspond to the matrix A in Equation (14), the regression coefficients $\beta_1, \beta_1^*, \ldots, \beta_n, \beta_n^*$ to the vector of activity levels α, and y to the vector of constraints b. The error terms $v_1, w_1, \ldots, v_T, w_T$ represent the introduction of $2T$ "slack" activities. The final constraint in Equation (15) corresponds to the vector of nonslack activity levels, $\beta_1, \beta_1^*, \ldots, \beta_n, \beta_n^*$ being nonnegative.

Although in this, the straightforward, formulation of the problem there are $2(n+T)$ activities in all, it will be noticed that in the big matrix in Equation (18) succeeding pairs of activities are dependent. Consequently, only one member of each of the pairs (β_j, β_j^*) and (v_i, w_i) for each i and j can be nonzero in any solution; otherwise the theorem that the activities in any basis must be

---

[9] For a discussion of transforming an unrestricted variable into the difference between two restricted ones, see Charnes *et al.* (1955, pp. 141–144).

$$(18) \quad
\begin{bmatrix}
x_{11} & -x_{11} & x_{12} & -x_{12} & \cdots & x_{1n} & -x_{1n} & 1 & -1 & 0 & 0 & \cdots & 0 & 0 \\
x_{21} & -x_{21} & x_{22} & -x_{22} & \cdots & x_{2n} & -x_{2n} & 0 & 0 & 1 & -1 & \cdots & 0 & 0 \\
 & & & & \vdots & & & & & & & & & \\
x_{T1} & -x_{T1} & x_{T2} & -x_{T2} & \cdots & x_{Tn} & -x_{Tn} & 0 & 0 & 0 & 0 & \cdots & 1 & -1
\end{bmatrix}
\begin{bmatrix}
\beta_1 \\ \beta_1^* \\ \beta_2 \\ \beta_2^* \\ \vdots \\ \beta_n \\ \beta_n^* \\ v_1 \\ w_1 \\ v_2 \\ w_2 \\ \vdots \\ v_T \\ w_T
\end{bmatrix}
=
\begin{bmatrix}
y_1 \\ y_2 \\ \vdots \\ y_T
\end{bmatrix}
$$

independent would be violated. Since only one of β_j and β_j^* can be nonzero, the inclusion of the negative of each independent variable is a device to enable the coefficients of the independent variables to be of either sign. Also, since v_i and w_i cannot both be nonzero, it is evident that the values taken by S in Equation (2) and S^* in Equation (17) will be equal. Moreover, in view of the fact that the activities corresponding to the independent variables have zero "cost" in the minimand, the independent variables will always appear in the optimal solution. This means that $T-n$ residuals (i.e., slack activities) will appear in the optimal solution, and that n residuals will therefore be zero. This corresponds to our earlier observation that the regression hyperplane is determined by a subset of n observations.

While the formulation of the problem just presented will (degeneracy aside) always yield a solution, it has the drawback that the computational procedure is cumbersome and lengthy if the number of observations is at all large. Wagner (1959) has shown that the number of activities and constraints can be substantially reduced by considering the dual to the above formulation and solving it as a problem in bounded variables using special simplex procedures developed by Charnes and Lemke (1954), Dantzig (1955), and Wagner (1958).[10]

II. Rudiments of A Distribution Theory for Least Absolute Error

Distribution of the "Solution" Subset of Observations

Once the linear programming problem referred to in Equations (17) and (18) has been solved, the system of equations for the solution can be written as

$$(19) \qquad \begin{bmatrix} y_{(1)} \\ y_{(2)} \end{bmatrix} = \begin{bmatrix} X_{(1)} & 0 \\ X_{(2)} & I \end{bmatrix} \begin{bmatrix} \hat{\beta} \\ \hat{u} \end{bmatrix},$$

where the subscripts 1 and 2 refer to the observations with zero and nonzero residuals, respectively. This corresponds to reordering the observations so that the first n are those lying in the regression hyperplane. Accordingly, $X_{(1)}$ is $n \times n$ in dimension and $X_{(2)}$ $(T-n) \times n$. The vector $\hat{u}$ refers to the nonzero residuals and, since these are $T-n$ in number, the dimension of the identity matrix is $(T-n) \times (T-n)$; 0 is a corresponding $n \times (T-n)$ submatrix of zeros, and $\hat{\beta}$ contains the n regression coefficients.

The second subset of equations in Equation (19) shows that $\hat{\beta}$ is obtained as the solution to the system of equations

$$(20) \qquad y_{(1)} = X_{(1)}\hat{\beta},$$

[10] For a clear exposition of the underlying theory, see Simmonard (1966, pp. 206–210). For description of a computing algorithm which yields bounded variable solutions, see Padberg and Wiginton (1969).

or

(21) $$\hat{\beta} = X_{(1)}^{-1} y_{(1)}.$$

Substitution in the first subset of equations then yields for $\hat{u}$

(22) $$\hat{u} = y_{(2)} - X_{(2)} X_{(1)}^{-1} y_{(1)}.$$

If we now reorder the observations in the original model in Equation (1) to conform to Equation (19), we will have for $y_{(1)}$

(23) $$y_{(1)} = X_{(1)} \beta + u_{(1)},$$

so that from Equation (21)

(24) $$\hat{\beta} = \beta + X_{(1)}^{-1} u_{(1)}.$$

It is useful to compare this expression with the analogous one for least squares,

(25) $$\hat{\beta}_{LS} = \beta + (X'X)^{-1} X'u.$$

While superficially Equations (24 and (25) might seem similar, there are major differences between them. In Equation (25), $\hat{\beta}_{LS}$ is a function of *all* of the u's and *all* of the observations on the independent variables, but $\hat{\beta}$ in Equation (24) is a function of only a subset of both. Moreover, and this is of critical importance, the subset of observations $X_{(1)}$ will, in general, vary from one realization of u to the next. Accordingly, $X_{(1)}$ must also be viewed as a random variable, or, more accurately, a random matrix. In view of this, it follows that the distribution of $\hat{\beta}$ will depend not only on the distribution of u as with least squares, but also on the distribution of $X_{(1)}$, the "solution" subset of observations. Consequently, a first step in deriving the distribution of $\hat{\beta}$ is to isolate the distribution of $X_{(1)}$.

At one time I had hopes that this distribution would turn out to be independent of the form of the distribution of u and to depend only on the values taken by the independent variables themselves. Some small-scale Monte Carlo results reported in a paper I delivered at the Cambridge World Congress of the Econometric Society in September 1970 seemed to be consistent with this view, but, as will be seen below, such is in fact not the case. The distribution of $X_{(1)}$ depends on the distribution of u as well as the values taken by X. However, the Monte Carlo results in my Cambridge paper yielded another conjecture that has subsequently been proved to be correct, namely, that there can be some subsets of observations that can never appear in the optimal solution. In the traditional language of linear programming, what this result states is that, for the "production technology" implied by the LAE problem, there can be certain combinations of activities that will never be used no matter what the resource availabilities.

To establish this result, it will be useful to recast the linear programming problem in Equations (17) and (18) in the traditional simplex tableau.

Accordingly, we define the initial tableau,

(26)

$$M = \begin{bmatrix} 0 & O_n & O_n & \iota_n' & \iota_{T-n}' & \iota_n' & \iota_{T-n}' \\ y_{(1)} & X_{(1)} & -X_{(1)} & I_n & O_{nx(T-n)} & -I_n & O_{nx(T-n)} \\ y_{(2)} & X_{(2)} & -X_{(2)} & O_{(T-n)xn} & I_{T-n} & O_{(T-n)xn} & -I_{T-n} \end{bmatrix},$$

where the subscripts on the vectors and matrices, except for those on y and X, refer to their respective dimensions. It is assumed that the observations have been partitioned as in Equation (19), and $y_{(1)}$, $y_{(2)}$, $X_{(1)}$, and $X_{(2)}$ have the dimensions defined there. The first row in M corresponds to the minimand in Equation (17), ι denoting a vector of ones, while the second and third rows correspond to the constraints in Equation (18) written according to the partitioning in Equation (19).

The task before us is to find the matrix Q yielding

(27) $$M^* = Q^{-1}M$$

such that the first n observations provide the LAE estimator. The appropriate Q will contain the T independent vectors from M corresponding to the optimal basis in M^*. As we already know, n of these vectors will be from X (or $-X$ as the case may be), while the remaining $T-n$ vectors will correspond to the observations with nonzero residuals. We are interested in the conditions on X (or, more particularly, on $X_{(1)}$) that must be satisfied if the observations for which this is the case are the last $T-n$.

In specifying Q, we must take into account the fact that a nonzero residual can be of either sign. To do this, let I^* be the $(T-n) \times (T-n)$ diagonal matrix whose every diagonal element is either $+1$ or -1, and let $\bar{I}$ be the set of all possible I^*. The matrix Q can therefore be written as

(28) $$Q = \begin{bmatrix} 1 & O_n & \iota_{T-n}' \\ O_n & X_{(1)} & O_{nx(T-n)} \\ O_{T-n} & X_{(2)} & I^* \end{bmatrix}$$

for some $I^* \in \bar{I}$. Note that Q here represents as many different matrices as there are elements in $\bar{I}$, namely, 2^{T-n}.

Using the rules for inverting a matrix by partitioning and noting that $(I^*)^{-1} = I^*$, we then have for Q^{-1}

(29) $$Q^{-1} = \begin{bmatrix} 1 & \iota'I^*X_{(2)}X_{(1)}^{-1} & -\iota'I^* \\ O_n & X_{(1)}^{-1} & O_{nx(T-n)} \\ O_{T-n} & -I^*X_{(2)}X_{(1)}^{-1} & I^* \end{bmatrix}.$$

Postmultiplication by M then yields for M^*

(30)

$$M^* = \begin{bmatrix} R_1 & 0 & 0 & \iota'+\iota'R_2 & \iota'-\iota'I^* & \iota'-\iota'R_2 & \iota'+\iota'I^* \\ X'_{(1)}y_{(k)} & I & -I & X_{(1)}^{-1} & 0 & -X_{(1)}^{-1} & 0 \\ R_3 & 0 & 0 & -R_2 & I^* & R_2 & -I^* \end{bmatrix},$$

where all matrices and vectors have the dimension of their corresponding place in Equation (26) and where

(31) $$R_1 = \iota'X_{(2)}X_{(1)}^{-1}y_{(1)} - \iota'I^*y_{(2)},$$

(32) $$R_2 = I^*X_{(2)}X_{(1)}^{-1},$$

(33) $$R_3 = -I^*X_{(2)}X_{(1)}^{-1}y_{(1)} + I^*y_{(1)}.$$

For M^* to be the terminal (i.e., optimal) tableau, the simplex criterion requires that all elements in the first row, except for R_1, be nonnegative. This condition is always satisfied by the two vectors, $\iota'-\iota'I^*$ and $\iota'+\iota'I^*$, since for any I^* every element in them is either 0 or 2. The crucial conditions for optimality are therefore given by

(34) $$\iota' + \iota'R_2 \geqslant 0, \qquad \iota' - \iota'R_2 \geqslant 0$$

or

(35) $$-\iota' \leqslant \iota'I^*X_{(2)}X_{(1)}^{-1} \leqslant \iota'.$$

We shall henceforth refer to this as Condition I.

If there exists an $I^* \in \bar{I}$ such that this condition is satisfied, then M^* is optimal (though we would still have to check for feasibility). On the other hand, if there is no $I^* \in \bar{I}$ that satisfies this condition, then the hyperplane containing the first n observations can never yield the LAE estimator. Thus, we have proven the following theorem.

THEOREM 1.   Let $X_{(1)}$ denote a subset of n observations on n independent variables. Then, in order for $X_{(1)}$ to yield the LAE estimator, it is necessary that $X_{(1)}$ satisfy Condition I.

Since Condition I is independent of the values taken by u, it is thus possible for some subsets of observations never to provide the LAE estimator. In particular, when the condition is applied to the matrix of explanatory variables used in the Monte Carlo experiments reported in my Cambridge paper, it was violated by precisely those four bases (out of ten) that never yielded an LAE estimate.

Let us now take up the question of feasibility. The simplex condition for feasibility is that all of the elements in the first column of M^* be greater than or equal to zero. The first n elements of this column are $X_{(1)}^{-1}y_{(1)}$, and it is clear that some of these might be negative. However, this does not create any problem since we can multiply the rows of M^* corresponding to negative elements in $X_{(1)}^{-1}y_{(1)}$ by -1, the effect of which is merely to replace columns of $X_{(1)}$ by the corresponding columns of $-X_{(1)}$ and thereby change the sign of the corresponding $\hat{\beta}_i$. Consequently, the crucial condition for feasibility is found in the last $T-n$ elements of the first column of M^*, which is that we must have

(36)
$$-I^*X_{(2)}X_{(1)}^{-1}y_{(1)} + I^*y_{(2)} \geqslant 0,$$

henceforth to be referred to as Condition II. This condition is seen to depend on y, and accordingly it is possible, depending on the form of the distribution of u, for it to be satisfied with very small, or even zero, probability.

Combining Conditions I and II, we finally arrive at the set of conditions necessary and sufficient for M^* to be both feasible and optimal.

THEOREM 2. Let $X_{(1)}$ be defined as in Theorem 1. Then, for $X_{(1)}$ to yield the LAE estimator, there must exist an $I^* \in \bar{I}$ such that

$$-\iota' \leqslant \iota'I^*X_{(1)}^{-1} \geqslant \iota'$$

and

$$-I^*X_{(2)}X_{(1)}^{-1}y_{(1)} + I^*y_{(2)} \geqslant 0.$$

Theorem 1 answers the important question of which subsets of observations can yield the solution basis for the LAE estimator, while Theorem 2 goes further and provides the link between the values taken by the dependent variable and the solution basis. This being the case, the importance of Theorem 2 can hardly be overemphasized, for, as will shortly become clear, it supplies the key ingredient for obtaining the distribution of $X_{(1)}$.[11]

To derive this distribution, let us begin by rewriting Condition II in terms of u,

(37)
$$-I^*X_{(2)}X_{(1)}^{-1}u_{(1)} + I^*u_{(2)} \geqslant 0.$$

---

[11] The derivation of Conditions I and II presented here was formulated by Gilbert Bassett of the University of Michigan as part of his Ph.D. thesis. In particular, the I^* matrix, which is crucial to the development of the two conditions, is his invention. Theorem 2, which embodies these conditions, is equivalent to Lemma 2 of Rosenberg and Carlson (1971). However, unlike Theorem 2, which is arrived at by considering the simplex criteria that must be met for the solution to the (primal) linear programming problem, the Rosenberg–Carlson lemma focuses on the slope of the objective function in the neighborhood of its minimum.

Next, let us number the $N\ [=T/n!\,(T-n)!]$ subsets of n observations from 1 to N, and denote the ith of these subsets by B_i. Let $g(B)$ be the probability density function of B. Then,

$$(38) \qquad g(B_i) = \int \int \cdots \int_A f(u_1, \ldots, u_T)\, du_1, \ldots, du_T,$$

where the region of integration A is defined by

$$(37) \qquad -I^* X_{(2)} X_{(1)}^{-1} u_{(1)} + I^* u_{(2)} \geq 0$$

for all $I^* \in I$ satisfying Condition I,

$$(35) \qquad -\iota' \leq \iota' I^* X_{(2)} X_{(1)}^{-1} \leq \iota'.$$

If there is no I^* that satisfies Condition I, then $g(B_i) = 0$.

Observe that from $g(B)$ in Equation (38) it is possible to derive the distribution of the LAE estimator, since to obtain the probability that $\hat{\beta}$ lies between two vectors b_0 and b_1 $(b_0 < b_1)$, we simply need to add the probabilities that $\hat{\beta}$ lies within these limits over all possible B_i. However, while this solves the problem of the distribution of $\hat{\beta}$ in principle, its practical value is probably not very great. The evaluation of $g(B)$ requires multiple integration over regions of the sample space of u, and, since these regions depend on the values taken by X, it is clear that the resulting distribution will be sample dependent. I shall return to this problem in Section IV.

Some Consequences of Conditions I and II

Conditions I and II have some readily obtainable consequences that we shall now proceed to derive. To begin with, observe that Equation (38) establishes a one-to-one correspondence between regions of the sample space of u and the B_i satisfying Condition I. Since (degeneracy aside) every u leads to a unique LAE estimate, it is clear that these regions constitute an exhaustive partition of the sample space. Unfortunately, it is not possible at present to say much about the form that these partitions take. However, as the following theorem establishes, it is clear that at a minimum they must consist of rays through the origin.

THEOREM 3.   Let H denote the sample space of u, and let H_i be the region of H associated with basis B_i. Then, if $u^* \in H_i$, so also is αu^* for any real α.

Proof.   To begin with, it is clear that for $u = 0$ any of the B_i will give the LAE estimate (even those that do not satisfy Condition I!); hence the origin is contained in H_i.

Next, assume $\alpha > 0$, and replace u in the left-hand side of (37) by αu.

We have

$$(39) \quad -I^*X_{(2)}X_{(1)}^{-1}(\alpha u_{(1)}) + I^*(\alpha u_{(2)}) = \alpha[-I^*X_{(2)}X_{(1)}^{-1}u_{(1)} + I^*u_{(2)}]$$
$$\geqslant 0,$$

since α is positive. Condition I in Equation (35) is not affected, hence we have established that if u^* leads to basis B_i, so also does αu^* for $\alpha > 0$.

Finally, note from Equation (35) that if B_i satisfies Condition I for I^*, it also satisfies Condition I for $-I^*$. In view of this, assume $\alpha u^* \in H_i$, and consider the left hand side of Equation (37) with I^* replaced by $-I^*$ and αu^* replaced by $-\alpha u^*$. Condition II is not affected, hence $-\alpha u^*$, too, is contained in H_i. From this, it follows that if $u^* \in H_i$, then so too is αu^* for $\alpha < 0$ as well as for $\alpha \geqslant 0$. This proves the theorem.

From Equation (24), the estimation error in $\hat{\beta}$ is given by

$$(40) \qquad\qquad\qquad \hat{\beta} - \beta = X_{(1)}^{-1}u_{(1)}.$$

Let $e = \hat{\beta} - \beta$. Then as a consequence of the preceding theorem, we have

THEOREM 4.   If u^* leads to estimation error e, then $-u^*$ leads to estimation error $-e$.

Proof.   The proof is immediate from the fact that u^* and $-u^*$ lead to the same solution basis of observations. Replace $u_{(1)}^*$ in Equation (40) by $-u_{(1)}^*$, and we have $-e$.

Note that it follows from this theorem that if the distribution of u is symmetrical about zero, then the distribution of e is also symmetrical about zero. In view of this, we have the following important result.

THEOREM 5.   In the regression model, $y = X\beta + u$, if the distribution of u is symmetrical about zero, then LAE provides an unbiased estimator of β, i.e., we will have

$$(41) \qquad\qquad\qquad E(\hat{\beta}) = \beta.$$

Since for given B_i, we have from Equation (24) that

$$(42) \qquad\qquad\qquad E(\hat{\beta} \mid B_i) = \beta,$$

it is tempting to conclude that unbiasedness follows directly simply by taking the expected value of Equation (42) over all possible B_i. However, this is not a valid procedure, since the estimator implicit in Equation (42) is not the LAE estimator. It is true that LAE *estimates* depend upon a subset of n observations, but the LAE *estimator* depends upon all T observations.[12] The essential ingredient in the proof of unbiasedness is symmetry of the error term.[13]

A well-known property of least squares is that, for models with a constant term, the estimated regression hyperplane contains the point of means of the variables. Unless the point of means should happen to coincide with one of the observations in the solution basis, this is, of course, not the case with LAE. Nevertheless, it is true that LAE estimates have the property that if the constant is chosen so as to force the fitted hyperplane though the point of means, they are still unbiased. This is proven in the next theorem.

THEOREM 6. In the regression model $y = X\beta + u$, where u is symmetrically distributed about zero and where the first vector of X is a vector of ones, ι. Let $X = [\iota, X^*]$, $\hat{\beta}' = (\hat{\beta}_1, \hat{\beta}^*)$, $\tilde{y} = y - \bar{y}$, and $\tilde{X}^* = X^* - \bar{X}^*$. Then, the LAE estimate of β, where $\hat{\beta}_1 = \bar{y} - \bar{X}^*\hat{\beta}^*$, is unbiased.

Proof. With $\hat{\beta}_1$ obtained as $\bar{y} - \bar{X}^*\hat{\beta}^*$, the estimation problem is to determine $\hat{\beta}^*$ so as to minimize

$$\sum_i \left| \tilde{y}_i - \sum_{j=2}^n \hat{\beta}_j \tilde{x}_{ij} \right|.$$

In this case, Conditions I and II become

(43) $-\iota \leqslant I^* \tilde{X}^*_{(2)} \tilde{X}^{*-1}_{(1)} \leqslant \iota,$

(44) $-I^* \tilde{X}^*_{(2)} \tilde{X}^{*-1}_{(1)} u_{(1)} + I^* u_{(2)} \geqslant 0,$

where the subscripts 1 and 2 denote the same as before, except that the solution basis in $\tilde{X}^*_{(1)}$ now contains $n - 1$ observations. Once again it is clear that replacement of I^* by $-I^*$ will not affect Equation (43), while simultaneous replacement of I^* by $-I^*$ and u by $-u$ leaves Equation (44) unaffected. Moreover, it is clear that formula (40) continues to hold for the estimation error in $\hat{\beta}^*$, e^*, with $X^{-1}_{(1)}$ replaced by $\tilde{X}^{*-1}_{(1)}$.

All of this being the case, it follows that, as in Theorem 4, if u^* leads to estimation error $e^* = \tilde{X}^{*-1}_{(1)} u^*_{(1)}$, $-u^*$ leads to estimation error $-e^*$. Since u is symmetrical about zero, so also is e^*. This establishes that $\hat{\beta}^*$ is an unbiased estimator of β^*.[14] Thus, it only remains to show that $E(\hat{\beta}_1) = \beta_1$. Now,

---

[12] This is a good place to dispel the erroneous view [cf. Wonnacott and Wonnacott (1970, p. 5)] that LAE is a "poor" estimator because it ignores observations. This simply is not true, for all observations enter into the determination of the optimal basis.

[13] Rosenberg and Carlson (1971, Theorem 2) prove that if the variables in X are symmetrical about their respective means, unbiasedness of the LAE estimator does not require the distribution of u to be symmetrical. However, since this is such a restricted case, I only mention it here in passing.

[14] The argument just presented can be employed to show that the LAE estimator of β^* is unbiased for movement of the origin to any point not the point of means.

$\bar{y} = \beta_1 + \bar{X}^*\beta^* + \bar{u}$, and $E(\bar{y}) = \beta_1 + \bar{X}^*\beta^*$, since $E(u) = 0$. Accordingly, $\beta_1 = E(\bar{y}) - \bar{X}^*\beta^*$. However, since $\hat{\beta}_1 = \bar{y} - \bar{X}^*\hat{\beta}^*$, $E(\hat{\beta}_1) = E(\bar{y}) - \bar{X}^*E(\hat{\beta}^*) = E(\bar{y}) - \bar{X}^*\beta^*$. Whence, $E(\hat{\beta}_1) = \beta_1$, and the theorem is proved.

Before leaving this theorem, it should be emphasized that the LAE estimates one obtains by shifting the origin to the point of means are not the same as the ones obtained by estimating the constant term as a "free" regression coefficient. Both procedures yield unbiased estimates, but the estimates are not identical since, in general, the LAE hyperplane does not include the point of means.

Let us now inquire into the effect on the LAE estimator of scaling the variables. To be specific, suppose that X is replaced by XD, where D is an $n \times n$ diagonal matrix. Since $(X_2 D)(X_{(1)} D)^{-1} = X_{(2)} D D^{-1} X_{(1)}^{-1} = X_{(2)} X_{(1)}^{-1}$, neither Condition I nor Condition II is affected, and so the solution subset of observations remains the same. The effect of the scaling is therefore to scale the regression coefficients inversely; that is, if $\hat{\beta}$ is the LAE estimate for X, then $D^{-1}\hat{\beta}$ is the LAE estimate for XD.

The foregoing reasoning, it is to be noticed, is in no way dependent on the matrix D being diagonal, but only nonsingular. Accordingly, we have established the following result.

THEOREM 7. Let $\hat{\beta}$ be the LAE estimate of β in the model $y = X\beta + u$. Then, for A an $n \times n$ nonsingular matrix, $\hat{\beta}^* = A^{-1}\hat{\beta}$ is the LAE estimate of β^* in the model $y = XA\beta^* + u$.

Theorem 7 is actually a special case of the following result, presented first by Rosenberg and Carlson (1971, Theorem 3):

THEOREM 8. Let $\Phi(e \mid X, F(u))$ be the cumulative distribution of the estimation error $e = \hat{\beta} - \beta$ as a function of the independent variables X and the cumulative distribution of the error term $F(u)$. Then, for $\delta > 0$ and A any nonsingular $n \times n$ matrix,

(45) $$\Phi(e \mid X, F(u)) = \Phi(\delta A^{-1} e \mid XA, F(\delta u)).$$

That is, the scale of the distribution of the estimation error varies proportionately with the scale of the distribution of the disturbance error, and any nonsingular linear transformation of the independent variables results in the inverse transformation of the estimation error.

Proof. By checking Conditions I and II, it is easily established, details being left to the reader, that the solution basis for X and u remains the solution basis for XA and δu. Consequently, from Equation (24) we have for the model $y = XA\beta^* + \delta u$

(46) $$\hat{\beta} = \beta^* + \delta A^{-1} X_{(1)}^{-1} u_{(1)}.$$

Hence, the estimation error for $\hat{\beta}^*$, $e^* = \hat{\beta}^* - \beta^*$, is equal to

$$e^* = \delta A^{-1} X_{(1)}^{-1} u_{(1)} = \delta A^{-1} e,$$

as was to be shown.

Our final effort in this section will be to present two results concerning the consistency of the LAE estimator in the situation where the original T observations have been grouped into k groups, $k > n$, with T^* observations in each group.[15] The model thus becomes

(47) $Gy = GX\beta + Gu,$

where G is the $k \times T$ grouping matrix,

(48)
$$G = \frac{1}{T^*}
\begin{bmatrix}
\overbrace{1 \cdots 1}^{T^*} & \overbrace{0 \cdots\cdots\cdots\cdots\cdots\cdots 0}^{T-T^*} \\
0 \cdots 0 & 1 \cdots 1 \quad 0 \cdots\cdots\cdots 0 \\
\vdots & \\
0 \cdots\cdots\cdots\cdots\cdots\cdots 0 \quad 1 \cdots 1
\end{bmatrix}.$$

As all along, assume that u is identically and independently distributed independent of X, and symmetrical about zero, and let $\bar{y}_{T^*} = Gy$, $\bar{X}_{T^*} = GX$, and $\bar{u}_{T^*} = Gu$.

THEOREM 9.   Let $\hat{\beta}_{T^*}$ be the LAE estimator of β in the model

(49) $\bar{y}_{T^*} = \bar{X}_{T^*}\beta + \bar{u}_{T^*}.$

Then, on the assumptions regarding u just stated and the further assumption that the elements of X are bounded,

(50) $\plim_{T^* \to \infty} \hat{\beta}_{T^*} = \beta.$

Proof.   This proposition hinges on the fact that, under the assumptions stated for u, the strong law of large numbers can be invoked to show that $\bar{u}_{T^*}$ goes to zero in probability as $T^* \to \infty$.[16] Consequently, since the elements of X are bounded,

(51) $\plim_{T^* \to \infty} \bar{y}_{T^*} = \lim_{T^* \to \infty} \bar{X}_{T^*}\beta.$

The consistency of $\hat{\beta}_{T^*}$ then follows from the fact that any n of the group means will yield the true β.

The proof of this theorem does not require the disturbance u to have a second moment. Had this been assumed, the weak law of large numbers could have been used in the proof in place of the strong law.

Let us now modify the model so as to assume that the random component

---

[15] The assumption of an equal number of observations in each group is one of convenience.
[16] See Gnedenko (1962, p. 245).

is in the independent variables rather than the dependent variable. That is, we shall now assume that $X = Z + V$, where $V = (v_1, \ldots, v_n)$. Each v_i is assumed to be independently and identically distributed, symmetrical about zero, and independent of Z. The model is then

(52)
$$y = Z\beta$$
$$= X\beta - v\beta.$$

However, we retain the assumption that the observations are grouped into k classes, $k > n$, with T^* observations in each class. Accordingly, the model to be estimated is

(53)
$$\bar{y}_{T*} = \bar{X}_{T*}\beta - \bar{V}_{T*}\beta,$$

where $\bar{y}_{T*}$ and $\bar{X}_{T*}$ are as defined above. Finally, we assume that the elements of Z are bounded.

Under the conditions imposed on V, the strong law of large numbers can once again be invoked to establish that $\bar{V}_{T*}$ converges in probability to a zero matrix as $T^* \to \infty$. Hence, since the elements of Z are bounded,

$$\lim_{T^* \to \infty} \bar{y}_{T*} = \plim_{T^* \to \infty} \bar{X}_{T*}\beta.$$

Consequently, we have proven the following theorem, due originally to Charnes *et al.* (1955).

THEOREM 10.   Let $\hat{\beta}_{T*}$ be the LAE estimator of β in Equation (53). Then, under the conditions just stated on V and Z, $\hat{\beta}_{T*}$ is consistent.[17]

Theorems 9 and 10, which apply to grouped data with a fixed number of groups, are the strongest results currently available concerning consistency of the LAE estimator for the general case of n independent variables. However, Rosenberg and Carlson (1971, Theorem 4) have established consistency, without recourse to grouping, for the model with just a single independent variable and, in view of this, a proof of consistency for the general case will almost certainly be forthcoming.[18]

III.   Geometrical Representation of Least Absolute Error

It is well-known property of least squares estimation that its estimator can be interpreted as a projection—in the spherical disturbance case, as the orthogonal projection of the vector lying in T-dimensional space defined by

---

[17] Once again, note that the v's are not assumed to have finite variances.

[18] Rosenberg and Carlson have also established (see their Theorem 4) for the single independent variable case that the distribution of the estimation error of the LAE estimator will have moments through order k if the distribution of the disturbance possesses absolute moments of order $(k/h + \delta)$ for some $\delta > 0$, where h is the smallest number such that for some combination of the indices $1, 2, \ldots, T$, denoted by $t_1, \ldots, t_T$,

$$\sum_{j=1}^{h} |x_{t_j}| > \sum_{j=h+1}^{T} |x_{t_j}|.$$

the observations on the dependent variable into the n-dimensional subspace spanned by the vectors defined by the observations on the independent variables. In particular, the least squares estimator can be viewed as the one that is obtained by expanding a hypersphere with center at y until it touches the hyperplane defined by the independent variables. The point of tangency yields the vector $\hat{y} = X\hat{\beta}_{LS}$, where $\hat{\beta}_{LS} = (X'X)^{-1}X'y$.

With LAE, the hypersurfaces of constant distance about y are not hyperspheres as with least squares, but rather regular polyhedrons whose corners lie in the rectangular coordinate axes emanating from y as the origin. The LAE estimator will then be defined as the $\hat{y} = X\hat{\beta}$ obtained by expanding the polyhedron of equal distance until it touches the hyperplane defined by the independent variables. If, for example, there were three observations, the polyhedron in question would have the shape of two identical regular four-sided pyramids butted base-to-base centered at the point $y' = (y_1, y_2, y_3)$ and whose eight faces are isosceles triangles of equal area. If there is only a single independent variable, the LAE estimate will be given by the point on the line defined by the origin and the point $x' = (x_1, x_2, x_3)$ which is cut by the expanding "double pyramid." A moments thought will convince the reader that this will occur, with probability unity, on one of the edges of the expanding double pyramid. This being the case, one of the residuals will be zero. On the other hand, if there are two independent variables, the LAE estimate will be given by the point where the expanding polyhedron hits the plane defined by the origin and the two points $x_1' = (x_{11}, x_{21}, x_{31})$ and $x_2' = (x_{12}, x_{22}, x_{32})$. Again, reflection will show that this will occur, with probability unity, at one of the corners of the double pyramid. A corner corresponds to two of the three residuals being zero.

Returning to the general case of T observations and n independent variables, it should, in view of the foregoing, be clear that the expanding polyhedron of equal distance will touch, with probability unity, the hyperplane defined by the independent variables at a point on the polyhedron that lies in as many edges of the polyhedron as there are dimensions to the hyperplane. Since each edge of the polyhedron corresponds to some residual being zero, there will therefore be n zero residuals in all.

IV. Concluding Observations

In view of its superior properties in the presence of fat-tailed disturbance distributions, LAE is finding increased empirical use. However, it is clear that until a distribution theory is developed that is suitable for testing hypotheses about the underlying population regression coefficients, LAE is going to lie outside of the mainstream of application. While Section II makes it clear that we now know a lot more about the statistical properties of the LAE estimator than was the case just a few short years ago, the shape of its distribution remains pretty much a mystery. As was noted at the end of the first subsection of Section II, the problem is that, since the probability that $\hat{\beta}$ is going to lie between the limits b_0 and b_1 must be obtained by summing the probability that $\hat{\beta}$ is within these limits for each solution basis over all possible bases, it is unlikely, even for fixed X, that the resulting distribution for $\hat{\beta}$ can be written as an analytic transform of the distribution of the error term. On the other hand, it seems just as unlikely, unless the number of possible solution bases is very small, that the distribution of $\hat{\beta}$, no matter what the values taken by X, not be reasonably smooth.

This being the case, a natural procedure is to attempt to approximate the distribution by some known distribution, say the multivariate normal. Rosenberg and Carlson (1971) have in fact tried this and have concluded, on the basis of extensive Monte Carlo experiments, that, for symmetrical distributions of the error term, the distribution of $\hat{\beta}$ is approximately multivariate normal with mean β and covariance matrix $\lambda (X'X)^{-1}$, where λ/T is the variance of the median of a sample of size T drawn from the distribution of u. The approximation appears to be especially good for distributions of the independent variables having low kurtosis. However, for independent variables having high kurtosis, Rosenberg and Carlson find the multivariate normal approximation to be much less adequate. Since fat-tailed distributions typically display high kurtosis, a fully satisfactory approximating distribution for $\hat{\beta}$ pretty much remains an open question.

In closing this survey of LAE, I should mention that, while LAE is clearly superior to least squares in the presence of fat-tailed distributions of the error term, it has not yet been established that LAE has any optimal properties (whatever optimal in this context might be taken to mean). It may be, for example, that least squares applied to a trimmed (or "Winsorized") sample will provide an estimator with even better properties than LAE.[19] Indeed, one can conceive of a combined LAE-LS estimation procedure in which LAE is used to begin with as a means of identifying outliers to be trimmed, and then least squares applied after the trimming has been done.

REFERENCES

Arrow, K. J. and M. Hoffenberg (1959). *A Time Series Analysis of Interindustry Demands*, North Holland Publ., Amsterdam.
Blattberg, R. and T. Sargent (1971). "Regression with Non-Gaussian Stable Disturbances: Some Sampling Results," *Econometrica* 39.
Charnes, A. and C. E. Lemke (1954). "Computational Theory of Linear Programming: The Bounded Variables Problem." Graduate School of Ind. Administration, Carnegie Inst. of Technol., Pittsburgh, Pennsylvania.

[19] For a recent survey of the literature on robust procedures in estimation, including trimming, see Huber (1972).

Charnes, A., W. W. Cooper and R. O. Ferguson (1955), "Optimal Estimation of Executive Compensation by Linear Programming," *Management Sci.* **1**, 138–151.

Dantzig, G. B. (1955). "Upper Bounds, Secondary Constraints, and Block Triangularity in Linear Programming," *Econometrica* **23**, 166–173.

Edgeworth, F. Y. (1887). "On Discordant Observations," *Phil. Magazine* **24**, 364–375.

Edgeworth, F. Y. (1888). "On a New Method of Reducing Observations Relating to Several Quantities," *Phil. Magazine* **25**, 184–191.

Edgeworth, F. Y. (1923). "On the Use of Medians for Reducing Observations Relating to Several Quantities," *Phil. Magazine* 6th ser., 1074–1088.

Fama, E. F. and R. Roll (1968). "Some Properties of Symmetric Stable Distributions," *J. Amer. Statist. Ass.* **63**, 817–836.

Fisher, W. D. (1961). "A Note on Curve Fitting with Minimum Deviations by Linear Programming," *J. Amer. Statist. Ass.* **56**, 359–361.

Glahe, F. R. and J. G. Hunt (1970). "The Small Sample Properties of Simultaneous Equation Least Absolute Estimators vis-a-vis Least Squares Estimators," *Econometrica* **38**, 742–753.

Gnedenko, B. M. (1962). *Theory of Probability*, Chelsea, New York.

Granger, C. W. J. and D. Orr (1972). "'Infinite Variance' and Research Strategy in Time Series Analysis," *J. Amer. Statist. Ass.* **67**, 275–285.

Huber, P. J. (1972). "Robust Statistics: A Review," *Ann. Math. Statist.* **43**, 1041–1067.

Karst, O. J. (1958). "Linear Curve Fitting Using Least Deviations," *J. Amer. Statist. Ass.* **53**, 118–132.

Mandelbrot, B. (1963). "New Methods in Statistical Economics," *J. Polit. Econ.* **LXXI**, 421–440.

Mandelbrot, B. (1967). "The Variation of Some Other Speculative Prices," *J. Bus.* **XL**, 393–413.

Meyer, J. R. and R. R. Glauber (1964). *Investment Decisions, Economic Forecasting and Public Policy*, Harvard Business School Press, Cambridge, Massachusetts.

Oveson, R. M. (1968). "Regression Parameter Estimation by Minimizing the Sum of Absolute Errors," unpublished doctoral dissertation, Harvard University, Cambridge, Massachusetts.

Padberg, M. and J. Wiginton (1969). "Efficient Computation of MSAE Regression Estimates Using the Dual Simplex Bounded Variables Technique," Graduate School of Ind. Administration, Carnegie-Mellon Univ.

Rhodes, E. C. (1930). "Reducing Observations by the Method of Minimum Deviations," *Phil. Magazine* 7th ser., 974–992.

Rosenberg, B. and D. Carlson (1971). "The Sampling Distribution of Least Absolute Residuals Regression Estimates," Working Paper No. IP-164, Inst. of Business and Econ. Res., Univ. of California, Berkeley, California.

Sharpe, W. F. (1971). "Mean-Absolute-Deviation Characteristic Lines for Securities and Portfolios," *Management Sci.* **18**, B1–B13.

Simmonard, M. (1966). *Linear Programming*. Prentice-Hall, Englewood Cliffs, New Jersey.

Singleton, R. R. (1940). "A Method for Minimizing the Sum of Absolute Errors," *Ann. Math. Statist.* **11**, 301–310.

Taylor, L. D. (1970). "On Estimation by Minimizing the Sum of Absolute Errors," paper presented at the Second World Congress of the Econometric Soc., Cambridge, England.

Wagner, H. M. (1958). "The Dual Simplex Algorithm for Bounded Variables," *Naval Res. Logist. Quart.* **5**, No. 3, 257–261.

Wagner, H. M. (1959). "Linear Programming Techniques for Regression Analysis," *J. Amer. Statist. Ass.* **56**, 206–212.

Wonnacott, R. J. and T. H. Wonnacott (1970). *Econometrics*. Wiley, New York.

Part III

MULTIPLE-EQUATION MODELS

Chapter Seven

Unobservable
variables in econometrics

ARTHUR S. GOLDBERGER[1]

UNIVERSITY OF WISCONSIN
MADISON, WISCONSIN

An unobservable variable is one that is measured with error. Sometimes, the error is due to inaccurate measurement in the narrow sense. More broadly, it arises whenever measurable quantities differ from their theoretical counterparts. In any case, unobservable variables, or errors of measurement, or errors in the variables, have a curious history in econometric theory. In the early days

[1] This paper derives from Goldberger (1971b, 1972b). My research has been supported in part by grants from the John Simon Guggenheim Memorial Foundation and the Graduate School of the University of Wisconsin.

of econometrics, equations were formulated as exact relationships among unobserved variables, and errors in the variables provided the only stochastic component in the observations. But since the days of the Cowles Commission, the emphasis has shifted almost entirely to errors in the equations, so much so that most current econometrics textbooks offer only a very casual treatment of errors in the variables. Goldberger (1964) has two pages, Christ (1966) has three, Dhrymes (1970) has none, Theil (1971) has nine, and Kmenta (1971) has sixteen. (Malinvaud (1970), on the other hand, offers a full chapter). A possible justification for this neglect is that measurement errors in economic data are negligible, at least in comparison with behavioral disturbances.

But the real explanation may lie elsewhere. Economists have taken the permanent income model as the prototype for the errors-in-variable set-up. As we know, this model is underidentified (at least without Friedman's special assumption that permanent consumption is proportional to, rather than merely linear in, permanent income). Consequently, we have come to associate errors in the variables with underidentification. Since underidentified models appear to present no interesting problems of estimation and testing, econometric theorists have turned away. In particular, several texts give the impression that combining measurement error with simultaneity creates intractable problems: see Johnston (1963, p. 294), Goldberger (1964, pp. 387–388), and Kmenta (1971, pp. 321–322, 596).

Neglect by the theorists elicits malpractice by applied econometricians. In empirical work, it is not uncommon to find "proxies" and "surrogates" used freely, with little attention paid to the consequences. (Measurement error is sometimes invoked as a last resort: If, after much experimentation with the choice of variables in a regression, I am still unable to get sensible results, I might remark that the variables were, after all, not measured accurately.) When nothing is possible in the way of rigorous model-building, identification, and inference, then everything is possible—anything goes—in the way of *ad hoc* rationalization.

Fortunately, as we shall see, the permanent income model is a misleading prototype. Unobservable variables do not preclude identification and do not preclude rigorous inference. Indeed, the proper modes of analysis for unobservable-variable models display striking parallels with those for the more familiar simultaneous-equation models.

I. Multiple Indicators

Consider the following model:

(1) $y_1 = \beta_1 x^* + u, \qquad y_2 = \beta_2 x^* + v, \qquad x^*, u, v$ independent.

Here y_1 and y_2 are observable indicators ($=$effects) of the unobservable x^*, while u and v are errors ($=$ disturbances). (Throughout the paper, we take all variables to have zero expectations.) If we set $\beta_1 = 1$ and let $y_1 =$ income, $y_2 =$ consumption, and $x^* =$ permanent income, we have the permanent income model. For present purposes, however, it is more convenient to normalize by setting the variance of x^* at unity: $\sigma_{**} = 1$.

Our model implies three equations relating population moments of the observable variables to the structural parameters:

$$(2) \qquad \sigma_{11} = \beta_1^2 + \sigma_{uu}, \qquad \sigma_{12} = \beta_1 \beta_2,$$

$$\sigma_{22} = \beta_2^2 + \sigma_{vv}.$$

These three equations do not suffice to determine the four parameters β_1, β_2, σ_{uu}, and σ_{vv}. The model is indeed underidentified.

But now suppose that we observed three, rather than only two, indicators of the unobservable:

$$(3) \qquad y_1 = \beta_1 x^* + u, \qquad y_2 = \beta_2 x^* + v, \qquad y_3 = \beta_3 x^* + w,$$

$$x^*, u, v, w \quad \text{independent.}$$

In conjunction with the normalization $\sigma_{**} = 1$, this model implies six equations relating population moments of the observables to structural parameters:

$$(4) \qquad \sigma_{11} = \beta_1^2 + \sigma_{uu}, \qquad \sigma_{12} = \beta_1 \beta_2, \qquad \sigma_{13} = \beta_1 \beta_3,$$

$$\sigma_{22} = \beta_2^2 + \sigma_{vv}, \qquad \sigma_{23} = \beta_2 \beta_3,$$

$$\sigma_{33} = \beta_3^2 + \sigma_{ww}.$$

These six equations just suffice to determine the six parameters β_1, β_2, β_3, σ_{uu}, σ_{vv}, and σ_{ww}. Explicitly, the solution is

$$\beta_1 = \left(\frac{\sigma_{12}\sigma_{13}}{\sigma_{23}}\right)^{1/2}, \qquad \beta_2 = \left(\frac{\sigma_{12}\sigma_{23}}{\sigma_{13}}\right)^{1/2}, \qquad \beta_3 = \left(\frac{\sigma_{13}\sigma_{23}}{\sigma_{12}}\right)^{1/2},$$

$$\sigma_{uu} = \sigma_{11} - \beta_1^2, \qquad \sigma_{vv} = \sigma_{22} - \beta_2^2, \qquad \sigma_{ww} = \sigma_{33} - \beta_3^2.$$

The model is just-identified, and readily estimated. (One qualification should be noted: There is an arbitrariness of sign associated with the fact that $-x^*$ is operationally equivalent to x^*.)

If a fourth indicator of the same type is available, overidentification results. Thus consider a general multiple-indicator model:

$$(5) \qquad y = \beta x^* + u, \qquad E(x^* u') = 0, \qquad E(uu') = \Theta \text{ diagonal},$$

where y is an $M \times 1$ vector of observable indicators, x^* is an unobservable scalar (normalized by $\sigma_{**} = 1$), u is an $M \times 1$ error vector, and Θ is the $M \times M$ diagonal matrix of error variances. The implied population covariance matrix of the observable variables is

(6) $$\Sigma = E(yy') = E[(\beta x^* + u)(\beta x^* + u)'] = \beta\beta' + \Theta.$$

There are $q = M(M+1)/2$ distinct elements in Σ, and only $p = 2M$ (nonzero) elements in β and Θ; thus there are $r = q - p = M(M-3)/2$ restrictions on Σ, a positive quantity when $M > 3$.

Given a random sample of observations $y(t)$, $t = 1, ..., T$, efficient estimates of β and Θ may be obtained by the maximum likelihood method. Under normality, the likelihood function is, apart from irrelevant constants, given by

(7)
$$L^* = |\Sigma|^{-T/2} \exp\left(-\tfrac{1}{2} \sum_{t=1}^{T} [y'(t)\Sigma^{-1}y(t)]\right)$$

$$= |\Sigma|^{-T/2} \exp[-\tfrac{1}{2}T \operatorname{tr}(\Sigma^{-1}S)],$$

where

$$S = \sum_{t=1}^{T} \frac{y(t)y'(t)}{T} = Y'Y$$

is the sample covariance matrix of y, with

$$T^{1/2}Y = [y(1), ..., y(T)]'$$

being the $T \times M$ observation matrix. To maximize L^* we may as well maximize

$$L = \log L^* = -\tfrac{1}{2}T[\log|\Sigma| + \operatorname{tr}(\Sigma^{-1}S)],$$

or indeed we may as well *minimize*

(8) $$F = \log|\Sigma| + \operatorname{tr}(\Sigma^{-1}S).$$

The minimization is to be carried out subject to $\Sigma = \beta\beta' + \Theta$.

Since $\Sigma = \beta\beta' + \Theta$ implies

$$|\Sigma| = |\Theta|(1 + \beta'\Theta^{-1}\beta) \quad \text{and} \quad \Sigma^{-1} = \Theta^{-1} - (1 + \beta'\Theta^{-1}\beta)^{-1}\Theta^{-1}\beta\beta'\Theta^{-1},$$

we can write the criterion as

(9)
$$F = \log|\Theta| + \log(1 + \beta'\Theta^{-1}\beta) + \operatorname{tr}(\Theta^{-1}S) - (1 + \beta'\Theta^{-1}\beta)^{-1}(\beta'\Theta^{-1}S\Theta^{-1}\beta)$$

$$= \log|\Theta| + \operatorname{tr}(\Theta^{-1}S) + \log(1 + f) - (1 + f)^{-1}g,$$

say, where

(10) $$f = \beta'\Theta^{-1}\beta, \qquad g = \beta'\Theta^{-1}S\Theta^{-1}\beta.$$

Differentiating Equation (9) with respect to β gives

$$\frac{1}{2}\frac{\partial F}{\partial \beta} = (1 + f)^{-1}\Theta^{-1}\beta - (1 + f)^{-1}\Theta^{-1}S\Theta^{-1}\beta + (1 + f)^{-2}g\Theta^{-1}\beta.$$

Setting this at zero gives

(11) $$(S\Theta^{-1} - \lambda I)\beta = 0,$$

where

(12) $$\lambda = 1 + \frac{g}{1+f}.$$

Equation (11) says that the solution value for β is a characteristic vector of $S\Theta^{-1}$ corresponding to the root λ. Multiplying Equation (11) through by $\beta'\Theta^{-1}$ gives $g = \lambda f$, which in conjunction with Equation (12) implies $f = \lambda - 1$; thus the vector should be normalized by $\beta'\Theta^{-1}\beta = \lambda - 1$. Inserting this solution into Equation (9) gives

$$F = \log|\Theta| + \text{tr}(\Theta^{-1}S) + \log\lambda - \lambda + 1,$$

which is decreasing in λ for $\lambda > 1$. Thus, to minimize F we should take λ as large as possible. We conclude that (conditional on Θ), the maximum likelihood estimate of β is the characteristic vector corresponding to the largest root λ of $S\Theta^{-1}$, and is normalized by $\beta'\Theta^{-1}\beta = \lambda - 1$.

Returning to Equation (9), we differentiate with respect to θ_m, the mth diagonal element of Θ, and get

(13) $$F_m \equiv \frac{\partial F}{\partial \theta_m} = \theta_m^{-1} - \theta_m^{-2}s_{mm} + (1+f)^{-1}(f_m - g_m) + (1+f)^{-2}gf_m$$

$$= \theta_m^{-1} - \theta_m^{-2}s_{mm} + f_m - \frac{g_m}{\lambda},$$

where s_{mm} is the mth diagonal element of S, $f_m \equiv \partial f/\partial\theta_m$, $g_m \equiv \partial g/\partial\theta_m$, and we have used $1+f = \lambda$ and $g = f(1+f)$. Defining e_m as the $M \times 1$ vector all of whose elements are zero except the mth, which is unity, we compute from Equation (10):

$$f_m = -\theta_m^{-2}\beta'(e_m e_m')\beta = -\theta_m^{-2}\beta_m^2,$$

$$g_m = -\theta_m^{-2}[\beta'\Theta^{-1}S(e_m e_m')\beta + \beta'(e_m e_m')S\Theta^{-1}\beta]$$

$$= -\theta_m^{-2}(\lambda\beta'(e_m e_m')\beta + \beta'(e_m e_m')\lambda\beta) = 2\lambda f_m,$$

where β_m is the mth element of β, and we have used $S\Theta^{-1}\beta = \lambda\beta$ from Equation (11). Thus $f_m - g_m/\lambda = -f_m = \theta_m^{-2}\beta_m^2$, and Equation (13) reduces to

$$F_m = \theta_m^{-1} - \theta_m^{-2}s_{mm} + \theta_m^{-2}\beta_m^2.$$

Setting this at zero gives the solution value

$$\theta_m = s_{mm} - \beta_m^2.$$

We can collect these values for $m = 1, ..., M$ into

(14) $\text{diag}(\Theta) = \text{diag}(S - \beta\beta')$.

Procedures for solving Equations (11) and (14) jointly are given in Lawley and Maxwell (1971, Chap. 4).

II. Factor Analysis

Our multiple-indicator set-up [Equation (5)] is a special case of the factor analysis model that has long been used in psychometrics. The general factor analysis model specifies a set of linear relationships in which M observable variables (indicators) $y_1, ..., y_M$ are determined by K unobservable variables (common factors) $x_1^*, ..., x_K^*$, and M independent disturbances (specific factors) $u_1, ..., u_M$. In matrix terms, the model is

(15) $y = Bx^* + u$, $E(x^*u') = 0$, $E(uu') = \Theta$ diagonal,

where y is the $M \times 1$ vector of indicators, B is the $M \times K$ matrix of factor loadings (i.e., structural coefficients), x^* is the $K \times 1$ vector of common factors, and u is the $M \times 1$ vector of specific factors. In a typical example, y gives the scores on a battery of tests, while x^* gives the underlying mental abilities.

The model implies that the covariance matrix of the observable variables is

(16) $\Sigma = E(yy') = B\Phi B' + \Theta$,

where $\Phi = E(x^*x^{*'})$. There is a trivial indeterminacy in the model since, for any nonsingular $M \times M$ matrix A, we may define

(17) $\bar{x}^* = Ax^*$, $\bar{B} = BA^{-1}$, $\bar{\Phi} = E(\bar{x}^*\bar{x}^{*'}) = A\Phi A'$,

whence $\bar{B}\bar{\Phi}\bar{B}' = B\Phi B'$. The transformed model is operationally indistinguishable from the original model. To remove the indeterminacy, the following normalization rules may be introduced:

(18) $\Phi = I$, $B'\Theta^{-1}B = \Delta$ diagonal.

Then Equation (16) represents a set of q equations in p unknowns, where $q = M(M+1)/2$ is the number of distinct elements in Σ, and $p = M(K+1) - K(K-1)/2$ is the number of free parameters. [The value of p is computed as follows: MK (elements in B) plus M (diagonal elements in Θ) plus K (diagonal elements in Δ) minus $K(K+1)/2$ (distinct equations in $B'\Theta^{-1}B = \Delta$.)] The presumption is that the model is identified if $r \geqslant 0$, where $r = q - p = [(M - K)^2 - (M + K)]/2$; further, if $r > 0$, the presumption is that there are r overidentifying restrictions on Σ. For example, if $M = 10$ test scores are expressed in terms of $K = 3$ abilities, there would be $r = 18$ restrictions on Σ. These presumptions, being merely counting rules, are subject to various qualifications; see Anderson and Rubin (1956, pp. 114–124) and Lawley and Maxwell (1971, Chap. 2).

It is not hard to see that the restrictions amount to requirements that certain submatrices of Σ have less than full rank, and are thus closely parallel to the restrictions on the reduced form of simultaneous-equation models; see Koopmans and Reiersøl (1950). Furthermore, in factor analysis the sample covariance matrix of y provides an unconstrained estimate of Σ, just as in simultaneous-equation analysis the sample regressions of endogenous on exogenous variables provide an unconstrained estimate of Π. (It is no coincidence that the Anderson–Rubin contribution to factor analysis was started while the authors were research associates of the Cowles Commission.) In factor analysis, as in econometrics, a large number of estimation methods have been developed. The list includes the counterparts of our full-information maximum likelihood [minimizing $\log|\Sigma| + \operatorname{tr}(\Sigma^{-1}S)$], simultaneous least squares [minimizing $\operatorname{tr}((S-\Sigma)^2)$], and weighted least squares [minimizing $\operatorname{tr}(C(S-\Sigma))^2$ for given diagonal C]. Jöreskog and Goldberger (1972) have developed a generalized least squares procedure {minimizing $\operatorname{tr}[(S^{-1}(S-\Sigma))^2]$} that is the factor-analytic counterpart of Malinvaud's (1970, pp. 682–684) minimum-distance method. In each of the methods, of course, minimization is carried out subject to Equations (16) and (18).

After the factor model has been estimated, it is customary to undo the normalizations [Equation (18)]—which were essentially arbitrary—by a series of transformations of the form of Equation (17). These transformations, called "rotations," are designed to isolate and reveal a simple parametric structure, that is, to make $\overline{B\Phi B}'$ more readily interpretable. This rotation phase occupies a good part of standard factor analysis textbooks; see Lawley and Maxwell (1971, Chap. 6) and Harman (1967, Chaps. 12–15).

In view of the many parallels to simultaneous-equation analysis, it is surprising to find that econometricians make so little reference to the factor analysis literature. Principal component analysis *has* been widely used, and—almost as often—confused with factor analysis. To suggest one distinction between the two procedures, consider Equation (11): The estimated factor loading vector β is the first characteristic vector of $S\Theta^{-1}$, while in principal component analysis one generally extracts the first characteristic vector of S itself. (If it were known *a priori* that the diagonal elements of Θ are equal, then the estimated factor loading vector β *would* be the first characteristic vector of S, but that situation is very special indeed.) Among the very few economic studies that really use factor analysis are those by King (1966) and Adelman and Morris (1967).

What explains this neglect of factor analysis? Economists, it appears, are not attracted to a model in which all observables are treated as mere indicators of anonymous factors, and in which variables and parameters are freely redefined *ex post facto*. These features of conventional, "explanatory" factor analysis do limit its interest for economists working with well-defined chains of causation and well-defined (if not necessarily well-measured) variables.

But these features are not inherent in factor analysis. It is possible to build *a priori* specifications (e.g., zero factor loadings) into the parameter matrices; these are quite analogous to the *a priori* specifications incorporated in simultaneous-structural-equation models. When enough such restrictions are made, rotation will be ruled out. In this manner one arrives at the models of "confirmatory" factor analysis, discussed in Lawley and Maxwell (1971, Chap. 7) and Jöreskog (1969); see also Anderson and Rubin (1956, pp. 122–123). Proceeding further in the same vein, it is possible to formulate a causal model (e.g., a recursive one) for the factors, so that the elements of Φ are derivable from more basic structural parameters. In this manner, one is led to "second-order" factor analysis, and to Jöreskog's (1970) "general covariance structure" model.

Algorithms for full-information maximum likelihood estimation (and likelihood-ratio testing) are available for these modern versions of factor analysis, whose potential in econometrics is virtually untapped.

III.　Multiple Causes

We have just seen how the introduction of multiple indicators of unobservables leads to a rich class of stochastic models. Another route is provided by the introduction of multiple causes. Consider the following model:

$$(19) \quad y_1 = \beta_1 x^* + u, \quad y_2 = \beta_2 x^* + v, \quad x^* = \alpha_1 x_1 + \cdots + \alpha_K x_K,$$

$$u \text{ and } v \text{ independent of } x_1, \ldots, x_K.$$

Here y_1 and y_2 are observable effects ($=$ indicators) of the unobservable x^*, which is an exact linear function of its observable exogenous causes ($=$ determinants) $x_1, \ldots, x_K$. An example was provided by Zellner (1970) in introducing this model: let $y_1 =$ income, $y_2 =$ consumption, $x^* =$ permanent income, and $x_1, \ldots, x_K =$ determinants of permanent income—"such variables as house value, educational attainment, age, etc." Solving for each indicator in terms of the observable exogenous variables, we find the reduced form:

$$y_1 = \beta_1 \alpha_1 x_1 + \cdots + \beta_1 \alpha_K x_K + u,$$

$$y_2 = \beta_2 \alpha_1 x_1 + \cdots + \beta_2 \alpha_K x_K + v.$$

The $q = 2K$ reduced-form coefficients are expressed in terms of $p = K+1$ structural parameters: K α's, 2 β's, less one normalization. A natural normalization is $\beta_1 = 1$, but $\sigma_{**} = \Sigma_j \Sigma_k \alpha_j \alpha_k E(x_j x_k) = 1$ is more convenient for present purposes. Since $r = q - p = K - 1$, we see that the model is identified for $K \geq 1$ and overidentified for $K > 1$. Zellner (1970) and Goldberger (1972a) develop generalized least squares and maximum likelihood algorithms under alternative assumptions about $E(uv)$.

Extending the model to cover the case of more indicators, we have

$$(20) \quad y = \beta x^* + u, \quad x^* = \alpha' x, \quad E(xu') = 0, \quad E(uu') = \Theta.$$

Here y is the $M \times 1$ vector of observable effects, x is the $K \times 1$ vector of observable exogenous causes, u is the $M \times 1$ vector of disturbances, α and β are respectively $K \times 1$ and $M \times 1$ parameter vectors, and the unobservable scalar x^* is normalized by

$$\sigma_{**} = E(x^* x^*) = \alpha' E(xx') \alpha = 1.$$

The reduced form is

$$(21) \qquad\qquad y = \beta \alpha' x + u = \Pi' x + v,$$

with

$$(22) \qquad\qquad \Pi = \alpha \beta', \quad v = u.$$

In Equation (22), the KM elements of the coefficient matrix Π are expressed in terms of $K + M - 1$ free structural parameters: K elements of α, M elements of β, less one normalization. Thus there are $r = KM - (K + M) + 1$ overidentifying restrictions on Π. To put it slightly differently, the $K \times M$ matrix Π, being the product of rank-1 matrices, has rank 1. These restrictions on Π are of the type that arise in limited-information analysis of a single structural equation in a conventional simultaneous-equation model. [To confirm this, consider, e.g., Goldberger (1964, p. 315): Equation (4.28b) reads $\Pi_{**,*}\gamma_* = 0$, meaning that a nontrivial linear combination of the columns of a submatrix of Π equals zero, i.e., this submatrix has less than full column rank.]

Under normality, the likelihood function for a sample of T joint observations on y and x is, apart from irrelevant constants, given by

$$L^* = |\Theta|^{-T/2} \exp\left(-\tfrac{1}{2} \sum_{t=1}^{T} [v'(t) \Theta^{-1} v(t)] \right)$$

$$= |\Theta|^{-T/2} \exp[-\tfrac{1}{2} T \operatorname{tr}(\Theta^{-1} W)],$$

where

$$W = \sum_{t=1}^{T} \frac{v(t) v'(t)}{T} = (Y - X\Pi)'(Y - X\Pi)$$

is the sample covariance matrix of reduced-form disturbances; here

$$T^{1/2} Y = [y(1), ..., y(T)]' \quad \text{and} \quad T^{1/2} X = [x(1), ..., x(T)]'$$

are the $T \times M$ and $T \times K$ observation matrices. To maximize L^* we may as well maximize its logarithm, or indeed minimize

(23)
$$F = \log|\Theta| + \operatorname{tr}(\Theta^{-1}W).$$

Conditional on Π, F is minimized by taking $\Theta = W$, in which case the function to be minimized with respect to α and β reduces to

(24)
$$F^* = \log|W|.$$

An alternative estimation criterion is the generalized least squares one, which calls for minimization of

$$G = \operatorname{tr}(S^{-1}W),$$

where

$$S = (Y - XP)'(Y - XP)$$

is the sample covariance matrix of residuals in the unconstrained reduced-form regressions,

$$P = (X'X)^{-1}X'Y$$

being the coefficient matrix for those regressions. Note that

$$W = S + (\Pi - P)'X'X(\Pi - P).$$

By extension of a theorem given in Goldberger and Olkin (1971), it can be shown that in the present model, ML and GLS produce the same estimate of Π; see Goldberger (1970, pp. 50–54). Proceeding in terms of G, which is more convenient, we have

$$G = \operatorname{tr}\{S^{-1}[S + (\Pi - P)'X'X(\Pi - P)]\}.$$

Inserting $\Pi = \alpha\beta'$ and discarding irrelevant constants, this becomes

(25)
$$G^* = (\alpha'X'X\alpha)(\beta'S^{-1}\beta) - 2\alpha'X'YS^{-1}\beta.$$

We seek α and β to minimize G^* subject to

$$\alpha'X'X\alpha = 1.$$

The derivatives are

$$\frac{1}{2}\frac{\partial G^*}{\partial \alpha} = (\beta'S^{-1}\beta)X'X\alpha - X'YS^{-1}\beta + \mu X'X\alpha,$$

$$\frac{1}{2}\frac{\partial G^*}{\partial \beta} = (\alpha'X'X\alpha)S^{-1}\beta - S^{-1}Y'X\alpha,$$

where μ is the Lagrangian multiplier. Setting these derivatives at zero, we find that $\mu = 0$, and then that

$$(26) \qquad \alpha = (\beta'S^{-1}\beta)^{-1}PS^{-1}\beta,$$

$$(27) \qquad \beta = Y'X\alpha = (\beta'S^{-1}\beta)^{-1}QS^{-1}\beta,$$

where

$$Q = Y'XP = Y'X(X'X)^{-1}X'Y = P'X'XP = Y'Y - S$$

is the sample covariance matrix of calculated values in the unconstrained reduced-form regressions. Rearranging Equation (27), we have

$$(28) \qquad (QS^{-1} - \lambda I)\beta = 0,$$

where $\lambda = \beta'S^{-1}\beta$. This says that the solution value for β is a characteristic vector of QS^{-1} corresponding to the root λ. Multiplying Equation (28) through by $\beta'S^{-1}$ gives $\beta'S^{-1}QS^{-1}\beta = \lambda\beta'S^{-1}\beta$. It follows that the vector should be normalized by $\beta'S^{-1}\beta = \lambda$. For, from Equation (26) the solution value for α is

$$\alpha = \lambda^{-1}PS^{-1}\beta,$$

whence

$$1 = \alpha'X'X\alpha = \lambda^{-2}\beta'S^{-1}P'X'XPS^{-1}\beta = \lambda^{-2}\beta'S^{-1}QS^{-1}\beta = \lambda^{-1}(\beta'S^{-1}\beta).$$

Next, inserting the solution values for α and β into Equation (25), we find

$$G^* = \lambda - 2\lambda = -\lambda,$$

which is decreasing in λ for $\lambda > 0$. Thus to minimize G^* we should extract the largest root of QS^{-1}. Note that β is the first principal component of QS^{-1}.

An interpretation is provided if we define the $T \times 1$ vector of estimated values of the unobservable $\hat{x}^* = X\alpha$. Regressing the indicators on this constructed variable will yield the coefficient vector β:

$$(\hat{x}^{*\prime}\hat{x}^*)^{-1}\hat{x}^{*\prime}Y = (\alpha'X'X\alpha)^{-1}\alpha'X'Y = \alpha'X'Y = \beta'.$$

For a further discussion in terms of canonical correlation theory and a numerical illustration, see Hauser and Goldberger (1971).

The present model can be extended in various ways. In one version some exogenous variables directly affect the indicators:

$$(29) \qquad y = \beta x^* + \Pi_1'x_1 + u, \qquad x^* = \alpha'x_2,$$

$$E(xu') = 0, \qquad\qquad E(uu') = \Theta.$$

Here

$$x_1 \text{ is } K_1 \times 1, \qquad x_2 \text{ is } K_2 \times 1, \qquad x = \begin{pmatrix} x_1 \\ x_2 \end{pmatrix},$$

$$\Pi_1 \text{ is } K_1 \times M, \qquad \alpha \text{ is } K_2 \times 1,$$

and the remaining symbols retain their previous meanings. The reduced form becomes

$$y = \Pi_1' x_1 + \beta(\alpha' x_2) + u = \Pi_1' x_1 + \Pi_2' x_2 + u = \Pi' x + v,$$

where

(30) $$\Pi_2' = \beta\alpha', \qquad \Pi = \begin{pmatrix} \Pi_1 \\ \Pi_2 \end{pmatrix}, \qquad v = u.$$

In contrast to Equation (22), only a portion of the reduced-form coefficient matrix is now constrained to have rank 1. This constraint is again of the type that arises in conventional limited-information analysis, and the algorithm of Equations (23)–(28) is readily adapted to produce maximum likelihood estimates; see Hauser (1972, Appendix).

As an illustration of an economic setting for Equation (29), we offer the following labor supply situation, suggested by the work of Christensen (1972) and Hall (1973). For a cross section of households, let $x^* = $ true wage rate, $y_1 = $ observed wage rate, $y_2 = $ hours worked, $x_1 = $ labor demand conditions, and $x_2 = $ socio-demographic characteristics. A related example can be found in the analysis by Griliches and Mason (1972, pp. S91–S97) of the effects of background and ability on income and occupation.

It is worth repeating that the models of the present section are closely related to conventional simultaneous-equation models, the implied restrictions on the reduced-form coefficients being of the same type. Another way of clarifying the connection between simultaneity and errors in variables was pointed out by Zellner (1970, p. 442).

We have now seen how the introduction of multiple causes of unobservables can lead to identification, and to a class of overidentified models. In applied work, no doubt, it will be useful to develop recursive models in which unobservables appear as effects of some observables and as causes of others. This style has already been adopted by sociologists working in the framework of path analysis; see, e.g., Duncan and Featherman (1972) and Hauser (1972).

IV. A Multiple-Indicator–Multiple-Cause Model

An interesting situation arises when we combine the independent-errors specification of Sections I and II with the multiple-cause specification of Section III. Consider the following multiple-indicator–multiple-cause

(MIMIC) model:

(31) $$y = \beta x^* + u, \qquad x^* = \alpha' x + \varepsilon,$$

$$E(xu') = 0, \qquad E(x\varepsilon) = 0, \qquad E(\varepsilon u') = 0, \qquad E(uu') = \Theta \text{ diagonal.}$$

Here again y is an $M \times 1$ vector of observable effects, x is a $K \times 1$ vector of observable causes, u is an $M \times 1$ vector of disturbances, α and β are respectively $K \times 1$ and $M \times 1$ parameter vectors, and x^* is the unobservable scalar. In contrast to Equation (20), we are now assuming that the elements of u are mutually independent, and are introducing a scalar disturbance ε into the equation determining x^*.

The reduced form is

(32) $$y = \beta(\alpha' x + \varepsilon) + u = \beta \alpha' x + \beta \varepsilon + u = \Pi' x + v,$$

where

(33) $$\Pi = \alpha \beta'$$

and

$$v = \beta \varepsilon + u,$$

so that

(34) $$\Omega = E(vv') = E[(\beta \varepsilon + u)(\beta \varepsilon + u)'] = \beta \beta' + \Theta,$$

adopting the normalization

$$\sigma_{\varepsilon\varepsilon} = E(\varepsilon\varepsilon) = 1.$$

In Equation (33) as in Equation (22), the reduced-form coefficient matrix is restricted to have rank $1: \Pi = \alpha \beta'$. But now, in Equation (34), we also have the reduced-form disturbance covariance matrix restricted, in the factor analysis pattern $\Omega = \beta \beta' + \Theta$ with Θ diagonal. (In effect ε plays the role of a single common factor, and u plays the role of the specific factors.) Further—and this is what makes the MIMIC model particularly intriguing—the factor-loading vector β which enters Ω coincides with the structural-coefficient vector β which enters Π. Thus the MIMIC model blends econometric and psychometric themes. We remark that a connection between regression coefficients and disturbance covariances arises in some of Theil's (1967, pp. 228–233) consumer demand models. But the present setting appears to be distinctive.

Under normality, the likelihood function for a sample of T joint observations on y and x is, apart from irrelevant constants, given by

$$L^* = |\Omega|^{-T/2} \exp\left(-\tfrac{1}{2} \sum_{t=1}^{T} [v'(t)\Omega^{-1}v(t)] \right) = |\Omega|^{-T/2} \exp[-\tfrac{1}{2}T \operatorname{tr}(\Omega^{-1}W)],$$

where

$$W = (Y - X\Pi)'(Y - X\Pi)$$

is again the sample covariance matrix of reduced-form disturbances. To maximize L^*, we may as well minimize

(35) $$F = \log|\Omega| + \text{tr}(\Omega^{-1}W).$$

Now $\Omega = \beta\beta' + \Theta$ implies

$$|\Omega| = |\Theta|(1 + \beta'\Theta^{-1}\beta), \qquad \Omega^{-1} = \Theta^{-1} - (1 + \beta'\Theta^{-1}\beta)^{-1}\Theta^{-1}\beta\beta'\Theta^{-1},$$

and $\Pi = \alpha\beta'$ implies

$$W = (Y - X\alpha\beta')'(Y - X\alpha\beta') = Y'Y - Y'X\alpha\beta' - \beta\alpha'X'Y + \beta\alpha'X'X\alpha\beta'.$$

We can write the criterion as

(36)
$$F = \log|\Theta| + \text{tr}(\Theta^{-1}Y'Y) + \log(1 + \beta'\Theta^{-1}\beta)$$

$$- (1 + \beta'\Theta^{-1}\beta)^{-1}[\beta'\Theta^{-1}Y'Y\Theta^{-1}\beta + 2\alpha'X'Y\Theta^{-1}\beta - (\alpha'X'X\alpha\beta'\Theta^{-1}\beta)].$$

The derivatives with respect to α are

$$\frac{1}{2}\frac{\partial F}{\partial \alpha} = -(1 + \beta'\Theta^{-1}\beta)^{-1}(X'Y\Theta^{-1}\beta - \beta'\Theta^{-1}\beta X'X\alpha).$$

Setting this at zero gives

$$\alpha = (\beta'\Theta^{-1}\beta)^{-1}P\Theta^{-1}\beta,$$

where $P = (X'X)^{-1}X'Y$, as in Section III. Again introducing

$$S = (Y - XP)'(Y - XP), \qquad Q = P'X'XP, \qquad Y'Y = S + Q,$$

we find that when the solution value for α is inserted into Equation (36), the criterion becomes

(37) $$F = \log|\Theta| + \text{tr}(\Theta^{-1}S) + \text{tr}(\Theta^{-1}Q) + \log(1 + f) - (1 + f)^{-1}g - f^{-1}h,$$

where

(38) $$f = \beta'\Theta^{-1}\beta, \qquad g = \beta'\Theta^{-1}S\Theta^{-1}\beta, \qquad h = \beta'\Theta^{-1}Q\Theta^{-1}\beta.$$

The derivatives with respect to β are

$$\frac{1}{2}\frac{\partial F}{\partial \beta} = (1 + f)^{-1}\Theta^{-1}\beta - (1 + f)^{-1}\Theta^{-1}S\Theta^{-1}\beta$$

$$+ (1 + f)^{-2}g\Theta^{-1}\beta - f^{-1}\Theta^{-1}Q\Theta^{-1}\beta + f^{-2}h\Theta^{-1}\beta.$$

Setting this at zero gives

(39) $$(R\Theta^{-1} - \lambda I)\beta = 0,$$

where

(40) $$R = \left(\frac{f}{1+f}\right)S + Q, \qquad \lambda = \frac{f}{1+f} + \frac{fg}{(1+f)^2} + \frac{h}{f}.$$

Multiplying Equation (39) through by $\beta'\Theta^{-1}$ gives $fg/(1+f)+h = \lambda f$, which in conjunction with Equation (40) implies $g = f(1+f)$ and $\lambda = f+h/f$. Inserting the solution values into Equation (37) gives

(41) $$F = \log|\Theta| + \mathrm{tr}(\Theta^{-1}S) + \mathrm{tr}(\Theta^{-1}Q) + \log(1+f) - \lambda,$$

which is decreasing in λ. Thus, conditional on f, to minimize F, we should take λ as large as possible. We conclude that (conditional on Θ and f), the maximum likelihood estimate of β is a characteristic vector corresponding to the largest root λ of $R\Theta^{-1}$. The appropriate normalization is $\beta'\Theta^{-1}Q\Theta^{-1}\beta = f(\lambda - f)$.

Returning to Equation (37), we differentiate with respect to θ_m, obtaining

$$F_m \equiv \frac{\partial F}{\partial \theta_m} = \theta_m^{-1} - \theta_m^{-2}(s_{mm} + q_{mm}) + (1+f)^{-1}(f_m - g_m)$$

$$+ (1+f)^{-2}gf_m - f^{-1}h_m + f^{-2}hf_m,$$

where s_{mm} and q_{mm} are the mth diagonal elements of S and Q, $f_m \equiv \partial f/\partial \theta_m$, $g_m \equiv \partial g/\partial \theta_m$, and $h_m \equiv \partial h/\partial \theta_m$. By adapting the development after Equation (13), we find that F_m reduces to

$$F_m = \theta_m^{-1} - \theta_m^{-2}(s_{mm} + q_{mm}) + \frac{\lambda\theta_m^{-2}\beta_m^2}{f}.$$

Setting this at zero gives

$$\theta_m = (s_{mm} + q_{mm}) - \frac{\lambda\beta_m^2}{f}.$$

For completion of this algorithm (including the determination of f) and a numerical illustration, see Jöreskog and Goldberger (1973). It is interesting to note how the matrix determining the estimate of β in Equation (39), namely R, is a mixture of the sample residual and regression moment matrices, corresponding to the fact that the parameter β enters both Ω and Π.

V. Unobservables in Simultaneous-Equation Models

Up to this point, our exploration has been confined to recursive models. To round out the discussion, we turn to the possibility of allowing for unobservable variables within a simultaneous-equation model.

First, we note that random measurement error in endogenous variables can be absorbed into the structural disturbances. Consequently, in the standard case where the structural disturbance covariance matrix is unrestricted, measurement error in endogenous variables should not affect the identifiability of the structural coefficients. Therefore, we focus attention on the situation where there is random measurement error in the exogenous variables.

Consider a conventional simultaneous-equation model

(42) $$y'\Gamma = x^{*\prime}B + u', \qquad E(x^*u') = 0,$$

with reduced form

(43) $$y' = x^{*\prime}B\Gamma^{-1} + u'\Gamma^{-1} = x^{*\prime}\Pi^* + v', \qquad E(x^*v') = 0.$$

We suppose that, were x^* observable, the model would be overidentified. That is, not only are the structural coefficients B and Γ uniquely determined by Π^*, but there are in fact restrictions on Π^*. Now suppose that x^* is not observable; what we do observe is x, which is related to x^* in the usual errors-in-variable manner:

(44) $$x = x^* + \varepsilon, \qquad E(x^*\varepsilon') = 0, \qquad E(\varepsilon\varepsilon') = \Theta, \qquad E(\varepsilon v') = 0.$$

For simplicity we will assume that Θ is diagonal, and further that some diagonal elements of Θ are zero, reflecting the accurate measurement of the corresponding exogenous variables.

Let

$$\Phi \equiv E(xx') = E[(x^*+\varepsilon)(x^{*\prime}+\varepsilon')] = E(x^*x^*) + \Theta$$

be the population covariance matrix of the observed x, and let

$$\Pi \equiv \Phi^{-1}E(xy') = \Phi^{-1}E[(x^*+\varepsilon)(x^{*\prime}\Pi^*+v')] = \Phi^{-1}E(x^*x^*)\Pi^*$$

be the coefficient matrix in the population linear regression of y on x. Then

$$\Phi\Pi = E(x^*x^*)\Pi^* = (\Phi-\Theta)\Pi^*,$$

so that

(45) $$\Pi^* = (\Phi-\Theta)^{-1}\Phi\Pi$$

is the relation connecting the observable moments and coefficients, Φ and Π, to the parameters, Π^* and Θ. This relation, in conjunction with the zeroes in Θ and the overidentifying restrictions on Π^*, may suffice to identify Π^*. If so, the structural parameters will be identified.

To illustrate, consider the supply-demand model:

$$y_1 = \alpha_1 y_2 + \alpha_2 x_1^* + u_1 \qquad \text{(demand)},$$

$$y_1 = \beta_1 y_2 + \beta_2 x_2^* + \beta_3 x_3^* + u_2 \qquad \text{(supply)},$$

where the endogenous variables are $y_1 =$ quantity and $y_2 =$ price, and the exogenous variables are $x_1^* = $ income, $x_2^* = $ wage rate, and $x_3^* = $ raw material price. The reduced form of the model is

$$(46) \qquad (y_1, y_2) = (x_1^*, x_2^*, x_3^*) \begin{pmatrix} \pi_{11}^* & \pi_{12}^* \\ \pi_{21}^* & \pi_{22}^* \\ \pi_{31}^* & \pi_{32}^* \end{pmatrix} + (v_1, v_2),$$

where

$$\pi_{11}^* = -\alpha_2 \beta_1/\delta, \qquad \pi_{12}^* = -\alpha_2/\delta, \qquad v_1 = (\alpha_1 u_1 - \beta_1 u_2)/\delta,$$

$$\pi_{21}^* = \alpha_1 \beta_2/\delta, \qquad \pi_{22}^* = \beta_2/\delta, \qquad v_2 = (u_2 - u_1)/\delta,$$

$$\pi_{31}^* = \alpha_1 \beta_3/\delta, \qquad \pi_{32}^* = \beta_3/\delta, \qquad \delta = \alpha_1 - \beta_1.$$

The reduced-form coefficient matrix is constrained by

$$\frac{\pi_{21}^*}{\pi_{22}^*} = \frac{\pi_{31}^*}{\pi_{32}^*} \quad (=\alpha_1),$$

that is, by

$$(47) \qquad \begin{vmatrix} \pi_{21}^* & \pi_{22}^* \\ \pi_{31}^* & \pi_{32}^* \end{vmatrix} = 0.$$

We suppose that there is a random error of measurement in x_1^*, but none in x_2^* nor x_3^*. Thus the observed exogenous variables are

$$x_1 = x_1^* + \varepsilon_1, \qquad x_2 = x_2^*, \qquad x_3 = x_3^*,$$

and the measurement-error covariance matrix takes the form

$$(48) \qquad \Theta = \begin{pmatrix} \theta & 0 & 0 \\ 0 & 0 & 0 \\ 0 & 0 & 0 \end{pmatrix},$$

where $\theta = E(\varepsilon_1^2)$. Applying Equations (45) and (48), we find

(49)

$$\begin{pmatrix} \pi_{11}^* & \pi_{12}^* \\ \pi_{21}^* & \pi_{22}^* \\ \pi_{31}^* & \pi_{32}^* \end{pmatrix} = \frac{1}{1 - \theta\phi^{11}} \begin{pmatrix} 1 & 0 & 0 \\ \theta\phi^{21} & 1 - \theta\phi^{11} & 0 \\ \theta\phi^{31} & 0 & 1 - \theta\phi^{11} \end{pmatrix} \begin{pmatrix} \pi_{11} & \pi_{12} \\ \pi_{21} & \pi_{22} \\ \pi_{31} & \pi_{32} \end{pmatrix},$$

where the ϕ^{ij} denote elements of Φ^{-1}. Then use of Equation (47) gives

$$\begin{vmatrix} \theta\phi^{21}\pi_{11} + (1 - \theta\phi^{11})\pi_{21} & \theta\phi^{21}\pi_{12} + (1 - \theta\phi^{11})\pi_{22} \\ \theta\phi^{31}\pi_{11} + (1 - \theta\phi^{11})\pi_{31} & \theta\phi^{31}\pi_{12} + (1 - \theta\phi^{11})\pi_{32} \end{vmatrix} = 0,$$

which reduces to

(50)

$$\theta = \frac{\pi_{22}\pi_{31} - \pi_{21}\pi_{32}}{\phi^{11}(\pi_{22}\pi_{31} - \pi_{21}\pi_{32}) + \phi^{21}(\pi_{11}\pi_{32} - \pi_{31}\pi_{12}) + \phi^{31}(\pi_{21}\pi_{12} - \pi_{11}\pi_{22})}.$$

Recalling that the ϕ's and π's are estimable from observations on y and x, we see that Equation (50) suffices to identify θ, whence Equation (49) suffices to identify the π^*'s, which in turn identify the α's and β's. The model in fact is now just-identified, and hence readily estimated. The single overidentifying restriction on Π^* has been traded off against the single measurement error variance in Θ.

This approach was applied to Tintner's meat-market data by Goldberger (1971a). The resulting reduced-form and structural coefficient estimates are reported below, along with the FIML estimates that result when all variables are assumed to be accurately measured; cf. Goldberger (1964, pp. 338–345).

Reduced-form estimates:

	Π^*, with measurement error			Π^*, without measurement error	
	y_1	y_2		y_1	y_2
x_1	−0.059	0.183	x_1	−0.049	0.119
x_2	−0.341	0.200	x_2	−0.215	0.044
x_3	0.742	−0.435	x_3	0.701	−0.145

Structural estimates:

	α_1	α_2	β_1	β_2	β_3	θ
With measurement error	−1.71	0.20	−0.32	−0.28	0.60	551
Without measurement error	−4.85	0.53	−0.41	−0.20	0.64	—

The estimated error variance in income, $\theta = 551$, represents about 15% of the total variance of income in the data. The careful reader will have noted that our reestimation did not correct the "wrong sign" on β_1—the supply curve remains downward sloping. While this is unfortunate in one respect—it suggests that the structural model was misspecified—in another respect it is fortunate: Allowance for measurement error did not automatically explain away an unattractive result. Hence, it is not an empty approach.

In any event, this example should suffice to indicate that it is possible to handle errors in the variables in a simultaneous-equation model. In general, the idea is that overidentifying restrictions on the reduced-form coefficients can be used up to identify measurement-error variances. Clearly, not only the number, but also the location of the error variances is critical. For example, in the supply-demand model above, if x_2^* rather than x_1^* were measured with error, identifiability would be lost. Operational rules for assessing the identifiability of parameters in a simultaneous-equation model with unobservable variables remain to be worked out. Anderson and Hurwicz (1949) sketched the subject; further results have since been obtained by Wiley (1973) and Geraci (1973).

Estimation of such models has been considered by Chernoff and Rubin (1953, pp. 204–206) and Sargan (1958), who rely on limited-information and instrumental variables, respectively. The full-information maximum likelihood algorithm for the case of independent measurement errors has recently been programmed by Jöreskog (1973). For empirical examples of simultaneous-equation models with measurement error, one must turn to the sociological literature; e.g., Duncan et al. (1968), Hauser (1972), and Duncan and Featherman (1972).

VI. Conclusions

It is possible to exaggerate the novelty of the ideas presented here. In distributed lag models, "desired stocks" and "anticipated sales" are unobservable variables and are regularly handled in a rigorous manner. In the variance-component models introduced by Balestra and Nerlove (1966) for panel data, a factor-analytic structure for regression disturbances appears. Various econometric studies have used instrumental variables to obtain estimates in the presence of unobservables. Nevertheless, our exploration may suggest a range of applications broader than econometricians have heretofore recognized. Also, it may discourage the practice of pulling instrumental variables out of the hat as the occasion arises. As our analysis indicates, assumptions of independence—or dependence—between observables and unobservables are best incorporated into the original specification of a stochastic model, rather than introduced as afterthoughts. Sociologists and educational psychologists, indeed, have been adopting the practice of conjoining the "measurement model" to the "main model" in structural equation systems. Examples can be found in books edited by Blalock (1971) and by Goldberger and Duncan (1973).

REFERENCES

Adelman, I. and C. T. Morris (1967). *Society, Politics, and Economic Development: A Quantitative Approach.* Johns Hopkins Press, Baltimore, Maryland.
Anderson, T. W. and L. Hurwicz (1949). "Errors and shocks in economic relationships," *Econometrica Suppl.* **17**, 23–25.
Anderson, T. W. and H. Rubin (1956). "Statistical inference in factor analysis," *Proc. Berkeley Symp. Math. Statist. Probability* Vol. V, pp. 111–150. Univ. of California, Berkeley, California.

Balestra, P. and M. Nerlove (1966). "Pooling cross section and time series data in the estimation of a dynamic model: the demand for natural gas," *Econometrica* **34**, 585–612.

Blalock, H. M., Jr. (ed.) (1971). *Causal Models in the Social Sciences.* Aldine-Atherton, Chicago, Illinois.

Chernoff, H. and H. Rubin (1953). "Asymptotic properties of limited-information estimates under generalized conditions," *Studies in Econometric Method* (W. C. Hood and T. C. Koopmans, eds.), Chapter 7, pp. 200–212. Wiley, New York.

Christ, C. F. (1966). *Econometric Models and Methods.* Wiley, New York.

Christensen, S. S. (1972). "Income Maintenance and the Labor Supply." Dept. of Econ. doctoral dissertation, Univ. of Wisconsin, Madison, Wisconsin.

Dhrymes, P. J. (1970). *Econometrics: Statistical Foundations and Applications.* Harper, New York.

Duncan, O. D. and D. L. Featherman (1972). "Psychological and cultural factors in the process of occupational achievement," *Soc. Sci. Res.* **1**, 121–145.

Duncan, O. D., A. O. Haller and A. Portes (1968). "Peer influences on aspirations: a reinterpretation," *Amer. J. Sociol.* **74**, 119–137.

Geraci, V. J. (1973). "Simultaneous Equation Models with Measurement Error." Dept. of Econ. doctoral dissertation, Univ. of Wisconsin, Madison, Wisconsin.

Goldberger, A. S. (1964). *Econometric Theory.* Wiley, New York.

Goldberger, A. S. (1970). "Criteria and constraints in multivariate regression," Workshop Paper EME 7026, Social Syst. Res. Inst., Univ. of Wisconsin.

Goldberger, A. S. (1971a). "Simultaneity and measurement errors: an example," Workshop Paper EME 7108, Social Syst. Res. Inst., Univ. of Wisconsin.

Goldberger, A. S. (1971b). "Econometrics and psychometrics: a survey of communalities," *Psychometrika* **36**, 83–107.

Goldberger, A. S. (1972a). "Maximum-likelihood estimation of regressions containing unobservable independent variables," *Int. Econ. Rev.* **13**, 1–15.

Goldberger, A. S. (1972b). "Structural equation methods in the social sciences," *Econometrica*, **40**, 979–1002.

Goldberger, A. S. and O. D. Duncan (eds.) (1973). *Structural Equation Models in the Social Sciences.* Seminar Press, New York.

Goldberger, A. S. and I. Olkin (1971). "A minimum-distance interpretation of limited-information estimation," *Econometrica* **39**, 635–639.

Griliches, Z. and W. Mason (1972). "Education, income, and ability," *J. Political Econ.* **80**, S74–S103.

Hall, R. E. (1973). "Wages, income, and hours of work in the U.S. labor force," In *Income Maintenance and Labor Supply: Econometric Studies* (G. C. Cain and H. W. Watts, eds.), Chapter 3, pp. 102–162. Markham, Chicago, Illinois.

Harman, H. H. (1967). *Modern Factor Analysis*, 2nd rev. ed. Univ. of Chicago Press, Chicago, Illinois.

Hauser, R. M. (1972). "Disaggregating a social-psychological model of educational attainment," *Soc. Sci. Res.* **1**, 159–188.

Hauser, R. M. and A. S. Goldberger (1971). "The treatment of unobservable variables in path analysis," In *Sociological Methodology 1971* (H. L. Costner, ed.), Chapter 4, pp. 81–117. Jossey-Bass, San Francisco, California.

Johnston, J. J. (1963). *Econometric Methods.* McGraw-Hill, New York.

Jöreskog, K. G. (1969). "A general approach to confirmatory maximum likelihood factor analysis," *Psychometrika* **34**, 183–202.

Jöreskog, K. G. (1970). "A general method for analysis of covariance structures," *Biometrika* **57**, 239–251.

Jöreskog, K. G. (1973). "A general method for estimating a linear structural equation system," In *Structural Equation Models in the Social Sciences* (A. S. Goldberger and O. D. Duncan, eds.), Chapter 5, pp. 85–112. Seminar Press, New York.

Jöreskog, K. G. and A. S. Goldberger (1972). "Factor analysis by generalized least squares," *Psychometrika* **37**, 243–260.

Jöreskog, K. G. and A. S. Goldberger (1973). "Estimation of a model with multiple indicators and multiple causes of a single latent variable," unpublished manuscript.

King, B. F. (1966). "Market and industry factors in stock price behavior," *J. Business* **39**, 139–190.

Kmenta, J. (1971). *Elements of Econometrics*. Macmillan, New York.

Koopmans, T. C. and O. Reiersøl (1950). "The identification of structural characteristics," *Ann. Math. Statist.* **21**, 165–181.

Lawley, D. N. and A. E. Maxwell (1971). *Factor Analysis as a Statistical Method*, 2nd ed. American Elsevier, New York.

Malinvaud, E. (1970). *Statistical Methods of Econometrics*. North-Holland Publ., Amsterdam.

Sargan, J. D. (1958). "The estimation of economic relationships using instrumental variables," *Econometrica* **26**, 393–415.

Theil, H. (1967). *Economics and Information Theory*. American Elsevier, New York.

Theil, H. (1971). *Principles of Econometrics*. Wiley, New York.

Wiley, D. E. (1973). "The identification problem for structural equation models with unmeasured variables," In *Structural Equation Models in the Social Sciences* (A. S. Goldberger and O. D. Duncan, eds.), Chapter 4, pp. 69–84. Seminar Press, New York.

Zellner, A. (1970). "Estimation of regression relationships containing unobservable variables," *Int. Econ. Rev.* **11**, 441–454.

Chapter Eight

Consistent and efficient estimation of systems of simultaneous equations by means of instrumental variables

JAMES M. BRUNDY[1]

FEDERAL RESERVE BANK OF SAN FRANCISCO
SAN FRANCISCO, CALIFORNIA

DALE W. JORGENSON[1]

HARVARD UNIVERSITY
CAMBRIDGE, MASSACHUSETTS

[1] This work was supported in part by National Science Foundation Grant GS-2635 to the Institute of Mathematical Studies in the Social Sciences, Stanford University and by the Federal Reserve Bank of San Francisco. The authors are grateful to Phoebus Dhrymes, Ray C. Fair, Franklin M. Fisher, Arthur S. Goldberger, Jerald A. Hausman, Lawrence K. Klein, Ejnar Lyttkens, Henri Theil, Herman O. A. Wold, and Paul Zarembka for comments helpful in preparing this paper. All responsibility for any remaining errors resides with the authors.

A solution to the problem of consistent and efficient estimation of systems of simultaneous equations can be obtained by applying the method of maximum likelihood.[2] Although this solution is very attractive from the point of view of statistical theory, the computational burden of maximum likelihood methods is so substantial that these methods are rarely applied in practice. The purpose of much of the statistical theory of simultaneous equations estimation is to design methods for consistent and efficient estimation that are easier to implement.

Two alternative lines of attack on the problem of consistent and efficient estimation can be distinguished. First, a reduced form for the system of simultaneous equations can be derived and estimated, possibly subject to constraint. This approach was originated by Haavelmo (1944) in his path-breaking monograph, "The Probability Approach in Econometrics." Second, the structural form can be estimated without first estimating the reduced form. This approach was originated by Tinbergen (1939) in his pioneering study of a complete econometric model for the United States.

Haavelmo's original proposal was to estimate the reduced form of a system of simultaneous equations by ordinary least squares and then to derive estimates for the parameters of the structural form by indirect least squares. For exactly identified systems Haavelmo (1943, 1944, 1947) showed that this method is equivalent to the method of maximum likelihood. Anderson and Rubin (1949, 1950) extended Haavelmo's approach to over-identified equations, introducing the method of limited information maximum likelihood. They proposed to estimate the reduced form, subject to the over-identifying restrictions on a single equation, and to derive estimates for the parameters of the structural form from constrained estimates of the parameters of the reduced form.

Tinbergen's approach to simultaneous equations estimation was to estimate the structural form by ordinary least squares. Although Tinbergen did not attempt to rationalize this approach by an appeal to statistical theory, this gap was filled by Bentzel and Wold (1946). Bentzel and Wold showed that for recursive systems of equations like those employed by Tinbergen, least squares applied to the structural form is equivalent to full information maximum likelihood.

The approach of Tinbergen and of Bentzel and Wold is consistent and

---

[2] Throughout this paper "efficient" means "asymptotically efficient." Application of the method of maximum likelihood to systems of simultaneous equations was first proposed by Haavelmo (1943). Maximum likelihood methods for systems of stochastic difference equations were developed by Mann and Wald (1943). The methods of Mann and Wald were extended by Koopmans et al. (1950). Computation of maximum likelihood estimates is discussed by Chernoff and Divinsky (1953), Durbin (1963), and Rothenberg and Leenders (1964).

efficient for systems of simultaneous equations that are recursive in the sense of Bentzel and Wold. However, the method of least squares applied to the structural form is inconsistent for systems of simultaneous equations like those considered by Haavelmo. An alternative method for direct estimation of structural equations that is consistent for systems like those considered by Haavelmo is the method of instrumental variables, originated by Reiersøl (1945) and Geary (1949).[3] The problem that remains is to obtain an instrumental variable estimator that is consistent and efficient.

In this paper our first objective is to characterize the class of consistent and efficient estimators for systems of simultaneous equations based on the method of instrumental variables. In Section I we present the statistical model and review the main results on efficient estimation of the parameters of this model available in the literature. In Section II we characterize the class of consistent and efficient instrumental variables estimators of the parameters of a single over-identified equation in a system of simultaneous equations. In Section III we characterize the class of consistent and efficient instrumental variables estimators of a system of simultaneous equations. Durbin's iterative method for calculating the full information maximum likelihood estimator can be interpreted as the reiteration of a consistent and efficient instrumental variables estimator for a system of simultaneous equations.[4]

Estimators based on repeated applications of the method of least squares can be interpreted as instrumental variables estimators. For these estimators the first stage, as in indirect least squares, is to estimate the parameters of the reduced form by ordinary least squares. The second stage is to substitute fitted values from the reduced-form equations for jointly dependent variables in the equations of the structural form and to apply least squares again. This results in the two-stage least squares estimator proposed by Theil (1958) and Basmann (1957). The two-stage least squares estimator can be interpreted as a consistent and efficient instrumental variables estimator for a single over-identified equation. The third stage is to apply generalized least squares to a system of equations as a whole. This results in the three-stage least squares estimator proposed by Zellner and Theil (1962). The three-stage least squares estimator can be interpreted as a consistent and efficient instrumental variables estimator for a system of simultaneous equations.

The repeated least squares estimators proposed by Theil, Basmann, and Zellner and Theil involve the ordinary least squares estimator of the parameters of the reduced form. For models of even moderate size, the number of independent variables entering each reduced-form equation is large, so that estimation of the reduced-form equations by ordinary least squares is very

---

[3] A definitive treatment of the method of instrumental variables for a single structural equation is given by Sargan (1958).

[4] See Durbin (1963).

cumbersome. The two-stage and three-stage least squares estimators are almost never employed in the form originally proposed. For example, although Klein has successfully applied full information maximum likelihood methods to the Klein–Goldberger model, he does not present two-stage least squares estimates for this model. He indicates that it was impossible to compute a satisfactory ordinary least squares estimate for the reduced form of the model.[5]

For moderate or large size econometric models, the repeated least squares estimators employed in practice are based on truncated lists of variables at the initial stage.[6] Alternatively, the repeated least squares formulas can be evaluated with fitted values of the dependent variables obtained from first-stage regressions of the dependent variables on a proper subset of the principal components of the independent variables.[7] The latter approach has been applied by Klein (1969) to the Klein–Goldberger model, by Evans and Klein (1968) to the Wharton model, by Leibenberg *et al.* (1966) to the OBE model, and by Mitchell (1971) to the Brookings model. This application of the method of repeated least squares produces an estimator that is inconsistent.[8]

Our second objective is to characterize repeated least squares estimators with initial estimation of the reduced form by methods other than ordinary least squares. In Section IV we provide necessary and sufficient conditions for consistency and efficiency of repeated least squares estimators. Essentially, we find that repeated least squares estimators are consistent if and only if they reduce to instrumental variables estimators. These estimators are efficient if and only if they coincide with estimators based on initial estimation of the reduced form by ordinary least squares. Many applications of repeated least squares methods involve a loss of consistency; almost all applications involve a loss of efficiency.

In Section V we compare alternative instrumental variables estimators with respect to efficiency. We estimate Klein Model I model of the United States from annual data for the period 1921–1941. We compare an ordinary instrumental variables (IV) estimator with an estimator that is efficient for a single equation or a limited-information instrumental variables efficient estimator (LIVE). We compare both with an estimator that is efficient for a system of equations or a full-information instrumental variables efficient estimator (FIVE). Efficient instrumental variables estimators do not require initial

---

[5] See Klein (1969, p. 175).

[6] Truncation of the list of predetermined variables at the initial stage has been discussed by Fisher (1965a,b), Mitchell and Fisher (1970), and Mitchell (1971).

[7] Repeated least squares estimators based on the use of principal components were proposed by Kloek and Mennes (1960). Related methods have been discussed by Amemiya (1966), Dhrymes (1970), Malinvaud (1970), and Mitchell (1971).

[8] See Section IV.

estimation of the reduced form by ordinary least squares; these estimators can be constructed for models of moderate or even large size.[9]

I. The Statistical Model

We consider a simultaneous-equations model with p equations; the structural form of the model is denoted

$$(1) \qquad\qquad Y\Gamma + X\mathrm{B} = \mathrm{E},$$

with Y the matrix of observations on the p jointly dependent variables, X the matrix of n observations on the q predetermined variables, and E the matrix of random errors; the matrices $\{\Gamma, \mathrm{B}\}$ of structural coefficients are unknown parameters to be estimated. The reduced form of the model may be written

$$Y = X\Pi + \Upsilon,$$

where the matrix $\Pi = -\mathrm{B}\Gamma^{-1}$ of reduced-form coefficients is unknown and $\Upsilon = \mathrm{E}\Gamma^{-1}$ is a matrix of random errors.

Following the notation of Zellner and Theil (1962), we may denote the individual structural equations by:

$$(2) \qquad\qquad y_j = Z_j\delta_j + \varepsilon_j, \qquad (j = 1, ..., p),$$

where

$$Z_j = [Y_j X_j], \qquad \delta_j = \begin{bmatrix} \gamma_j \\ \beta_j \end{bmatrix}.$$

In this notation y_j is a vector of observations on the jth column of Y; the structural coefficient of this variable is normalized at unity; Y_j is a matrix of observations on the other jointly dependent variables included in the equation, X_j is a matrix of observations on the included predetermined variables, and ε_j is the jth column of E. The vectors $\{\gamma_j, \beta_j\}$ are structural coefficients of the included jointly dependent variables (other than the variable with coefficient normalized at unity) and the included predetermined variables, respectively.

Combining the p equations into a system of simultaneous equations, we may denote the system by

$$(3) \qquad\qquad y = Z\delta + \varepsilon,$$

[9] Our presentation is based on Brundy and Jorgenson (1971); our methods of estimation were proposed, independently, by Dhrymes (1971). An alternative approach to simultaneous equations estimation based on the approach of Tinbergen and Bentzel and Wold, is the fixed-point method of Wold (1965). Estimators based on the fixed-point method have also been discussed by Lyttkens (1970), Maddala (1971), and Mosbaek and Wold (1970). The method of iterative instrumental variables proposed by Lyttkens (1970) is closely related to the methods we present in Section II. The problem of estimation of large models has also been discussed by Fisher and Wadycki (1971) and Theil (1971).

where

$$y = \begin{bmatrix} y_1 \\ y_2 \\ \vdots \\ y_p \end{bmatrix}, \quad Z = \begin{bmatrix} Z_1 & 0 & \cdots & 0 \\ 0 & Z_2 & \cdots & 0 \\ \vdots & \vdots & & \vdots \\ 0 & 0 & \cdots & Z_p \end{bmatrix}, \quad \delta = \begin{bmatrix} \delta_1 \\ \delta_2 \\ \vdots \\ \delta_p \end{bmatrix}, \quad \varepsilon = \begin{bmatrix} \varepsilon_1 \\ \varepsilon_2 \\ \vdots \\ \varepsilon_p \end{bmatrix}.$$

In this notation we write the reduced form as

(4) $$y = [I \otimes X]\pi + v,$$

where $\otimes$ is the Kronecker product and

$$I \otimes X = \begin{bmatrix} X & 0 & \cdots & 0 \\ 0 & X & \cdots & 0 \\ \vdots & \vdots & & \vdots \\ 0 & 0 & \cdots & X \end{bmatrix}, \quad \pi = \begin{bmatrix} \pi_1 \\ \pi_2 \\ \vdots \\ \pi_p \end{bmatrix}, \quad v = \begin{bmatrix} v_1 \\ v_2 \\ \vdots \\ v_p \end{bmatrix}.$$

The vector π_j is the jth column of Π and the vector v_j is the jth column of Υ.

In addition to matrices of observations on the jointly dependent variables Y and the predetermined variables X we suppose the existence of a matrix of observations W on t instrumental variables. Instrumental variables may include the predetermined variables X together with variables such as dummies that divide the sample into subsamples—seasons, phases of the business cycle, geographical regions, and so on. In addition, the instrumental variables may include composite variables constructed from the predetermined variables such as principal components of these variables or fitted values of the jointly dependent variables calculated as linear combinations of the predetermined variables by means of estimates of the reduced form parameters.

The statistical specification of the simultaneous equations model, including the instrumental variables, is given by the following list of assumptions:

(i) Each structural equation is identifiable.
(ii) The vector ε of errors in the structural equations is normally distributed with mean zero and variance–covariance matrix $\Sigma \otimes I$, where Σ is a positive definite matrix of order p.

Under this assumption:

$$\operatorname{plim} n^{-1} E'E = \Sigma.$$

(iii) The matrices of observations on the predetermined variables and instrumental variables $\{X, W\}$ are distributed independently of ε and

$$\operatorname{plim} n^{-1} X'E = 0,$$
$$\operatorname{plim} n^{-1} W'E = 0.$$

(iv) The matrices $X'X$, $W'W$, and $W'X$ have ranks q, t, and $\min(q,t)$, respectively, with probability one, and the following probability limits exist are finite, and have full rank:

$$\operatorname{plim} n^{-1} X'X = \Sigma_{x'x},$$

$$\operatorname{plim} n^{-1} W'W = \Sigma_{w'w},$$

$$\operatorname{plim} n^{-1} W'X = \Sigma_{w'x}.$$

(v) The vector $n^{-1/2}[I \otimes X]'\varepsilon$ is asymptotically normal with mean zero and variance–covariance matrix $\Sigma \otimes \Sigma_{x'x}$; the vector $n^{-1/2}[I \otimes W]'\varepsilon$ is asymptotically normal with mean zero and variance–covariance matrix $\Sigma \otimes \Sigma_{w'w}$.

Some comments on these assumptions may be useful at this point. Assumptions (iii) and (iv) embody the most important properties of instrumental variables, namely, that these variables are uncorrelated (asymptotically) with errors E and that they are correlated (asymptotically) with the predetermined variables X. From the reduced form we can deduce that

$$\operatorname{plim} n^{-1} W'Y = \operatorname{plim} n^{-1} W'X\Pi + \operatorname{plim} n^{-1} W'\Upsilon = \Sigma_{w'x} \Pi,$$

so that the instrumental variables are correlated (asymptotically) with the jointly dependent variables.

Assumptions (ii), (iii), and (iv) provide a partial characterization of the joint distribution of the errors, the predetermined variables, and the instrumental variables. These assumptions would obviously be satisfied for fixed predetermined variables or fixed instrumental variables provided that the limits—$\lim n^{-1} X'X$, $\lim n^{-1} W'W$, $\lim n^{-1} W'X$—exist and are finite. They would be satisfied for random predetermined variables, including variables generated by a stationary stochastic process, provided that the usual hypotheses of the law of large numbers are satisfied for cross products of the predetermined and instrumental variables with themselves, with each other, or with the errors.[10] Similarly, assumption (v) provides a characterization of the asymptotic distribution of the random vectors $n^{-1/2}[I \otimes X]'\varepsilon$ and $n^{-1/2}[I \otimes W]'\varepsilon$. This assumption would be satisfied for fixed predetermined variables and instrumental variables provided that the usual hypotheses of the central limit theorem are satisfied for cross products of these variables with the errors.[11] The assumption would be satisfied for random predetermined variables and instrumental variables under similar conditions.

Assumption (ii), that the errors have a joint normal distribution, is essential

---

[10] For further details, see Malinvaud (1970, esp. pp. 369–373).

[11] For further details, see Malinvaud (1970, esp. pp. 250–253); see also Eicker (1963).

for consideration of the problem of efficient estimation.[12] Under this assumption and the other assumptions we have made the full-information maximum likelihood estimator attain the Cramer–Rao lower bound for the asymptotic variance–covariance matrix of (essentially) any consistent estimator of the structural parameters.[13] This bound, stated in terms of the asymptotic information matrix, depends on the likelihood function. Without an explicit likelihood function, such as that associated with a normal distribution of the errors, it is impossible to discuss efficient estimation. Of course, the asymptotic distribution theory we develop for instrumental variables estimators is valid whether or not the errors are normally distributed, provided that our other assumptions on the distribution of the errors are satisfied.[14] While alternative estimators may be compared with regard to relative efficiency, no lower bound is available that would enable us to characterize any estimator as efficient in the class of consistent estimators.

The main results on asymptotic efficiency available in the literature are that within the class of (essentially) all consistent, asymptotically normal estimators:

(1)   The full information maximum likelihood estimator is efficient.[15]

(2)   With no restrictions on the variance–covariance matrix of the errors, full information maximum likelihood and three-stage least squares converge in distribution, so that three-stage least squares is efficient.[16]

(3)   The limited-information maximum likelihood estimator is efficient among estimators that depend only on identifying restrictions for a single equation.[17]

(4)   Limited-information maximum likelihood and two-stage least squares converge in distribution, so that two-stage least squares is efficient within the same class of estimators.[18]

We consider estimation of the structural coefficients δ in the absence of restrictions on the variance–covariance matrix Σ of the errors; the full-

[12] The problem of efficient estimation for the simultaneous equations model is discussed in detail by Rothenberg (1966).

[13] For further discussion, see Rothenberg (1966); properties of the method of maximum likelihood are analyzed by Rao (1965, esp. pp. 289–301). The Cramer-Rao bound is discussed by Rao (1965, pp. 283–287).

[14] Similarly, it is possible to characterize the asymptotic distribution of an estimator that has the same form as the maximum likelihood estimator without assuming that the errors are normally distributed, as in the quasi-maximum likelihood estimators of the Cowles Commission. See Koopmans and Hood (1953, pp. 146–147), and the references listed there.

[15] Koopmans and Hood (1953, pp. 146–147).

[16] See Rothenberg and Leenders (1964) and Sargan (1964).

[17] See Rothenberg (1966).

[18] See Theil (1958, pp. 230–232).

information maximum likelihood and three-stage least squares estimators are efficient. The asymptotic variance–covariance matrix of these estimators, also the Cramer–Rao bound, is

$$\{\Sigma'_{\bar{x}'z}(\Sigma \otimes \Sigma_{x'x})^{-1}\Sigma_{\bar{x}'z}\}^{-1},$$

where d is an efficient estimator of δ, $\bar{X} = I \otimes X$, and the matrix $\Sigma_{\bar{x}'z}$ has the form,

$$\Sigma_{\bar{x}'z} = \begin{bmatrix} \Sigma_{x'z_1} & 0 & \cdots & 0 \\ 0 & \Sigma_{x'z_1} & \cdots & 0 \\ \vdots & \vdots & & \vdots \\ 0 & 0 & \cdots & \Sigma_{x'z_p} \end{bmatrix}.$$

Further,

$$\Sigma_{x'z_j} = [\Sigma_{x'y_j}\Sigma_{x'x_j}] = [\Sigma_{x'x}\Pi_j\Sigma_{x'x_j}], \qquad (j = 1, ..., p).$$

In this expression $X'X_j$ is a submatrix of $X'X$ and Π_j is a submatrix of Π, corresponding to the reduced form equations,

$$Y_j = X\Pi_j + Y_j.$$

We also consider estimation of the structural coefficients of a single equation δ_j, subject only to the identifying restrictions for that equation; the limited-information maximum likelihood and two-stage least squares estimators are efficient. The asymptotic variance–covariance matrix of these estimators, also the Cramer–Rao bound, is

$$\sigma_{jj}\{\Sigma'_{x'z_j}\Sigma_{x'x}^{-1}\Sigma_{x'z_j}\}^{-1}, \qquad (j = 1, ..., p),$$

where d_j is an efficient estimator of δ_j. This completes our discussion of the simultaneous equation model.

II. Instrumental Variables Estimation of a Single Equation

The method of instrumental variables for estimation of a single equation in a system of simultaneous equations is the following: We suppose that r_j jointly dependent and s_j predetermined variables are included in the jth equation and that a subset of $t_j = r_j + s_j - 1$ instrumental variables W_j is selected from the set of t instrumental variables W. The instrumental variables estimator d_j of δ_j is obtained by solving the equation

$$W_j'y_, = W_j'Z_jd_j,$$

thus obtaining

(5) $$d_j = (W_j'Z_j)^{-1}W_j'y_j.$$

Examples of instrumental variables follow: (a) The indirect least squares estimator,

$$d_j = (X'Z_j)^{-1}X'y_j,$$

where $t = p = r_j + s_j - 1$. (b) The two-stage least squares estimator,

$$d_j = \{Z_j'X(X'X)^{-1}X'Z_j\}^{-1}Z_j'X(X'X)^{-1}X'y_j,$$

where $W_j = X(X'X)^{-1}X'Z_j$, the fitted values from a regression of the right-hand side variables in the equation Z_j on the matrix of predetermined variables X.

We first observe that any instrumental variables estimator d_j is consistent since

$$\text{plim } d_j = \delta_j + \text{plim}(n^{-1}W_j'Z_j)^{-1}\,\text{plim } n^{-1}W_j'\varepsilon_j = \delta_j,$$

where

$$\text{plim}(n^{-1}W_j'Z_j) = [\Sigma_{w_j'x}\Pi_j\Sigma_{w_j'x_j}] = \Sigma_{w_j'z_j}$$

is a nonsingular matrix of constants by assumptions (iii) and (iv) and where

$$\text{plim}(n^{-1}W_j'\varepsilon_j) = 0,$$

by assumption (iii). Second, this estimator is asymptotically normal, since the vector $n^{-1/2}W_j'\varepsilon_j$ is asymptotically normal by assumption (v). Further,[19] this estimator is asymptotically unbiased and its asymptotic variance–covariance matrix is $\sigma_{jj}\{\Sigma_{w_j'z_j}'\Sigma_{w_j'w_j}^{-1}\Sigma_{w_j'z_j}\}^{-1}$.

The first problem is to select a matrix of t_j instrumental variables such that the instrumental variables estimator is efficient. Obviously, this can always be done by selecting $W_j = X(X'X)^{-1}X'Z_j$ as in two-stage least squares.[20] The remaining problem is to select the instrumental variables so as to avoid the use of the method of ordinary least squares to estimate the coefficients Π_j of the reduced form. To solve this problem we select W_j as follows:

(6) $$W_j = [X\hat{\Pi}_j\,X_j],$$

where $\hat{\Pi}_j$ is any consistent estimator of the reduced form coefficients,

$$\text{plim } \hat{\Pi}_j = \Pi_j.$$

Of course, the ordinary least squares estimator is consistent, but there are many consistent estimators, some of which are far easier to compute than the ordinary least squares estimator. We discuss possible consistent estimators of the reduced form parameters below.

---

[19] These properties of an instrumental variables estimator of a single equation are derived by Sargan (1958).

[20] This is pointed out by Klein (1955) and Sargan (1958). For further discussion, see Malinvaud (1970, pp. 713–717).

At this point we must show that the matrix of instrumental variables W_j, as given in Equation (6) results in an efficient instrumental variables estimator of the structural coefficients δ_j. The asymptotic variance–covariance matrix becomes

$$(7) \quad \sigma_{jj}\{\Sigma'_{w_j'z_j}\Sigma^{-1}_{w_j'w_j}\Sigma_{w_j'z_j}\}^{-1} = \sigma_{jj}\Sigma^{-1}_{w_j'w_j} = \sigma_{jj}\begin{bmatrix} \Pi_j'\Sigma_{x'x}\Pi_j & \Pi_j'\Sigma_{x'x_j} \\ \Sigma_{x_j'x}\Pi_j & \Sigma_{x_j'x_j} \end{bmatrix}^{-1}$$

Similarly, the Cramer–Rao bound may be written

$$\sigma_{jj}\{\Sigma'_{x'z_j}\Sigma^{-1}_{x'x}\Sigma_{x'z_j}\}^{-1} = \sigma_{jj}\begin{bmatrix} \Pi_j'\Sigma_{x'x}\Pi_j & \Pi_j'\Sigma_{x'x_j} \\ \Sigma_{x_j'x}\Pi_j & \Sigma_{x_j'x_j} \end{bmatrix}^{-1}.$$

We obtain the following theorem:

THEOREM 1. A necessary and sufficient condition for the efficiency of an instrumental variables estimator (Equation (5)) is that the matrix of instrumental variables can be transformed by means of a nonsingular matrix into a matrix of instrumental variables that includes two subsets, $W_j = (W_{j1} W_{j2})$:

(a) A set of instrumental variables W_{j1} such that

$$\operatorname{plim} n^{-1}W_{j1}'X = \Pi_j'\Sigma_{x'x}.$$

(b) A set of instrumental variables W_{j2} such that

$$\operatorname{plim} n^{-1}W_{j2}'X = \Sigma_{x_j'x}.$$

These variables may be selected such that $W_{j1} = X\hat{\Pi}_j$, where $\hat{\Pi}_j$ is a consistent estimator of Π_j, and $W_{j2} = X_j$, the matrix of predetermined variables included in the jth equation.

The hypothesis of the theorem is obviously sufficient since under this hypothesis the instrumental variables estimator (5) attains the Cramer–Rao bound. The hypothesis is necessary for if the instrumental variables take some other form, the asymptotic variance–covariance matrix is different from the Cramer–Rao bound; hence, the estimator (5) is inefficient. We refer to the estimator (5) associated with the instrumental variables of Theorem 1 as the limited information instrumental variables efficient (LIVE) estimator.[21]

To construct a consistent estimator of the reduced form coefficients Π we may choose any consistent estimator of the structural coefficients since

$$\operatorname{plim} \hat{\Pi} = -\operatorname{plim} \hat{B} \cdot \operatorname{plim} \hat{\Gamma}^{-1} = -B\Gamma^{-1} = \Pi,$$

where the matrices $(\hat{B}, \hat{\Gamma})$ are consistent estimators of the structural coefficients.

---

[21] We are indebted to Arthur S. Goldberger for bringing to our attention an error in our original statement of this theorem and Theorem 2, below; see Brundy and Jorgenson (1971, pp. 211, 213).

As examples, we consider some consistent but possibly inefficient instrumental variables estimators:

(A)   Let $W_j = [X_j^* X_j]$, where X_j is the matrix of predetermined variables included in the jth equation and X_j^* consists of any $r_j - 1$ additional predetermined variables. These variables could be selected from the variables included in the structural equations determining the jointly dependent variables Y_j by the method of structural ordering devised by Fisher.[22]

(B)   Let $W_j = [P_j X_j]$, where P_j is a subset of the principal components of X, equal in number to $r_j - 1$. The principal components could be selected in order of magnitude of the associated characteristic values. This method is proposed by Taylor (1962). Taylor's instrumental variables estimator should be carefully distinguished from the truncated two-stage least squares method of estimation, also using principal components of the predetermined variables, proposed by Kloek and Mennes (1960).[23]

(C)   Let $W_j = [\hat{Y}_j X_j]$, where $\hat{Y}_j$ is a set of fitted values for regressions of Y_j on a set of predetermined variables, including X_j. If all the predetermined variables are included in the regressions, the resulting instrumental variables estimator is identical to two-stage least squares. Provided only that X_j is included in the regressions, the instrumental variables estimator is identical to a possibly truncated two-stage least squares estimator with the fitted value $\hat{Y}_j$ as regressors at the second stage.[24]

(D)   Let $W_j = [\hat{Y}_j X_j]$, where $\hat{Y}_j$ is a set of fitted values for the jointly dependent variables, obtained by fitting the structural form of a simultaneous equations model by ordinary least squares and solving for the jointly dependent variables. This method for constructing instrumental variables in the first step of the iterative instrumental variables (IIV) estimator proposed by Lyttkens (1970) and analyzed by Maddala (1971).

Given estimates of parameters of all the structural equations, the next step is to construct a set of fitted values for the jth equation $X \hat{\Pi}_j$, corresponding to a consistent estimator of the structural coefficients. The fitted values can be obtained from a simulation of the model over the sample period. The final step is to construct a complete set of instrumental variables for each equation by

[22] See Fisher (1965a, b). Fisher proposes to employ a proper subset of the predetermined variables as the set of initial regressors in a truncated version of two-stage least squares, as discussed in Section IV. Fisher's original proposal results in a consistent estimator only if all the right-hand side jointly dependent variables included in a given equation are fitted to the same set of predetermined variables as initial regressors. In general this condition will not be satisfied. The proposal is amended by Mitchell and Fisher (1970, pp. 226, 229–232), to achieve consistency of the resulting estimator of the structural coefficients. The revised proposal is employed by Mitchell (1971).

[23] See footnote 26.

[24] See Theorem 3 in Section IV.

combining the fitted values for the jointly dependent variables $X\hat{\Pi}_j$ with actual values of predetermined variables included in the equation X_j. The resulting instrumental variables estimator is equal in efficiency to limited information maximum likelihood and two-stage least squares estimators.

The two-stage least squares estimator with $W_j = X(X'X)^{-1}X'Z_j$ is a limited information efficient instrumental variables (LIVE) estimator. If the instrumental variables in (C) above are constructed by including all predetermined variables X in the initial regressions, the first-stage instrumental variables estimator is identical to two-stage least squares. A second-stage instrumental variables estimator produces no gain in efficiency. A convenient feature of the two-stage least squares estimator is that it can be modified to produce a consistent estimator for the parameters of a single equation in a system of simultaneous equations without estimating the entire system. A similar modification is possible for any limited-information efficient instrumental variables estimator. Given a single structural equation, the remaining equations in the system can be replaced by reduced form equations for the jointly dependent variables Y_j, appearing as right-hand side variables. The reduced-form equations could be replaced in turn by regression equations for the jointly dependent variables Y_j; the list of regressors need not include all the predetermined variables. A similar modification can be made to produce a consistent estimator for the parameters of a subsystem consisting of several structural equations.

Another interesting member of the class of limited-information efficient instrumental variables (LIVE) estimators is the iterative instrumental variable (IIV) estimator studied by Lyttkens and Maddala. We have outlined the first step of the construction of this estimator in (D) above. Lyttkens and Maddala propose to repeat this step until the process converges and the instrumental variables used at each stage are equal to the fitted values of the jointly dependent variables at that stage. They observe that the limiting instrumental variables estimator is asymptotically equivalent to a two-stage least squares estimator. By Theorem 1 a two-stage instrumental variables estimator indicated by a consistent estimator of the structural parameters is both consistent and efficient. The second iteration of the iterative instrumental variables estimator is asymptotically equivalent to the limiting estimator considered by Lyttkens and Maddala. Reiteration of the process beyond the two-stage instrumental variables estimator is superfluous from the point of view of gains in efficiency.

III. Instrumental Variables Estimation of a System of Equations

We are now prepared to confront the problem of efficient instrumental variables estimation for a system of simultaneous equations. The method of instrumental variables for a system of simultaneous equations is the following:

we suppose that $\sum_j (r_j + s_j - 1) = r + s - p$ variables are included in the p equations, where $\sum_j r_j = r$, $\sum_j s_j = s$, and that instrumental variables are now defined so that each one contains an element corresponding to each observation in each equation. We may denote the set of instrumental variables by

$$\overline{W} = \begin{bmatrix} W_{11} & W_{12} & \cdots & W_{1p} \\ W_{21} & W_{22} & \cdots & W_{2p} \\ \vdots & \vdots & & \vdots \\ W_{p1} & W_{p2} & \cdots & W_{pp} \end{bmatrix},$$

where each submatrix W_{ij} has $r_j + s_j - 1$ columns. The instrumental variables estimator d of δ is obtained by solving the equation[25]

$$\overline{W}'y = \overline{W}'Zd,$$

obtaining

(8) $$d = (\overline{W}'Z)^{-1}\overline{W}y.$$

Examples of instrumental variables estimators for a system of simultaneous equations follow.

(a) The instrumental variables estimator for a single equation applied to each equation in the system. In this example, the matrix $\overline{W}$ of instrumental variables becomes

$$\overline{W} = \begin{bmatrix} W_1 & 0 & \cdots & 0 \\ 0 & W_2 & \cdots & 0 \\ \vdots & \vdots & & \vdots \\ 0 & 0 & \cdots & W_p \end{bmatrix}.$$

(b) The three-stage least squares estimator,

$$d = \{Z'\overline{X}(S \otimes X'X)^{-1}\overline{X}'Z\}^{-1}Z'\overline{X}(S \otimes X'X)^{-1}\overline{X}'y,$$

where $\overline{X} = I \otimes X$ and S is a consistent estimator of the variance–covariance matrix Σ constructed from the residuals from structural equations estimated by two-stage least squares; in this example, the matrix $\overline{W}$ becomes

$$\overline{W} = \overline{X}(S \otimes X'X)^{-1}\overline{X}'Z.$$

This interpretation of the three-stage least squares estimator is due to Madansky (1964).

[25] Instrumental variables estimators for a system of equations are discussed by Madansky (1964). Note that the rank of the matrix $\overline{W}'Z$ must be equal to $r+s-p$ with probability one. Under assumption (iv), this condition is easily seen to be satisfied for the instrumental variables estimator of Theorem 2, provided that the number of observations n exceeds the number of equations p.

We first observe that if each submatrix W_{ij} satisfies assumptions (iii), (iv), and (v), the instrumental variables estimator d is consistent, since

$$\text{plim}\, d = \delta + \text{plim}\,(n^{-1}\overline{W}'Z)^{-1}\cdot \text{plim}\, n^{-1}\overline{W}'\varepsilon,$$

where $\text{plim}\,(n^{-1}\overline{W}'Z)$ has typical submatrix,

$$\text{plim}\,(n^{-1}W'_{ji}Z_j) = [\Sigma_{w'_{ji}x}\Pi_j\Sigma_{w'_{ji}x_j}] = \Sigma_{w'_{ji}z_j},$$

so that $\text{plim}\,(n^{-1}\overline{W}'Z) = \Sigma_{\overline{w}'z}$ is a nonsingular matrix of constants by assumptions (iii) and (iv), and the vector $\text{plim}\, n^{-1}\overline{W}'\varepsilon$ has typical element,

$$\text{plim}\, n^{-1}\sum_j W'_{ji}\varepsilon_j = \sum_j \text{plim}\, n^{-1}W'_{ji}\varepsilon_j = 0,$$

by assumption (iii). Further, the estimator is asymptotically normal, since the vector $n^{-1/2}\overline{W}'\varepsilon$ is asymptotically normal. The vector $n^{-1/2}\overline{W}\varepsilon$ has typical element $\sum_j n^{-1/2}W'_{ji}\varepsilon_j$, so that $n^{-1/2}\overline{W}'\varepsilon$ is asymptotically normal by assumption (v). The typical submatrix of the asymptotic variance–covariance matrix of the vector $n^{-1/2}\overline{W}'\varepsilon$ takes the form

$$\sum_k \sum_l \sigma_{kl}\Sigma_{w'_{ki}w_{lj}}.$$

The first problem is to select a matrix of $r + s - p$ instrumental variables such that the instrumental variables estimator is efficient. This can always be done by selecting $\overline{W} = \overline{X}(S \otimes X'X)^{-1}\overline{X}'Z$ as in three-stage least squares. The remaining problem is to select the instrumental variables so as to avoid estimation of the reduced form by the method of ordinary least squares. To solve this problem we select W_{ij} as follows:

(9) $$W_{ij} = \hat{\sigma}^{ij}W_j, \qquad (i, j = 1, \ldots, p),$$

where

$$W_j = [X\hat{\Pi}_j X_j], \qquad (j = 1, \ldots, p);$$

as before $\hat{\Pi}_j$ is any consistent estimator of the reduced form parameters Π_j. The scalar $\hat{\sigma}^{ij}$ is a typical element of $\hat{\Sigma}^{-1}$, where $\hat{\Sigma}$ is any consistent estimator of the variance–covariance matrix Σ. We discuss possible consistent estimators of the reduced-form parameters and the variance–covariance matrix below.

We must now show that the matrix of instrumental variables $\overline{W}$, as given by Equation (9), results in an efficient estimator of the structural coefficients δ. The typical submatrix of the asymptotic variance–covariance matrix of the vector $n^{-1/2}\overline{W}'\varepsilon$ takes the form

$$\sum_k \sum_l \sigma_{kl}\Sigma_{w'_{ki}w_{lj}} = \left(\sum_k \sum_l \sigma_{kl}\sigma^{ki}\sigma^{lj}\right)\Sigma_{w_{i'}w_j}$$

$$= \sigma^{ij}\Sigma_{w_{i'}w_j},$$

since $\sum_k \sigma_{kl} \sigma^{ki}$ equals unity if $i = l$ and zero otherwise. Further, this submatrix may be written

$$\sigma^{ij} \Sigma_{w_i' w_j} = \sigma^{ij} \begin{bmatrix} \Pi_i' \Sigma_{x'x} \Pi_j & \Pi_i' \Sigma_{x'x_j} \\ \Sigma_{x_i'x} \Pi_j & \Sigma_{x_i'x_j} \end{bmatrix}.$$

Similarly, the typical submatrix of $\Sigma_{\bar{w}'z}$ may be written

$$\Sigma_{w_{ji}'z_j} = \sigma^{ij} \Sigma_{w_i'z_j} = \sigma^{ij} \begin{bmatrix} \Pi_i' \Sigma_{x'x} \Pi_j & \Pi_i' \Sigma_{x'x_j} \\ \Sigma_{x_i'x} \Pi_j & \Sigma_{x_i'x_j} \end{bmatrix}.$$

We conclude that the asymptotic variance–covariance matrix becomes $\Sigma_{\bar{w}'z}^{-1}$. The matrix $\Sigma_{\bar{x}'z}'(\Sigma \otimes \Sigma_{x'x})^{-1} \Sigma_{\bar{x}'z}$ occurring in the Cramer–Rao bound has a typical submatrix,

$$\sigma^{ij} \Sigma_{x'z_i}' \Sigma_{x'x}^{-1} \Sigma_{x'z_j} = \sigma^{ij} \begin{bmatrix} \Pi_i' \Sigma_{x'x} \Pi_j & \Pi_i' \Sigma_{x'x_j} \\ \Sigma_{x_i'x} \Pi_j & \Sigma_{x_i'x_j} \end{bmatrix}.$$

We can now verify the following theorem.

THEOREM 2. A necessary and sufficient condition for the efficiency of an instrumental variables estimator (8) is that the matrix of instrumental variables can be transformed by means of a nonsingular transformation into a matrix of instrumental variables that has a typical submatrix including two subsets, $W_{ij} = (W_{ij1} W_{ij2})$:

(a)   A set of variables W_{ij1} such that

$$\text{plim } n^{-1} W_{ij1}' X = \sigma^{ij} \Pi_j' \Sigma_{x'x};$$

(b)   A set of variables W_{ij2} such that

$$\text{plim } n^{-1} W_{ij2}' X = \sigma^{ij} \Sigma_{x_j'x}.$$

These variables may be selected such that $W_{ij1} = \hat{\sigma}^{ij} X \hat{\Pi}_j$, where $\hat{\Pi}_j$ is a consistent estimator of Π_j and $\hat{\sigma}^{ij}$ is a typical element of $\hat{\Sigma}^{-1}$, where $\hat{\Sigma}$ is a consistent estimator of Σ, and $W_{ij2} = \hat{\sigma}^{ij} X_j$, where X_j is the matrix of predetermined variables included in the jth equation.

The hypothesis of the theorem is obviously sufficient since under this hypothesis the instrumental estimator (8) attains the Cramer–Rao bound. The hypothesis is necessary for if the instrumental variables take some other form, the asymptotic variance–covariance matrix is different from the Cramer–Rao bound; hence, the estimator (8) is inefficient. We refer to the estimator (8) associated with the instrumental variables of Theorem 2 as the full-information instrumental variables efficient (FIVE) estimator.

To construct consistent estimators of the reduced form coefficients Π and the variance-covariance matrix Σ we may choose any consistent estimator of the structural coefficients, say $\hat{\delta}$. A consistent estimator of a typical element of the variance–covariance matrix is given by

(10) $\hat{\sigma}_{ij} = n^{-1}(y_i - Z_i\hat{\delta}_i)'(y_j - Z_j\hat{\delta}_j),$ $(i, j = 1, \ldots, p),$

since

$$\text{plim}\,\hat{\sigma}_{ij} = \text{plim}\,n^{-1}\varepsilon_i'\varepsilon_j = \sigma_{ij},$$

by assumptions (ii), (iii), and (iv). We have discussed consistent but possibly inefficient instrumental variables estimators of the structural coefficients above.

The computational steps for efficient estimation of simultaneous equations by instrumental variables are summarized in Table 1. The process of efficient estimation is initiated by evaluation of any consistent estimator for the coefficients of the structural equations. For example, the process can be initiated by a consistent but possibly inefficient instrumental variables estimator. The associated consistent estimators (10) of the elements of the variance–covariance matrix Σ can then be evaluated.

The second step in efficient estimation is to simulate the model for the sample period to obtain fitted values of the jointly dependent variables. At this point the computational steps for limited-information instrumental variables (LIVE) and full-information instrumental variables (FIVE) estimators diverge. Both employ fitted values for the jointly dependent variables obtained by simulation. In addition, the full-information estimator uses as weights elements of the inverse of the consistent estimator $\hat{\Sigma}$ of the variance–covariance matrix Σ. The fitted values for each jointly dependent variable in the matrix Y are the same for all submatrices (Equation (9)) of the matrix $\overline{W}$ in which these variables are included. Only the weights $\{\hat{\sigma}^{ij}\}$ differ from submatrix to submatrix. The second step is completed by selecting the variables to be included in each matrix W_j $(j = 1, \ldots, p)$ for the limited information estimator or in each submatrix W_{ij} $(i, j = 1, \ldots, p)$ of the matrix $\overline{W}$ for the full information estimator. For the full information estimator these variables are combined with the weights $\{\hat{\sigma}^{ij}\}$ to obtain the matrix of instrumental variables $\overline{W}$.

The third step in efficient estimation is to construct the instrumental variables estimator (5) or (8). For statistical inference about the structural parameters, an estimator of the variance–covariance matrix for either limited-information or full-information estimators of these parameters is required. The estimator of either variance–covariance matrix requires a consistent estimator of the variance–covariance matrix Σ; in the fourth step of efficient estimation the initial consistent estimator of this matrix from the first step of the computation may be employed.

TABLE 1

Computational Scheme for Efficient Estimation of Simultaneous Equations by Instrumental Variables

Computational steps	Limited information (LIVE)	Full information (FIVE)
(1) Construct a consistent estimator of the structural parameters $\{\delta, \Sigma\}$.	(1) E.g., use a consistent but possibly inefficient instrumental variables estimator.	(1) Same.
(2) Construct instrumental variables for efficient estimation. Fitted values of Y obtained by simulation of the model for the sample period.	(2) $W_j = [X\hat{\Pi}_j X_j]$, $(j = 1, \ldots, p)$.	(2) $W_{ij} = \hat{\sigma}^{ij} W_j$, $(i, j = 1, \ldots, p)$; $\overline{W} = \{W_{ij}\}$.
(3) Construct instrumental variables estimates of the structural parameters δ.	(3) $d_j = (W_j'Z_j)^{-1}W_j'y_j$, $(j = 1, \ldots, p)$.	(3) $d = (\overline{W}'Z)^{-1}\overline{W}'y$.
(4) Construct estimate of the variance–covariance matrix. Estimate $\hat{\Sigma}$ of Σ obtained from (1).	(4) Estimate of the asymptotic variance–covariance matrix of the vector $n^{1/2}(d_J - \delta_j) = \hat{\sigma}_{jj}(n^{-1}W_j'W_j)^{-1}$, Estimate of the asymptotic covariance matrix of the vectors $n^{1/2}(d_i - \delta_i)$ and $n^{1/2}(d_J - \delta_j) = \hat{\sigma}_{ij}(n^{-1}W_j'W_j)^{-1}$ $\times (n^{-1}W_i'W_j)(n^{-1}W_i'W_i)^{-1}$ $(i, j = 1, \ldots, p, i \neq j)$.	(4) Estimate of the asymptotic variance–covariance matrix of the vector $n^{1/2}(d - \delta) = \{\hat{\sigma}^{ij} n^{-1}W_i'W_j\}^{-1}$.

TABLE 1—continued

Computational step	Limited information (LIVE)	Full information (FIVE)
(5) Construct corresponding estimates of the reduced form parameters; $\hat{\Sigma}$ from (1).	(5) $\hat{\Pi} = -\mathbf{B}\hat{\Gamma}^{-1}$, $\hat{\Omega} = \hat{\Gamma}^{-1\prime}\hat{\Sigma}\hat{\Gamma}^{-1}$.	(5) Same.
(6) Construct corresponding estimates of the variance–covariance matrix. Estimate of Γ from (3), Π from (5), and asymptotic variance–covariance matrix of $n^{1/2}(d-\delta)$ from (4).	(6) Estimate of the asymptotic variance–covariance matrix of the vector $$n^{1/2}(\hat{\pi} - \pi) = \left[\hat{\Gamma}^{-1} \otimes \begin{pmatrix} \hat{\Pi}' \\ I \end{pmatrix}\right]'$$ $\times$ [Estimate of the asymptotic variance–covariance matrix of the vector $n^{1/2}(d-\delta)$] $$\times \left[\hat{\Gamma}^{-1} \otimes \begin{pmatrix} \hat{\Pi}' \\ I \end{pmatrix}\right].$$	(6) Same.

233

For prediction or "multiplier" analysis of a system of simultaneous equations, an estimator of the reduced-form coefficients Π and the variance–covariance matrix of the reduced-form errors is required. The reduced-form errors take the form $\Upsilon = E\Gamma^{-1}$, so that we may write

$$v = [\Gamma^{-1\prime} \otimes I]\,\varepsilon,$$

and

$$V(v) = [\Gamma^{-1\prime} \otimes I]\,V(\varepsilon)[\Gamma^{-1} \otimes I]$$

$$= [\Gamma^{-1\prime}\Sigma\Gamma^{-1} \otimes I]$$

$$= \Omega \otimes I,$$

where $\Omega = \Gamma^{-1\prime}\Sigma\Gamma^{-1}$ is a positive definite matrix of order p. Estimation of the parameters of the reduced form in the fifth step of the computation is perfectly analogous for the limited-information and full-information instrumental variables estimators.

The final computational step in efficient estimation is to construct an estimator of the variance–covariance matrix for either limited-information or full-information estimators of the reduced-form coefficients. The estimator of either variance–covariance matrix requires a consistent estimator of the variance–covariance matrix of the corresponding estimator of the structural coefficients from the fourth step of the computation, and consistent estimators of the structural coefficients Γ and reduced-form coefficients Π from the third and fifth steps, respectively. The computational steps for efficient estimation of simultaneous equations by instrumental variables are summarized in Table 1.

The three-stage least squares estimator with $\overline{W} = \overline{X}(S \otimes X'X)^{-1}\overline{X}'Z$ is a full-information efficient instrumental variables (FIVE) estimator. The fitted values of the jointly dependent variables used at the second step of the computation are obtained from the ordinary least squares estimator of the reduced-form coefficients. The estimator of the variance–covariance matrix Σ used at the second step is obtained from the two-stage least squares estimator of the structural coefficients. For efficient instrumental variables methods of estimation, least squares estimation of the reduced-form coefficients can be replaced by evaluating an initial consistent estimator of the structural coefficients δ. Least squares estimation of the reduced-form parameters involves a number of regressions equal to the number of jointly dependent variables. Each regression includes all the predetermined variables as regressors, but the regressors are the same for all regressions. The initial estimation of the structural equations by instrumental variables involves a computational burden equivalent to the same number of regressions. However, each regression involves a number of regressors equal to the number of variables included in the corresponding structural equation less one. The regressors are not the same from equation to equation.

The full information maximum likelihood estimator can be interpreted as an iterative version of the full-information efficient instrumental variables (FIVE) estimator. At each stage in the computations, the fitted values of the jointly dependent variables and the estimator of the variance–covariance matrix Σ used at the second step in Table 1 can be taken from the preceding stage. This iterative procedure was proposed by Durbin (1963) and has been discussed by Malinvaud (1970), Lyttkens (1971), and Hausman (1973). The first iteration of the full-information efficient instrumental variables estimator is asymptotically equivalent to the limiting estimator considered by Durbin. Reiteration of the process is superfluous from the point of view of gains in efficiency. Reiteration of the three-stage least squares estimator, with only the variance–covariance matrix modified at each stage and with the fitted values obtained from the ordinary least squares estimator of the reduced form, fails to produce the full-information maximum likelihood estimator, as Dhrymes (1973) has pointed out.

IV. Repeated Least Squares Estimation

The computational burden of implementing two- and three-stage least squares estimators is substantial, especially in estimation of the reduced-form coefficients by ordinary least squares. Repeated least squares estimators can be adapted to circumvent the use of ordinary least squares at the initial stage by truncating the initial list of regressors. Our next objective is to characterize the repeated least squares estimators that result from truncation of the list of regressors at the initial stage.

In the method of truncated two-stage least squares, the ordinary least squares estimator of the reduced form is replaced by a regression of the jointly dependent variables included in the equation on a proper subset of the predetermined variables, or a basis for a proper subspace of the space spanned by the predetermined variables such as a subset of the principal components of the predetermined variables, say X_1. The fitted values of the included jointly dependent variables, say $\hat{Y}_j$, are given by

$$\hat{Y}_j = X_1 (X_1' X_1)^{-1} X_1' Y_j.$$

Applying the method of ordinary least squares with the fitted values $\hat{Y}_j$ and the actual values of the predetermined variables included in the equation X_j, we obtain the estimator

$$\hat{\delta}_j = \begin{bmatrix} \hat{Y}_j'\hat{Y}_j & \hat{Y}_j'X_j \\ X_j'\hat{Y}_j & X_j'X_j \end{bmatrix}^{-1} \begin{bmatrix} \hat{Y}_j'y_j \\ X_j'y_j \end{bmatrix}$$

$$= \begin{bmatrix} Y_j'X_1(X_1'X_1)^{-1}X_1'Y_j & Y_j'X_1(X_1'X_1)^{-1}X_1'X_j \\ X_j'X_1(X_1'X_1)^{-1}X_1'Y_j & X_j'X_j \end{bmatrix}^{-1}$$

$$\times \begin{bmatrix} Y_j'X_1(X_1'X_1)^{-1}X_1'y_j \\ X_j'y_j \end{bmatrix}.$$

From this expression we obtain the following result.

THEOREM 3.   The truncated two stage least squares estimator reduces to an instrumental variables estimator if and only if the initial regressors X_1 include a basis for the subspace spanned by the columns of the included predetermined variables X_j. Further, the instrumental variables may be taken to be

$$W_j = [X_1(X_1'X_1)^{-1}X_1'Y_j \quad X_j].$$

Verification of this theorem proceeds by observing that under the hypothesis of the theorem the truncated two-stage least squares estimator can be represented in the form

$$\hat{\delta}_j = (W_j'Z_j)^{-1}W_j'y_j = \begin{bmatrix} Y_j'X_1(X_1'X_1)^{-1}X_1'Y_j & Y_j'X_1(X_1'X_1)^{-1}X_1'X_j \\ X_j'Y_j & X_j'X_j \end{bmatrix}^{-1}$$

$$\times \begin{bmatrix} Y_j'X_1(X_1'X_1)^{-1}X_1'y_j \\ X_j'y_j \end{bmatrix}.$$

Further, the truncated two-stage least squares estimator may be represented as an instrumental variables estimator only if

$$X_j'X_1(X_1'X_1)^{-1}X_1' = X_j',$$

which implies the hypothesis of the theorem. Our next result is as follows.

THEOREM 4.   The truncated two-stage least squares estimator is consistent if and only if *either*

(a)   it reduces to an instrumental variables estimator as in Theorem 3; *or*
(b) $(X_1'X_1)^{-1}X_1'Y_j$ is a consistent estimator of the nonzero reduced form coefficients in Π_j.

To verify this theorem we first observe that condition (a) is obviously sufficient since an instrumental variables estimator is consistent.[26] Second, condition (b) implies

$$\text{plim}\,\hat{\delta}_j = \left[\begin{array}{cc} \Pi_j'\Sigma_{x'x}\Pi_j & \Pi_j'\Sigma_{x'x_j} \\ \Sigma_{x_j'x}\Pi_j & \Sigma_{x_j'x_j} \end{array}\right]^{-1} \left[\begin{array}{cc} \Pi_j'\Sigma_{x'x}\Pi_j & \Pi_j'\Sigma_{x'x_j} \\ \Sigma_{x_j'x}\Pi_j & \Sigma_{x_j'x_j} \end{array}\right]\delta_j = \delta_j.$$

If the truncated two-stage least squares estimator $\hat{\delta}_j$ is not an instrumental variables estimator and condition (b) is not satisfied, this probability limit becomes

$$\text{plim}\,\hat{\delta}_j = \left[\begin{array}{cc} \Pi_j'\Sigma_{x'x_1}\Sigma_{x_1'x_1}^{-1}\Sigma_{x_1'x}\Pi_j & \Pi_j'\Sigma_{x'x_1}\Sigma_{x_1'x_1}^{-1}\Sigma_{x_1'x_j} \\ \Sigma_{x_j'x_1}\Sigma_{x_1'x_1}^{-1}\Sigma_{x_1'x}\Pi_j & \Sigma_{x_j'x_j} \end{array}\right]^{-1}$$

$$\times \left[\begin{array}{cc} \Pi_j'\Sigma_{x'x_1}\Sigma_{x_1'x_1}^{-1}\Sigma_{x_1'x}\Pi_j & \Pi_j'\Sigma_{x'x_1}\Sigma_{x_1'x_1}^{-1}\Sigma_{x_1'x_j} \\ \Sigma_{x_j'x}\Pi_j & \Sigma_{x_j'x_j} \end{array}\right]\delta_j$$

which is different from δ_j, so that the truncated least squares estimator is inconsistent.

We are now prepared to state and prove our main result on estimation by the method of truncated two-stage least squares.

THEOREM 5.   The truncated two-stage least squares estimator is consistent and efficient if and only if condition (b) of Theorem 4 is satisfied.

If condition (b) is satisfied, the truncated two-stage least squares estimator converges in distribution to the two-stage least squares estimator and is, therefore, efficient. Conversely, if condition (b) is not satisfied, this estimator is consistent only if condition (a) of Theorem 4 is satisfied, so that the truncated two-stage least squares estimator is an instrumental variables estimator with instruments, as given in Theorem 3, that do not satisfy the hypotheses of Theorem 1. Considered as an instrumental variables estimator, the truncated two-stage least squares estimator is inefficient.

As a practical matter condition (b) of Theorem 4 would be applicable only if variables other than those included in the list of initial regressors do not enter the reduced-form equations determining the included jointly dependent variables Y_j. In these rather special circumstances, a consistent estimator of the reduced form coefficients Π_j may be constructed by setting certain elements

---

[26] This sufficient condition for consistency is discussed by Amemiya (1966). It is satisfied for the truncated two-stage least squares estimator based on principal components proposed by Kloek and Mennes (1960) and discussed by Amemiya (1966). It is not satisfied for the truncated two-stage least squares estimator discussed by Dhrymes (1970) and Malinvaud (1970, pp. 717–718). The second version is not consistent if the number of principal components used as initial regressors is fixed as sample size increases. For further discussion, see McCarthy (1971).

equal to zero and estimating the rest by ordinary least squares applied to a proper subset of the predetermined variables. Except for these special circumstances, the truncated two-stage least squares estimator is inconsistent unless it reduces to an instrumental variables estimator. Even if the truncated estimator reduces to an instrumental variables estimator, it is inefficient.

In extending these results to truncated versions of three-stage least squares, we first observe that the consistency of a truncated version of three-stage least squares is assured by the conditions of Theorem 4 for each equation together with consistency of the second stage estimator of the variance–covariance matrix Σ; the latter condition requires only consistency of the truncated two-stage least squares estimator, so that the conditions of Theorem 4 for each equation are necessary and sufficient for the consistency of the corresponding truncated three-stage least squares estimator. The truncated three-stage least squares estimator is consistent and efficient if and only if condition (b) of Theorem 4 is satisfied for each equation.

Our principal conclusion is that with the minor exceptions noted above, the two- and three-stage least squares estimators are consistent and efficient if and only if they can be reduced to efficient instrumental variables estimators. In practice this implies that the initial stage must be carried out without truncation of the list of predetermined variables entering each least squares regression. Direct application of the method of efficient instrumental variables reduces the computational burden considerably, as we have already demonstrated. Our second conclusion is that truncated two- and three-stage least squares estimators are consistent if and only if they can be reduced to instrumental variables or if the initial estimator of the reduced form coefficients Π is consistent. Under the first of these conditions direct application of the method of instrumental variables reduces the computational burden. Under the second condition application of the method of instrumental variables reduces the computational burden and produces an efficient estimator.

V.   Example: Klein Model I

To illustrate a consistent and efficient estimation of systems of simultaneous equations by means of instrumental variables, we present estimates for the structural coefficients of Klein Model I.[27] This model has been estimated by the methods of two- and three-stage least squares,[28] which are consistent and efficient instrumental variables estimators. We present instrumental variables

---

[27] See Klein (1950, pp. 58–66). In an earlier paper, Brundy and Jorgenson (1971), we presented estimates of the structural coefficients of a model of moderate size, the Liu quarterly model of the U.S. economy.

[28] See, for example, Rothenberg and Leenders (1964).

estimates based on initial estimation of the structural form of the model by means of instrumental variables rather than initial estimation of the reduced form by ordinary least squares. Klein Model I has three behavioral equations and three identities. The model determines six jointly dependent variables from eight predetermined variables, including a dummy variable corresponding to the intercept in each behavioral equation. To condense the presentation of this model, we employ the names of equations and the notation for the variables used by Klein. Estimates of the structural parameters of Klein Model I from annual data for the period 1921–1941 are given for three methods of estimation in Table 2.

TABLE 2

ALTERNATIVE ESTIMATES AND THEIR STANDARD ERRORS, KLEIN MODEL I, 1921–1941

Equations	Coefficients (Standard errors)		
Variables	IV	LIVE	FIVE
(1) Consumption (C)			
*Profits (P)	0.0611	−0.1153	0.0532
	(0.140)	(0.118)	(0.108)
Profits, lag 1 (P_{-1})	0.1650	0.3105	0.2234
	(0.122)	(0.107)	(0.100)
*Wages (W)	0.8248	0.8217	0.7932
	(0.041)	(0.040)	(0.038)
Intercept	16.05	16.77	16.54
	(1.34)	(1.32)	(1.30)
(2) Investment (I)			
*Profits (P)	0.0671	0.1062	−0.0131
	(0.255)	(0.173)	(0.162)
Profits, lag 1 (P_{-1})	0.6874	0.6537	0.7473
	(0.229)	(0.163)	(0.153)
Capital stock, lag 1 (K_{-1})	−0.1694	−0.1639	−0.1805
	(0.045)	(0.036)	(0.033)
Intercept	22.84	21.63	25.44
	(9.49)	(7.54)	(6.79)
(3) Private wages (W*)			
*Private product (E)	0.4035	0.4254	0.3866
	(0.039)	(0.036)	(0.032)
Private product, lag 1 (E_{-1})	0.1801	0.1593	0.1922
	(0.041)	(0.039)	(0.034)
Time trend (T)	0.1390	0.1337	0.1577
	(0.029)	(0.029)	(0.028)
Intercept	1.686	1.571	1.996
	(1.15)	(1.15)	(1.12)

* Jointly dependent variable.

The initial consistent estimator from the first step of the computational scheme described in Table 1, above, are obtained by the method of instrumental variables. For each equation we use all the predetermined variables included in that equation as instrumental variables. We construct further instrumental variables by regressing all jointly dependent variables included in each behavioral equation on the five predetermined variables included in the behavioral equations—lagged profits, lagged capital stock, lagged private product, time trend, and a dummy variable corresponding to the intercept. If we had included three additional predetermined variables in the initial regressions—government expenditures, government wage bill, and net exports—the resulting instrumental variables estimator would be identical to two-stage least squares. Estimates obtained by means of instrumental variables and their standard errors are presented in the first column (IV) of Table 2.

Estimates of the standard errors of the instrumental variables coefficient estimator require a consistent estimator of the variance–covariance matrix Σ; we compute estimates of the elements of this matrix from the residuals of the structural equations calculated from our initial instrumental variables estimator of the structural coefficients. Our next step is to obtain fitted values for the jointly dependent variables required for construction of new sets of

TABLE 3

GENERALIZED VARIANCE MEASURES FOR ALTERNATIVE ESTIMATORS,
KLEIN MODEL I, 1921–1941

Equation	Method of estimation		
	IV	LIVE	FIVE
(1) Consumption (C)			
Sum	1.695	1.643	1.599
Trace	1.839	1.772	1.725
Determinant	4.737×10^{-9}	3.239×10^{-9}	2.389×10^{-9}
(2) Investment (I)			
Sum	88.61	56.07	45.47
Trace	90.16	56.95	46.21
Determinant	1.312×10^{-8}	6.067×10^{-9}	4.756×10^{-9}
(3) Private Wages (W*)			
Sum	1.312	1.305	1.232
Trace	1.327	1.321	1.248
Determinant	7.811×10^{-12}	6.676×10^{-12}	4.600×10^{-12}
All equations			
Sum	97.45	62.66	51.42
Trace	93.32	60.04	49.18
Determinant	1.724×10^{-29}	7.456×10^{-30}	2.204×10^{-30}

instrumental variables. We then compute limited-information instrumental variables efficient (LIVE) and full-information instrumental variables efficient (FIVE) estimates of the structural coefficients. The resulting estimates are presented in the second (LIVE) and third (FIVE) columns of Table 2 together with their standard errors. This completes the third step of the computational scheme described in Table 1.

To provide a quantitative comparison of the efficiency of our three instrumental variables estimators we estimate the asymptotic variance–covariance matrix of each of these estimators of the structural coefficients. For each equation in the model and for the system as a whole, the trace, determinant, and sum of elements of the estimated variance–covariance matrix are given for each method of estimation in Table 3. These three functions of the elements of the variance–covariance matrix provide alternative measures of the relative efficiency of the three estimators. Comparison of the three measures of relative efficiency suggests that there is a substantial gain in efficiency, proceeding from the initial instrumental variables (IV) estimator to the limited-information instrumental variables efficient (LIVE) estimator and, finally, to the full-information instrumental variables efficient (FIVE) estimator. The gains in relative efficiency for Klein Model I are comparable to gains we reported earlier for the Liu model, a moderate-size quarterly model of the United States.

VI. Suggestions for Further Research

Our results suggest a number of possible directions for further research.

First, efficient instrumental variables estimators can be compared with alternative methods for estimation of systems of simultaneous equations. As presented in the literature, many of these methods are based on truncated versions of repeated least squares estimators. By Theorems 3 and 4, almost any consistent estimator of this type can be represented as an instrumental variables estimator. A comparison of consistent repeated least squares estimators would involve comparisons similar to that we have given between our initial instrumental variables (IV) estimator and the corresponding limited-information efficient (LIVE) and full-information efficient (FIVE) instrumental variables estimators in Tables 2 and 3.

Second, Fair (1972) has demonstrated that efficient instrumental variables estimators must be modified for application to time series simultaneous equations models with lagged dependent variables and autocorrelated disturbances. The problem that remains is to compare the resulting efficient instrumental variables estimators with alternatives proposed in the literature such as the corresponding modifications of two- and three-stage least squares estimators.

Third, alternative instrumental variables estimators can be compared with respect to finite sample properties. Sargan and Mikhail (1971) have developed finite sample approximations to the distributions of instrumental variables estimators. Their results can be applied directly to the evaluation of relative bias and efficiency of alternative estimators in finite samples. Sargan has provided finite sample approximations for the distributions of maximum likelihood estimators so that instrumental variables and maximum likelihood estimators can be compared with regard to performance in finite samples.[29]

Fourth, we have presented consistent and efficient estimators based on instrumental variables only for linear systems of simultaneous equations. For these systems the reduced form can be represented in closed form; our proofs have made use of this explicit representation. Perhaps the most important direction for further research is to extend our results by constructing consistent and efficient estimators based on instrumental variables for nonlinear systems of simultaneous equations.

REFERENCES

Amemiya, T. (1966). "On the Use of Principal Components of Independent Variables in Two-Stage Least-Squares Estimation," *Int. Econ. Rev.* **7**, No. 3, 283–303.

Anderson, T. and H. Rubin (1949). "Estimation of the Parameters of a Single Equation in a Complete System of Stochastic Equations," *Ann. Math. Statist.* **20**, 46–63.

Anderson, T. and H. Rubin (1950). "The Asymptotic Properties of Estimates of the Parameters of a Single Equation in a Complete System of Stochastic Equations," *Ann. Math. Statist.* **21**, 570–582.

Basmann, R. (1957). "A Generalized Classical Method of Linear Estimation of Coefficients in a Structural Equation," *Econometrica* **25**, No. 1, 77–83.

Bentzel, R. and H. Wold (1946). "On Statistical Demand Analysis from the Viewpoint of Simultaneous Equations," *Skand. Aktuarietidskrift* **29**, 95–114.

Brundy, J. and D. Jorgenson (1971). "Efficient Estimation of Simultaneous Equations by Instrumental Variables," *Rev. Econ. Statist.* **53**, No. 3, 207–224.

Chernoff, H. and N. Divinsky (1953). "The Computation of Maximum Likelihood Estimates of Linear Structural Equations," In *Studies in Econometric Method* (W. Hood and T. Koopmans, eds.), pp. 236–302. Wiley, New York.

Dhrymes, P. (1970). *Econometrics: Statistical Foundations and Applications.* Harper, New York.

Dhrymes, P. (1971). "A Simplified Structural Estimator for Large Scale Econometric Models," *Aust. J. Statist.* **13**, No. 3, 168–175.

Dhrymes, P. (1973). "Small Sample and Asymptotic Relations between Maximum Likelihood and Three Stage Least Squares Estimators," *Econometrica* (forthcoming).

Durbin, J. (1963). "Maximum-Likelihood Estimation of the Parameters of a System of Simultaneous Regression Equations," unpublished manuscript.

---

[29] See Sargan (no date). On the basis of Rao's results on second-order efficiency, the maximum likelihood estimators are not only asymptotically efficient, but efficient to a second-order of approximation to the exact sampling distribution; see Rao (1965, p. 289).

Eicker, F. (1963). "Asymptotic Normality and Consistency of the Least Squares Estimators for Families of Linear Regressions," *Ann. Math. Statist.* **34**, 447–456.

Evans, M. and L. Klein (1968). *The Wharton Econometric Forecasting Model.* Econ. Forecasting Unit, Dept. of Econ., Wharton School of Finance and Commerce, Philadelphia, Pennsylvania.

Fair, R. C. (1972). "Efficient Estimation of Simultaneous Equations with Auto-Regressive Errors by Instrumental Variables," *Rev. Econ. Statist.* **54**, No. 4, 444–449.

Fisher, F. (1965a). "The Choice of Instrumental Variables in the Estimation of Economy-wide Econometric Models," *Int. Econ. Rev.* **6**, No. 3, 245–274.

Fisher, F. (1965b). "Dynamic Structure and Estimation in Economy-Wide Econometric Models," *In The Brookings Quarterly Econometric Model of the United States* (J. Duesenberry, G. Fromm, L. Klein, and E. Kuh, eds.), pp. 589–636. Rand McNally, Chicago, Illinois.

Fisher, W. and W. Wadycki (1971). "Note on Estimating a Structural Equation in a Large System," *Econometrica* **39**, No. 3, 461–466.

Geary, R. (1949). "Determination of Linear Relations between Systematic Parts of Variables with Errors of Observation the Variances of which are Unknown," *Econometrica* **17**, No. 1, 30–58.

Haavelmo, T. (1943). "The Statistical Implications of a System of Simultaneous Equations," *Econometrica* **11**, No. 1, 1–12.

Haavelmo, T. (1944). "The Probability Approach in Econometrics," *Econometrica Suppl.* **12**, pp. 1–115.

Haavelmo, T. (1947). "Methods of Measuring the Marginal Propensity to Consume," *J. Amer. Statist. Ass.* **42**, No. 237, 105–122.

Hausman, J. (1973). "An Instrumental Variables Interpretation of FIML and Associated Estimators," unpublished manuscript.

Klein, L. (1955). "On the interpretation of Theil's Method of Estimating Economic Relationships," *Metroeconomica* **7**, No. 3, 147–153.

Klein, L. (1969). "Estimation of Interdependent Systems in Macroeconometrics," *Econometrica* **37**, No. 2, 171–192.

Kloek, T. and L. Mennes (1960). "Simultaneous Equations Estimation Based on Principal Components of Predetermined Variables," *Econometrica* **28**, No. 1, 45–61.

Koopmans, T. and W. Hood (1953). "The Estimation of Simultaneous Linear Economic Relationships," In *Studies in Econometric Method* (W. Hood and T. Koopmans, eds.), pp. 112–199. Wiley, New York.

Koopmans, T., H. Rubin and R. Leipnik (1950). "Measuring the Equation Systems of Dynamic Economics," In *Statistical Inference in Dynamic Economic Models* (T. Koopmans, ed.), pp. 53–237. Wiley, New York.

Leibenberg, M., A. Hirsch and J. Popkin (1966). "A Quarterly Econometric Model of the United States: A Progress Report," *Survey Current Business* **46**, No. 5, 13–39.

Liu, T-C. (1963). "An Exploratory Quarterly Econometric Model of Effective Demand in the Postwar U.S. Economy," *Econometrica* **31**, No. 3, 301–348.

Lyttkens, E. (1970). "Symmetric and Asymmetric Estimation Methods," In *Interdependent Systems* (E. Mosbaek and H. Wold, eds.), pp. 434–459. North-Holland Publ., Amsterdam.

Lyttkens, E. (1971). "The Iterative Instrumental Variables Method and the Full Information Maximum Likelihood Method for Estimating Interdependent Systems," unpublished manuscript.

Madansky, A. (1964). "On the Efficiency of Three-Stage Least-Squares Estimation," *Econometrica* **32**, No. 1–2, 51–56.

Maddala, G. (1971). "Simultaneous Estimation Methods for Large and Medium-Size Econometric Models," *Rev. of Econ. Stud.* **38** (4), No. 116, 435–445.

Malinvaud, E. (1970). *Statistical Methods of Econometrics*, 2nd rev. ed. North-Holland Publ., Amsterdam.

Mann, H. and A. Wald (1943). "On the Statistical Treatment of Linear Stochastic Difference Equations," *Econometrica* **11**, No. 3, 173–220.

McCarthy, M. (1971). "Notes on the Selection of Instruments for Two Stage Least Squares and *k*-Class Type Estimators of Large Models," *Southern Econ. J.* **37**, No. 3, 251–259.

Mitchell, B. (1971). "Estimation of Large Econometric Models by Principal Component and Instrumental Variable Methods," *Rev. Econ. Statist.* **53**, No. 2, 140–146.

Mitchell, B. and F. Fisher (1970). "The Choice of Instrumental Variables in the Estimation of Economy-Wide Econometric Models: Some Further Thoughts," *Int. Econ. Rev.* **11**, No. 2, 226–234.

Mosbaek, E. and H. Wold (1970). *Interdependent Systems*. North-Holland Publ., Amsterdam.

Rao, C. (1965). *Linear Statistical Inference and Its Applications*. Wiley, New York.

Reiersøl, O. (1945). "Confluence Analysis by Means of Instrumental Sets of Variables," *Ark. Math. Astron. Fys.* **32**.

Rothenberg, T. (1966). "Efficient Estimation with A Priori Information," unpublished Ph.D. dissertation, Massachusetts Inst. of Technol.

Rothenberg, T. and C. Leenders (1964). "Efficient Estimation of Simultaneous Equation Systems," *Econometrica* **32**, No. 1–2, 57–76.

Sargan, J. (1958). "The Estimation of Economic Relationships Using Instrumental Variables," *Econometrica* **26**, No. 3, 393–415.

Sargan, J. (1964). "Three-Stage Least-Squares and Full Maximum Likelihood Estimates," *Econometrica* **32**, No. 1–2, 77–81.

Sargan, J. (no date). "Finite Sample Distribution of FIML Estimators," unpublished manuscript.

Sargan, J. and W. Mikhail (1971). "A General Approximation to the Distribution of Instrumental Variables Estimates," *Econometrica* **39**, No. 1, 131–170.

Taylor, L. D. (1962). "The Principal-Component-Instrumental-Variable Approach to the Estimation of Systems of Simultaneous Equations," unpublished Ph.D. dissertation, Harvard Univ., Cambridge, Massachusetts.

Theil, H. (1958). *Economic Forecasts and Policy*. North-Holland Publ., Amsterdam.

Theil, H. (1971). "A Simple Modification of the Two-Stage Least-Squares Procedure for Undersized Samples," Rep. 7107, Center for Math. Stud. in Business and Econ., Univ. of Chicago, February.

Tinbergen, J. (1939). *Statistical Testing of Business Cycle Theories, Vol. II, Business Cycles in the United States of America, 1919–32*, League of Nations, Geneva.

Wold, H. (1965). "A Fix-Point Theorem with Econometric Background, I–II," *Ark. Mat.* **6**, Nos. 12–13, 209–240.

Zellner, A. and H. Theil (1962). "Three-Stage Least Squares: Simultaneous Estimation of Simultaneous Equations," *Econometrica* **30**, No. 1, 54–78.

Author Index

Numbers in italics refer to the pages on which the complete references are listed.

Subject Index

Page numbers followed by *n* indicate that the citation appears in a footnote.

250